VODKA-COLA

ABOUT THE BOOK

Vodka-Cola is a witty, amusing, thought-provoking, sensational look at the East–West détente.

Charles Levinson strips off the mask of "cold war," which is everyman's newspaper headline, to show that trade relations between the "Vodka" block and the "Cola" front have flourished and boomed, even stimulated by U-2, Berlin Wall, Cuban Missile or Vietnam crises.

We may think of détente as the outcome of political efforts to secure peace, but Mr. Levinson shows that détente has been a response to economic relations which reach back far beyond the overtures of Nixon and Willy Brandt. Western investors discovered the advantages of Communist low-paid, strike-free labour as early as the Eastern bloc discovered its need for Western technology and investment. Together they developed a sophisticated system of buy-back agreements to side step non-convertible Eastern currencies.

"You bottle our Coke and we'll buy your Vodka"—*Vodka-Cola*.

The authoritarian élites on both sides operate an "Overworld" of organized conspiracy which mirrors the "Underworld" of organized crime. Richard Nixon even managed to bring the two together through his ties with Pepsi-boss Kendall and Mafia-boss Lansky. Levinson paints a witty and lively portrait of the money deals and trade agreements concocted by the Overworld financiers.

The gradual penetration of European Communist interests into the shareholding of Western companies echoes Western investment in the Communist block. Italy has spearheaded the development of Vodka-Espresso. Levinson shows that this convergence of Vodka-Cola institutions has been coordinated by various private foundations, which actually direct foreign policy.

The Vodka-Cola, Vodka-Espresso Overworld uphold détente as a positive convergence between East and West. It is certainly a convergence, but Levinson has amassed a convincing body of evidence to show that it is unlikely to bring greater personal freedom to the East or increased common ownership in the West. The Vodka-Cola cocktail is reinforcing authoritarian structures demanded by business efficiency on both sides.

ABOUT THE AUTHOR

Charles Levinson was born in Ottawa in 1920. He earned an M.A. in Toronto and a doctorate in Paris. Formerly Deputy Director of the European office of the CIO and Assistant General Secretary of the International Metal Workers Federation, he is now Secretary General of the International Federation of Chemical, Energy and General Workers Unions (ICEF). He has written a number of books on industry and economics and has been an innovator of international trade union programmes.

VODKA
Cola

Charles Levinson

*The author thanks
Christine Hauch
for her collaboration in the
preparation
of this edition.*

Gordon & Cremonesi

Designed by Heather Gordon
Set in 10 on 11 pt Century
by Input Typesetting Ltd.
Printed in Great Britain by The Anchor Press Ltd
and bound by Wm Brendon & Son Ltd,
both of Tiptree, Essex.

British Library Cataloguing in Publication Data
Levinson, Charles
    Vodka Cola.
    1. East-West trade (1945-) 2. Communist
countries—Foreign economic relations
    I. Title II. Hauch, Christine
382.1'09171'7   HF1411   78-40401

LCCN: 78-040401
ISBN: 0-86033-070-2

                Gordon & Cremonesi
                Publishers
                London and New York
                New River House
                34 Seymour Road
                London N8 OBE

Contents

Introduction

It is the central thesis of this book that the political and ideological phenomenon of détente is the post-facto servant of an economic reality. For the USSR and the East-bloc countries détente has never been about avoiding nuclear war. It has been about acquiring from the capitalist West sophisticated technology and know-how, modern, more efficient machinery and, of course, the credits to finance them and exports to pay for them. For the USA and the Western world, détente has facilitated the extension of the international rationalization of production, characterized by the multinational companies and their financial shadows. The ritualistic mouthings of the political détente are deployed on behalf of the ensconced power élites of East and West in a determined campaign to alter the consciousness of the wider public (the meso-world) in line with the practice of economic cooperation.

The chronology of détente is evident. Since 1917 the Soviet régime's ideological commitment to the destruction of the political and social system of the West produced a counter-hostility of anti-Communism towards the USSR and its satellites on the part of the West. This has continued fundamentally unchanged despite certain modifications to meet temporary convergencies and tactical expediency. The warmer periods of Soviet–American relations, such as the NEP period of Lenin, showed the possibility of capitalist technology transfer to the USSR, heralding the flood to follow in the 1960s. Other periods of warmer relations, such as the alliance against Hitler and Khrushchev's brief search for "peaceful co-existence," temporarily modified but did not alter the basic element of official doctrines—the commitment to replace capitalism by Bolshevism or new Bolshevist régimes. The only hard contacts between East and West in the very late fifties and early sixties were through foreign trade. In most other areas, the cold war was at cryogenic temperature: wars rumbled on in Korea and Vietnam, confrontations persisted in the near-East, the Cuban missile crisis threatened disaster and there was relative stalemate in disarmament negotiations.

Most governments, and most politicians in the West, except for the ubiquitous anti-capitalist minuscules or groupuscules, were manning cold-war battle stations, supported by the opinion manufacturers of the commercial media. In the West there were a scattering of anti-American, pro-socialist voices: Olof Palme of Sweden, a minister or two of the Tribune group within the British Labour Party, and, of course, some traditionally contre-tous French under the reign of Charles de Gaulle. In the East there was a strident unison of highpitched anti-West, anti-imperialist and anti-American propaganda.

Economic relations as of the middle fifties were already surging in the opposite direction, however, towards contacts, cooperation, and amicability. The initial period of economic thaw was marked by such first contacts as between Valletta of Fiat (Fascism's most decorated manager), Hammer of Occidental Oil (Communism's best-loved millionaire), and Beitz of Krupp (loved by militarists the world over). From then on until the late sixties—while the cold war was at its coldest—the great economic wave from Europe gathered way. Most of the large deals and projects were concocted directly by individual companies without the governmental trimmings and trappings of the latter détente period. "Framework agreements" between governments (proclamations of commitment to détente, cooperation, joint undertakings in research, prospecting joint ventures, etc.) and cooperation agreements between the Eastern Foreign Trade Organisations (FTOs) and the capitalist monopolists were added subsequently.

The initial cooperation ventures were direct and unadorned—usually enveloped in the thickest secrecy and largely unreported by the media. A striking example of this cloak of invisibility was the scant attention accorded the gigantic deals of Fiat by its domestic Italian media, especially by those such as *La Stampa*, *Il Globo*, and Italian Television RAI, which were a part of the Fiat empire. Similarly, the comrades and workers of the Communist Party-controlled trade union confederation, the Italian CGIL, called upon to strike and struggle for wages, jobs and socialism against the clearest symbol of Italy's corrupt and decadent capitalism which was Fiat, were not told of the numerous reciprocal flights being made by their boss, Valletta, and Soviet and Polish officials to plan the building of assembly lines to produce the Fiat 124 Model in Eastern Europe. Since the Italian Communist Party (CPI) was involved in the operation through its extensive network of Party-owned trading companies (which were and remain the source of most of the CPI's funds), it is highly unlikely that the Communist Party leadership of the CGIL was unaware of this negotiation.

As European and Japanese eastward traffic increased, so American companies took the first steps towards involvement using their subsidiaries for back-door access to the new opportunities. As totally legal corporate citizens of their respective host countries (Opel-GM in Germany, IBM in France, ITT in Switzerland, DoW in Holland, Exxon in Italy, and many others), the corporate subsidiaries joined the economic *Drang nach Osten* provided with European passports and immunity from the impotent American regulations which prohibited their parent companies in Detroit, New York and tax-haven Delaware from engaging in such activities. Progressively, the economic imperative became too strong for the obstructive political and ideological barricades, which collapsed and were replaced by "détente" traffic signals showing: *go, go, go*.

Publisher's Note. In this book 'billion' signifies 1000 million, i.e. an American billion or one milliard. Some American spellings are retained (center, program, license, defense; for centre, programme, licence, defence).

Part I

1

The Ideological Façade

The mythology pursued and propounded by world leaders and political scientists (particularly in the USA) is based upon the proposition that morals, ethics and religion—the folklore foundations of their political stance—are dominant factors in international relations. The same ethic which views the successful millionaire as being an earthly manifestation of God's bounty, also projects that the compounded moral positions of politics determine the direction for economic development. This is the antithesis of the basic tenet of Marxian and Socialist theory which is that political and social structures are largely determined by economic relations. Certainly, such economic determinism is essential to dialectical materialism and the theory of class struggles as the driving force of social evolution.

The contest between the official doctrines of East and West can be explained in another way than by the classical view that the capitalist class is consciously working to shield its true economic rapaciousness and domination behind the virtues of political abstractions. The alternative view holds that in the Soviet Union and the East European régimes official political dogma and economic power are both vested in and identified with the same power group. The Communist Party, the military establishment and the intelligence and surveillance departments of the KGB are components of an integrated system—the unitary state. Economic and political functions are official, identical and integrated doctrinally and administratively, as are the overt and covert faces of government. The myth that pervasive class struggle as in the West, deriving from the capitalist or private ownership of the means of production, is absent from the countries with collective or social ownership of the means of production is official doctrine of both the governing élitists and the compliant masses.

Similarly, in the West the dichotomy between the allotted power of the official and visible meso-world in the political sphere and the invisible power in economic spheres of what we have called the "Overworld" results inevitably in efforts to advance the supremacy of politics or political determinism in official doctrine. The exercise of clandestine power in the economic sphere necessarily requires the pretended subordination or trivialization of private economics to public politics in the democratic market-economy systems.

This is at least a partial explanation for the continuous emphasis to date upon the political aspects as compared to the fundamental economic aspects of East–West relations. In the official version, political détente is claimed to have engendered trade and not the reverse. In this framework, the succession of peaks and troughs in East–West relations or Soviet–US relations is related almost exclusively to political events. Yet, as suggested above, business contacts continued throughout the period of apparent ideological antagonism. American capitalists travelled to Russia to trade in the twenties and thirties on a steady individual basis. Credits, the key of Soviet foreign trade and the most important constant of its foreign policy, were also secured, notably from Germany.

Even in face of the ideological hostility and the military confrontations, both direct and between satellites (NATO–US—Warsaw Pact, Berlin blockade, Korean War, Vietnam, Cuban missile crisis, Angola), the Soviets have always sought trade and credits. Pacific coexistence for the Soviets has always been pursued as a double-level policy, permitting political and ideological aggression to run parallel to the peaceful search for credits and trade. For the capitalist or market economies such a double-standard policy has always been a normal state of affairs. With effective economic power ensconced in the secretive reaches of the Overworld élite and in the boardrooms of the banks and ,large enterprises, the official political ideology has remained effectively secondary and apart from economic considerations. This weaker, supportive role has permitted at all periods of history and in most political conflicts with rightwing and conservative régimes not seeking the overthrow of the capitalist economic order, economic coopera- tion and collaboration with ideological and political opponents: Nazi Germany, Fascist Italy, Franco Spain, Salazar Portugal, Chile, South Africa, and the military régimes of Latin America, Greece, etc. Business has been largely free of ideological and political restraints of the nation state, even in the era before the multinational companies, which have rendered the last *coup* to the power of national politics to govern international economic enterprises.

The contradictions of Communism

Given the affinity of the economic organizations of East and West to hierarchical, authoritarian structures and systems, and their superiority over proclaimed political policy, the question arises as to why there had been so little economic interpenetration until relatively recent times. The meagre extent of trade relations in the past might appear to prove the contrary thesis that politics do determine economics.

The explanation for such an apparent contradition in fact lies in the economic strategies of the Soviet bloc and the systems introduced after the Second World War to implement these plans. These characteristics of economic development virtually sealed off the Soviet economy from substantial interpenetration and cooperation. In point of fact, many of the elements of the successive plans were intended to achieve isolation and autarky for a siege economy.

Foreign trade as such has never been important in the Soviet economy. Even today, it represents only about 5% of GNP. Endowed with vast national and colonized resources, energy sources, and a huge land mass, the Soviets considered foreign trade merely a stop-gap function to procure foreign exchange for critically needed imports to build the new economy. This has been in keeping with the ideological fundamentals of the tightly controlled central planning of the economy. Marx and Lenin wrote abundantly about the threats and inherent evils of international monopolies, and especially the interna- tional dominance of monopolies and finance, which Lenin described as "the highest stage of capitalism." Though Marx in his time considered the emerging American joint stock company as a possible instrument for transforming private capital into social property, Lenin lived through the period which proved the unreality of such an expecta- tion. Most of the giant firms he attacked repeatedly and explicitly as symbols of the new imperialism are among today's leading giant multinationals and leaders in the penetra- tion of the modern imperialism into the socialist motherland: Standard Oil, Shell Oil, General Electric, Siemens, Krupp, and some of today's leading multinational banks such as Morgan Guaranty Trust, Deutsche Bank, Crédit Lyonnais, PARIBAS, and especially Chase Manhattan and the oil banks of the Rockefellers.

It was, nevertheless, natural that in protecting the newly-established centrally- planned economy against economic as well as political and military threats from the predatory anti-Communist international monopolies, politics should serve the economic purpose of internalizing development to the greatest degree possible. The cold war philosophy provided a stern defence for the vulnerable Eastern economies against the theoretical encroachments of the capitalist monopolies. The Iron Curtain and an internalized non-convertible monetary policy ensured isolation better than the more traditional import barriers.

To facilitate the importation of desperately needed technology without laying open the nascent economy to the perceived dangers of capitalist exploitation, trading systems were evolved on the basis of commodity exchange in kind rather than upon the basis of money and prices. Such an arrangement also suited the capitalist monopolies, anxious in defence of their property rights and wary of the monetary policies of the bankrupt Russian economy. The Labour Theory of Value, which posits that the amount of socially necessary labour time incorporated in a product is its real value, was accepted, if never measured, as a planning criterion. Prices in the domestic economy became and still remain mere clearing devices to effect balances between available goods and consumers. They are useless as indicators for policy or as standards of values of goods and services. Therefore utility, availability and quality are the factors which determine consumer choices rather than prices. The same strategy has been applied to money in general. Though the NEP period ushered in a function for money and credit in planning policy, it was soon abandoned in favour of central and administrative controls for steering the economy. Growth at all levels in the centrally planned economy was delineated in input–output terms and in real magnitudes rather than in monetary terms. Thus both the function of money and prices are held to be of secondary importance and intrinsically different from—even antithetical to—their role in capitalist market economies. The chief function of money within the centrally planned economies appears to be as an accounting aggregate for the production and distribution of the national product. Other major functions of money and prices—as a standard of value, settlement of obligations or a method of payment as in the capitalist system—are of minor importance. Only in the consumer markets do prices and money play an important role. In the area of production and inter-relationship between enterprises its primary use is in cost accounting given that the production plan is geared to maximization of extensive developmental factors: labour, national resources, physical plant, etc. The current approach of the Soviet Union to the control function of pricing and profits is given by Leonid I. Brezhnev, General Secretary of the CPSU, in his presentation to the 25th Party Congress in early 1976: "Another area of the work is more skilful use of economic incentives and levers: cost accounting, profit, prices and bonuses. In other words, it is necessary to improve the entire system of basic indicators for the assessment of the work of ministries, associations and enterprises, above all the efficiency and quality of their work." Commodity exchange or barter therefore remains the essential means for producing and distributing the social product in the absence of a meaningful monetary vehicle. Domestic currencies were blocked to protect the planned economies from external world-market forces and interest rates above minima of 3–4% were considered as a part of surplus value or capitalist exploitation. Under these ideologico-economic conditions, the ruble was never permitted to become a convertible currency. Because money was a secondary factor in production and distribution, and was not a meaningful measure of the relative values of products, it could never be exposed as a commodity to the dangers of international trading on foreign exchange markets. More than any other factor, the different roles assigned to money and the price system in the capitalist and collectivist economies made barter plus gold the essential form of trade with the Soviet Union. A characteristic of underdeveloped economies, the unconvertibility of money and the consequent dependency upon barter in foreign trade has remained the most serious obstacle to East–West trade and the cause of the limited economic cooperation of the past.

On the other hand, foreign trade has always been more important to the smaller more industrially advanced associates in COMECON—Hungary, for example, depends upon exports for around 40% of its national product. Nevertheless, because the ideological fundamentals of the different, centrally-planned economies were patterned upon the dominant Soviet super-power model, barter became the basis of most COMECON trade. Clearings of import–export balances are done bilaterally. Just as in trade with the West, the non-convertible currencies of the different countries of COMECON cannot be used for multilateral clearings. The so-called "clearing ruble," used as a medium of commodity exchange among the COMECON countries, and the "transferable ruble," used for clearing bilateral trade balances, are both solely accounting units representing prices in rubles for offer on the world market in harder currencies. They in no way reflect real or true prices of the internal value of goods in the domestic market.

The limitations posed by non-convertible currencies and the necessities of straight-forward bilateral barter deals conditioned the initiatives of the Communist countries to expand trade and secure longer credits. Few of the products available in the COMECON bloc for exports were saleable in Western markets, because of poor quality, lack of sophistication and even unavailability. Such exports as were made from the Soviet Union were of agricultural and semi-finished goods with restricted possibilities in the West. Inter-COMECON trade reflects the structure of the planned economies with the USSR supplying energy and commodities in exchange for machinery and equipment from the satellites. As long as the Soviet economy remained limited and in a primitive state, there was slight potential for overall growth in trade with the West. This was the general situation up to the late fifties. During this period, therefore, politics and ideology were largely directed at bolstering economic imperatives in limiting East–West trade.

Problems of the Soviet economy

The needs for enhanced and transformed trade relations kept intensifying; the Soviet economic system as a whole was deteriorating with dangerous potential for social and political stresses. In an age of science and technology, despite its much-published achievements in space technology and weaponry, the domestic levels of technology and productivity in Soviet agriculture and industry were lamentable. A visiting delegation of young US farmers to the USSR reported that agricultural efficiency was very low and that Soviet farms used ten times more labour than American farms for comparable outputs. Average lags in the industrial technology of the USSR are usually put at twenty years in service industries, fifteen years in chemicals, ten years in light industry and at least ten years in data processing. A similar comparison applied to the other COMECON countries to varying extents, with the possible exception of the GDR, which has consistently been by far the most industrially developed of the still relatively underdeveloped region of COMECON. Doctrinal emphasis on heavy industry led to inadequacies in the light, modern, high-technology industries. The top central planners were represented by the sixty-to-seventy age group and the stultified plant and enterprise managers were oppressed by antiquated revolutionary, political and quantitative economic steering instruments. As a result, they completely missed the start of the greatest revolution of all time, the technotronic revolution, by at least twenty-five years.

Far from catching up and overtaking the USA, as Krushchev boasted, the relative position of the USSR and its satellites was receding catastrophically. Wallpaper for foreign edification, decorated with self-praising slogans about the absence of inflation and economic unemployment could not cover over the cracks and fissures completely. The long food queues in Russia, Poland and Czechoslovakia in 1975 and 1976, the universal inadequacy of even minimal social housing, the rapid increase in personal savings due to a mass consumer boycott of shoddy, unattractive, poor-quality products symptomize a system in deep structural trouble.

A recurring and growing complaint of Communist political leaders has been the inefficiency of industrial management and the poor quality of most products which have proved unsaleable in the West with catastrophic consequences for trade. As late as February 1976, Brezhnev was telling the Party faithful: "It is necessary to close all the loopholes that still allow slack executives to remain in the front ranks, despite breaches of contract commitments and low-grade output."

These internal constraints are evident in the COMECON pattern of trade. Exports of the Communist countries to the West are largely composed of raw materials, mineral fuels and food and drink products (over 65%). Capital goods constitute less than 10%. The commodity composition of its trade and its barter-based bilateral trading practices are typical of developing countries, with which the Soviet Union in fact competes. As it will not be possible to increase the raw material and food product exports because of domestic demand, stagnation and deficit are inevitable without increased exports of manufactured and capital goods to Western markets. But internal stresses have hampered attempts at such reorganization. Shortages of labour, especially skilled labour, have become acute in most COMECON countries, including the Soviet Union. Clandestine wages, consumer shortages, poor quality and manipulation of products to evade price regulations have created serious if unacknowledged inflation.

The overall inferior quality of equipment and products restricts access to Western markets, especially for Hungary, Rumania, Poland and Czechoslovakia. In the spring of 1976, the Soviets for the first time felt compelled to criticize Hungary openly for the inferior quality of its clothing, shoes and manufactured products exported to the USSR.

On the other hand, Hungarian agencies reported rejecting 20–30% of the consumer items imported from other East European countries. The Hungarian Chamber of Commerce publication "Magyar Import" recently reported that imports from other Socialist countries were rejected and turned down for sale to the public by the Trade Control Institute (KERMI) and the National Electrotechnical Control Institute (MEEI). The items referred to included refrigerators, vacuum cleaners, washing machines, spin driers and electric razors imported from the Soviet Union, the GDR and Poland to make up for shortages in domestic production. None of them met the Hungarian quality and safety requirements, which have been modelled on standards applied in the West. However, the Hungarians note with satisfaction that a 20–30% share of rejects represents a vast improvement over previous years when the control institutes turned down up to 60% of consumer goods imported from COMECON countries because of obvious deficiencies. Among the worst offenders were the Soviet-made Saratov refrigerators, the door handle of which delivered an electric shock when touched, and electric hazards in electric razors and spin driers, where wiring was not adequately insulated. Czechoslovak hot-water heaters also came in for criticism as unsafe.

The Polish Government officially put managers on notice, in September 1976, that failure to correct the impossibly poor quality of goods and mismanagement and waste of Western capital obtained under license or through cooperation could be considered and treated as criminal negligence. Czechoslovakia announced that priority attention in the current Plan would be given to importing capital equipment which can turn out goods capable of finding hard currency export markets. But the domestic need for these goods is also growing. Poland, Rumania and Czechoslovakia, beset by growing discontent like the USSR, cannot divert superior products made from imported plant and equipment into exports.

Viewed on a sector-by-sector basis, rather than macroscopically, the picture looks even bleaker. The deficiencies, bottlenecks and inter-sector planning discontinuities have become endless and chronic. Food processing in Rumania is primitive, transportation in Bulgaria rudimentary, the agricultural infrastructure for storing, processing and distributing crops in the USSR is catastrophic. Printing and publishing services, information processing, and, above all, technology coefficients of most specific processes in the electrical, chemical, paper, rubber and glass industries are extremely inefficient. Consequently, the pressures upon these sectors will increase as they fall farther behind.

Dominance of the multinationals

For the West the beckoning mass markets of 400 million undersupplied consumers stretching from Berlin to Vladivostok had become hypnotic. Difficulties in the Western domestic economies from strikes, high wages and inflation, despite unemployment, more stringent anti-trust regulations threatening from leftist and reformist anti-capitalist régimes, and, above all, the trend towards protectionism in industrialized countries, stimulated interest in the market potential of the Communist economies. Key to the intensifying interest was the fact that the multinational company (as Lenin predicted on the basis of entirely false premises) had "inherited the earth."

Around 1,000 industrial multinationals account for over 50% of world trade and about 75% of the Western world's productive capital. A recent survey by the European Economic Community (EEC) estimates approximately 10,000 Western multinational companies (defined as a company with "links" in two or more countries). It reported further that multinationals whose headquarters are based in Europe have nearly 50,000 "links" abroad, compared with US-originating firms, which have very nearly 24,000 such "links" with 113 companies throughout twenty or more countries. The Commission estimated that the top 200 companies represented 32.9% of the combined Gross Domestic Product of all OECD countries. In terms of national importance, the MNCs' proportion of national Gross Domestic Product was 69% in Holland, 53% in the UK, 41% in the US, 30% in Japan, 27% in the FRG, 23% in Switzerland, and 18% in France. But in value terms even these figures understate the real position of multinationals. For example, while American multinationals are fewer in numbers, their turnover is 43% higher.

The concentration of power is even greater than these figures would suggest due to the fact that the 1,000 leading multinationals have extensive participations, partnerships, and joint ventures with each other. In the petroleum industry, the nine or ten largest companies have common links probably exceeding 20,000. Similarly, multinationals in the chemical, rubber, plastics, paper, electronic, nuclear and service industries have massive joint ventures and participations with each other. Most are controlled today by some thirty to forty banking and financial institutions, who wield effective decision-making power over operational management.

The multinational companies are, therefore, the core of modern capitalism and have replaced the Western nation-state as the real political power centers of the age. This transfer of power to the multinationals has caused a profound structural reformation of the entire Western system and by the late fifties was already emerging as the critical element of industrial societies. Both the authoritarian Eastern bureaucracy and the authoritarian Western multinational clearly perceived mutual advantages in greatly expanded East–West trade.

For the East, facing an age of technology and capital-intensive industry, the technology gap had become an unbridgeable chasm. Internal self-corrections had failed. The only way out of the critical dilemma of how to upgrade the Soviet economic system qualitatively was to shift economic priorities from ideological isolation and the economics of surplus-value and public ownership of the means of production, towards integration into the new science-based global economy of the capitalist international monopolies (as multinational companies are termed by Stalinist orthodoxees). The Soviets sought to repeat the Japanese experience of borrowing licensing and incorporating foreign capitalist technology, thus saving an estimated twenty to twenty-five years on catch-up through the alternative of separate self-development. There was the added realization that self-generated catch-up was likely to prove impossible in any case, considering the retrograde point of departure and the accelerating rate of technological progress in the West.

Only the traditional impediments of the inconvertibility of Communist currencies and the inadequacy of simple barter deals as a basis for massive transfers of capital goods and services stood in the way of such integration. The Soviets were unable to use their important reserves of gold as a means of financing purchases of technology and equipment on the necessary scale. The trading of gold on the free market naturally causes the price to fall if large quantities are introduced, making the terms of trade less favourable and the operation therefore self-defeating, except for specific emergencies such as the financing of the USSR's 1975 wheat purchases. A substantial drop in the gold price would also undercut the USSR's credit rating with Western lending agencies, since gold is by far that country's main source of foreign earnings and solvency. It is said among commodity dealers that whenever the price of gold falls below £150 an ounce, the Soviets stop selling it. For the other, goldless COMECON countries, even this secondary source of hard foreign exchange is not available.

But, it was discovered, the eastern Europeans did possess one other resource which was deemed of high value to the capitalist multinationals—massive supplies of skilled, highly disciplined and very cheap labour!

Money finds a way

In comparison to Western salaries the workers in the COMECON countries earn from ten to twenty times less. In addition, the workers in the centrally planned economies do not belong to free trade unions and have no collective bargaining rights in respect of wages, hours of work or determination of working conditions. Above all, they do not have the right to strike. All levels of management belong to the union along with the workers, whilst both managers and union leaders belong to the unique Party. Thus the principal challenges to and checks upon management authority and prerogatives in the West are entirely absent.

It is the unprecedented and creative discovery of how to fuse this fund of cheap, skilled, strikeless labour into a new form of economic cooperation which made Communist-based profits possible for multinationals, and catalysed the détente. By innovating a new form of foreign exchange, permitting the multinational companies to earn exceptionally high profits in hard dollars, marks, francs, sterling and yen, the historical economic bottlenecks were broken and the West's political barricades against Communism dismantled.

The creation of this new "Eldorado of détente" supplied the element missing during previous surges of East–West economic cooperation and pacific coexistence campaigns. Profits commensurate with modern mammoth-scale projects became feasible. The techniques were even applicable to medium and small-scale projects. For the first time, a quantum leap out of the containments of barter and *in natura* commodity exchanges (despite the absence of comparable price mechanisms and the unconvertability of Eastern currencies), became a fact and reality of modern economic relations of the détente. The era of Vodka-Cola imperialism had arrived. And just as Fiat and Krupp had signalled the breakthrough in trade during the fifties, making necessary the *Ostpolitik* of Willy Brandt as a political concomitant, so the Pepsi–Vodka deal became the public relations symbol of the Nixon–Brezhnev détente.

The underlying techniques of Vodka-Cola cooperation are described in greater detail later in this chapter. At this point, we may simply point out that cooperation is a method which permits the Communist régimes to acquire voluminous credits from Western government and private bank suppliers to finance plant, technology and managerial know-how importations, including a vast range of supporting inputs such as training, technical documentation, servicing systems, etc., from the capitalist monopolies, as part of a package deal which provides for guaranteed repayment facilities through the buy-back and counter-purchase of goods by the capitalist partner. These "counter-purchases" may either be of other stipulated products or of products from the plant established under the deal. Deals often cover entire production processes, specific types of advanced machinery and equipment and even complete factories and industrial complexes called "turn-key plants" (all delivered, built and presented, key in hand). The interest costs of these credits are incorporated into the final costs of the project.

The Western associate and the government foreign trade monopoly responsible for the appropriate Eastern industrial sector create a partnership to effect this strategy, which may range from a simple form of association with no formal or legal corporate status (being governed merely by a contractual relationship) up to an integrated venture on a 49/51% or even a 50/50% basis. These relationships make possible the Vodka-Cola enterprise giving mutual advantages to both the Eastern and Western partners. Such dealings are therefore quite distinct from normal or traditional foreign trade, which is based upon exports paid for by clearances made at international level through the normal capitalist methods of connecting balances to monetary aggregates and paying or receiving them in negotiable currencies. In the new form of cooperation only goods are exchanged as payments and receipts, not money. Although fundamentally based upon the barter technique, this development is more sophisticated and flexible than anything known in the past. The apparent form of such deals permits the maintenance of a closed autarkical system of economic isolationism by the Eastern élite and the perpetuation of its authoritarian industrial and political system. Numerous recent declarations by Soviet and satellite leaders claim officially that such deals have no relationship to the permanent ideological commitments and political objectives of helping to destroy capitalism and supporting workers' revolutions to overthrow exploitation for the final victory of socialism.

Again, the words of CPSU General Secretary Brezhnev are illustrative of the rhetorical defense by association with concepts of "socialism" and "peace" rather than by the exercise of logic:

> No one should expect that because of the détente Communists will reconcile themselves with capitalist exploitation or that monopolists will become followers of the revolution. On the other hand, strict observance of the principle

of non-interference in the affairs of other states and respect for their independence and sovereignty, are one of the essential conditions of détente.

We make no secret of the fact that we see détente as the way to create more
favourable conditions for peaceful socialist and Communist construction.
This only confirms that socialism and peace are indissoluble.

All such rapports, except in the case of Yugoslavia, are claimed to be external to the
centrally steered economy and hermetically sealed off from the socialist structure. The
dangers that cooperation will cause changes in the system in Eastern Europe because of
technological and technocratic imperatives or stimulated tastes among Eastern consumers for greater creature comforts, especially the "democratizing individual ownership of an automobile," are considered impossible. As long as prices and currencies
remain purely administrative and unconnectable, it is held, there can be no significant
transformations within the integrated economico–politico–social system.

Integration of interests

These arrangements meet all the economic criteria demanded by Eastern technological
growth, whilst allowing monetary protectionism to persist. Previously, the extension of
bank credits to would-be Eastern purchasers was totally hampered by the inability of
capitalist firms to generate profits within the Eastern economy to repay and enhance
their advances. Cooperation deals make possible the lucrative fulfilment of these credits
without violating the currency barrier. Furthermore, they facilitate the transfer of
critically needed technology to the East without large, self-defeating outlays of gold and
without changing the monetary system. Eastern governments can, therefore, avoid
integration into the currencies, banking systems and credit networks of the capitalist
free market system. Repayment in project production and other export goods is an
intrinsic feature of the deal, enabling the "capitalist-monopolists" to form a guaranteed
export market for a part of the products produced by the cooperation project (often
ranging between 30–60%) as well as supplying badly-needed export outlets for other
products usually unsaleable in the West through normal trade channels. Only a very
small portion (usually 10–15%) is paid for in hard currencies. The remainder is repaid in
goods. In a time when the Eastern economic systems have retrograded into deepening
crisis, both qualitatively and quantitatively, as reflected in ominously growing trade
deficits and debts to the West, barter-based cooperation, through licensing, buy-back,
counter-purchase, co-production, joint association by partnership contract and joint ventures, is a life-saver. It may provide the means of propping up the discredited élitists of
the Eastern ruling class, composed of the Party, the bureaucracy and the KGB. Providing supportive Western technology, without opening up Eastern systems to the vicis-
situdes of capital market forces certainly provides a breathing space, at least for the
moment. Whether this step represents an implicit and unconscious sapping of the fortress of privilege in the East, with consequences for the future, is not yet apparent.
Clearly the ruling caste itself has no such anxieties. They expect the capitalists to sell
them the rope with which they may eventually hang them. It has never been suggested
or indicated that the Gosplanners have been infiltrated by anti-Communist elements to
promote self-annihilating capitalist technology in order to dislocate or disrupt the system from within.

If cooperation, or economic détente, serves the aims of Eastern economic development
without encroaching too harshly upon their flexible ideological barrage, the counter-
ideologists of the West find the new arrangements equally easy to accommodate. For the

monopoly capitalists or multinationals, détente has never, we repeat, been about avoiding nuclear war, nor about promoting constructive "convergencies" between the best
socialist and democratic features of both systems. Least of all has it been about catalys-
ing liberalism, human rights, and the market economy into the Communist countries.
Slogans such as "Peace through Trade," "Economics—the Arms of Peace," "Make Love
and Profits, not War," are promoted by lawyers on commission hustling deals for personal profits, as in the case of Samuel Pisar or the call-boys of the media and of academe.
These jaded hacks are paid their hire by the call-houses of the Rockefellers, the banks
and the oil companies, to apply the cosmetics of Madison Avenue and the advertising
world to the motivations of the Western ruling élite. As with the Soviets, Poles, Czechs,
East Germans and others, these motivations are entirely pecuniary and secular:
accumulating more profits and cash flow by exploiting workers in the East in order
better to exploit workers in the West. The business of big business is to make profits or
surplus value. The rulers of the East are making it their business to help them.

Cooperation, not trade, has made profits possible and enabled multinationals to
capitalize on Communism. An argument often heard is that, in overall balances, cooperation represents only a small amount compared to East–West import–export figures.
Companies, governments and the domesticated multinational media, of course, have an
obvious interest in playing down the relative importance and significance of cooperation
deals. Should the true impact of this departure become widely realized, opposition would
grow from all sides: from workers because of the growing threats of dumping, loss of jobs
and production to low-wage non-union economies; from consumers because of the contribution of cooperation deals to raising interest rates, to inflation and to high prices for
consumer products; and from concerned free people everywhere, already disturbed by
the decreasing number of democratic countries in the world, who would raise questions
about the quasi-clandestine, conspiratorial dealings between Eastern politico–economic
and Western economic authoritarians.

From this perspective, the control systems of both partners in cooperation seem to
have a great deal in common: the internal power structures of both the Eastern régimes
and of the ruling Western multinational enterprises are based on hierarchical,
military-type principles. The trend towards integration in a secret monopoly control of
power would seem to underscore their external economic cooperation. For example, it is
hard to see how a joint venture or association with a state-owned, monopoly Foreign
Trade Organization (FTO) can fail to extend the degree of monopolization and cartelization in the world economy. Shell, Exxon and BP are all signatories to a cooperation deal
with the same Soviet FTO for oil, Soyuznefteexport—as an example of competition this
is patently absurd. All their services, practices and procedures will unavoidably con-
verge into an unified undertaking. When one side of such a deal is already a total and
complete monopoly, and all FTOs are simply divisions of the central state monopoly, it
is impossible to argue that competition will not be progressively reduced and administrative control over systems in the West expanded. When A, B and C are organically
linked to D, in the area of their common interests, how can there be competition—it
would be quite irrational and inoperable.

It is obvious that the superstructures and ramifications of the cooperation system are
becoming heavy and extensive. The more public and private credits that are advanced,
the more "investments" the multinationals make, the more powerful interests tie into
cooperation deals, the greater the political and economic pressure will be to expand
commitment. The Western multinationals are, therefore, likely to use their already
predominant strength over the political and economic policies of the nation state in
support of the unhindered perpetuation of the Eastern régimes with whom they have

an ever-growing financial and economic community of interests. Obviously, with investments in the $50–100 billion range and debts on the same scale, the multinationals and the banks would definitely not be content at the prospect of a change in the Eastern régimes. In economic terms, such a change would probably result in the repudiation of all external obligations and debts contracted by the present undemocratic, non-elected, oppressive régime. Similarly, the introduction of free trade unions, collective bargaining, industrial democracy, the right to strike and any other feature of democratic trade unions, is not something the Western partners of the present authoritarian firms would foresee with tranquillity and pleasure. The multinationals and banks, therefore, have a vested, direct, financial interest in the perpetuation of these oppressive régimes and must be among their most solid, if tacit, supporters.

A debt of $50–100 billion is a large one and a lot of concessions to authoritarianism will be made to ensure its repayment. Basic considerations of individual rights, freedom of speech, free expression of opinions, etc., weigh lightly in the billion dollar universe of the Overworld. Few analogies exist in history of the depth and extent of the repercussions triggered by the integration process which is détente; few movements in history were as pregnant with consequences, for better or worse, as the détente of co-production is for our future. Its influence is behind the apparent political *volte-face* of the still ideologically opposed superpowers. One direct result of the economic need for détente was the Vodka-Cola cooperation in achieving a cease-fire and beginnings of peace talks in the Kippur War. Another linked outcome was the cessation of hostilities in Vietnam through the abrupt American withdrawal and the concession of South Vietnam to the North. Many in the West, like the present author, unconditionally opposed the American intervention from the beginning of the Vietnam tragedy, but regardless of the original rights or wrongs of the involvement only prior agreement between the multinationals of the US military–industrial complex and the power structure of the East could account for such a complete withdrawal and termination. Neither Henry Kissinger's small-step, near-East diplomacy nor his Vietnam negotiations could have been conducted without Soviet support and approval. It was necessary for both parties to eradicate areas of overt confrontation in order to pursue unhindered the grand design of Vodka-Colanization and the economic cooperation so ardently promoted by the Overworld élitists. It appears that Mao Tse-Tung, for one, never did understand how the American fight against Communism had become subordinated to economic realities if a report in *Time* magazine by Henry Kissinger of the statements by Mao on Vietnam are true. Mao is reported to have said he "could not comprehend how a nation as big and powerful as the US would give up after having lost only 50,000 men." He did not understand its apparently weak withdrawal, surrendering South Vietnam to its enemy. Nor did he understand how a great country could "allow such as Watergate to happen" (*Time*, 20 September 1976). Being programmed for power in essentially political and executive terms, Mao apparently did not fathom the real power structures of the US and their motivations. He obviously could not connect the fall of Nixon to an attempt by an anti-détente faction in the CIA to stem the headlong rush into détente by the Kissinger–Rockefeller faction for whom Nixon was fronting, as our earlier discussion of this interlude in American politics discloses. Nor apparently did Mao appreciate that the large economic empires of the multinationals had calculated that profits from the Vietnam war had reached the point of diminishing returns when balanced against the awaiting bonanza in East–West cooperation which could not be seriously mined until the US pulled out completely.

While politicians or militarists may conduct their affairs on short-term operational considerations, long-term, billion-dollar economic programs are not formulated and implemented without ensuring the maximum degree of very long-term guarantees and safeguards. The critical and essential safeguard of the financier is stability—that there should be no serious confrontation capable of stopping the grand design. Local skirmishes, such as Angola and Portugal, media and verbal aggression to maintain the ideological façade are a part of that design and act as safety valves or sops to extant ideological sentiments. Like Mao, most of the other political so-called leaders have not yet grasped the dimension of the design nor the scale of its probable impact.

Strategy and solvency

East–West trade has increased tremendously since the late fifties. The average rate of growth since 1960 is close to 18%—much higher than that for world trade as a whole, which in 1975 and 1976 rose only by about 11%. The rise has been even faster than that in inter-COMECON trade—almost double, in fact. Progressively the embargo was lifted from strategic exports on the so-called Coordinating Committee on Export Control (or COCOM) list. This list of strategic commodities and technologies is maintained by the secretariat of the fifteen-nation committee (all NATO members, minus Iceland and plus Japan) in Paris. From an original list of thousands of items it has been reduced down to a hard core which includes munitions, nuclear energy materials and a highly selective list of high technology equipment which could have military applications. Not surprisingly, it has been the USA which has requested the greatest number of exceptions to the COCOM list. In 1970–1971, 1,700 embargoed items and licensed commodities were removed from the USA's own unilateral stop list. In 1972, the number of items was reduced to 400, whilst 1973 saw a reduction to a mere 70 items. Even large-scale computers, barred to exports in 1970, are now permitted to be exported to Eastern Europe. Except for items on the COCOM list, France, West Germany, Italy and the UK no longer require export licences for goods destined for Eastern Europe.

It is known that much of the advanced technology sought by the East has military as well as civilan uses. According to *Newsweek*, a former Soviet trade official now living in Israel reported that every Soviet foreign trade organization has a military–scientific unit attached to it for the purpose of examining the possible application of imported technology for military use. But in addition, most advanced technology is largely common to both civilian and military purposes. Only the actual hardware and weapon systems are uniquely applicable. In the Soviet Union and other COMECON countries, such as the GDR or Czechoslovakia, the military-industrial complex appears quite as extensive as it is in the West. In addition to its mass array of military-owned and operated armament factories, the army runs many factories producing civilian goods: automobile firms, electrical firms, metal-working and numerous consumer goods plants. When a Western firm such as GM, Ford, Fiat, etc., enters into agreements with the Eastern foreign trade organizations which are the only contractors or agents, they are virtually entering into an operational partnership with the military forces. That this is entirely known to and approved by Western governments and the capitalist multinationals cannot be doubted. It illustrates the degree to which economics and trade have triumphed in setting military considerations aside—a situation which is not likely to be reciprocated in the East.

Despite their lip-service to bilateral balancing of trade, the Eastern foreign trade monopolies have never achieved equilibrium in their overall trade with capitalist countries, for reasons previously described. This failure has meant continued unbalanced trade and mounting deficits for Eastern economies. By September 1976 the overall deficit of the East European countries was nearly $50 billion. Soviet long-term indebtedness to the West is generally estimated to be around $10–12 billion, with an annual servicing debt of some $800 million. The Morgan Guaranty Trust, one of the world's largest banks and heavily engaged in Vodka-Cola financing, reported an Eastern deficit figure in August 1976 of $32 billion, and this is probably an understatement to avoid panicking the capitalist money markets. A confidential NATO report which put the figure at over $50 billion released a public figure of only $35 billion, as part of the same concern to prevent doubts as to the solvency of the Communist countries and so forestall a consequent universal run on the private capitalist banks who were so deeply involved in this financing. In reality the actual debt figure is probably higher than $50 billion when the under-reporting of credit by countries such as Italy and France is considered.

The current rate of increasing hard-currency indebtedness to the West is estimated to be in the region of $1–2 billion monthly or $12–24 billion in a full year. These chronic deficits are financed mainly from Western credits and from sales of gold by the USSR ($700–800 million annually). Most of these credits are for financing debts incurred in connection with cooperation projects over the last ten years. As in most under-developed economies, the USSR's debt servicing has risen enormously; it represents about 20% of the Soviet Union's hard currency exports—a level at which bankers start asking searching questions.

It is an article of Wall Street faith and the current financial certainty of the City of London that the Soviet Union and the other centrally-planned State-owned economies are gilt-edged credit risks. The Soviet Union is proud of a fifty-year record of never defaulting on a debt. As all industry is state-owned, the guarantor of last resort is the government itself and, therefore, admirably credit-worthy. But now the upper threshold limits on financing of debt are being reached and outstanding long-term deficits are increasing. Actual gold reserves of the Soviet Union correspond approximately to its total indebtedness or slightly less. For the moment it is solvent and liquid, but any attempt at large-scale extension of that current outstanding debt would induce a tremor through Western money markets. Though it cannot really provide a serious comparison, North Korea with over $700 million of debt to Western bankers has already made history as the first Communist country to have defaulted. Requests for payment of agreed annual instalments are being ignored—a fact which the large US banks like First National City and Chase Manhattan and leading Swiss banks are keeping quiet. These bastions of capitalism seem anxious not to besmirch the legend that the centrally-planned Communist régimes never default on the repayment of debts. Social-ist honour in this matter seems in safe hands—no self-respecting capitalist banker is going to raise a question of confidence in a debtor.

This precarious situation adds a new dimension to the importance of buy-back or barter-based counter-purchase cooperation. The Prime Ministers of Poland and Czechoslovakia have declared that such counter-trade projects are to become the princi-pal means of foreign trade in order to boost exports and hard-currency revenues. Only counter-trade barter deals offer the prospect of keeping open the flow of capitalist tech-nology and maintaining the détente. Despite being granted most favoured nation (MFN) trading status by most Western countries (excepting the USSR, Czechoslovakia and Hungary at present by the USA), the Eastern bloc still finds it wholly impossible to off-load poor quality, over-priced home made products on to Western markets through the means of direct exports. While the Soviet Union can gain little currency to relieve its credit position from its exports of agricultural and raw materials, it has a far greater interest in co-production deals for more finished, sophisticated commodities. Such deals bring more profits for the Western multinationals either from the production returned for sale in the American markets or from the portion of the output of the Soviet partner also exported to the West. In the first case, the multinational will be content to proceed further with investment on which it is receiving a direct, tax-free return, whilst in the second instance hard currency can be used to pacify and encourage agencies to grant further financial credit. The urgency with which the Soviets regard the situation was highlighted in Brezhnev's keynote address to the 25th CPSU Congress in late February 1976: "Among the key economic problems, the promotion of foreign economic relations acquires growing importance," he asserted. "The time is ripe," he declared, "to extend compensation agreements to processing industries as well." Most buy-back deals have been in the area of commodities and agricultural products. This announcement of the greater emphasis on buy-back and counter-purchase in processing industries is an accurate barometer of the pressures rising under cooperation.

2

The Importance of Credits

The USSR, in a dispatch by Tass, has publicly recognized the existence of the problem of COMECON debts to the capitalist banks (Tass, 20 September 1976). It inveighed against the prospect of any freeze in credits which would be fatal to détente and to Soviet overall strategy. The article was a reaction to the deepening concern in the West about the basic solvency of the East-bloc countries just explained. For the first time Western bankers were beginning to question the soundness of continuing credits on such a scale from the point of view of prudent banking practice. Deficits of this magnitude could only be repaid through some equally large expansion in attractive exports. Both parties are therefore agreed that an enormous expansion must take place in the re-export of the products stemming from the credit-financed plant and technology in the East, adding the benefits of low-wage labour.

In the current and foreseeable future inflation, unemployment and restrictions on imports will continue in the West. Just how increased dumping of Eastern exports is received without retaliation from Western workers, politicians and nationally-based industry will certainly be the next phase of the dilemma. Credits have often been used in economic warfare. The rise and fall in credits has occurred simultaneously with the rise and fall in political confrontation in US–Soviet relations. Immediately after the Second World War, for a brief period, the US granted large credits to Poland and Czechoslovakia and even considered generous grants to the Soviet Union. By 1959, the climate had cooled in response to the final choice of the USSR to withdraw into autarky, as already described, rather than to join in the capitalist-dominated international monetary and trade system. Of all the East-bloc countries only Rumania has joined the IMF.

In keeping with the general climate, the USA put a tight ban on credits and guarantees. But this *cordon sanitaire* did not last long. As the first large-scale cooperation projects took shape, the European multinational firms and banks quickly changed their governments' credit policies through 180 degrees to meet the perceived demand potential in the Communist countries. Even the most reactionary anti-Socialists in high office, most of whom were associated or tied up with the banks and business interests in one way or another declared against economic warfare with the Communist states and supported cheap long-term credits to back up their investments.

Italy began an aggressive pro-Eastern credit policy in the late fifties to finance the pioneering Vodka-Colanization of giant firms such as Fiat, Pirelli, Montedison and Olivetti, although it was chronically short of domestic capital for financing its own development in backward regions like the Mezzogiorno. The large-scale credit to finance Fiat's construction of the Togliattigrad factory was the most important given by any Western country up to that time. Successively, all the West European countries, under pressure from the multinationals and their banks, cast off the prudence one would expect of visceral anti-Communist bankers of the City of London, Bahnhofstrasse, Frankfurt, and Place de la Bourse, Paris, to enter joyously into the profitable streaming of capitalist credits into the Communist countries to finance capitalist–Communist joint undertakings.

In 1963, France granted the Soviet Union a major credit of 3.5 million francs. From 1963 to 1970, France extended over one billion francs in credits to finance the activities of Renault, Rhône-Poulenc, Péchiney and others in the East-bloc countries. Maturity periods also began to extend from five to seven, and finally to ten, years.

The first British Government Export Credit Guarantee was granted to Czechoslovakia in June 1964 with a repayment period of twelve years. This was followed by a credit of fifteen-years maturity to the USSR.

West Germany was prohibited by the Allied military authorities from granting credits to the East up until 1963, with the exception of Poland. But since 1964, it has become the most extensive purveyor of credits to Communist regions, with most being tied to specific goods and buy-back corporation deals. Its credit generosity to the Soviets exceeded by far all other offers, until by 1976, half of all FRG foreign credits were going to the Soviet Union.

The rapid extension of credit and cooperation by West European countries forced the USA to follow suit and in August 1971 it too removed most restrictions and started extending credits on an unprecedented scale.

A large portion of the current outstanding Eastern debt to the West represents debt associated with extended long-term credits in what represented a profound change in previous policy. Instead of opposing financial ties and involvement with capitalist banking groups, out of fear of losing political independence and suspicion of the destabilizing infiltration of the Communist economies by Western capital, the Eastern régimes now energetically sought such links. During the early sixties some very large projects were promoted by the Soviet Union on the basis of capitalist credits on a new scale. Italy's $100 million credit in 1961 and the follow-up $363 million credit for the Fiat automotive plant in 1966, was paralleled in France by the granting of 3.5 billion francs for financing equipment for the petroleum and petro-chemical industries, a further 1.5 billion francs in 1971 for Renault's participation in the construction of the Kama River truck factory, and an 800 million francs credit for a joint cellulose factory. Great Britain agreed that 80% of all capital goods deliveries to the East would be financed by credits, but the longest-ever credit facility has been from the USA in the form of the $500 million Commodity Credit Corporation grant, involving an additional subsidy of $500 million for grain purchases and a $225 million loan with sixteen-years maturity to back the Kama River scheme.

Studies have been made for a mammoth project for the development of raw material reserves in Siberia estimated at $45 billion. $500 million of Japanese credit was already advanced in 1976 for other raw material projects in Siberia.

Interest rates

The East European countries, with the Soviet Union at their head, have succeeded not only in keeping interest rates far below their real level in their own countries (around 2%) but in having rates on Western credits fixed well below the astronomically high levels prevailing on the capitalist markets. To encourage further integrated business, credits are granted at rates much below Western prime rates and very much below those prevalent in markets for average businessmen and borrowers.

Despite this incentive, the Soviet Union continues in its efforts to have the rates lowered still further. It feels that to go beyond 6% or at most 7% for interest rates on credits would be intolerable for ideological reasons. A compromise is often struck by the

Western banks nominally granting the lower rates whilst tacitly recouping the difference in prices. This saves face ideologically but still ensures a return at the going commercial rate for commercial banks. The Federal Republic of Germany insists upon applying commercial interest rates, except in the case of Yugoslavia, which was given DM 1 billion with thirty-years credit at 2%. The high commercial rate (now 9%) is usually buried in the price of the project.

All such direct and indirect preferential interest rates are, of course, ultimately subsidized by the various governments and borne by the tax-payer. Canada, Great Britain, France and Japan subsidize interest rates on Communist credits officially. The official discounts are accompanied by a number of different risk protections for the national lender, including guarantees against inflation and exchange rate fluctuations. France, Great Britain, Italy and Japan also extend concessionary official credit lines running into billions, at interest rates ranging from 6.5–7.5%. Almost all these official credit lines are for backing exports to Eastern Europe as part of cooperation deals. Only a small amount (10%) is used for financing straight exports of goods and services.

Except in the case of the USA, credit lines of all leading governments finance up to 85% of each project. The US Export–Import (Exim) Bank, the agency which finances and promotes US foreign trade, employs another technique for providing subsidized credits. The Bank advances credits to cover 45% of the cost of each project. Private commercial banks cover another 45% and the recipient produces a cash payment of 10%. The Exim Bank's interest rate rose from 6% in 1974 to 7% in mid-1976. This rate, when blended with the normal commercial rate of the other 45% still provides an effective rate well below that of the market. For example, if the commercial rate is 12% and the Exim rate is 7%, the loan would be at an effective 9.5%, added to which, the higher commercial interest is repaid first in order that the private banks can make their profits as they would in the western credit market. Cheap insurance against defaults is also available.

Many ordinary businessmen have openly criticized the anomaly of a large country like the USSR being susidized by the USA and other governments at interest rates much cheaper than they themselves can get.

In Great Britain, where government trade officials have been pleading with the Soviet Union to take their full quota of the £950 million export credits on offer for 1976, home-based manufacturing industry, which is in deep recession, must now borrow at rates between 13% and 14%, following a 1.5% rise in base lending rates. This has prompted comment that the fervently-awaited recovery in British industry will be slowed yet further, despite cooperation by trade unionists in their government's extended policy of wage and public expenditure restraints, ostensibly aimed at transferring scarce resources into needed industrial investment. British workers must pay up to 16% for personal loans, whilst the latest round of public expenditure reductions is targeted to "save" just over the £950 million extended to the Soviet Union.

US trade unions have sharply criticized the concessionary rates of the Exim Bank, rightly pointing out that an American worker wishing to finance the purchase of a car or a house has to pay interest at almost double the rate extended to the Soviets. As a tax payer, of course, the average American is penalized a second time when the subsidy reappears as a charge against the public budget. He feels it again as a consumer, for shortage of capital leads to higher prices. Indeed, capital scarcity and demand, high interest rates and the cost of capital credits are the principal pressures under modern inflation. The extent of the capital shift to the East is substantial. In 1971, according to UN estimates, total indebtedness of East European countries to the West was around $7 billion compared with the present $50 billion. Most of this growth is matched by credits, transferred out of the Western capital markets to the Eastern countries. How much of the inflation and rising consumer prices is due to this capital transfer is impossible to estimate accurately, but the scale of this trend shows that its effects must have been very significant.

Banking cooperation

In his pamphlet *Imperialism: The Highest Stage of Capitalism,* Lenin cited the Crédit Lyonnais as an example of the "imperialist" banks. It is ironic that this was also the first foreign bank to open a branch in a socialist country. As the multinational companies expanded into Eastern Europe, their banking shadows followed them. The Crédit Lyonnais was the pioneer for many others, especially German and Italian banks. Ostensibly and commercially, their presence was established to facilitate the transfer of credits and to assist in working out the financing arrangements for cooperation deals. Obviously, without the existence of a private money and capital market in the East they could not transact business such as taking deposits, financing mergers, raising debt capital, making loans or speculating in foreign exchange and real estate which cover the range of normal banking activities in the West. By the end of 1973, twenty banks had already submitted applications to the Soviet Gos bank. Another thirty applications from the largest capitalist banks were submitted to the other central banks. The Chase Manhattan Bank—first located in Vienna to coordinate exploratory Eastern business long dabbled in by the various interests of its President, David Rockefeller—was also the first US bank to open a branch in Moscow and was followed by others including Wells Fargo, the Bank of America, First National, Morgan Guaranty Trust, and others. Even the New York Stock Exchange (which effectively provides cover for banking control over large segments of American industry through mysterious "Street Name" holding companies) organized discussions in Moscow in November 1972 on how the NYSE could become involved in advancing Vodka-Colanization.

A very large proportion of Western capitalism, especially the multinational companies, is controlled by the large banks. The trust and stock equity holdings of leading German, French, British and American banks exercise effective voting control over most of the companies involved in East–West cooperation. It is normal that the banks whose profits come not only from interest rates and charges on the financing of credits, but ultimately from the dividends and value of the stock of the non-banking multinationals which they control, should seek to become more directly involved. The extensive presence of so many capitalist banking concerns in Eastern Europe is therefore not an insignificant nor secondary aspect of Vodka–Colanization. It is, indeed, of fundamental importance to the process in view of the real power and control which these financial empires exercise over the industrial enterprises, nationally and internationally. The leading banks all have representation on the boards of directors or supervisory boards of major multinationals. This fact increases the degree of direct banking participation in the economic and political decisions of industry. The industry–banking complex is, therefore, a tightly knit, cohesive power structure. It further explains the complete parallelism between the liberalization of credit policies and the growth of cooperation, as well as the alacrity of the switch to détente by previously hostile political establishments.

Certainly, the first-stage presence of so many representatives of the financial power élite of capitalism is of great significance for future developments in East–West relations. This presence and related influence will grow as trade expands. The cooperation of these denizens of the Overworld of capitalism with their leading counterparts at the top of the political and financial hierarchy of the Eastern régimes will decisively affect the direction of future trends. Progressive association and collaboration between these élitist power centers will fashion a new and unchallengeable Overworld system, before which all of the West's meso-world political structures will become even more impotent and ineffectual than they are today.

While awaiting permission to set up operations directly, many Western banks have begun branch operations in Vienna through which to coordinate East–West business. Financial Square in Vienna is now an important center for East–West activities. Over 200 branches and representatives of foreign banks are located there. This includes around twenty large international banks and nearly ninety American companies. Combined into national and international consortia, the leading banks have become powerful lobbyists for removing obstacles to deals with the East in which they are so directly concerned. It is in these most politically retrograde, anti-socialist, anti-worker and anti-union circles that the most unconditional pro-Soviet pressurizing and lobbying takes place. Representatives of the big banks are constantly pressing for the granting of MFN status to the Soviet Union, for the removal of the obligation that the US Congress should be consulted on credits to the USSR of more than $300 million, for increasing Exim Bank lending possibilities, for relaxing export quotas and for removing more sensitive items from the COCOM strategic embargo list. In West Germany, the UK, France, Italy, Sweden, Austria, and elsewhere, the banking–Brezhnev coalition has succeeded in subduing most political opposition to Vodka-Colanization.

In many fields, the power of vested-interest groups in the West has a curious, but perhaps necessary, double standard in regard to tolerance of East European institutions. The major one, of course, is permitting Communist political parties and Communist-Party dominated trade unions to function freely within a democratic, pluralistic political system. The Soviets maintain that this is an expression of the will of the workers to have a revolutionary Communist Party to lead them from capitalist bondage and is not the result of any Soviet intervention in the internal affairs of other countries. But no reciprocal rights for testing whether the Soviet workers would like to have a Social-Democratic or Liberal Party to lead them out of neo-Stalinist bondage are demanded as a *quid pro quo*. This is dismissed as utopian, naïve and dangerous for peaceful coexistence.

In the same vein, Communist international and national trade unions are permitted to operate freely in the West to maintain agents and representatives, to disseminate propaganda, to organize rallies and meetings, to agitate and to establish separate, sectarian trade unions. No reciprocal rights are permitted to Western national and international organizations in Eastern Europe, where such notions are rejected as counter-revolutionary attempts to intervene in East European internal affairs.

The same dual standard is now accepted also in banking. While Western banks in Eastern Europe are not permitted to undertake banking transactions nor to function within the state banking system, although this is changing, Eastern European state banks are permitted full and unlimited banking privileges in the West. The Moscow Narodny Bank in London (with assets larger than the National Bank of Ireland) and its branches in Singapore and Beirut, the Soviet Banque Commerciale pour l'Europe in Paris, the Vozkhod Trade Bank in Zürich, the East–West Bank in Frankfurt, the Bank Russo-Iran in Teheran, the Donaubank in Vienna and the Soviet East–West United Bank in Luxembourg, though specializing in East–West foreign trade transactions, operate as fully licensed domestic banks and offer comprehensive traditional banking services. These services, of course, include many foreign exchange dealings and speculations, tax evasion services, etc., on behalf of their proprietors: the Soviet Union.

All the other COMECON nations carry out similar banking operations in the West with the exception of Bulgaria and the GDR. A few of the branches have been established for some time, but most of the expansion has taken place since 1970. Poland is relatively the most indebted and most capitalist-dependent Eastern country, with a third of its economy and labour still agricultural, high food costs, few exports, and a run-down, inefficient industry turning out low-quality goods. West Germany and the United States are its principal medium-term hopes for acquiring sufficient high-technology plant and know-how. Poland is forced to pay higher interest rates than other countries for specially needed equipment (up to 10 and 11%) and this is provoking a Soviet reaction for fear that these higher rates may be used as a springboard to raise the entire interest rate structure for all countries of the Eastern bloc.

Under pressure to find more credits, the Soviet Union, which sold 328 tons of gold in Switzerland in 1976 for slightly over $1 billion, has turned to issuing five-year promissory notes to raise more credit. During 1977 the Soviets raised up to $2 billion in the form of 6.5–7.5% interest-bearing promissory notes. The real interest is, however, approximately 10%, as the prices of the capital imports raised to provide the difference between the "ideological" rate and the market rate. As these notes are discounted to the Western banks they provide an alternative to direct lending and a supplementary source of medium-term credits. This constitutes another device for circumventing the US credit restrictions—lending to the Soviet Union—of the Jackson–Vanek amendment, as in the case of leasing. Raising hard currency loans and credits is a major parameter in the Polish Five-Year Plan, which makes banking cooperation particularly important. Western Banks in Poland include: the First National Bank of Chicago, Banca Commerciale Italiana, and two French banks, Crédit Industriel et Commercial and Banque Nationale de Paris. The Polish foreign trade bank, Bank Handlowy Warszawie SA maintains branches in Belgrade, London and New York. Bank PKO (Personal Service Bank) has branches in France and Israel engaged in personal money transfers for Polish citizens and nationals of Polish origin. As for other Eastern countries: the GDR has permitted two French banks and one Italian bank to set up in East Berlin; Hungary has one Austrian bank, the Creditanstalt-Bankverein; Rumania one American bank, Manufacturers Hannover Trust; and Bulgaria, the Italian Banco di Napoli. Only Czechoslovakia opposes the presence of foreign banks, a reflection of the persistent effects of the trauma following the Dubcek era of "Socialism with a human face."

Besides the Soviet and Polish banks mentioned above, Hungary has banks or banking representatives in Vienna and London, Rumania in London, Paris, Frankfurt, Rome and Zurich, whilst even Bulgaria has banking offices in London and Beirut.

Western banks operate extensively through networks of international correspondent banks through which foreign banking cooperation is carried out. A correspondent is a foreign bank which agrees to cooperate on an item-by-item basis for fees on behalf of another bank. This method is particularly utilized by banks with no directly-owned subsidiaries in certain countries and in foreign cities and financial centers. Correspondent foreign banks thus permit providing services for clients which otherwise could not be done, due to the bank's limited implantation abroad, especially smaller and medium-sized banks.

During the current phases of East–West economic cooperation, the practice of establishing networks of correspondent banks through the West has expanded rapidly. Most important East European banks have built up large numbers of such correspondent banking chains. It represents an important additional link between East and West banking, supplementary to the partnerships and direct investments described in this Section.

Below is an example of the correspondents which the Polish National Bank advertises itself as possessing in the West:

Osterreichische Landerbank A.G., Wien
Banque de Bruxelles S.A., Bruxelles
Den Danske Landmansbank, Copenhagen
Skandinaviska Enskilda Banken, Stockholm
Algemene Bank Nederland N.V., Amsterdam
Deutsche Bank A.G., München
Dresdner Bank A.G., Frankfurt/Main
Mitteleuropäische Handelsbank A.G., Frankfurt/Main
Union de Banques Suisses, Zürich
Banca Nationale del Lavoro, Roma
Barclays Bank International Ltd., London
Commonwealth Trading Bank of Australia, London
The Chase Manhattan Bank, New York
The First National Bank of Chicago, Chicago
First National City Bank, New York
Girard Trust Bank, Philadelphia
Irving Trust Company, New York
Bank of America NTrust and SA, San Francisco
The Royal Bank of Canada, Montreal
Commonwealth Trading Bank of Australia, Sydney

An indicator of the growing collaboration between the giants of financial monopoly capitalism and the Communist foreign trade monopoly banks (trade and credit are usually kept separate and distinct in the East) is the trend toward creating East–West banking consortia. The Polish Bank Handlowy, for example, joined six major capitalist banks on an equal share basis to create Centrobank AG in Vienna in 1971. The six banks were Banque Popular Español (of Franco's Spain), Kleinwort Benson of London, Banque Occidentale pour l'Industrie et le Commerce of Paris, Banco Sicilia of Palermo, Bank of Tokyo, and the Austrian trade union and Socialist Party-owned Bank für Arbeit und Wirtschaft. Two years later, Poland became a partner in the German–Polish Central European Bank in Frankfurt. This was the first joint venture between a West German bank and an Eastern bank, being formed on the basis of 70% ownership by the Polish Bank Handlowy and 30% by the Hessische Landesbank-Girozentrale.

Rumania also has been a leader in joint-venture Vodka-Cola banking. The Rumanian Foreign Trade Bank entered a joint venture with eight important French banks in 1972 to create the French–Rumanian Bank in Paris, and a 50/30/20 partnership in the Anglo–Rumanian Bank in London along with Barclays Bank and the American Manufacturers Hanover Trust respectively. Another joint venture with West German banks was established in Frankfurt in August 1976. Hungary has a joint venture in Austria with the Austrian Kontrolbank and another in London, the Hungarian National Bank, with 25% of its shares held by other Austrian banks.

Branches of foreign capitalist banks in Hungary were authorized by a decree issued on 24 January 1977. According to the new regulations these banks, which are exonerated from paying Hungarian taxes, may employ "non-Hungarian" personnel. They will be permitted to conclude banking business, but not to promote business in Hungary. They are chiefly permitted to arrange import–export business for their Western parent banks with Hungarian enterprises, but excluded as yet from conducting normal domestic banking functions such as opening accounts, extending credit and issuing cheques. Some Western banks have pointed out that such banking privileges accorded Hungarian banking subsidiaries in the West may improve the possibilities of reciprocal rights in Hungary. The thinking is that, as cooperation expands, the willingness to extend such reciprocal rights to Western banks will grow, especially as the US has authorized the National Bank of Hungary to open a branch on Wall Street with full banking rights under American law: raise loans, issue bonds and solicit deposits, etc.

Yugoslavia is both the least integrated of the Communist-bloc countries and the most interrelated to Western economies and enterprises. Not a member of COMECON, it was the leader in cooperative ventures with multinational companies. At least numerically Yugoslavia has the most East–West banking links abroad. Its foreign trade bank, Beogradska Bank, has branches in Frankfurt, London and Paris and the Yugoslavian Investment Bank branches in London and Paris. Most of the banking institutions whose clients are involved in Yugoslavian joint undertakings have representation or agents in Belgrade. By far the most important joint Yugoslavian capitalist banking venture is the International Investment Corporation for Yugoslavia (IICY). The headquarters of this organization, originally in London, are now shared between London and Yugoslavia. In the consortia are such multinational banks as the Amsterdam–Rotterdam Bank, Banco di Napoli, Creditanstalt of Austria, Commerzbank, Deutsche Bank, Dresdner Bank, Westdeutsche Landesbank-Girozentrale (all of the Federal Republic of Germany) and the Cunard Co. and Marine Midland Banks of the US. The IICY has been the primary bank for promoting, financing and implementing Western investments in Yugoslavia, frequently by way of a direct participation.

The Moscow Narodny Bank offered "Capitalist Eurodollars" to customers as early as 1954 and 1955 as did its sister Soviet bank in Paris. Since then Eastern Communist banks have regularly increased their participations in management and underwritings of bond issues for both capitalist as well as Communist borrowers in the Eurodollar market. The first bond issue of a Communist country, in capitalism's most licentious money market, was floated by Hungary in 1971. Over seventy-five leading capitalist banks underwrote the issue for $25 million. This was followed by a second bond for $50 million carrying 8.5% and a fifteen-years maturity, headed by a consortium composed of the Moscow Narodny Bank, London's Morgan Grenfell, the Bank of America and the Frankfurter Bank of the Federal Republic of Germany. Since that beginning, issues by Eastern countries have grown. The International Bank for Economic Cooperation (IBEC), the COMECON coordinating banking agency, has been in the Eurodollar market since 1972. One of its functions is to generate medium-term bank-to-bank credits to assist in financing East–West deals. The method is to cooperate with various capitalist banking consortia to put together issues of between $20–40 million. East European ideologues and Western Stalinists may still be able to argue that the number of Western banks and industrial joint venture projects in the East do not represent a real capitalist presence. On the other hand, the number of capitalist debtors or bondholders of Communist commercial papers has become very important—perhaps a portent of actual capitalist stockholders buying and selling Communist companies on the villainous, depraved, capitalist New York Stock Exchange! The margin of transition from debt to equity is not very wide in the West. Initial discussions on issuing Communist government bonds on the New York market have already taken place. And since the New York Stock Exchange has already indicated its readiness to play a role in furthering East–West economic relations, what better role could it play in furthering international peace, détente, and human happiness?

The second COMECON bank, actually a dual bank to the IBEC, the International

Investment Bank (IIB) has also been actively raising bond currency Euroloans in cooperation with Western consortia: $50 million under the syndicate leadership of the British National Westminster Bank; $50 million along with Crédit Lyonnais of France; $60 million through a Belgian group. Participating within these syndicates in the issues were all of the leading 100 investment banks of the Western world. Both COMECON banks, IBEC and IIB, have nearly 300 representations, links and ties with Western banks.

The growth in recent years of multinational consortia banking stimulated by the growth and domination of the economic system by multinationals has probably been the most important development in banking. Involving leading banks from different countries, the consortium provides a multinational structure of total banking services for its clients around the world. It has prompted a qualified estimate that ten to twelve multinational banking consortia will completely dominate the world's credit and money markets by the end of the century. All of the world's most powerful national banks are today intrinsically multinational in their own structure and are further integrated internationally through their common membership in these consortia. The fifty leading banks account for nearly 75% of international financing, including the nearly $70 billion annual bond issues for debt capital. Together they have hundreds of branches around the world. The Bank of America alone has 100 branches in 58 countries and earns 60% of its profits abroad. The Chase Manhattan Bank of the Rockefellers has 57 branches in 44 countries, the Deutsche Bank 65 branches in 32 countries, and Barclay's Bank has 48 branches in 33 countries. British, Swiss and German banks have, if anything, been more international than even the American giants in terms of the amount of business transacted abroad.

A first UK–USSR banking joint venture was established in 1978:

> Morgan Grenfell, the Bank of Scotland and Moscow Narodny Bank yesterday signed an agreement to set up a joint venture banking operation in Moscow, aimed at providing for their customers a service in the Soviet Union. The new venture will combine the expertise of Moscow Narodny in the financing of East–West trade with the experience of Morgan Grenfell and the Bank of Scotland in the arrangement of ECGD-backed loans and the financing of major projects. The Bank of Scotland, with experience in the oil industry, hopes to expand business in that sector, particularly in Soviet offshore oil development. It also hopes to increase funding of ECGD-backed deals which Morgan Grenfell would manage.
>
> Moscow Narodny, a Soviet-owned but British-registered international bank, would continue to specialise in documentary credits and play an important role in providing assistance within the Soviet Union. The office in Moscow will be managed by Moscow Narodny's representative there. Morgan Grenfell, with traditional ties in Eastern Europe, will continue to arrange buyer credits and intends to expand Eurodollar lending and management, while looking at new methods of financing such as leasing, an area in which Moscow Narodny has recently been active.

Given their domination of the West's money and credit markets, it is natural that the banking consortia should also dominate the Vodka-Cola financial markets. A growing volume of credits for East European cooperation is channelled through syndicates of the consortia. Most of the large capitalist banks have established branches in East European countries either directly or through some variation of the joint venture arrangement.

Confronted by the mounting debt of East European banks, arrangements for a $200 million UK Euromarket loan to IBEC fell through following an opinion by British lawyers that IBEC had no juridical validity in the UK. In case of default, the opinion held, the lender banks would have no recourse in law for recovery. Such is the thrust for co-production banking business, however, that shortly after IBEC was able to secure a $400 million Euromarket loan from Western banks for financing sections of a long pipeline, from which revenues will be laid off against the loan. Instead of squeamish British banks, the German Dresdner Bank operated as lead bank for some ten other capitalist banks with confidence in Communist solvency. To evade all forms of legal trivia, the loan is to be registered under Luxembourg law—which excludes the risk of legal interpretation.

There is scarcely a Western bank of any importance (commercial multibanks or investment banks) which is not involved in the huge new market of raising East European credits. Most of the debt, present and future, of Eastern Europe to the West represents private bank loans, effectively about two-thirds. As the Federal Republic of Germany, Canada, the UK, France, Belgium, Austria, Japan, etc., favour private or non-governmental bank loans extended under government guarantees, the debt will continue to accrue to the private or semi-public money market.

Two salient features emerge: (1) The Western banking system, capitalism's strategic underpinning, is totally and critically extended or "loaned" into the Communist system and dependent upon its stability as condition of repayment; (2) the size of the debt-overhang will be so enormous in 1980 (US$ 100 billion) that any serious threat of default by any one Communist country would induce tremors and possible collapse of the West's monetary and financial system. Together they compel capitalist support and protection of the political status quo.

This compulsion toward support and protectionism contains another dimension which enlarges the Vodka-Cola syndrome by several magnitudes. Outstanding and largely unrecoverable debts of the less developed countries, estimated at around $250 billion, towards the industrialized world's banking system will exceed the East European level by two or three times. Although of lesser proportion, this debt is still substantially due to the same major banks. Cumulatively, under normal banking criteria, the debt-overhang should place the private system's solvency in question—theoretically, of course, for governments could not permit a crash of any significant scale to occur and would supply the liquidities necessary to seal a breach before a major run got underway. But increasingly warnings of the dangers building up are being expressed in concerned banking circles. They allege that if the present rate of expanding credits is maintained, and doubts grow on the solvency of the East European countries due to scarcity of hard currency and inadequacy of counter-purchase and co-production schemes to cover debt repayment, the situation could quickly become unstable and accident-prone. A major default in one sector or country in such a situation could trigger a sequence of runs in others which even governments and international lending institutions could not plug. Under such circumstances, political policy must inevitably be directed to protection and maintenance of existing régimes and systems regardless of their social and humanitarian characteristics.

The following Table provides a schematic overview of the involvement of the West's leading banks in raising dollar and Eurocurrency loans for COMECON countries and Yugoslavia. Actually, the list could be extended to include hundreds of other less important banks in many countries. Either as lead banks or participants in syndicated

Leading Western Banks in Eastern Europe

US	Bank of America	Moscow
	First National City Bank	Moscow — Budapest
	First National Bank of Chicago	Warsaw
	Chase Manhattan Bank	Moscow
	Manufacturers Hanover Trust	Bucharest
Federal Republic of Germany	Commerzbank	Moscow
	Deutsche Bank	Moscow
	Dresdner Bank	Moscow
United Kingdom	Barclay's Bank	Moscow
	Lloyd's Bank	Moscow
	Midland Bank	Moscow
	National Westminster Bank	Moscow
France	Banque de Paris et des Pays-Bas	Moscow
	Banque Nationale de Paris	Moscow — Warsaw
	Crédit Industriel et Commercial	Warsaw
	Crédit Lyonnais	Moscow — East Berlin
Italy	Banca Commerciale Italiana	Moscow — Warsaw — East Berlin
	Banco di Napoli	Moscow — Sofia
	Credito Italiano	Moscow
Austria	Creditanstalt-Bankverein	Budapest
Sweden	Svenska Handelsbanken	Moscow
Finland	Korsallis-Osake Pankki	Moscow
Japan	Bank of Tokyo	Moscow

placements, medium and long-term loans of short-term deposits and placing East European bonds with customers has become a major banking activity of the capitalist system.

Czechoslovakia has not been included because of the limited volume of direct bank loans which have been placed. Following the Russian invasion of the country, Czechoslovakia has preferred to provide itself with hard currency credits through the COMECON banks rather than directly through bank-to-bank or bank-to-foreign-trade organization loans. However, this policy is now changing and Czechoslovakia is increasingly coming to the Western banks and Eurocurrency market for capital funds.

Leading Western banks involved in Eastern credit placements either as lead banks or syndicate participants

Bank	Head office	Total assets ($ US million 1/75)	USSR	Pol	Hun	Rum	GDR	Bul	Yug	IBEC IIB
Bank of America	San Francisco	59,369	X		X	X	X	X	X	X
First National City Bank	New York	55,499	X		X	X	X		X	X
Chase Manhattan Bank	New York	41,714	X	X	X	X	X	X	X	X
Banque National de Paris	Paris	35,780	X	X	X	X	X	X	X	X
Barclays Bank	London	33,334	X	X	X	X	X	X	X	X
Deutsche Bank	Frankfurt	32,418	X	X	X	X	X		X	X
National Westminster Bank	London	31,899	X	X	X	X	X	X	X	X
Dai-Ichi Kengyo Bank	Tokyo	31,187	X	X	X		X	X	X	
Crédit Lyonnais	Paris	29,737	X	X	X	X	X	X	X	X
Société Générale	Paris	28,507	X	X	X	X	X	X	X	X
Fuji Bank	Tokyo	27,603	X	X	X	X	X	X	X	X
Sumitomo Bank	Osaka	27,051	X	X	X	X	X	X	X	X
Mitsubishi Bank	Tokyo	25,747	X	X	X	X	X	X	X	
Morgan Guaranty Trust Co.	New York	25,641	X	X	X	X	X		X	X
Dresdner Bank	Frankfurt	25,526	X	X	X	X	X	X	X	X
Sanwa Bank	Osaka	25,187	X	X	X	X	X	X	X	
Manufacturers Hanover Trust Co.	New York	24,960	X	X	X	X	X	X	X	X
Westdeutsche Länderbank-Girozentrale	Dusseldorf	23,654	X	X	X	X	X		X	X
Bank of Tokyo	Tokyo	23,536	X	X	X	X	X	X	X	
Midland Bank	London	23,340	X	X	X	X	X		X	X
Royal Bank of Canada	Montreal	21,823	X	X	X	X	X	X	X	X
Chemical Bank	New York	21,651	X	X	X	X	X	X	X	X
Industrial Bank of Japan	Tokyo	21,124	X	X	X	X		X	X	
Lloyds Bank	London	21,026	X	X	X	X	X	X	X	X
Banca Commerciale Italiana	Milan	20,091	X	X	X	X	X			X
Banca Nazionale del Lavoro	Rome	19,863	X	X	X	X	X		X	
Canadian Imperial Bank of Commerce	Toronto	19,700	X	X	X		X	X	X	X
Tokai Bank	Nagoya	19,560	X	X	X	X		X	X	

Bank	Head Office	Total assets ($ US million 1/75)	USSR	Pol	Hun	Rum	GDR	Bul	Yug	IBEC IIB
Bankers Trust Co.	New York	19,193	X	X	X	X	X	X	X	X
Continental Illinois National Bank	Chicago	18,899	X	X		X	X		X	X
Mitsui Bank	Tokyo	18,316	X	X	X	X	X	X	X	
Taiyo Kobe Bank	Kobe	18,293	X		X	X		X	X	
Commerzbank	Düsseldorf	18,276	X	X			X	X	X	X
First National Bank	Chicago	18,164	X	X	X	X	X		X	
Bank of Montreal	Montreal	17,680	X	X	X	X	X	X	X	
Bayerische Vereinsbank	Munich	17,088	X	X			X	X		X
Long-Term Credit Bank of Japan	Tokyo	16,410	X	X	X	X	X	X	X	
Swiss Bank Corporation	Basle	16,159	X	X	X		X	X	X	X
Union Bank of Switzerland	Zurich	16,029	X	X	X		X		X	X
Daiwa Bank	Osaka	15,685	X		X	X		X	X	
Security Pacific National Bank	Los Angeles	15,256		X			X	X		X
Cooperatieve Centrale Raiffeisen	Utrecht	14,935	X		X	X	X	X	X	
Bayerische Landesbank-Girozentrale	Munich	14,763	X	X	X	X	X	X		X
Banco di Rome	Rome	14,160	X	X	X	X		X	X	
Algemene Bank Nederland	Amsterdam	13,969	X	X	X		X		X	X
Credito Italiano	Milan	13,709	X	X	X	X	X	X	X	
Amsterdam—Rotterdam Bank	Amsterdam	13,473	X	X			X	X	X	X
Bayerische Hypotheken-u. Wechsel-Bank	Munich	13,379	X	X	X	X	X	X	X	
Hessische Landesbank-Girozentrale	Frankfurt	13,326	X	X	X		X			X
Société Générale de Banque	Brussels	13,175	X	X	X	X	X		X	X
Bank of Nova Scotia	Toronto	12,962	X	X	X			X	X	X
Kyowa Bank	Tokyo	12,863	X	X	X	X	X	X	X	X

Partial list of Western loans to Eastern Europe

Year	Debtor	Loans in millions of dollars	Year	Debtor	Loans in millions of dollars
1969	IBEC	60	1975	Hungary	50
1970	IBEC	20	1975	Czechoslovakia	60
1973	IIB	50	1975	Poland	490
1973	Poland	50	1975	GDR	250
1974	Poland	509	1975	Hungary	349
1974	Hungary	150	1975	Bulgaria	106
1974	Bulgaria	160	1975	IBEC	420
1974	IIB	150	1976	IIB	600
1974	IBEC	50	1976	IIB	300
1975	USSR	100	1976	Yugoslavia	200
1975	Hungary	100	1976	Poland	50
1975	GDR	75	1976	Hungary	25
1975	IIB	70	1976	Poland	30
1975	Poland	240	1976	Rumania	240
1975	USSR	250	1977	IIB	500
1975	Poland	50	1977	Hungary	200
1975	GDR	50	1977	Poland	208
1975	IBEC	240	1977	Bulgaria	150
1975	IIB	240	1977	Rumania	50

3

Forms of Cooperation

Imagine a scene in the boardroom of a large Western multinational. The results of a sophisticated computer analysis are presented to the directors: the problem analysed is the optimum global configuration of the company's production and sales over the next twenty-five years. The computer's answer is a shocker: produce in the world's most favourable cost-efficiency region, i.e. Eastern Europe, and sell in the world's best comparative sales-profits region, i.e. the industrialized West. Mind-blowing—yet simple and logical. Very low wages, long hours, plus relatively skilled, disciplined and no-strike unions to produce company products at the lowest costs, for sale in the high-wage, high-price, mass consumer markets of Europe, the USA, Japan, Canada and Australia. A dream—mathematically logical but politically unthinkable.

In early 1950 such a scenario was virtually unimaginable. Both peacenicks and hawks were looking to Eastern Europe, especially the Soviet Union, as a vast opening of a market of 400 million demanding consumers with new aspirations to which the régimes now would have to start responding with more than their constantly postponed promises of a better tomorrow. But this "official" vision soon turned out to be a mirage. For hard-nosed, pragmatic businessmen, little inclined to believe their own propaganda, the Eastern markets were a sociological phenomenon but an illusion from the perspective of the balance sheet. There were no big profits to be made. First, the "masses" were not effective consumers: not only did they not have enough money to buy extra goods, but the little they did have was not convertible to Western balance sheet currencies. So sales in the vast Eastern markets were a profitless potential. *But*, (the computer logic holds) if the same unprofitable consumers can be turned into low-cost *producers* and their output sold in the company's normal hard-currency markets, the circle could be squared. The inversion of the perspective of the Communist East as a consumer market and sales area to that of a primarily production and manufacturing area provided the key to the most important transformation of the world's economic and political relations. This key was *co-production*, a new and highly sophisticated form of barter. Co-production would permit the linking of the Russian citizen–worker to the American, West-German, Dutch, Italian, French, Canadian, and other Western citizen–consumer, thereby completing the profits cycle. Initiated timidly and experimentally at first, the technique quickly proved viable and efficient and expanded very rapidly.

Simply described, co-production deals involve the Western enterprise bringing its technology and managerial know-how to an East European country and setting up a partnership of one of various types with a foreign trade organization of the Eastern government who supplies land, buildings, sometimes simple components, but, above all, *labour*. Low-interest, hard-currency credits to finance the manufacture and transport of equipment, machines, dies, training of operatives, and so on, are usually furnished by the Western company's government either entirely or in conjunction with private banks as a loan to the Eastern partner or associate. Once the project goes on stream, the end products are shared by the partners according to proportions fixed in the contract. A share of the production is allocated to the Eastern partner for the domestic market or the export market, the proportions depending upon the nature of the products and upon government priorities. A large, usually the major, part is normally earmarked for direct exports to earn continuing hard currency. From these exports the original loans contracted in connection with the project are repaid to the Western banks.

For the Western partner, of course, the supply of credits, plant and know-how generates no profit of itself. These inputs are regarded rather as straight investment costs to be amortized and to lead forward to profits once the plant begins producing. The Western firm disposes of its share of output according to the contracted proportions either in Eastern markets, in its Western export markets, or in its domestic market. As the product of this modern plant usually is identical with the product manufactured at home, it is readily assimilated into its distribution network. Frequently, the Western partner also handles the Western sales of the Eastern partner's share if it is a final product.

The range of possible forms of production is very extensive. Plants may produce components and parts to be integrated into a final product, large elements of heavy machinery or of an entire product ranging from an automobile through tires and glass window shields. Plants have been established for products as diverse as calculating machines and furniture, to chemicals and petro-chemical products. The principal input from the Western multinational is the transferred technology and management know-how, which contribute to enhancing the average quality of the manufactured products. Goods closely patterned and controlled to Western specifications may readily be merged into the multinational's world-wide distribution networks, to be sold in Western markets to recoup the hard currency returns from its original investment. By this device the barrier to monetary convertibility is neatly overcome.

Industrial cooperation

Statistically the new form of relationship between centrally-planned and market economies still does not account for a substantial share of East–West trade. Most East–West business is still on the regular buying and selling basis of foreign trade cleared in currencies or through strict barter deals. But such a classical yardstick is misleading. Static macroscopic averages are inaccurate criteria for measuring dynamic phenomena. Small percentages in certain circumstances can be important—even decisive. For example, 10% inflation, 10% unemployment, 10% overall or specific environmental pollution or 10% of cancer cells in the body could spell crises and dysfunctions of the system. One cannot speak of one's average health being good if the 10% which is sick is represented by the heart.

It is the rate of growth which will determine the impact of a new phenomenon. Given the overwhelming political and economic influence of the multinationals and international banks upon world policy, their specific commitments to cooperation will decisively influence developments.

In 1973 East–West industrial cooperation was estimated to account for 1.5–2% of overall trade. By 1975, this estimate rose to 5% and should rise by extrapolation to 9% or 10% by 1979. But given the renewed emphases and pressures upon capitalist firms by East European governments to accept cooperation agreements, the proportion could easily exceed 15–20% by 1980. Only 300 agreements were in force in 1970. Their number rose to 600 in 1973 and 1,000 in 1974. It is estimated that they will number 3,000 by 1979. This would mean a quantum change in East–West trade and in the related consequences.

Recent Congresses of East European Communist Parties (USSR, Bulgaria, Poland, Czechoslovakia) have articulated the position clearly to Western firms: either accept to cooperate in manufacturing or assembling, in whole or at least in part, in the East European country and cooperate in distributing a share of the production for the account of the Eastern partner, or risk having a contract refused or given to a competitor. But these political threats are largely vain. The issue has long been resolved by total agreement between the power centers of industry and finance. Such cooperation agreements are the only highways for transporting Eastern profits to the West and they will therefore be kept wide open. So both sides benefit, if we are to recognize the narrow parochial interests of the authoritarian states and multinational power élitists as still constituting separately identifiable "sides." But what is manifestly good for the new joint venture of General Motors and the Polish and Soviet motor vehicle trust is not necessarily good for American, Polish or Russian workers and citizens.

For the Eastern partner some of the most obvious economic advantages include:
– Long-term, low-interest credit to finance equipment and technology procurement
– Self-financing of most projects through payment in plant output
– Hard-currency exports of share of plant output usually sold by Western partner, thus giving immediate entry to Western markets
– Management know-how and training in specific areas of maximum need
– Long-term cooperation contributes to improved organization and administration of production and distribution
– Cooperation can be integrated into central plans to plug shortcomings and gaps and continued Western advances in technology can be regularly introduced
– Modern technology gained in these enterprises can be emulated and copied throughout the Eastern industrial sector
– More modern and up-to-date products—both for domestic and export markets.

Advantages for the Western firms are similarly numerous and hold few risks. Here are some of the more obvious:
– Labour costs the major advantage: beyond the offset costs of transport, import duties, etc., labour cost differentials are still 5:1 to 10:1
– Cooperation arrangement or license sale frequently opens access to Eastern markets
– Unions are integral to government and enterprise systems, are subservient to the Party and include all levels of management in the union. This compels strict observance of cooperation agreements by workers
– Strikes and demonstrations not permitted, assuring production stability and accurate long-term forecasting of profits
– Possible access to profitable markets in developing countries through joint ventures owing to lower labour costs and prices which Western firms could not match from Western plants
– Cover facilitated for commercial deals in "socialist" regions of the world still ideologically opposed to capitalism and multinational firms
– Monopoly advantages facilitated in Eastern markets and underdeveloped markets as Eastern partner is already a legal and total monopoly
– Protection provided for Western firm against anti-trust prosecution in its area of joint activities in Western markets because of the "legal monopoly" nature of the partner
– Substantial protection against dumping regulations for its Eastern-produced products. Costs of the Eastern components and products are used to undercut prices applying to West-produced products. Margins result in higher cash-flow and profits. For inferior quality products or to undercut competition, Eastern domestic prices and cost estimates make it very difficult to apply dumping regulations by traditional standards, especially the criterion that exported goods must not be priced lower than their prices on domestic markets. These products do not benefit from subsidies, special export

inducements, etc., but are cheap because wage costs are extremely low and because prices are fixed by administrative rather than market instruments

- Long-term access to low-cost extra capacity operations and bottlenecks or substitutes for costlier, less profitable new plants at home
- Prolonged commercial life of quasi-obsolete products and processes and especially continued sales of obsolete lines in less exacting consumer markets abroad. This applies particularly to first and second-generation models replaced in home markets by new third-generation versions
- Cooperation agreements may prevail in which East European partner specializes in producing less sophisticated components and Western firm produces the more sophisticated items. This permits lower unit costs and longer production runs.

Like the term "cooperation," the term "technology" is also an umbrella concept and techniques of technology transfer are necessarily complicated. According to the United Nations' Economic and Social Council (ECOSOC) industrial technology can be briefly defined

> ... as the set of processes whereby raw or semi-finished materials are transformed into a final product which may be either goods or services. Industrial technology comprises all the processes (principal and subsidiary) required for (i) designing, (ii) constructing, (iii) operating and (iv) maintaining production facilities.
>
> The production facilities required for the operation of a given technology may be (i) a shop, (ii) a plant, (iii) an enterprise, or (iv) a group of enterprises performing jointly given functions.
>
> Depending on the state of the art and the R and D which is performed, technology may be new and rapidly-evolving or mature and relatively stable, adapted to the requirements of mass production or tailored to serve specific needs, easily divisible into its constituent elements (and therefore 'segmentable') or indivisible (and accordingly provided in a 'packaged' form).
>
> Technical as well as managerial elements are included in a comprehensive definition of technology, which, therefore, should not be identified exclusively with the specific operations executed by means of a given piece of machinery and equipment. R and D work aimed at developing new or improved products and processes, as well as the specific techniques involved in the marketing of corresponding output (including the provision of adequate after-sales service), are an important and, indeed, in some cases decisive part of industrial technology.

Given that all the different components of technology are being transferred through the process of industrial cooperation, a variety of forms have been developed and still others will surely be developed in the future. The concept is, therefore, necessarily flexible and we cannot determine as yet an "official" definition of East–West "cooperation." As it is of very recent origin, seldom going back more than eight or ten years, and there is a tacit "official" understanding not to emphasize it publicly, there are no international terms yet agreed upon.

Certain characteristics, however, are common to most forms of cooperation deals. The most important feature is the establishment of a lasting and formal relationship between an Eastern and Western industrial enterprise for enduring purposes which distinguish cooperation from the normal *ad hoc* or independent importing and exporting of foreign trade. "Industrial cooperation" implies a lasting relationship between enterprises and does not include agreements between governments. It is important to emphasize this point to avoid the confusion deliberately created by the Eastern governments (particularly the Soviet Union) regarding the role of inter-governmental agreements.

Inter-governmental economic agreements

The purpose of economic agreements between Eastern and Western governments is to provide a framework for promoting favourable conditions for inter-enterprise deals. Though they have proliferated rapidly in the last five years, inter-governmental agreements definitely postdate the surge of inter-enterprise cooperation agreements. They are, therefore, mere political window-dressing, facilitating agreements rather than providing real stimuli. For the Soviet Union their value lies in the surface veneer they give to Eastern propaganda that détente is essentially a process between governments and the consequence of a successful offensive for peace "imposed by the forces of peace upon the revanchist anti-Communist monopolists." Ideologically, détente is maintained at the political level of government. Its declared purpose is to transfer free-floating, disembodied "technology," apparently unrelated to capitalism, monopolists or Marxian considerations of surplus value, socially necessary labour time and other official Soviet-Marxian dogmas. Of course, "technology" does not exist as an abstract concept, but as the hardware of the multinational powerhouses of capitalist production. Seldom, however, is there specific reference in the pronouncements of the Eastern leaders to such "peace loving" supporters of détente as ITT, the oil companies, General Motors, and the rest.

The first inter-government agreement to lay down certain procedures and conditions for capital credits and interest rates was signed between Belgium and Poland during 1965 and 1966. Especially following the ice-breaking visit of Richard Nixon and thirty leading businessmen to the USSR in 1972, such inter-governmental agreements have been concluded by nearly all major and many less powerful Western governments, embracing both democratic and rightwing authoritarian régimes. These have included Spain in Franco's time, Greece in the Colonels' time, and Brazil in the Generals' time. The USA has such agreements with the USSR, Poland, Rumania, and Yugoslavia, the UK with eight countries, France with nine, the Federal Republic of Germany with eight, Italy with eight.

The agreements are basically intended to give official sanction and legal and political support to firms wishing to enter into new relations with East-bloc foreign trade organizations. A type of international status and recognition is provided for the East European countries by these government-level agreements. Inter-governmental joint commissions under long-term general economic accords have emanated from these framework agreements. These were sought by the East Europeans as another means of establishing recognition of the status quo and of setting favourable ground rules for future cooperation. The commissions created extensive personal ties and formed planning groups to push for the exchange of research and information and for more concrete forms of cooperation. Most agreements eventually provide for technical and sectorial sub-groups involving specialists, technicians, and managers. This furthers integration and commitments under existing ground rules which facilitate the exchange of information and technology between two amoral, apolitical, fundamentally different social systems.

Industry cooperation agreements

Another intermediate form of framework agreements associated with industrial cooperation has developed as between individual multinational corporations and state bodies
at the ministerial level responsible for coordinating scientific and technological
research and development. The alleged purpose of these industry cooperation agreements is to promote the exchange of information and experience, including research
projects of mutual interest. Some, in fact, have resulted in original joint research ventures between the multinationals and the Eastern research and development agencies.
But mostly these periodic meetings seem designed to test the real commitment of a
Western firm to East–West cooperation and to elicit a prior contribution of technological
data before the conclusion of profit-generating cooperation deals. Most of the large
companies have hesitantly entered into such agreements, even though they are aware
that they do not necessarily produce hard money deals and that they could lead to an
intelligence breach in the company's defense of valuable information. Nearly 200 such
agreements have been entered into with the USSR State Committee for Science and
Technology, whose Vice-President, G. Vishioni, is simultaneously co-chairman of the
US–Soviet Trade and Economic Council. The agreements thus help to strengthen the
network of Vodka-Cola relationships and the framework of détente against those who
still remain hesitant or opposed to the process. They are also effective transmission belts
for the political objectives and strategies elaborated by the high-level Vodka-Cola
institutions seeking to transform the perspectives and consciousness of operational
management and of technicians habituated to the basic ideology that capitalism is still
an adversary of class-based international socialism.

Cooperation at level of plant and production

As we said above, because of the numerous pragmatic and ad hoc relations which can be
created by cooperation deals, precise definition is not possible. There are, however, some
main types of cooperation which have developed that can be usefully categorized. All
have the common base that they entail lasting relations between enterprises and
involve the exchange of goods for technology. There is little legislation in the West
governing industrial cooperation of a specific nature. Partly, this is because such deals
grew independently of government and faster than official awareness and concern, but
partly also, it is due to the insistence of its promoters upon as little public discussion as
possible in order not to provoke ideological traumas or public opposition. As both
Eastern and Western protagonists stress the need for secrecy and non-intervention in
their affairs as a normal condition, maintaining public ignorance has been relatively
simple.

   In the East, however, the reverse is the case. Virtually all the COMECON countries
have adopted strict legislative provisions governing the various forms of East–West
cooperation. The most detailed is a Yugoslavian law, reflecting that country's greater
experience and development of this form of undertaking. As cooperation expands, legislative cover will increase. Cooperation in practice is, therefore, a controlled and formal
expression of Eastern state policy which explicitly spells out its limits and conditions its
relationship to the centrally-planned economy. Within such a relationship, the more
cohesive, carefully controlled Eastern approach will invariably impose itself upon the
still disparate, private and competitive positions of the Western multinationals. Both in
economic and political terms such a biased strength favours the East in exacting conces-

sions and advancing its interests. And the legislative framework of the deals is more binding than the simple commercial contracts.

The following descriptions of the major types of cooperation center around the fundamental ingenuity of transforming barter, previously a trait of primitive and underdeveloped economies, into a modern technique for overcoming the problems posed by the impenetrable monetary policy of the Eastern countries, and for transferring profits—the sustenance of wealth and private ownership—from the heartland of socialism.

Barter and switching

Every exchange of goods between foreign customers which omits any currency element from the transaction represents classic barter. In varying degrees barter underpins industrial cooperation. Apart from the credits advanced for financing the purchase of machine tools, the inputs of equipment and know-how, and the overheads of training, supervision and transport, for example, are valued and repaid proportionately in the sharing of goods output. Classic barter transactions or quasi-barter forms are still prevalent. In détente jargon barter is called "counter-purchase." Under counter-purchase a Western firm has to take products as part of full payment for its exports, and this usually means accepting payment in kind from a list of goods selected for export by the foreign trade organizations. This form of cooperation has been strongly emphasized by the USSR and is being increasingly demanded by all other Eastern countries in face of the growing credit deficits and their inability to export, already discussed.

Many of the products offered for counter-purchase are general goods or difficult-to-sell machinery and equipment, relatively unsophisticated industrial products being generally pushed hardest by most countries. Most often the Western exporters cannot use such products and turn to a Western trading house (or "switchhouse") specializing in finding customers for such items at an appropriate discount. Counter-purchase barter covers a wide range of transactions: in one such case, Greek lemon and orange juices were accepted in part-exchange for selling Fiat Polish-made automobiles.

Counter-purchase, already urgently demanded of Western suppliers by the USSR, is to be greatly intensified to become the basis of all Soviet–West cooperation deals. Though not more than 30% of the value of Western exports is presently demanded for repayment in this form, the proportion will in practice be very much higher, especially for industrial projects under which the Western firm is paid with the products of his equipment. More than fifty major and over a hundred minor counter-purchase projects have been concluded. Eastern Germany is putting more pressure on Western firms to agree to counter-purchases and to accept a large percentage of the price in products. In many cases they are looking for levels approaching 100%. Poland's critical situation is also compelling the government to press for more counter-purchases. Some experts predict that counter-purchases will cover between 60% and 75% of total imports within five or six years. Rumania requires the highest percentage of counter-purchase for plant, equipment and other products supplied by Western firms, who often complain that artificially high prices and poor quality make "switching" Rumanian products particularly difficult.

French firms like Renault, Michelin and Rhône-Poulenc, and Italian firms like Fiat, Pirelli or Montedison, have concluded such accords. Renault, Fiat and BMW have received components and automobile supplies to be sold in their home markets under counter-purchase conditions. An example of the extent to which barter and switch-trade can reach, is the use of barter between Gulf Oil and Rumania for the sale of a nuclear reactor in 1973. Gulf General Atomic, a subsidiary of Gulf Oil, contracted for the supply of a Triga-type dual-core nuclear reactor to become operational in 1976 or 1977. Gulf Oil is owned by the Mellon interests and the Mellon Bank who have major participations in Westinghouse. The project, worth $4.1 million, was financed by the US Exim Bank and private banks. In return, Gulf agreed to accept Rumanian products for the equivalent of the purchase price over a period of ten years.

In a recent cooperation barter-deal between General Motors and the Bulgarian state-concern Balkancar, heavy duty trucks are to be traded for fork-lift trucks. According to General Motors' British subsidiary, Bedford Trucks, who are to supply the new range of GM vehicles, the attraction of the deal is that it gives access to Europe's largest truck fleet. Between 3,500 and 4,000 Bulgarian trucks operate on international routes. In return, Balkancar will be supplying to GM fork-lift trucks for use in its own plants throughout the world, providing therefore a guaranteed outlet. The Bulgarian state organisation obviously expects this exchange to lead to wider outlets in the West through GM's world-wide marketing network. It will be interesting to observe whether the might of GM will be able to achieve such a breakthrough for its Bulgarian partner's truck (which is already causing concern on grounds of quality) in a crowded European market already offering 160 different makes of fork-lift trucks.

Subcontracting and contracting capacity

A more complex form of counter-purchase or buy-back is the growing practice of sub-contracting and direct contracting for manufacturing between a Western firm and an Eastern enterprise. Under these agreements the Eastern enterprise produces finished products or parts according to the Western firm's specifications for incorporation into the Western sales and distribution plan. Payment is usually in output over and above the delivery quotas required by the West. Most frequently, the Western firm supplies only specifications and design blueprints for production on Eastern machinery. Such agreements offer Western firms expanded capacity without supplementary investment and enable them to profit from lower labour costs. If capacities are large and the ability exists to produce efficiently up to Western quality control standards and specifications, the Western firms sometimes agree to sell an extra portion of the output as exports in their markets for the account of the Eastern firm. The opportunity to earn hard currency from this exchange of commodities has stimulated keen interest in Eastern Europe for this type of contracting. It is difficult to know how many such deals have been quietly concluded, but it can be conservatively estimated to run to several hundred. Though it is a political principle in Eastern Europe that available plant and products are used exclusively for internal consumption, Communist authorities are increasingly award-ing such contracts and turning plant capacity over to production for capitalist markets. A more recent type of sub-contracting openly uses the more efficient management sys-tems of Western firms in Eastern Europe. This new means of merging capitalism directly into the local economy is particularly evident in the construction industry. For example, department stores in Prague, foreign trade centers in Moscow and East Berlin, Olympic Games projects in Moscow, hotels in Warsaw, Budapest and Prague, and apartment buildings in Moscow and Yugoslavia are being built by Western contractors. Reciprocally, where labour costs are the determining factor, construction labour from Yugoslavia and Bulgaria is being employed in the West under the direction of Eastern contractors who ensure lower wages and social benefits than prevail for Western work-ers.

Licensing

Classical Soviet ideology held invention and scientific discovery to be a collective achievement belonging to society as a whole and therefore not subject to individual reward by payments or royalties but by bestowing honours and position. On this premise the Soviets not only repudiated individual rewards at home, but refused to acknowledge any patent obligations when appropriating Western innovations and discoveries. In the present situation of urgently needed, intensive qualitative expansion rather than extensive quantitative development, Eastern policy on licensing has changed. Recognizing that Western licenses could be a major means of acquiring modern technology, the Soviet Union (followed by all the other COMECON countries) has given top priority to buying licenses from the West. All the East-bloc countries have established special agencies to develop such licensing deals. Since the early sixties when there were only a few important Western licenses utilized in Eastern industry, licensing has assumed important proportions. Sales of licenses in the last five years actually exceeded all previous similar sales. Over 2,000 Western licenses have been bought since 1960, the largest number by Yugoslavia (nearly 600), followed by the USSR, Poland and Hungary (around 300 to 400 each). The product ranges cover virtually all branches of industry, but recently issued licenses have tended to concentrate in the advanced technology industries: communication equipment, quality controls, chemicals and electronics in particular. This invasion of capitalist technology has been an important factor in the overall growth in East–West trade as licenses cover about 90% of the total machinery and equipment transferred along with designs and specifications. One of the reasons for such swift development in this area has been an early willingness on the part of the East to pay in cash, necessarily in hard currencies. Both lump-sum or royalty payments for licenses in cash have been the exceptions to the insistence on barter-based cooperation. Only Bulgaria and Poland pressurized Western firms to allow at least partial payment in exported local products.

However, there have been important exceptions to this policy, particularly in respect of very large projects from which long-term benefits could be expected to flow westwards. Most automobile deals, for example, were negotiated on the basis of licenses and have been repaid in cars, parts or supplies: the operations of Fiat in the USSR, Poland and Yugoslavia, Renault in the USSR and Poland, and Volkswagen in Yugoslavia are examples. British Leyland and Berliet (Renault) bus deals were similarly arranged. In cases where "turn-key" plants have been provided, licenses covering some of the processing technology have also been subject to repayment in production from the plants in the wider context of the larger contract or co-production deal. In these circumstances licensing may also become a form of barter or buy-back. Advantages to the internal economics of the receiving Eastern licensee of Western technology are extensive:

– Speeds up application of new techniques and permits production of higher quality products, especially in the case of consumer goods
– Allows large economies to be made in Research and Development expenditures
– Permits concentration of own R and D effort on limited, high potential objectives
– Facilitates import-substitution and hard currency earnings from exports of licensed products.

Poland, which has over 20% of its industrial production based upon Western licenses, has directed that future purchases be tied to export-promotion. Hungary and Czechoslovakia too intend to substitute export-oriented and buy-back arrangements for the payment of royalties in hard cash. So far Western firms have been happy to sell licenses to Eastern Europe, because the licenses released have generally covered relatively dated technology and not the most up-to-date modifications. If licenses are now to be tied to export-connected products which must be re-sold in hard currency markets before profit accrues, and if the East is to insist upon having the most up-to-date technology, the growth of licensing as such is likely to slow down. But the amount of production already taking place on Western monopolist licenses indicates the pervasive dependency on Western multinational invention which exists in the East and which is likely to seek cooperation of the more integrative type in order to maintain the flow of technology.

Even Czechoslovakia has now abandoned its iron policy of self-sufficiency in the face of weak economic standing relative to its COMECON neighbours. Together with East Germany, Czechoslovakia began its period as a Communist satellite of the USSR as the most advanced industrial country of the bloc. Its role as principal supplier of machinery and equipment to other COMECON countries was enhanced by its being virtually the sole East European country able to export significant quantities of manufactured goods to the West. In recent times, however, its refusal to purchase up-to-date Western technology or to engage in cooperative ventures with Western firms and its consequent separation from Western sources of credit have caused a visible decline in Czechoslovakia's internal and external economy. This is especially apparent when compared to the rapid growth which its COMECON partners have achieved by piggy-backing Western enterprise. According to Czechoslovak Premier Strougal:

> Czechoslovakia in 1965 accounted for 18% of all engineering goods exports in COMECON: by 1975 our share had decreased to a mere 12%. The research and development basis of our engineering industry has at its disposal considerable resources capable of tough international competition, but international comparison of results is far from favourable. The result is that numerous goods are exported to the world market at prices considerably below the going price and numerous industries are unable to sell their production at all. The principal reason for this state of affairs is the low technico-economic level of our goods.

The remedy was finally presented to the meeting of the Czechoslovak Communist Party Central Committee by Strougal in September 1976:

> The necessity of speeding up technical innovation is closely connected with our licensing policy. Czechoslovak engineering and research employ as many resources per capita as the most developed Western countries. However, there are important differences between the share of expenditures on research and on purchases of licenses. In Czechoslovakia, *we allocate on licenses for the engineering sector only 4% of total expenditure on research and development. Most other countries at a similar level of development allocate some 30–40% of total research and development expenditures.* Much too often we prefer our own research, which can be very expensive and without concrete results, against relatively cheap purchases of licenses which already represent verified results of R & D. *Therefore we have to activate our policy for sales and purchases of licenses. We have to reconsider our R & D targets, compare them with the possibilities of purchasing licenses and try to find the most effective solution.* Our engineering and metallurgy sectors, enterprises and the Federal Ministry for Technical Development are now required to propose a new concept for license purchases coordinated with the plan of technical development and reflected in targets for production and foreign trade.

So fell a final Eastern bulwark against the encroachments of capitalism.

Leasing

Leasing is a recent innovation even in Western economies. The technique consists simply of renting or leasing equipment to a user instead of selling it directly. This permits the user to utilize the plant, equipment, computer, hotel, boat, aeroplane, etc., without having to dispense large lump sums of capital. The ownership, of course, remains with the lessor. Leasing is most widely practised in the electronics industries, where IBM, ITT and Rank-Xerox, for example, rent equipment in preference to selling it. Many large banks and financial institutions have entered leasing on a large scale. Its extension to East–West cooperation is just beginning, but will probably extend. First, the technique offers the enterprises in Eastern Europe the possibility of securing modern technology without having to dispense scarce hard currency reserves. Leasing can also be made self-financing if goods or services produced from the leased equipment are used for rental payments. For the lessor, cheap, low-wage operations make some buy-back deals an attractive form of rental, as the difference between buying and selling prices on the Eastern goods can be manipulated to turn a handsome profit.

Several joint East–West leasing companies have been established. One is a UK company called City Leasing in which the very conservative capitalist Morgan Guaranty Trust Company is involved with the Moscow Narodny Bank. A second is Promalease, founded in Paris by the Crédit Lyonnais, a French state-owned bank, and the Paris–Soviet Banque Commerciale pour l'Europe du Nord. The operations of these companies raise some interesting theoretical and ideological conundrums. Though such companies as IBM and ITT, for example, widely implanted in the East, are known to be pressing for leasing rights in COMECON, there is still understandable hesitation on the part of the Eastern governments, for they fully realize that a lessee is not an owner—title to the ownership over the means of production remains with the lessor. Leasing would, therefore, represent a new form of effective capitalist ownership *within* the socialist economy. Despite the ideological subversion which leasing will represent, however, ways will be found to cosmetize the facts for ideological home consumption, simply because the technique will probably prove too attractive economically to be refused in the face of mounting Eastern indebtedness. In the meantime, the two mixed leasing companies mentioned above are concentrating on financing leasing deals for a series of products and equipment (including hydrofoils, Russian-made Fiats and Yak aircraft) in the United States, where such ideological hangups do not prevent a profit. Exploiting capitalist markets for capitalist currency in partnership with capitalists seems now a tenet of neo-Marxist–Leninist doctrine.

A number of leasing deals in transport and shipping are holding the door open to future expansion of this particularly fascinating example of cooperation. Container Transport International of the USA, for instance, has leased 2,500 sea-freight containers to the Soviet Union over a three-year period at a total leasing fee of around $2 million. Soninfiot also leases some 4,000 containers from the Belgian Company Brugeoise et Nivelles.

In another container leasing deal, Interpool of the USA has leased 2,000 intermodal cargo containers to the Soviet Far Eastern Shipping Company (FOSECO), which has only recently — and half-heartedly — agreed to join the world shipping "conference" (or cartel) for its region of operation, having previously bought its way into a 7% share of the US ocean-freight market at give-away rates. FOSECO will pay $5.5 million in advance monthly payments to lease the containers for five years, with an option to buy them on expiration of the lease.

The Soviet-owned Baltatlantic Line is still the target of strong charges of "dumping" for its cut-price traffic in roll-on/roll-off vessels between the East Coast of America and Northern Europe. Among the most strident critics are West German shipowners. Nevertheless, a joint venture company between Soviet and West German interests, Transnautik, which operates from the FRG, has leased 400 chassis to Sovinflot over an eight-year period for handling huge cargoes on the Baltatlantic Line.

Though the USSR has used leasing only to acquire containers and ships so far, it is certain that the capitalist technique will expand rapidly. For one thing it will help the Vodka-Cola deals avoid the US Jackson–Vanek Amendment limiting credits to the USSR. Leasing will make it possible to enlarge the number of US Banks and credit organizations which could take part in financing Soviet projects on a leasing rather than formal credit basis, thus evading the letter of the law. For another, it facilitates a *de facto* joint venture for the life of the lease which could run from fifteen to twenty years, if necessary, with legal ownership vested in the capitalist "lessors" but with a physical "unowned" existence in the USSR.

In February 1977 Tass News Agency reported the study of a project which, if completed, would represent a major breakthrough in leasing deals.

The Lummus Corporation, a major engineering multinational, it reported, is studying the possibility of supplying plant and equipment to the USSR under a leasing arrangement. Lummus believes that lease financing would be compatible with the compensation deals that Western suppliers conclude with Soviet importing organizations under which the suppliers accept payment in the products made with their equipment.

Lummus, according to Tass, believes that a lease could run ten to fifteen years or longer, and when the term expires the Soviet Union would have the right to buy the leased property at the present price. One of the questions under study is how to preserve the lender's right of ownership.

According to Tass, the Lummus proposal caused interest among Soviet specialists and banks and is now being studied. A working group has been formed to prepare specific recommendations which will certainly be accepted, thus ushering in the "leasing" era of socialism: capitalist ownership of the means of production located in a socialist state.

Co-production

The foregoing forms of East–West cooperation, based in varying degrees on barter and counter-purchase, stop short of creating a physical and lasting presence of the Western multinationals within the Communist economy. Barter, licensing, sub-contracting and production agreements involve little or no physical presence beyond the loan of representatives or technical personnel necessary to carry out contracts. A major impediment to the further expansion of cooperation has been the reluctance of multinationals to provide up-to-date technology without safeguards over their proprietary and commercial rights. Technology in modern industry is, after all, the most valuable asset of a company and it will not be merely handed over to the Eastern partner to exploit as he wishes. Related concern over the quality of output and over the universal exploitation of licensed processes throughout the country stemming from even a single purchase, increase Western fears about loss of control. Therefore, in most of the previously described forms of cooperation, Western firms have provided less than up-to-date technology.

Recognizing, however, that imported technology was the key to further development of their economies, East European countries have understood the importance of conceding proprietary and corporate rights to the Western partner. This has led to two forms of corporate presence in Eastern Europe, *co-production* and *joint ventures*. The essential difference between these forms is that joint ventures entail equity ownership by the Western firm in a joint undertaking, while co-production does not. Co-production involves arrangements whereby the cooperating parties to a project agree by contract to carry out complementary production using Western techniques, tools and dies. The output is then shared between them in differing ways. Although no equity sharing is involved, co-production usually entails the presence of the Western firm in the management, production and distribution of the total undertaking. An example of the complexity of some of the co-production projects is a major nitrogen fertilizer complex being built in East Germany:

> Soviet ammonia will be used as feedstock. Plans call for the construction of a new storage terminal at Rostock, the big East German port on the Baltic. Ammonia will be taken 10km by a pipeline to a new grass-roots fertilizer complex comprising nitric acid, ammonium nitrate and calcium ammonium nitrate units. Cost of the whole scheme—terminal, pipeline and fertilizer complex—will be in the region of $200m.
>
> Ammonia shipments will total 350 000 ton annually and the complex will produce 2400 ton/day of nitric acid (two lines), 3 400 ton/day of calcium ammonium nitrate (also in two lines), 150 ton/day of porous ammonium nitrate and 70 ton/day of crystalline ammonium nitrate. Both ammonium nitrate units will produce explosive grade material.
>
> Six groups are involved in the bidding for the complex in the prequalification stage. These will be whittled down to three by the middle of [1978]. The contract is expected to be signed before the end of [1978].
>
> The contractors are Creusot-Loire (France); Voest Alpine (Austria); Klöckner of Vienna in a consortium with Davy Powergas GmbH and International Handling of Amsterdam; Thyssen Rhinestahl Technik with Uhde of West Germany; Mitsui/Toyo of Japan and Coppée Rust of Belgium.
>
> *Payment will be mostly in product and several contractors have incorporated traders into their consortia* [in order to organize Western distribution].

The Soviet Union is especially favourable to this form of cooperation as it saves face ideologically by denying the legal existence of Western equity capital. Co-production principles have been operative as the base for a number of major undertakings between leading Western multinationals and the East. Among the most important have been the planning of huge deals with the American Occidental Petroleum Company, to develop natural resources in Siberia, the new large-scale resource development projects with a Japanese consortium of firms in the Yakutsk region, the massive petro-chemical complexes, aluminium works and automobile plants being constructed in collaboration with such firms as Montedison of Italy, Pechiney of France, Fiat of Italy and soon General Motors of the USA. In the Soviet version the practice is referred to as compensation rather than co-production. This is due to the Soviet emphasis on getting the Western partner to accept goods, *in toto* or in part, other than those produced by the new Western technology. For example, some 400 French companies have created a new Association for Compensation Trading (ACECO) which has been set up under the sponsorship of the Employers' Association, a number of professional organizations and several state banks. At present only French companies are eligible to join, and they pay a membership fee of 2,000 francs a year. The new organization resembles Vienna's Evidenzburo which was set up primarily at the instigation of Austria's Association of Industrialists in 1968 to assist local companies in carrying out countertrade commitments in Eastern Europe. ACECO's basic function is to inform trading firms and banks of goods which the association's members (unnamed) have to offer. ACECO charges a commission only when its services result in a sale.

Compensation deals involving purchase of Western plant equipment, with repayment in end products and self-liquidating credit arrangements, account for roughly 40% of the Soviet overall Western debt, which in 1976 amounted to around $14 billion.

Soviet Deputy Foreign Trade Minister Vladimir Sushkow stated that more than fifty large industrial projects are under way in the Soviet Union with Western participation based on compensation arrangements. Projected exports of six major product groups under such arrangements are as follows (in millions of dollars):[1]

| | Export Income | |
Product	1975–1980	1980–1985
Natural gas	4,700	10,000
Chemicals	700	1,600
Timber and paper	1,300	100
Aluminium	100	400
Coal	80	700
Steel products	450	1,000
	7,330	13,800

As with the various other forms of cooperation, co-production is also based upon the Western firms supplying management know-how, licences, machines and equipment, and the Eastern firms supplying labour, physical plant and components. Co-production arrangements cover all aspects of production and are virtually limitless in application. Though the beginnings of equity cooperation have taken place, it can be assumed that non-equity forms of cooperation of this type will remain the most important vehicle for capitalist participation in East–West trade. Currently, co-production agreements cover most sectors of production in Eastern Europe from automotive vehicles, nuclear installations, computer manufacturing, metal alloys and fabricated machine tools to consumer articles, such as cosmetics, publications, and even including the recent Western export of pornography. According to ECE (Sc. Tech./10/p.19) the following co-production arrangements are observed in East–West relations:

(i)   co-production of a final product by specialization in components
(ii) co-production in which each party manufactures components belonging to a final product, the technology coming from one of the parties
(iii) co-production in which each party manufactures component parts according to its own technology
(iv) co-production in which each party manufactures component parts of the final product, the technology being the result of joint R and D. Co-production thus defined may involve the provision of joint sales and services.

1 East–West Markets, March 7/77

As the following table indicates, co-production is the leading form of cooperation in the GDR, Hungary, Poland and Yugoslavia.[1] From the size and scope of the co-production ventures already identified in the USSR, that country will not lag behind for long.

Classification of East–West cooperation agreements

Cooperation agreement: Country	(A) Supply of licence in exchange, at least partially, for products or components	(B) Delivery of plants and equipment in exchange, at least partially, for parts or components	(C) Co-production and specialization	(D) Sub-contracting	(E) Joint venturing	(F) Joint tendering or joint projects	(G) Total
	%	%	%	%	%	%	%
Bulgaria	62.5	25	12.5	—	—	—	100
Czechoslovakia	35.7	—	28.6	7.1	—	28.6	100
German Democratic Republic	—	—	66.7	—	—	33.3	100
Hungary	32.3	13.2	44.1	7.4	—	3.0	100
Poland	25.0	16.1	37.5	3.6	1.8	16.0	100
Rumania	22.8	34.3	8.6	14.3	14.3	5.7	100
USSR	—	56.6	34.8	4.3	—	4.4	100
Total	26.1	21.7	33.3	6.8	2.9	9.2	100
Yugoslavia	18.5	9.2	20.0	3.0	47.7	1.5	100
Total	24.2	18.7	30.2	5.9	13.6	7.4	100

Because of the combination of different forms of cooperation together, in single projects, it is difficult to set an exact figure on the number of co-production based agreements. But general cooperation figures provide a reasonable measure of their frequency by the fact that they are already qualitatively and quantitatively the most important form of East–West industrial cooperation. The total number of agreements concluded can be estimated at 300 in 1970, 300 in 1973, 1,000 in 1974, 3,000 in 1976 and 4,000 in 1977.

The approximate figures at the head of p. 54 for cooperation agreements refer to 1977.

The list of major Western multinationals involved in these deals is constantly expanding and includes practically the whole of the 1,000 leading world companies, which account for around 80% of total production in the West. Co-production is particularly appropriate for the large-scale projects which the Soviets favour and for the predilection of all East European countries to deal with the larger multinationals.

To pretend that integration with these new global enterprises has no impact on the Socialist integrity of the economic and social system is to play with words. To claim (as do the Soviets) that East–West economic relations are a matter of political, government-to-government cooperation is transparent window-dressing, and to allege that all that is entailed in détente is acquiring capitalist technology without conditions and strings is whistling Dixie in Siberia.

[1] ECE/UN, *Sc. Tech.*, Sem. 3, 1975.

Bulgaria	70	active projects
Czechoslovakia	40	active projects (over half with FRG) with
	60	permits issued
German Democratic Republic	22	active projects with
	60	permits issued
Hungary	350	active projects with
	450	permits issued
Poland	350	active projects with
	300	permits issued
Rumania	300	active projects
USSR	200	active projects with
	250	permits issued
Yugoslavia	525	active projects

Western multinationals with Moscow offices
(by countries of origin)

USA
American Express—Arthur Andersen—Caterpillar Tractor—Chromalloy American Corp.—Dow Chemical—E.I. du Pont de Nemours and Company Inc.—Engelhard Minerals Chemicals—First National City Bank—General Electric—Grace Italiana SpA—Hewlett-Packard—International Business Machines (IBM)—International Harvester Co.—ITT—Occidental Petroleum Corp.—Pullman Inc.—Honeywell Bull—Allis Chalmers—Armco Steel—Brown & Root—Cooper Industries—Oilfield Technology International—Sperry World Trading Inc.

FRANCE
Casacrus—Cefri—CGE Internationale—Cifal—Comef-France—Cie Générale d'Electricité—Cie Générale Transatlantique—Cie Internationale pour l'Informatique (CII)—Creusot-Loire—Etex—Magra-France—Honeywell Bull—Olivier—Renault Régie Nationale des Usines—Rhône-Poulenc—Sonocom—Sorice—Speichim & Creusot-Loire Entreprises—Thomson-CSF—Union of French Machine Builders (Comité de Coordination des Constructeurs Français de Machines Outils)—CIT Alcatel—Codevintec Oliver—Compagnie Générale de Constructions Téléphoniques—Compagnie Générale Maritime—Sofracop.

JAPAN
Ataka Sangyo—Chori Co. Ltd—Gunze Sangyo Inc.—Ishikura Sangyo—C. Itoh & Co. Ltd—Japan Sea Trading Co. Ltd (Nihonkai Boeki)—Kanematsu Gosho—Kawakami Trading Co. Ltd—Kyoho Tsusho—Marubeni Corp.—Mitsui Co.—Nichimen Jitsugyo—Nissho-Iwai Co. Ltd—Mitsubishi Corp.—Progress Trading Co. Ltd—Sumitomo—Tokyo Boeki—Toyo Menka Kaisha—Wako Koeki—International Trading Co.—Toray Ind.

FRG
AEG Telefunken—BASF—Bison-Werke Baehre & Greten GmbH—Deutsche Babcock & Wilcox—Gildemeister & Co. AG—Gutehoffnungshütte Aktienverein—Alfred Hempel KG—Farbwerke Hoechst AG—Industriewerke Karlsruhe-Augsburg AG—Salzgitter AG—Siemens AG—Otto Wolff—Kühne & Nagel—Mannesmann AG—AMK Anlagenvertrieb Mueller & Korff—Bochako Bochum Chemie—Bruker-Physik AG—M & D Gert-

ner KG—Gertner Fuhrmeister & Co.—Glahe International GmbH & Co.—Alfred Hempel KG—HOMAG Hornberger Maschinenbau—ILM Handelskontor—IPS International Processing System—Kloeckner & Co./KHD AG—Dr Knab & Co.—Liebherr Holding GmbH—Linde AG—Machintorg Maschinenhandels GmbH—Magra—Metorg KG/Invex—NUR Neckermann & Riesen—Anton Ohlert—Carl Prior Internationale Spedition—TB-Frankfurt

ITALY

Ente Nazionale Idrocarburi (ENI)—Fiat—Finsider/Istituto per la Ricostruzione Industriale—Grace Italiana SpA—Montedison—Ing. C. Olivetti & Co. SpA—Snia Viscosa—Coe & Clerici SpA—Cogis— IMEX-Compagnia per il Commercio—Intercoop—Italimpex—Merzario—Novasider—Rest-Ital

UK

International Computers Ltd (ICL)—Rank Xerox Ltd—M. Golodetz (Overseas) Ltd—Oxy Metal Industries—Quest Automation Ltd

FINLAND

Converta—Enso-Gutzeit—Kaukomarkkinat Oy—Valmet Oy—Nokia-Kone

SWEDEN

ASEA—The Axel Johnson Group—Alfa Laval—Bo Billing—BPA—Kährs Maskiner—Sandvik—Skanska Cementgjuteriet—Stansaab

THE NETHERLANDS

Investronic V.BV—Peja Holdings NV—Necoma—Wisse & Co.

BELGIUM

Eurintrade SA—Tracosa SA

SWITZERLAND

Ciba Geigy Ltd—Industrial Trading Trust SA—Inter-Indreba Co. Ltd

SPAIN

Waimer SA—Prodag SA—Sovhispab SA

AUSTRALIA

Commercial Bureau Pty

AUSTRIA

Delta Industrieberatung—Sytco

INDIA

Hind Exports International

A giant modern multinational will not usually be beguiled from its present and future technology, whatever its willingness to sell its out-of-date and uneconomical garbage. To secure modern technology and its regular improvements in a lasting manner, Brezhnev will have to accept into the Communist bosom both the multinational companies and their cabals of Overworld strategists. Current resistance to permitting legal, private-property joint ventures in countries like Yugoslavia, Hungary, Rumania and Poland is receding rapidly. For the smaller countries, a capitalist presence through co-production and joint ventures is fundamental to the development of their semi-industrialized economies. The Soviet Union is viewing such ideological dilution and closer bilateral relations between its satellites and the power centers of capitalism with growing concern and misgiving. It would like to arrest the speed of integrated production forms and to extend the old counter-purchase and buy-back deals which would protect socialist autarky from capitalist penetration, at least in appearance and for its ideological stance and credibility, particularly in the eyes of China and Western Communist Party members. The latter are not likely to grasp the nuance that whilst to the West of Berlin the multinationals are the ideological adversary and oppressors of the working class, yet somehow their transmigration to the East of Berlin sanctifies them as the technological architects of a new Communism.

However, initial sensibilities to ideological virtues have rapidly given way to the imperatives of Vodka-Cola economies. In May 1977, a decree issued by the Hungarian Finance Ministry explicitly extended joint ventures to production. Henceforth, production joint ventures will be encouraged beyond sales and service organizations, in which Western partners may hold up to 49% of the equity.

A major reason for this drastic change of policy in respect to capitalist ownership of the means of production has been the painful failure to attract joint ventures under the prevailing regulations. Despite almost 500 cooperation agreements, the failure to permit capitalist ownership and control of technology resulted only in three joint ventures up to 1977. In addition to explicitly permitting joint ownership of production facilities, the decree authorizes three key changes:

(1) majority control for Western partners in investment companies, whose main role would be to raise capital for Hungarian enterprises and other joint ventures
(2) a standard tax of 40% on profits with reductions for reinvestment
(3) a flat 35% payroll tax on wages and salaries to cover all other tax and social security obligations.

"The purpose [of the decree] is not to raise capital," a spokesman for the National Bank of Hungary explained. "But we recognize that some Western firms are reluctant to become involved without being able to manage the product as well. The new decree offers conditions comparable to those for setting up joint ventures in Western Europe." The number of Hungarian joint ventures rose to nine by 1978.

Italy's extensive involvement

Despite its chronic financial instability requiring increasingly larger injections of Western foreign loans, Italy is a major supplier of credits to Communist Europe. Elsewhere we describe the almost simultaneous acceptance of a $530 million IMF loan to bolster its shaky if not insolvent monetary system and announcement of another massive credit line of $650 million being opened to the Soviet Union. All the COMECON countries and Yugoslavia have extended Italian credits with the largest part allocated to the Soviet Union. The cumulative debt of the USSR to Italy is—or will soon be—around $3 billion while the combined acknowledged debt of the others stood at around $2 billion as from the end of 1976. Most of this debt of the Communist countries is the counterpart of credits for Vodka-Cola multinational co-production and cooperation deals. Along with the Federal Republic of Germany, Italy has led the movement to cooperation with the Communist countries. Besides the well-publicized deals of Fiat, virtually all of Italy's leading enterprises, including those of the Italian Communist Party, were into Vodka-Cola early.

The Pirelli Rubber Company was in the Soviet Union along with Fiat in the fifties (six rubber plants worth $50 million), while Olivetti was one of the first capitalist advisers to the Soviets on automation of office systems. Olivetti computerized the Pirelli Tyre plants, using American General Electric equipment and processes, and later concluded a $100 million deal for production of automation equipment and office machines (exact replicas of Italian models) at Oryol, south of Moscow. In Rumania Pirelli built a $12 million rubber plant and has operations in Hungary, Czechoslovakia, Yugoslavia and Poland as well. It scored a *coup* in 1975 with Soviet contracts worth $63 million. One was to furnish production lines for steel-belted radials: the other, a turn-key plant for manufacturing components for Fiat-built auto plants at Togliatti and on the Volga. Pirelli's trade with the Russian FTO Techmashinimport since 1960 is close to $200 million. Like all such projects they entailed massive public credits and compensation or buy-back arrangements much of which took place at a time when Pirelli was restructuring operations and laying off personnel in Italy.

ENI, the state-owned oil and energy monopoly, has signed cooperation agreements with most of the COMECON countries. Its overseas engineering subsidiary, SNAM Progetti has been extensively involved in the petroleum, petro-chemical sectors. SNAM Progetti has, for example, built refineries in the USSR, Poland and Rumania, and has put up Czechoslovakia's first ethylene glycol plant followed by similar plants in Poland and East Germany.

Total Italian projects in Eastern Europe, including all degrees of importance, number nearly 400—many of them implemented through the Italian Communist Party trading organizations at profitable commissions "to finance the overthrow of capitalism at home."

But even more than Fiat, ENI and Pirelli, it was Montedison which pioneered the co-production-compensation deals in the COMECON countries and buy-back deals in the Soviet Union. It has, in fact, become the major foreign partner of the USSR in chemicals. Montedison's relations with the USSR extend back nearly forty-five years and it was one of the first capitalist companies to establish an office in Moscow in 1968. This despite the fact that the Vatican and American banks were important shareholders with seats on the boards of directors while the anti-clerical, anti-American ideological hysteria was at a peak in Eastern Europe.

In June 1971, Montedison signed a contract for two complete plants worth around $50 million for producing triacetate of cellulose and polypropylene and other copolymers. Plants for producing vinyl chloride, methanol terphtalic acid and synthetic fibres followed. Subsidiaries under the parent umbrella, such as Industrie Macchine Elettronite (IME) which does about 20% of total USSR imports of table calculating machines, Farmitilia, its pharmaceutical subsidiary, Standa, its supermarket and department store chain, and Pavesi, its restaurant and bar division, have expanded activities in the Soviet Union, and progressively throughout the region. In 1973, an important corporation agreement with the Polish Ministry for the Chemical Industry called for long-term cooperation covering nearly all chemical branches, industrial cooperation and joint exploitation of markets in Third World countries. Concluded for an initial period of five years with renewals thereafter, the execution of the program is supervised by a special joint committee. With the Hungarian Chemolimpex, Montedison and its associated textile company (SNIA Viscosa) have set up a joint company to market Hungarian chemical goods in Italy and internationally. Initially Chemolimpex will supply an annual $7 million worth of olefins and aromatic compounds while Montedison will furnish $20 million of synthetic raw materials and organic and inorganic chemicals and SNIA aromatic compounds and petro-chemical materials for transformation and marketing of $8–10 million annually.

Montedison's "Russian Manager," Mario Reale, told TASS in April 1977 that the company "had some seven chemical plants under construction in the USSR based upon the buy-back principle." Taking into account sales of equipment, buy-back of products, Reale "reckoned the total value of the seven-plant deal at $1.2 billion." (*Soviet Business and Trade*, 24th April, 1977.)

The total two-way trade in 1976 with Soviet FTOs, including buy-back, added up to about $150 million with the figures expected to rise to nearly $200 million in 1977 and $300–400 million in 1978—if Italian credits still remain available in 1978.

Among the Montedison-Soviet cooperation projects are joint plants for:
– Ethylene-propylene rubbers

- Chemical fibres and textiles
- Fertilizers
- Joint development of a second-generation sulphamide drug
- Polycarbonate plastic plant and PUC plant

All these products are admittedly cheaper to produce in the USSR than in Italy and there are in addition no strikes nor union problems to contend with. The eventual sale of this production in Italy is one of the causes for closure of plants and increased layoffs.

Colourful and controversial Eugenio Cefis submitted his resignation as chairman of Montedison to the 1977 stockholders' meeting after he pushed through a contested $400 million share-capital expansion. Before this, his attempt to split off the company's profitable, though patently illegal, banking network failed, forcing him to threaten retirement. Cefis worked closely with the CP both politically and commercially in many sectors. But with near bankruptcy of its Montefiltre Division, need to shut down obsolete plants, its diversion of new plants to off-site locations in the United States, UK, Belgium and, above all, Communist Europe, and its cash-flow manipulation in friendly tax-free havens such as Luxembourg, Switzerland, the Bahamas, Liechtenstein, etc., profits have turned to massive losses—a $104 million loss on sales of $5.4 billion in 1976. Even in Italy, the land of ultra refinement in business manipulations and fiscal and monetary evasion, this is some performance. With Montedison shares down to a dismal low, few private stockholders (outside of the Rovelli group buying shares on the Swiss market secretly) are willing to risk investing in the vanishing Italian part of the company. Unfortunately, its Russian plants and Luxembourg holding companies are still not capitalized in share capital. When will there be a Kremlin stock exchange for trading in shares of the profitable part of Montedison instead of its loss-leaders in the West? The question of the share of the state in Montedison, which has a direct 18% interest, became a very litigious issue, but it will stay with the state and be limited to 18%. As for the private owners, and probably the ICP, including Fiat, Pirelli, the Vatican, Lazaire Stores, Rovelli, etc., they know that the most profitable way is to continue supplying the Russian and East Communist partners with credits for co-production deals for supplying the Italian market and hiding profits in tax havens, and accelerate the closure of Italian plants.

In Western markets today success lies not only in productive technology and production management, but also in marketing and distribution skills. An ECE research paper (research note on industrial cooperation, p. 8, iii) on industrial cooperation, states "given the disparity between market conditions and types of techniques employed, between the East and West European countries, it is quite natural that East–West industrial cooperation agreements of a more advanced type should include the marketing stage." Co-production gives partners the opportunity of penetrating the trade area to which they do not belong and may also involve sales networks in third countries. For Eastern companies this permits the extension of after-sales services which are important for establishing regular markets for their production. In general, therefore, it can be said that the leading multinationals and the leading banks which dominate Western production, sales and finance are all involved to some degree in co-production projects in Eastern Europe. Most indeed have direct participations in several countries. Facing is a list of the East European participations of the top world corporations.

The computer experience is a particularly good example of Vodka-Cola's rerouting of Western technology back to the West under Communist labels. Soviet authorities openly admitted in the late sixties to hopes of improving hopelessly inefficient sectors of the economy through the wide-scale application of computers. Previous reforms around decentralization begun in the early sixties were discarded in favour of merging firms

Cooperation in Eastern Europe among leading world corporations

Company	Country of origin	Industry sectors	1975 sales ($000s)	Bul	Czech	GDR	Hun	Pol	Rum	USSR	Yug
Exxon	US	oil, petrochemicals	44,864,824	✓					✓	✓	
General Motors	US	autos, trucks, arms	35,724,911				✓	✓		✓	✓
Royal Dutch/Shell	UK/Neth	oil, petrochemicals	32,105,096	✓	✓	✓	✓	✓	✓	✓	
Ford Motor	US	autos, trucks	24,009,100		✓		✓				✓
Mobil Oil	US	oil, petrochemicals	20,620,392				✓	✓	✓	✓	
British Petroleum	UK	oil, petrochemicals	17,285,854	✓		✓	✓	✓	✓	✓	
Unilever	UK	food, chemicals	15,015,994		✓		✓	✓			✓
IBM	US	computers, office machines	14,436,541	✓	✓	✓	✓	✓	✓		
Gulf Oil	US	oil, petrol products	14,268,000						✓	✓	
General Electric	US	electrical engineering	13,399,100		✓		✓		✓	✓	✓
ITT	US	telecommunications	11,367,647	✓	✓		✓	✓	✓	✓	
Philips	Neth	electronics	10,746,485		✓		✓	✓	✓	✓	
Ciê Française des Petroles	France	oil, petrochemicals	9,145,778							✓	
August Thyssen-Hütte	FRG	metallurgy	8,764,899		✓					✓	
Hoechst	FRG	chemicals	8,462,322	✓	✓	✓	✓	✓	✓	✓	
ENI	Italy	petrochemicals	8,334,432	✓	✓	✓		✓	✓	✓	
Daimler-Benz	FRG	autos, trucks	8,194,271			✓	✓	✓		✓	
US Steel	US	metals, mining	8,167,269							✓	
BASF	FRG	chemicals	8,152,318			✓	✓	✓	✓	✓	
Renault	France	autos, machinery	7,831,330		✓		✓	✓	✓	✓	
Siemens	FRG	electricals, electronics	7,759,909	✓		✓	✓	✓	✓	✓	
Volkswagenwerk	FRG	autos	7,680,786				✓		✓	✓	
Bayer	FRG	chemicals	7,223,302	✓	✓	✓		✓	✓	✓	✓
Du Pont	US	chemicals	7,221,500			✓	✓	✓		✓	
Toyota	Japan	autos, trucks	7,194,139		✓		✓				
ELF—Aquitaine	France	oil, petrochemicals	7,165,390							✓	✓
Nestlé	Switz	food products	7,080,160				✓				
ICI	UK	chemicals	6,884,219	✓	✓	✓	✓	✓	✓	✓	✓
Hitachi	Japan	construction	5,916,135		✓					✓	
Westinghouse	US	electronics	5,862,747				✓	✓			✓
Mitsubishi	Japan	engineering	5,693,994	✓	✓	✓	✓	✓	✓		
Union Carbide	US	chemicals	5,665,000		✓				✓	✓	
Tenneco	US	petrochemicals	5,599,709							✓	
Montedison	Italy	chemicals	5,417,741	✓	✓	✓	✓	✓	✓	✓	✓
British Steel	UK	iron and steel	5,340,183	✓				✓	✓	✓	✓
Fiat	Italy	autos, trucks, etc.	4,881,600	✓	✓	✓	✓	✓	✓	✓	✓
Krupp	FRG	engineering				✓	✓	✓	✓	✓	✓
Pepsi Cola	US	beverages, services	2,280,759	✓	✓	✓	✓		✓		✓
Coca-Cola	US	beverages, services	2,575,000	✓	✓	✓	✓		✓		✓
Mitsui	Japan	engineering, trading									

into very large units in two or three level structures: ministry–industrial production association–enterprise. The coordination of the system at the very top level of party-controlled planning was made dependent upon computers.

In 1969 Soviet computer equipment and methodology was admitted to be primitive by Western standards, estimated twenty years behind in equipment and twenty-five years behind in systems engineering. To close the gap, COMECON countries pressed IBM to expand its presence—which it did by making its 360 computer-system available along with instruction manuals, training of personnel, etc. With the exception of Rumania, all COMECON countries began co-production manufacture of IBM's 360s which were integrated into a program called the "unified system" and hailed as an advance in "socialist integration."

Despite poor input/output software, the system was sold not only in the area but as far as Belgium, Holland, Finland and India. The basic design of IBM's system has been improved progressively by some copying of IBM's up-dated models. To compensate for inadequacy of peripheral devices and software, the basic "up-copied" unit is coupled to Western products for commercial promotion. The Soviets have two testing laboratories in the West, one in Finland the other in Holland, where Western computer and data peripherals can be tested for adjunction to Soviet-IBM models.

However, this is only the Western visible tip of the computer iceberg. Virtually all major computer companies have concluded lasting commercial co-production relationships with Eastern Europe: in addition to IBM and Control Data, Sperry-Rand, UNIVAC, Honeywell and General Electric have established co-production links as have Olivetti of Italy, GEC and Ferranti of the UK, Siemens of West Germany, Honeywell-Bull and Co. EG of France, Philips of Holland, Eriksson of Sweden, Mitsubishi and Mitsui of Japan—to name only the most prominent among numerous others. An example of the state of the relationship is the recent permission by the US National Security Council for transfer of the latest strategic computer systems. Control Data in a six-million-dollar deal thereupon installed its Cyber 73 computer system, the world's largest strategic computer (estimated at fifteen to twenty years ahead of domestic computer capabilities) in the USSR. Such systems are basic to all phases of modern weapon systems through building, integration, testing, deployment, maintenance and operation as well as to specific technologies revolutionizing warfare-avionics, missile guidance, satellite surveillance, etc. The stated purpose of the system is for seismic computations of oil prospection.

Control Data, it is reliably reported, is urging a joint venture plant and is negotiating joint development of next generation computers. For a starter, Control Data has agreed to manufacture 100 megabit disk memories in the USSR. As there are only a dozen of these Cyber 73 systems in existence in such top-secret organizations as the US Air Force, the NASA Space Agency and National Security Agency, its installation in the Soviet Union seems to bring American and Russian defense establishments into a much closer and more intimate relationship. As long as people are not aware of this convergence, apparently military "defense" spending against the enemy can continue to grow. However, US military authorities objected to the sale on the grounds that it was suitable for nuclear weapons calculations, anti-submarine systems, phased-scatter tracking of ICBMs and manifold other military applications. The Cyber 73 like the IBM 370–155 systems are, however, only advanced strategic computers in military use. NATO defense establishments have deployed over 20,000 general-purpose computers. Almost all have applicability to wide varieties of civilian functions and industrial research and development, and almost all basic systems have been transferred to the USSR and the other COMECON countries.

Proportional breakdown of East–West industrial cooperation contracts by type: Total and individual countries (percentages)

Country	Total	comprising															
		A.1	A.2	A.1+A.2	B.1	B.2	B.1+B.2	C.1	C.2	C.1+C.2	D.1	D.2	D.1+D.2	E.2	F.1	F.2	F.1+F.2
Bulgaria	100.0	62.5	—	62.5	25.0	—	25.0	—	12.5	12.5	—	—	—	—	—	—	—
Hungary	100.0	22.0	10.3	32.3	13.2	—	13.2	39.7	4.4	44.1	5.9	1.5	7.4	—	3.0	—	3.0
Poland	100.0	17.9	7.1	25.0	16.1	—	16.1	35.7	1.8	37.5	—	3.6	3.6	1.8	10.6	5.4	16.0
German Democratic Republic	100.0	—	—	—	—	—	—	66.7	—	66.7	—	—	—	—	33.3	—	33.3
Romania	100.0	17.1	5.7	22.8	34.3	—	34.3	5.7	2.9	8.6	2.9	11.4	14.3	14.3	5.7	—	5.7
Czechoslovakia	100.0	21.4	14.3	35.7	—	—	—	28.6	—	28.6	—	7.1	7.1	—	28.6	—	28.6
USSR	100.0	—	—	—	39.2	17.4	56.6	34.8	—	34.8	4.3	—	4.3	—	—	4.3	4.3
TOTAL	100.0	18.8	7.2	26.1	19.8	1.9	21.7	30.4	2.9	33.3	2.9	3.9	6.8	2.9	7.2	1.9	9.2
Yugoslavia	100.0	15.4	3.1	18.5	7.7	1.5	9.2	18.5	1.5	20.0	1.5	1.5	3.0	47.8	1.5	—	1.5
TOTAL	100.0	18.0	6.2	24.2	16.9	1.8	18.7	27.6	2.6	30.2	2.6	3.3	5.9	13.6	5.9	1.5	7.4

Legend: Licensing: A.1 – Supply of licences and/or know-how (sometimes also some special equipment), in exchange – at least partially – for products or components; A.2 – Same as (1) but the supply also includes parts in varying percentage of the final product in exchange for produce or components. *Delivery of plant or equipment:* B.1 – Supply of plant or equipment, including the appertaining technology, in exchange for produce or components (at least partially); B.2 – For the exploitation of natural resources, same as (1) plus studies of the availability and accessibility of the resources and research connected with the application of technology to particular circumstances. *Co-production and specialization:* C.1 – Co-operation, including or not including sales, in which each party manufactures parts, components or entities belonging to a final product, the technology coming from one of the parties or from both; C.2 – Co-operation in which each party specializes in part of the manufacturing programme and then exchanges units in order to complete each other's range of products. *Sub-contracting:* D.1 – Short-term agreements providing for the delivery of an agreed quantity of finished or semi-manufactured goods produced through the use of documentation and know-how (and sometimes parts, machinery and equipment) provided by the contractor (do not necessarily have a repetitive character); D.2 – Long-term agreements providing for the delivery on a continuing basis same as above. *Joint ventures:* E.2 – Joint ventures involving production, marketing and R and D. *Joint tendering or joint projects:* F.1 – Customer located in a third country; F.2 – Customer located in one of the countries.

Countries' shares of the total number of East-West industrial co-operation contracts, with breakdown by type of contract (percentages)

TYPE OF CONTRACT	TOTAL FOR SEVEN COUNTRIES	comprising							TOTAL (including Yugoslavia)	Yugoslavia
		Bulgaria	Hungary	Poland	German Democratic Republic	Romania	Czechoslovakia	USSR		
A.1	100.0	12.8	38.5	25.6	–	15.4	7.7	–	100.0	20.4
A.2	100.0	–	46.7	26.7	–	13.3	13.3	–	100.0	11.8
A.1 + A.2	100.0	9.3	40.7	25.9	–	14.8	9.3	–	100.0	18.2
B.1	100.0	4.8	22.0	22.0	–	29.2	–	22.0	100.0	10.8
B.2	100.0	–	–	–	–	–	–	100.0	100.0	20.0
B.1 + B.2	100.0	4.4	20.0	20.0	–	26.7	–	28.9	100.0	11.8
C.1	100.0	–	42.9	31.7	3.2	3.2	6.3	12.7	100.0	16.0
C.2	100.0	16.7	50.0	16.7	–	16.6	–	–	100.0	14.3
C.1 + C.2	100.0	1.5	43.5	30.4	2.9	4.3	5.8	11.6	100.0	15.8
D.1	100.0	–	66.7	–	–	16.7	–	16.6	100.0	14.3
D.2	100.0	–	12.5	25.0	–	50.0	12.5	–	100.0	11.1
D.1 + D.2	100.0	–	35.7	14.3	–	35.6	7.1	7.1	100.0	12.5
E.2	100.0	–	–	16.7	–	83.3	–	–	100.0	83.8
F.1	100.0	–	13.3	40.0	6.7	13.3	26.7	–	100.0	6.2
F.2	100.0	–	–	75.0	–	–	–	25.0	100.0	–
F.1 + F.2	100.0	–	10.5	47.3	5.3	10.5	21.1	5.3	100.0	5.0
TOTAL	100.0	3.9	32.8	27.1	1.4	16.9	6.8	11.1	100.0	23.9

Legend: See p. 61, foot of table.

East–West industrial co-operation contracts, broken down by type of contract, industry and country (percentages)

Type of contract: Country / Industry:	A.1 + A.2											B.1 + B.2											C.1 + C.2										
	(1)	(2)	(3)	(4)	(5)	(6)	(7)	(8)	(9)	(10)	Total	(1)	(2)	(3)	(4)	(5)	(6)	(7)	(8)	(9)	(10)	Total	(1)	(2)	(3)	(4)	(5)	(6)	(7)	(8)	(9)	(10)	Total
Bulgaria	40.0	–	–	20.0	20.0	20.0	–	–	–	–	62.5	–	50.0	–	–	–	–	–	–	–	25.0	50.0	–	–	–	–	–	–	–	100.0	–	–	12.5
Hungary	–	13.6	–	4.6	18.2	40.8	–	4.6	9.1	9.1	32.4	–	–	11.1	11.1	–	–	–	11.1	44.5	11.1	13.2	–	13.3	–	30.0	–	36.7	13.3	6.7	–	–	44.1
Poland	–	7.1	7.2	21.4	7.1	21.4	14.3	7.2	7.1	7.2	25.0	11.1	–	33.3	–	–	–	–	11.1	11.1	22.3	16.1	–	–	9.5	9.5	14.3	42.9	9.5	–	9.5	–	37.5
German Democratic Republic	–	–	–	–	–	–	–	–	–	–	–	–	–	–	–	–	–	–	–	–	–	66.6	–	–	–	–	50.0	50.0	–	–	–	–	66.6
Romania	–	25.0	–	50.0	–	25.0	–	–	–	–	22.9	–	16.7	8.3	8.3	–	8.3	–	16.7	8.3	34.2	22.9	–	–	–	100.0	–	–	–	–	–	–	8.6
Czechoslovakia	–	40.0	–	40.0	20.0	20.0	–	–	–	–	35.7	–	–	–	–	–	–	–	–	–	–	35.7	–	–	–	25.0	–	50.0	–	25.0	–	–	28.6
USSR	–	–	–	–	–	–	–	–	–	–	7.7	12.5	53.8	15.4	–	–	–	–	–	7.7	15.4	56.5	12.5	–	–	12.5	12.5	50.0	12.5	–	–	–	34.8
TOTAL	3.7	14.6	1.9	20.4	11.1	29.5	3.7	3.7	5.6	5.6	26.1	1.5	24.4	13.6	4.4	–	2.2	–	8.9	13.6	17.8	21.7	–	7.2	2.9	23.2	7.3	39.2	10.1	5.8	2.9	–	33.3
Yugoslavia	–	8.3	–	33.3	–	25.0	8.3	8.3	16.8	–	18.5	–	15.4	33.2	–	–	16.7	–	16.7	16.7	9.2	18.7	–	15.4	–	46.1	7.7	7.7	–	7.7	7.7	7.7	20.0
TOTAL	3.0	13.6	1.5	22.8	9.1	28.8	4.5	4.5	7.6	5.6	24.3	1.2	21.7	17.6	3.9	–	3.9	–	9.8	13.7	17.6	18.7	8.5	2.4	28.9	7.3	34.2	8.5	6.1	3.7	1.2	30.1

Continued on p. 64.

Continued from p. 63.

Type of contract: Country / Industry:	D.1 + D.2 (1)	(2)	(3)	(4)	(5)	(6)	(7)	(8)	(9)	(10)	Total	E.2 (1)	(2)	(3)	(4)	(5)	(6)	(7)	(8)	(9)	(10)	Total	F.1 + F.2 (1)	(2)	(3)	(4)	(5)	(6)	(7)	(8)	(9)	(10)	Total	Overall Total A.1-F.2
Bulgaria	–	–	–	–	–	–	–	–	–	–	–	–	–	–	–	–	–	–	–	–	–	–	–	–	–	–	–	–	–	100.0	–	–	100.0	100.0
Hungary	–	–	–	20.0	20.0	20.0	–	–	40.0	–	7.4	–	–	–	–	–	–	–	–	–	–	–	–	–	–	–	–	–	–	100.0	–	–	2.9	100.0
Poland	–	–	–	–	–	100.0	–	–	–	–	3.6	–	33.3	33.3	–	–	–	–	–	–	–	1.8	–	33.3	33.3	–	–	22.2	–	–	–	1.2	16.0	100.0
German Democratic Republic	–	–	–	–	–	–	–	–	–	–	–	–	–	–	–	–	–	–	–	–	–	–	–	–	–	–	–	100.0	–	–	–	–	33.4	100.0
Rumania	–	–	–	–	100.0	–	–	–	–	–	14.3	–	40.0	–	–	–	20.0	40.0	–	–	–	14.3	–	–	–	–	–	100.0	–	–	–	–	5.7	100.0
Czechoslovakia	–	–	–	–	–	100.0	–	–	–	–	7.1	–	–	–	–	–	–	–	–	–	–	–	–	–	–	–	–	75.0	–	–	–	–	28.6	100.0
USSR	–	–	–	–	–	–	–	100.0	–	–	4.3	–	–	–	–	–	–	–	–	–	–	–	–	–	100.0	–	–	–	–	–	–	–	4.4	100.0
TOTAL	–	–	–	7.1	42.9	28.6	–	7.1	14.3	–	6.8	16.7	33.3	–	–	–	16.7	33.3	–	–	–	2.9	–	15.8	21.1	5.3	–	42.0	–	10.5	–	5.3	9.2	100.0
Yugoslavia	–	–	–	–	–	–	–	50.0	50.0	–	3.1	16.1	35.5	9.7	12.9	3.2	9.7	3.2	–	9.7	–	47.7	–	–	–	–	–	100.0	–	–	–	–	1.5	100.0
TOTAL	–	–	–	6.2	37.5	25.0	–	12.5	18.8	–	5.9	16.2	35.2	8.1	10.8	2.7	10.8	6.1	–	8.1	–	13.6	–	15.0	20.0	5.0	–	45.0	–	10.0	–	5.0	7.4	100.0

Legend: For A.1 to F.2, see p. 61, foot of table.

(1) – Food and agricultural industry (including beverage); (2) – Chemical industry (including pharmaceuticals); (3) – Metallurgy (including mining); (4) – Transport equipment: includes aircraft, automobiles, lorries, tractors (even for agriculture), rolling stock, earth-moving equipment, diesel engines (even stationary); (5) – Machine tools; (6) – Mechanical engineering (all other non-electrical engineering); (7) – Electronics (computers and other office equipment, radio and television sets, communications equipment); (8) – Electrical (locomotives and household appliances); (9) – Light industry (textiles, footwear, rubber, glass, furniture, consumer goods); (10) – Other, such as construction, hotel management, tourism, etc.

* The totals "A.1 + A.2", "B.1 + B.2", etc. relate to the over-all total "A.1-F.2".

Examples of Western multinationals in Bucharest

Austria
Evidenzbüro
Friedrich Wilhelm
Gerhard Schiesser
Indupromat
Richard Klinger
Sandvik
Turmöl
Martin Maimann & Co.
Unifer
Vereinigte Edelstahlwerke

Belgium
Fertibel
In-Diam-Ka
Unit International

Denmark
Novo Industri

France
Alliance Constructeurs
Cie Générale d'Électricité
Comptoir de Commerce
Le Carbona Lorraine
Maxime Poirier
Régie Nationale des Usines Renault
UNCEA

Greece
Impexport

Italy
Agind
Arcos
CEPMI
Ing. Celli
La Puntimatic
Montedison
Pietro Bove
Terressana Veneta Carni

Japan
Chori
C. Itoh
Kanematsu
Kokusai Koeki
Kowa

Koyo International
Marubeni Corp.
Mitsubishi Corp.
Mitsui & Co.
Nichibu Baleast
Nichimen
Nissho Iwai
Okura
Sumitomo
Tokyo Boeki
Toyo Menka

Netherlands
Juned
Organon

Sweden
Airco
ASEA
HEFA
Pharmacia

Switzerland
Brown-Boveri
Castolin
Ciba-Geigy
Coexsu
Copechim Trading
Gebrüder Sulzer
Georg Fischer
Interacid
Intersofax
Robinco
Sandoz
Waltrade

UK
Anglocentrop
Burmah Engineering Co. Ltd
Dominions Export Co.
Eastern Industrial Corp.
ICI
Rank Xerox
Shell International

US
AMP
Atalanta

US (cont.)
Dow Chemical
Hewlett Packard
IBM
Control Data
Ingersoll-Rand (Austrian subsidiary)
ITT
Moody International
Monsanto
Engelhard Minerals & Chemicals Corp.
Pfizer
Prudential Lines
Stafford International Corp.
Rollway Bearing International Inc.

West Germany
BASF
Bayer
Boehringer

Comex
C.C. Carroll
Demag
Ervin van Hazelbrouck
Franz Kirchfeld GmbH
Glahe International
Hoechst
IWKA
IFG-Interregional Flug GmbH
Klein, Schanzlin & Becker
Klockner
Metallgesellschaft
Ransburg
Robert Christians
Chemische Werke Hüls
Grachten & Söhne
Siemens
Teka
Novatex

Examples of some multinationals' cooperation deals in Bulgaria

Volvo (Sweden)	Vehicles and auto parts
General Motors (USA)	Exchange trucks against forklifts
Daimler-Benz (FRG)	Forklift trucks
Fiat (Italy)	Vehicles and auto parts
Renault (France)	Vehicles and auto parts
Voest Alpine (Austria)	Technical and industrial cooperation
Nippon Electric Co. (Japan)	Electronics and telecommunication
Akzo (Holland)	Pharmaceuticals, pesticides, synthetic fibres
Montedison (Italy)	Chemicals and marketing
ENI (Italy)	Chemicals, textiles, marketing
Lurgi (FRG)	Oil-shale exploitation
SA de Telecommunications (France)	Equipment, telecommunication
Nihon Kaihatsu (Japan)	Hotel construction
Finnish Food Consortium (Finland)	Deep-frozen foods
Thomson-Brandt (France)	Hotel construction
Technip (France)	Chemicals
Friedrich Uhde (FRG)	Polyester plant, chlorine plant
Tejin and C. Itoh (Japan)	Polyester plant
Thyssen Rheinstahl (FRG)	Metal foundry
ITT (USA)	Television licenses
Siemens (FRG)	Telephone exchanges
R.J. Reynolds (USA)	Winston-brand cigarettes
Philip Morris (USA)	Marlboro cigarettes
BAT	HB cigarettes
Austria Tabakwerke (Austria)	Memphis cigarettes
HF & PhF Reemtsma (FRG)	Astor cigarettes

Major contracting chemical projects in hand as of July 1977

Western contractor	USSR	Other Eastern Europe
Air Liquide	*	*
Ammonia Casale		*
Badger		
Catalytic International		*
Chemtex		*
Comprimo		*
Constructors John Brown	*	
Coppee-Rust	*	*
Crawford & Russell		*
Creusot-Loire	*	*
Davy Powergas GmbH	*	
Davy Powergas Ltd	*	*
Fluor		
Foster Wheeler	*	*
Heurtey		*
Krobs	*	
Krupp-Koppers	*	*
KTI		*
Linde	*	
Litwin	*	
Lummus	*	*
Lurgi	*	*
Matthew Hall		
McKee (including CTB)		
PEC Engineering	*	*
Petrocarbon Developments		*
Petrole-Chimie		*
J.F. Pritchard		
Pullmann Kellogg	*	*
Rivoira		
Salzglitter	*	
Sim-Chem		
Sirycon	*	*
SNAM Progetti	*	*
Speichim	*	*
Stone & Webster		*
Technip	*	*
Tecnimont	*	*
Toyo Engineering	*	
Uhde	*	*
Woodhall Duckham		*
Zimmer		*

MAJOR CHEMICAL COMPENSATION DEALS SIGNED WITH THE SOVIET UNION

Company	Year signed	Description of contract	Value	Products to be taken back	Year products will start coming in
Salzgitter, West Germany	1972	Supply of 120 000 ton/year low density polyethylene plant for Kazan	DM126m	Repayment in low density polyethylene. Between 150-250 000 tons in total. Bochako markets production in the West. Until 1983/84	1971
Salzgitter, West Germany	1973	Supply of 240 000 ton/year low density polyethylene plant for Severodonetsk	DM174m	Marketing by Bochako of 250-350 000 tons of low density polyethylene in the West. Until 1986	1973
Litwin, France	1973	Supply to the USSR of plants to produce 300 000 ton/year styrene. 100 000 ton/year high impact polystyrene and 100 000 ton/year expandable polystyrene for Shevchenko	$120m	Polystyrene to be bought back over a period of 85 years beginning in 1979. At present prices the deal works out at around 24 000 ton/year polystyrene	1979
Montedison, Italy	from 1973	Supply to the USSR of several plants to be repaid in product. So far the company has signed for 11 plants, the original 7 were valued at $500m. By now the value is thought to be in the region of $800m. The plants include: 42 000 ton/year cellulose triacetate at Fergana for completion 1977; 30 000 ton/year polypropylene, Guryev (1977); 270 000 ton/year sodium chloride crystallization, Sterlitamak (1977); 500 000 ton/year urea, Gorlovka (1978); 150 000 ton/year acrylonitrile Saratov (1978); 40 000 ton/year chloroflouromethanes, Volgograd (1979); 40 000 ton/year chloroflouromethanes, Yavan (1979); 100 000 ton/year polypropylene, Tomsk (1980); 500 000 ton/year urea, Berezniki (1979); 500 000 ton/year urea, Kemerovo (1979) and a 5 000 ton/year dyestuffs complex	$800m	250 000 ton/year of ammonia to be received back as well as a "symbolic" amount of acrylonitrile and some urea	1981

Company	Year signed	Description of contract	Value	Products to be taken back	Year products will start coming in
Occidental, US	1974	Supply to the USSR of 1 million ton/year of super-phosphoric acid over a period of 20 years beginning in 1978. Deliveries: 1978 1979 1980 superphos-phoric acid 000 ton 10 480 1000	$ 20 billion	In return Occidental will receive 2.1 million ton/year of ammonia for 10 years starting in 1978, about 1.5 million ton/year in the next 10 years and 1 million ton/year each of urea and potash for the entire 20 years. In the first few years the tonnages will be smaller: in 000t 1978 1979 1980 ammonia 350 1200 2100 urea 250 250 1000 potash 380 830 1000	1978
Creusot Loire, France	1974	Supply of equipment, engineering and basic design for four 1 350 ton/day ammonia plants for Togliatti	FF1 billion	Repayment in ammonia over 10 years. About 300 000 ton/year. Some 40 000 ton/year of this will be taken by Rhône-Poulenc	
Klöckner, West Germany	1975	Supply to the USSR of 250 000 ton/year PVC plant for Zima	DM154m	To be repaid with 10 000 ton/year of vinyl chloride monomer for 10 years begin-ning in 1977 also 8 000 ton/year PVC for 10 years starting in 1980	1977
SNAM Progetti/ Anic, Italy	1975	Supply to the USSR of 3 urea plants each with a capacity of 1 500 ton/day to be located at Togliatti (2 plants) and Novo-moskovsk	$ 200m	In return Anic will take 100 000 ton/year of ammonia over 10 years. With its own recent problems with ammonia plant it will apparent-ly need much of the material	1981
Snia Viscosa, Italy	1975	Supply to the USSR of 80 000 ton/year caprolactam plant based on toluene to be located near Tashkent	$ 180m	To be repaid in caprolactam. At current prices the amount should be over 200 000 ton	1980/81
Klöckner/ Davy Powergas GmbH, West Germany	1976	Supply to the USSR (Perm) of a 60 000 ton/year phthalic anhydride plant and a 3 000 ton/year fumaric acid unit. Also catalyst plant	DM100m	Repayment with 5 000 ton/year of phthalic anhydride. 3 000 ton/year fumaric acid (total amount of plant) and 15 000 ton/year of urea over a period of 10 years	1980

Company	Year signed	Description of contract	Value	Products to be taken back	Year products will start coming in
Klöckner/ Davy Powergas GmbH, West Germany	1977	Supply to the USSR (Rubezhnoye, Donetsk) of 60 000 ton/year of phthalic anhydride plant and 3 000 ton/year maleic anhydride plant	DM100m	Repayment with 5 000 ton/ year of phthalic anhydride, also 3 000 ton/year of maleic anhydride (total plant capacity) and 15 000 ton/year of urea over 10 years	1980
Salzgitter, West Germany	1976	Construction in the USSR (Gorkii) of a 200 000 ton/ year ethylene oxide plant	DM200m	Repayment mainly in mono ethylene glycol, some other chemicals as well. Until 1989	1979
Technip, France	1976	Construction in the USSR (Omsk and Ufa) of two aromatics complexes each producing 125 000 ton/year benzene, 165 000 ton/year orthoxylene and 165 000 ton/year paraxylene	$500m	The original contract provides for the purchase over a period of 10 years of: orthoxylene 20 000 ton/year paraxylene 20 000 ton/year fixed tonnage benzene 50 000 ton/year diesel oil 290 000 ton/year naphtha 250 000 ton/year flexible part	1980/81
Rhône-Poulenc, France	1976	Signed a three part agreement with the USSR: 1. Sale to the USSR of technology and equipment to produce pesticides, fertilizers to the value of FF2.5 billion 2. Receive chemicals from the USSR to the value of FF2.5 billion over a period of 10 years beginning in 1980 3. Sale to the USSR of Rhône-Poulenc products to the value of FF1 billion So far Speichim has signed a contract with the USSR to use Rhône-Poulenc technology in fertilizer plants (value FF450m) and Krebs in phosphoric acid plant (value FF90m).	Total value FF6 billion	Deliveries of oil products including naphtha as well as some chemical products. These will include about 40 000 ton/year of ammonia from the Creusot Loire deal, methanol and orthoxylene. The company is still in negotiations on this	1980

Company	Year signed	Description of contract	Value	Products to be taken back	Year products will start coming in
CJB, UK	1977	Construction of a 200 000 ton/year high density poly-ethylene plant in Kazan based on Union Carbide technology. Neither company involved in buy-back. A third party will market production in the West	£50m	Third party to market the product, about 160 000 ton in total	1981
Krupp-Koppers, West Germany	1976	Supply to the USSR of a 60 000 ton/year dimethyl-terephthalate plant for Mogilev. Licensor Dynamit Nobel	DM150m	Products involved: DMT paraxylene and other petro-chemical products. Dynamit Nobel will take a small amount of DMT, also paraxylene and other petrochemical products	1981
Uhde/Hoechst, West Germany	1977	Supply of 35 000 ton/year of polyester staple fibre plant for Mogilev. First one in a series of 230 000 ton/year total capacity	DM140m	Products involved: DMT paraxylene, methanol, crude cotton. Brenntag will market DMT, paraxylene, methanol and other products. Adix und Cordes will market crude cotton. Hoechst will take products it can use in own plants including DMT, paraxy-lene and others	1980/81
Davy Powergas/ ICI/Klöckner, UK	1977	Construction in the USSR (Gubakha and Tomsk) of two 2 500 ton/day methanol plants based on ICI technology	over $250m	ICI and Klöckner will market about 300 000 ton/ year of methanol over a period of 10 years. Of the 300 000 ton/year about 200 000 ton/year will be used in the UK. For the first two years (1981-82) a minimum of 280 000 ton/year will be shipped in	1981

Source: European Chemical News

Joint ventures

Up until August 1976, when Poland decreed the right to 100% foreign ownership of medium and small-scale enterprises, joint ventures represented the deepest penetration of equity capital or private ownership of the means of production into the Communist countries. Despite the very strong position taken by the Soviet Union against equity ownership in enterprises on her territory and in COMECON generally, Hungary, Rumania and Poland permit the creation of joint ventures and seem intent upon expanding such forms of cooperation rapidly. Joint ventures are equity arrangements among two or more independent firms. The degree of equity of the participants can vary from very little, say 90/10, to 50/50. Because of the many advantages, joint venturing is at present a very dynamic practice of the multinationals in their expansion of the global economy. Some firms, usually holding companies or corporations, possess hundreds of joint ventures with other firms in the West. Even the fiercest market competitors may have joint ventures with one another in new or non-competitive markets. The joint venture permits extending capital into more activities than would be possible in strictly independent operations. It also offers access to already established technology, products and markets, thus saving on substantial R and D expenditures, avoiding the risks of new product innovation and opening up new distribution networks.

Politically, the joint venture with a local company or government organization allows the global corporation to meet nationalistic demands for participation, to evade anti-trust prosecution and to keep a low profile on its dominant market positions. Economically, the joint venture facilitates achieving economies of scale and critical mass and brings earlier experience curve benefits. Overall, it extends available choices and options in planning strategies, particularly in relation to activities which are adjuncts or ancillary to the main operational area. It has become a proliferating form of multi-national cooperation in the West. The number of joint ventures among the 1,000 largest multinationals certainly exceeds 100,000.

For many of the same reasons the joint venture has numerous supporters as a significant form of East–West cooperation. But it has rather special characteristics for Eastern and Western enterprises. For the East, it raises the problem of the symbiotic coexistence in a single enterprise of national and private ownership, or socialist and captialist co-habitation. The question is whether limiting the number quantitatively effaces the contradiction, or whether even a limited entry of capitalist spermatozoa will effect the impregnation of the socialist cell and lead to the gestation of a Communo-capitalist hybrid economic system. At the present stage the issue is in full discussion with no final options taken. Only the USSR, Czechoslovakia, the GDR and Bulgaria explicitly forbid foreign ownership in domestic enterprises at present.

For the Western multinational firms all the advantages inherent in the other forms of cooperation are inherent in the joint venture. But this type has one further outstanding feature of fundamental importance to multinationals: equity ownership guarantees direct control and full rights in decision making, which permits the protection of up-to-date technology. The absence of such protection in all other forms of cooperation, as we have already discussed, has been a deterrent to and inhibitor of Western cooperation in sharing their most advanced technologies with the East. This is why in seminars, conferences and discussions on East–West economic cooperation, Western companies are stressing the need for equity joint ventures as a condition of a new leap ahead. Many projected deals have failed or were allowed to lapse in the past out of fear that technology would be directed and applied outside the contract area. Given that the state is the single true proprietor in East European countries and that all industry branches, sectors and plants ultimately operate under the centrally-planned structure, agreements with an Eastern enterprise or foreign trade organization are, despite the façade of independence, agreements with the entire economy. There is no way in which transfer of the technology to other sub-divisions of the central authority could be prevented, since it could be copied, resold or leased quite freely. It is the general consensus among multinational management that only the joint venture equity relationship offers some protection from these possibilities and that valuable and economically viable technology should not be transferred without the guarantee of control through equity participation, preferably 51%.

The "Cas Renault"

The French state automobile firm Régie Renault's joint ventures with Yugoslavia and Rumania now produce "national" cars and are its most successful penetrations of the COMECON market aside from its major involvement in the Soviet automobile and truck industry.

Renault–Yugoslav cooperation dates back to 1969. Sales led to signing of a cooperation agreement, which resulted in production of the Renault R4 model by Yugoslavia's IMV at a factory at Novo Mesto. This helped IMV to grow and become the country's second largest automobile manufacturer (it is the largest builder of caravans) with 1976 output reaching 15,000 units. The joint venture has announced plans to manufacture 150,000 Renault motors in Yugoslavia by the end of 1980. Approximately 100,000 of these will be marketed in Yugoslavia with the remainder being exported throughout the Renault network, including France. The IMV plan will also produce spare parts for Renault in France. Financing will be provided by the two partners and a number of private banking credits.

Renault is discreet about expansion plans in COMECON—there are complicated negotiations with the Soviets about the next round of Renault technical assistance, plans to help the Rumanians double production of their local version, the Dacia, and plans to resume production of Renaults in Bulgaria. Renault sources, however, said that Yugoslavia was one of the areas slated for development of a relationship similar to that established with Rumania.

The Pitesti plant in Rumania has been producing gearboxes and other parts for the Renault Estafette utility vehicle, made in France. The Rumanians have exported more than 26,000 gearboxes and parts. Renault hopes that the Rumanians will be able to double their current 60,000-unit annual output of the Dacia. Renault plans to develop a similar trade pattern with the Yugoslavs. "We are going to 'buy' parts from them. In addition, our engineering branch, Seri, is studying joint projects." Besides the Renault 4, Yugoslavia now produces the Renault 12 and 16 models. Another form taken by the two-way cooperation is the rising volume of specialized steel sales to the Yugoslav industry by Renault's speciality steel division, Société des Aciers Fins de l'Est (SAFE).

Renault signed a protocol agreement with the Bulgarian Foreign Trade Ministry in 1976. It covers cooperation in automobiles, trucks, and other vehicles for industry and agriculture over a five-year period. The possibility of starting a new assembly of Renault cars in Bulgaria has been discussed recently in Paris. In 1969 and 1970 the Bulgarians started assembly of the R8 and R10 models, but Renault did not consider it a profitable proposition. The company's views have changed, and a new joint production agreement with the Bulgarians is very much on the cards. Berliet, one of Renault's truck divisions, already active in the Bulgarian market, is eager to help the Bulgarians reorganize their national and international trucking system. Bulgaria is heavily engaged in international trucking, notably between Europe and the Middle East. Renault also hopes to sell engineering services and machinery to the Bulgarians.

In the Soviet Union Renault comes second to Fiat in the actual production of automobiles, but the company has done well with multifaceted agreements involving various divisions. The 1966 protocol produced contracts for the modernization of Moskvich plants in Moscow, construction of a new bodywork and assembly plant at Ijevsk and an engine plant at Ufa. The original 250 million francs deal was followed by a 1.2 billion francs protocol in 1971 which mainly covered engineering work on the engine plant at Kamaz. Renault's machine tool division won more than 25% of these contracts. The second 1.2 billion francs protocol was signed in 1976, and 250 million francs has been allotted to new projects.

Other joint ventures

Yugoslavia is considerably in advance of COMECON in respect of its joint venture arrangements. The first joint venture was created in Yugoslavia pursuant to a law passed in 1967. By 1973 their number had climbed to eighty-five and in September 1976 some 137 joint ventures with Western firms were in operation. By contrast, there were only two joint ventures with other East European enterprises. Under the 1967 law the foreign partner was allowed to have a maximum 49% share of capital. Motor vehicles and metalworking, iron and steel, chemicals and rubber received the larger share of foreign investment of this type.

Yugoslavian joint ventures with new $1 million investment

Western Multinationals	Nationality	Product or Activity
Fiat	Italy	automobiles
Daimler-Benz	W. Germany	heavy vehicles
Klöckner-Humboldt-Deutz	W. Germany	commercial vehicle motors and tractors
Volkswagen	W. Germany	automobiles
Citroën	France	automobiles
Renault	France	forged parts
Rhône-Progil	France	PVC
Bayer	W. Germany	pharmaceuticals and cosmetics
International Flavors & Fragrances	US	scents and aromas
Ciba-Geigy	Switzerland	chemicals and pharmaceuticals
Solvay/LaPorte	Belgium/UK	chemicals
Chemetex Fibres Inc.	US	polyesters
Hoechst	W. Germany	pharmaceuticals
Dow Chemical	US	petrochemicals
Henkel	W. Germany	detergents
Mira Lanzia	Italy	detergents
Storey Bros & Co.	UK	vinyl wallpaper
Ker-Domus	Italy	ceramic tiles

Western Multinationals	Nationality	Product or Activity
Viano Impianti	Italy	ceramic tiles
Trade & Business Brokers	Luxembourg	ceramic tiles
Eaton	US	control devices
Bell Telephone	US	electrical goods
EGO Elektrogerate AG	Switzerland	electro equipment
Tower International	US	soya processing
SKF	Sweden	bearings
Thyssen	W. Germany	rolling mill
Tecmo SpA	Italy	aluminium process
Trievel & Co.	Austria	iron and steel products
Armco Steel, General Electric, Production Machinery Corp., Waterbury Farrell	US	steel
Tragergesellschaft	W. Germany	pulp and paper
Buttes Gas & Oil Co. Isa Challenger Oil & Gas	US	oil prospecting
Dunlop	UK	high-pressure pipes
Semperit	Austria	tyres
Kleber-Colombes, Cifal, Setilex	France	tyres

Yugoslavia is the least restricted of all the Eastern economies. By a complicated scheme of retention quotas for earnings and foreign exchange allowances, Western partners were permitted to repatriate profits up to the extent of hard currency exports. But the Yugoslavs soon learned that the Western firms were interested in investing management know-how rather than cash and technology. They also found that the multinationals would rather sell their share of the goods produced in Yugoslavia than export them, and so the scale of most of the 137 joint ventures established since 1967 remains small. New regulations introduced in 1976 stiffened the conditions of 50/50 joint venture contracts.

The one exception to this general experience of small-scale, local market orientation was the large-scale venture negotiated by the American multinational Dow Chemical Company. A first $17 million project in 1974 for production of polystyerene was followed by a second project in August 1976 covering a $700 million petrochemical complex to be built jointly with Industrija Nafte (INA). This is a joint venture landmark, involving both the largest US investment and the largest joint venture in Eastern Europe. It is also the largest investment by a Yugoslav enterprise with a foreign partner. When completed in 1982, the Dow–INA petrochemical complex on the island of Krk, near the Adriatic port of Rijeka, will turn out annually products worth about $550 million, some $200 million worth of which are to be exported.

Western joint ventures in COMECON

Joint Enterprise	Western Partner	Year Established	Product or Activity
Rumania			
Romcontroldata	Control Data (US)	1973	peripheral elements for computers
Resita-Renk	Renk-Zahnradfabrik (West Germany)	1973	marine gear units
Rifal	Romalfa (Italy)	1973	acrylic fibers
Roniprot	Dai Nippon (Japan)	1974	protein-rich yeast
Elarom	L'Electronique Appliquée (France)	1974	electronic medical equipment
Romelite	Franz Kohmaier KG (West Germany)	1975	chains for industrial use
Hungary			
Volcom	Volvo (Sweden)	1974	cross-country vehicles
Sicontact	Siemens (West Germany)	1974	servicing Siemens equipment
Radelcor	Corning (US)	1976	blood analysers

Dow holds 50% of the equity, the maximum permitted under the Yugoslav joint venture law and has equal representation on the six-member management board. The general manager and the chairman of the board are appointed by the Yugoslav partner and the deputy general manager by Dow. As the chairman does not have a casting vote, all decisions must be unanimous.

The process used in the complex will be based on technology developed by Dow and there will be complete interdependence with Dow's manufacturing base in Western Europe, which will supply feedstocks during the initial stages. Dow is committed to continually update the technology used at the complex in line with best Western practice.

The Yugoslav partner's 23,000 workers also had to grant authority to the director general to sign the agreement. But once signed, the self-management rights stipulated in the constitution become superseded by the need for unanimous decisions by the management board except on matters concerning the distribution of wages and social allocations.

Despite this precedent-setting joint venture, Yugoslavia has learned the hard reality that even under the most liberal regulations the multinationals are very careful to put in the minimum and extract the maximum and that no firm offers technology gratuitously even under a 50/50 deal. For this reason co-production deals are now specifically required to increase exports and to ensure that the Western firm's profits are paid out of export proceeds. The new regulations will also make it difficult to provide outdated technology. Only modern Yugoslavian enterprises possessing approximately the same technological level as the foreign partner will be allowed to conclude joint ventures. The previous practice of Western firms was to form joint ventures with inefficient local firms willing to take obsolete Western technology and to ensure that it was not given the ability to manufacture sophisticated parts. This tension between the Eastern government requirement for only up-to-date efficient technology and the multinationals' attempts to transfer outmoded technology is bound to become a stronger factor in future East–West relations.

In the summer of 1976, after two years of study, Poland announced new joint venture regulations which go much beyond those prevailing in any other country. Avoiding excessively detailed legislation such as exists in Hungary and Rumania, the decree for the first time permits a 100% foreign-owned company. Joint ventures between multinationals and Polish organizations of presumably any proportion from 10–90% to 60–40% is authorized. Up to 50% of the company's after-tax profits calculated upon Polish income-tax regulations can be repatriated in hard currency. The decree further permits 100% owned or joint ventures to be undertaken by persons or corporation *domiciled abroad*. In case of liquidation, the Western firms can repatriate the original investment plus its share of capital gains.

Following Yugoslavia, Hungary and Rumania introduced joint venture legislation in 1971–1972. To date, ten joint ventures have been established in Rumania. These are for the most part 51% Rumanian, 49% Western firm equity shares. Firms involved include Control Data (US), Demag AG (FRG), Roma-Alfa (Italy), Dai Nippon (Japan), L'Electronique Appliquée (France) and Franz Madmaier (Austria).

The first Western company to establish a joint venture in Hungary was Sweden's Volvo automobile firm which concluded a deal with the Csepel Automotive Works in October 1972. Under the contract, the Volvo's four-wheel drive, cross-country, all purpose vehicle, the Lapplander, is being assembled in the Csepel works from Swedish-made components. Profits are divided 48% for Volvo and 52% for its Hungarian partners. Thus Volvo stockholders can legally claim to be capitalist proprietors of the means of production in Socialist Hungary and to be securing dividends from Socialist property. The Hungarian-assembled vehicles are delivered to South American customers. They are not, therefore, available to Hungarians.

Following the Volvo deal, the giant West German electrical multinational, Siemens AG, signed a second Hungarian joint venture agreement with Hungary's Intercorporation Ltd. Based upon equity shares of 51% for Intercorporation and 49% for Siemens, the venture provides technical assistance in the electrical and electronic industries. The joint venture itself is not the production unit. It merely provides management, technology and services for wholly State-owned factories, thus technically remaining removed from actual plant ownership, direction of labour, etc. Payment for these services, as in the case of Volvo, is 49% of the Siemens type products produced by the Hungarian factories. Siemens technicians are authorized to supervise production and to carry out quality controls. The aim of the Hungarian legislation is to effect a judicial separation of joint ventures from the economy proper in order to present the façade of socialist ownership over all the means of production. Rumania, Yugoslavia and Poland all consider their joint ventures as fully integrated parts of their economies.

The Soviet Union still opposes foreign equity or capitalist presence within its territory. It has instead stressed counterpurchase and buy-back relationships based upon licensed capitalist technology. Pressures for easing this anachronistic ideological hang-up have been rising owing to prospects of major deals with such firms as General Motors for the construction and management of the world's biggest truck factory in Siberia, a new very large-scale project with Occidental Petroleum in chemicals and fertilizers, resource development with the oil majors, such as Exxon, Shell, and BP and construction of large vehicle plants with Daimler Benz. Other ventures include Siberian wood and raw materials projects estimated at over $450 million with a consortium of Japanese multinationals; and a joint wide-body airframe construction project with Boeing, Lockheed and MacDonnell Douglas of the USA. Earlier discussions had taken place on further cooperation between the Soviet foreign trade organization for the aircraft industry and leading American aviation firms, all of whom are also leading armaments manufacturers of anti-Soviet weapon systems. The talks broke down because of the disinclination of the firms to accept technology transfers without full corporate presence and controls on Soviet territory. The failure of the talks shocked the USSR which was counting heavily on this cooperation to pioneer joint production of aircraft for the US and Western markets at present largely monopolized by these airframe giants. It had also planned on using the deal as a transmission belt for the export of wholly Russian-made civilian aircraft such as the Yak 40, to be manufactured to meet US Air Safety Regulations. Planes as weapons are now clearly distinguished from planes as profits in the East just as in the West.

These problems have caused the Soviet Union to re-evaluate the question and studies have been carried out to determine the legislative changes which may be necessary to allow foreign corporate presence, ownership and control along with the company's technology which is being sought.

Though Brezhnev went out of his way to refute such changes in his speech to the 25th Party Congress in February 1976, one can predict with confidence that the way will be found to permit joint ventures, whatever official descriptions of the relationship may be found in order to save face. The formula will entail maintaining Socialist ownership over the capitalist means of production as a legal and formal proposition while permitting all the functional aspects of joint management controls, rights of decision-making, distribution and repatriation of profits from the sharing of the ensuing production. In the case of the planned huge GM/Soviet truck deal in Siberia, the trend is toward a form of management service contract such as has been invented by the oil companies in their Near East operations. Instead of owning the oil fields as they did in the old days of concession, the companies operate, manage and administer the Arab-owned industry under a management service arrangement. Outside of legal ownership and new profit-sharing systems, their activities functionally are entirely as before. Such an arrangement would permit Brezhnev to deny that General Motors and its banking interests led by David Rockefeller were encroaching upon socialist means of production while, in fact, encouraging them to do so. In the Vodka-Cola era, what is good for General Motors has obviously become good for the Kremlin.

An interesting facsimile of this Vodka-Cola symbiosis occurred recently in connection with a requested $200 million US Exim Bank Credit to Poland to finance a General Motors–Polish joint venture for the manufacture of trucks. The incident occurred at the same time as a strike of the United Automobile Workers' Union in the USA which closed down the Ford Motor Company. Given that most of the vehicles produced under the Polish arrangement are intended for export by the partners, perhaps General Motors is preparing for the future when most of its cars and trucks might be produced in

COMPENSATION AGREEMENTS IN USSR
(recorded as of 1975)

Commodity	Contractor	Estimated Value of Soviet Imports (Million US $)	Year of Initial Purchases	Year of Initial Soviet Exports	Value of Project-Associated Exports (Million US $) 1975-80	1981-85
Natural Gas	Austria (OeMV, VOEST Alpine Montan)	110	1969	1969	900	1,000
Natural Gas	West Germany (Ruhrgas, Mannesmann)	1,500	1970	1974	2,800	4,700
Natural Gas	Italy (ENI, Finsider)	190	1971	1974	1,200	3,200
Natural Gas	France (Gaz de France, Vallourec)	250	1972	1976	700	1,462
East Siberian Forestry Project	Japan	163	1969	1969	Deal completed in 1974	
East Siberian Wood Chip Plant	Japan	45	1972	1972	145	50
Ust-Illimsk Timber Complex	France (Parsons & Whitemore)	60	1974	1977	34	50
Kuybyshev Ammonia and Urea Complex	United States (Occidental Chemicals)	400	1975	1978	2,000	2,500
Chemical Plants	Italy (Montedison)	500	1975	1977	175	250
South Yakutian Coal at Chulman	Japan	450	1975	1989	80	860
Kursk Iron Ore Pelletization Plant	West Germany (Krupp, Korf, Salzgitter, Siemens, Demag)	1,000	1975	N.A.	450	1,000
Second East Siberian Forestry Project	Japan	550	1975	1975	1,100	—
Chemical Plants	Italy (ENI)	1,000	1975—1980	N.A.	N.A.	N.A.
Chemical Plants	France (Litwin)	100	1974	1977	50	60
Aluminium Complex	France (PUK)	600—1,000	1976	N.A.	N.A.	N.A.
Chemical Plants	France (Creusot-Loire)	220	1975	1979	100	225

Source: U.S. Central Intelligence Agency

the efficient strike-free Communist countries safe from the disruption of undisciplined, free workers organized in free unions.

The new Exim Bank president, Stephen DeBrul Jr, was brought into his position from Lehman Brothers (where Petersen, Ball and other Overworld ex-anti-Communist apostates foregather) by pro-détente US Secretary of the Treasury, William Simon. DeBrul requested that the Poles pay 9% interest which, he claimed, "is competitive when all the facts are taken into consideration" (*New York Herald Tribune*, 19 September, Rowland Evans and Robert Novak). The Poles, of course, protested the high rate insisting upon the prevailing Exim Bank 7%. This resulted in an unprecedented intercession in the form of a confidential letter from US Deputy Secretary of Defense, William Clements (a long-standing resident of the Overworld society), supporting the Poles against DeBrul Jr. General Motors, besides being the world's leading automobile company is also a major Pentagon supplier of military equipment. Invoking reasons of national security, Clements wrote: "For some years the inactive tool industry, a major element of the defense industrial base, has suffered erosion of its relative position due primarily to the competition of members of the European Economic Community and from Japan." A Republican representative, John Anderson, (reported Evans and Novak in their column) warned that the bank "may be setting conditions that could jeopardize the $200 million in machine tool orders and 6,000 jobs were at stake." So the claim appears to be that in the interest of military and defense security against the Communist enemy, it is vital that Poland be given a $200 million General Motors assembly plant from which to export heavy trucks to the US. Why not credits for production of American Nuclear Missile MIRV's in the USSR on a buy-back deal? Not only would such an arrangement be good for the US electronics and space industry, and cheaper, but also an agreement might be reached on a leasing arrangement. The missile could remain in the USSR and reduce travelling time in case of the need for a second-strike response to a Russian nuclear attack on the USA!

In general joint ventures have not proved very successful. We have already commented upon the Yugoslav experience with out-of-date technology transfers until its launching of the mammoth Dow Chemical venture. On the other hand the restrictive definition of management control and ownership rights and the separation of the ventures from the economic main-stream of the Eastern countries limits the interest of multinationals in large-scale projects involving up-to-date technology. Another impediment to Western enthusiasm has been the Rumanian requirement that the joint ventures pay export wages to the foreign trade monopoly in hard currency. Artificially high wage rates are set by the Rumanian negotiating authorities and paid into a special fund, of which the workers receive only a small fraction, in local currency. These higher rates are still very much lower than "export rates" in the West—often no more than a quarter or less. Continuous shift work is obligatory with only minor premium payment, whilst the normal work week is between forty-six and forty-eight hours. The companies are forbidden to raise wages beyond the official national wage rates and cannot use wages as incentives or for recruiting more skilled workers. It was entirely due to such comparatively low wages that Control Data established Rumania's first joint venture to produce relatively outmoded computer hardware which had been discontinued in the US as being too costly.

Nevertheless, despite the overall present dissatisfaction with certain aspects of equity share cooperation, this form will undoubtedly continue to grow with modifications being introduced as necessary, because it is the only basis upon which the multinationals will consent to furnish their constantly improving up-to-date technology to Eastern Europe, without which the Communist élite is unlikely to survive economic and social disruption.

During the London meeting of the Anglo–Cuban Joint Trade Commission, a senior Cuban foreign trade official announced that Cuba is preparing to sign agreements with British and other Western companies, including American, willing to set up joint ventures. The most likely fields for this type of cooperation will be the development of tourism in northern Cuba and mining, especially of Cuban reserves of zinc, lead and copper in the western province of Pinar del Rio. These two sectors are potential large earners of foreign currency during a time when the poor Cuban sugar harvest and the fall in the price of sugar on the world market has proved detrimental to the Cuban economy. American pharmaceutical companies, chemical companies, Coca-Cola and sugar interests are already at work preparing for joint ventures and the new era of Rhum-Cola is about to set in. When it has matured, and despite Cuban intervention in Africa, and US Senators led by Senators McGovern, Church, Sarits, *et al.*, the position of the congress will also begin shifting away from a hard time towards economic cooperation.

Indicating the trend which has enveloped the world, the Vietnam government has announced it will allow foreign investment of up to 49% in selected joint ventures, possibly including oil exploration with Western multinationals; and recently North Korea, totally bankrupt and incapable of paying external debts, has followed suit.

Communizing the market economy

The Soviet Union, as we have seen, is extremely concerned about the formal establishment of capitalist, equity-owned ventures within its centrally planned economies. It displays less qualms about the establishment of joint-owned and Soviet-controlled ventures in the capitalist market economies. Already it has created a number of such capitalist-based companies of different types. Though not as yet numerous, these companies violate by their existence another fundamental tenet of Communist doctrine: namely, opposition to all forms of capitalist exploitation of workers through the creation of surplus value, high interest rates and capitalist pricing of products based upon monetary, speculative and market monopoly rather than upon socially necessary labour time. Again we may make an analogy with the impossibility of only a "partial pregnancy"—everything grows in time. The Soviet Union and the other East European countries have established *capitalist* bases in the capitalist West, not socialist beachheads. Regardless of their relative numbers, these beginnings definitely represent a fatal negation to the official declarations of Socialist virtue.

The most significant Western presence which we have observed by Eastern State ventures is in the banking sector. But important Soviet operations in the West have taken place also in sales and distribution over the last few years and notably in joint distribution with Western firms of the obligatory exports of co-production output. Through a variety of marketing companies, Soviet watches, cameras, tractors, aerofoils, Vodka, etc., are sold in the USA and in European countries. The Soviet-owned Nafta oil chain, for example, operates a distribution network for oil products in South-East England, whilst Belgium and Liechtenstein are supplied by its 100%-owned oil refinery in Antwerp. Other fully-owned or equity-shared capitalist Soviet enterprises include: the Scalda–Volga 95%-owned auto-assembly plant in Belgium; the Anglo–Soviet Shipping Company in London; insurance companies in London and Vienna; another oil refinery in Brazil; a steel company and numerous trading companies in France; and innumerable import–export trading, insurance, publishing, transport and shipping companies in Italy and Belgium.

Similar capitalist companies have been established by the satellite countries, including: a Polish phosphate undertaking in Montreal, Canada; a Hungarian potash mine in Saskatchewan; Yugoslavian engineering enterprises in Mexico; Rumanian building contractors in the Federal Republic of Germany; a Comecon–Benelux Trucking Company. There are also numerous joint trading companies, including 50/50 Bulgarian–Italian, Polish–Italian, West German–Polish, Hungarian–Austrian ventures, and a Rumanian–Irish concern, to refer to just a few examples from a myriad.

Eastern joint ventures established in the West are gaining ground, though limited mostly to marketing or to banking, as already described. For example: Arcode (London) is a 50/50 British–Rumanian chemical marketing firm; Tjecke-SUEA (Stockholm) is a 49/51 Swedish–Czech machinery marketing firm; Russalmaz (Antwerp) a 80% Soviet–Belgian diamond-marketing firm; Chemapol Svenska (Stockholm) a 49/51 Swedish–Czech chemical marketing firm.

The first major Soviet joint marketing venture in North America was the Satra Corporation of New York, a small American firm set up to import Soviet cars and later, hydrofoils. Together with the Soviet FTO Traktor export, it established Belarus Equipment of Canada Ltd in Toronto in which 80% of the shares are owned by the Soviet partner. Created to market Soviet tractors, Belarus extended its sales and servicing network right across Canada. Satra is currently safety-testing the Fiat 124-based Lada automobile for a major import operation. The vehicle will be equipped with American-made equipment such as catalytic exhaust correctors which will be added during assembly in the USA.

The Soviet Union created its first 50/50 joint venture in 1976 in the Federal Republic of Germany to market Linotype printing equipment, manufactured in a Leningrad factory under Western licence, but it has approached the issue of joint ventures in the USA very carefully. It is expected, however, that this prudence will relax somewhat to allow the establishment of a number of potentially significant joint ventures. During September 1975 the chairman of the Electronorgtecknica, the Soviet FTO responsible for the electronics industry, discussed possible agreements with an American partner for setting up a sales organization and subsequently assembling products from Russian-made components to side-step the huge tariffs on finished industrial goods.

COMECON COUNTRY SUBSIDIARIES IN ADVANCED CAPITALIST ECONOMIES

(These include officially acknowledged firms only and not clandestine participation in Western Communist Party-controlled firms and other proxy-held companies)

COMECON country	Aust	Bel—Lux	Can	Fin	Fr	FRG	It	Jap	Neth	Sp	Swed	Switz	UK	US	Joint Vent.	100% owned	Unknown
Bulgaria	2	1	1	—	2	11	4	2	1	1	1	2	4	—	18	5	9
C.S.S.R.	—	2	1	—	1	1	2	—	1	—	3	—	10	—	12	2	7
G.D.R.	3	1	—	—	4	—	—	—	1	—	1	—	5	—	12	—	3
Hungary	11	—	1	1	4	13	3	1	3	2	2	2	8	—	41	8	3
Poland	4	5	1	1	4	12	1	1	3	2	2	2	7	5	39	4	8
Romania	2	—	2	—	6	7	5	—	1	—	—	1	3	2	27	1	1
U.S.S.R. *	3	10	5	9	11	10	5	2	4	2	4	1	10	4	58	18	7
Total	25	19	11	11	32	54	20	6	14	7	13	8	47	11	207	38	38

(FORM OF OWNERSHIP spans Joint Vent., 100% owned, Unknown)

* 3 in Norway

Source: Institute of Soviet and East-European Studies Working Paper No. 7 February 1977
Carleton University, Ottawa, Canada

Soviet multinational joint ventures in West (acknowledged)

Argentina
Corann South America
Electrical apparatus

Australia
Opal Maritime Agency (Sovinflot)
Ships

Austria
Asotra
Transportation
Garant Versicherung
Insurance

Belgium
Belgium-Soviet Trade Co-Belso
Consumer goods, food products
Belgo-Marine (Sovinflot)
Transportation
Elorg-Belgie NV
Electronics
EWA Technical & Optical Equipment
Optical equipment
Ferchimex SA
Fertilizers, phosphates, oils
Nafta (B) SA
Oil products
Russalmaz NV
Diamonds
Scalda-Volga
Automotives, machine tools,
metalworking equipment
Transworld Marine Agency NV
Transportation

Canada
Belarus Equipment Ltd (Tractorexport)
Agricultural & industrial equipment
EMEC Trading Ltd
Electrical equipment
Morflot Freight Liners
Transportation
Socan Aircraft Ltd
Sales & service: aircraft equipment
Stan-Canada
Machine tools

Ethiopia
Ethos Trading
Electrical products

Finland
Converta
Packaging
Elorg-Data
Technical services (electronics)
Kaukomarkkinat Oy
Sales agency

Koneisto AB
Machinery & equipment
Konela-Belarus
Sales & service: tractors
Konela Oy
Sales & service: vehicles
Perusyhtymä
Construction
Saimaa Lines Ltd
Transportation
Suomen Petrooli Oy
Oil products
Teboil Oy
Oil products

France
Actif-Avto SA
Agricultural & construction
equipment
Fransov
Fishing vessel service
Interagra SA
Miscellaneous products
Promolease, affiliate of Banque
Commerciale pour l'Europe
du Nord
Renting & leasing of equipment
Rusbois
Wood, pulp & paper
Sagmar-Société d'Agences Maritimes
Franco-Soviétique (Sovinflot)
Transportation
Slava (Mashpriborintorg)
Assembly & sales: watches
Sogo & Cie SA
Chemicals, pharmaceuticals
Stanko-France
Machine tools, metalworking
equipment

Italy
Dolphin Agenzia Maritima
Transportation
Ruslegno
Wood products
Sovitalmare di Navigazion SpA
Transportation
Sovitpesca
Fish products
Stanitaliana SpA
Machinery

Japan
Aurora
Publishing
United Orient Shipping & Agency Co.
   Ltd
Transportation

Morocco
Marino Export
Machinery

Netherlands
East-West Agencies
Electric, optical & photographic
equipment
Elorg BV
Technical service (electronics)
Gremi Autoimport BV
Vehicles
Transworld Marine Agency NV
Transportation

Nigeria
Waatego Lagos
Trucks

Norway
Belarus-Norge
Tractors
Koneisto Norge A/S
Machinery & equipment
Konela Norge Bil
Sales & service: automobiles

Spain
Intramar SA
Transportation
Pesquerias Españolas Sovieticas
Conjuntas SA-Pesconsa
Technical services (fishing)
Sovhispan SA
Fish products & fishing vessel service

Sweden
Matreco Bil AB
Sales & service: automobiles
Metrevo-Bil AB
Pulp & paper machinery
Scansov Transport AB
Transportation

United Kingdom
Anglo-Soviet Shipping Co. Ltd.
Transportation
East-West Leasing (Moscow Narodny
   Bank)
Leasing
Nafta (GB) Ltd
Oil products
Razno & Co. Ltd
Food products
Russian Wood Agency Ltd
Wood, pulp & paper
Sovfracht (London) Ltd
Transportation
Technical & Optical Equipment Ltd
Electrical & optical equipment
UMO Plant Ltd
Sales & service: construction equipment

United States
Amtorg Trading Corp.
Agent
Morflot America Inc.-Moram
Transportation
Sovfracht (USA) Inc.
Transportation

West Germany
Deutsch-Sowjetische Teppich GmbH
Carpets
Neotype Techmashexport
Printing machinery
Plodimex Aussenhandels GmbH
Food products
Russalmaz AG
Precious stones
Russische Holz
Wood
Sobren Chemiehandel GmbH
Chemicals
Transglobe Container Services GmbH
Container leasing
Uberseeschiffahrtsagentur
Transportation
Wesotra Spedition and Transport GmbH
Transportation

A small Belgian company, Pachon, concluded a barter deal with the Soviet foreign trade company Soyuzkoopvneshtorg for the delivery of $11 million worth of carpets to the USSR. In turn, Pachon takes various Soviet goods worth $13 million. These goods include petroleum products, viscose waste, textile waste, wood and various raw materials. In Brussels the company is known to have organic links with the Communist party. This political orientation is a clear plus for their success on the Soviet market just as Italian, French and British CP-related firms prosper in East–West trade.

The deal is a good example of the fact that even a small CP company outcompetes larger Western producers for contracts. This is the case with carpets. Western producers were anticipating the complete refurbishing of Moscow hotels in view of the 1980 Olympic Games and had been trying very hard to obtain important Soviet contracts.

For Pachon the deal is already the third carpet deal with the Soviets. The first provided for the delivery of 500,000 square metres, the second for the delivery of 1 million square metres and the current deal also provides for the delivery of 1 million square metres.

The company employs only twenty-two people and was established some twenty-three years ago to trade with Eastern Europe. Its involvement is not restricted to the USSR. It imports a large volume of shoes from Hungary, for example, and exports hosiery articles to Czechoslovakia. Other articles that it trades with Eastern Europe include various textiles and wood, in particular. In reality the company is primarily known as a wood-trading agent for the Soviet Union in Belgium.

One of the reasons for the company's ability to take important amounts of Eastern European barter goods is that it does not sell them only on the Belgian market, but in most of Western Europe. The UK, the FRG and Italy are the most important markets.

Perhaps the most spectacular joint venture operations in North America are two Rumanian investment projects. One involved the construction of the Brasov tractor assembly plant in Saskatchewan, Canada, in 1972 and the other constituted an agreement with Occidental Petroleum to invest $50 million in a one-third participation in a coal mine belonging to Occidental's Island Creek coal company. The agreement provides for a further option to eventually acquire another third in the Virginian mine.

> An unusual loan has been obtained by the Rumanian Foreign Trade Bank from a group of banks led by First Chicago [to] help finance investment in a coal mine in Virginia, which is operated by Island Creek Coal, a subsidiary of Occidental Petroleum, and it is believed to be the first ever investment by Romania in the U.S.
>
> Under the contract agreed between the Romanian state company, Mineralimportexport, and Occidental Petroleum, the first-named has agreed to buy, over the long term, up to 27.3m. tons of coal, which could be worth up to $2bn.
>
> The coal will be sold by the U.S. company at market prices and used by Romania for its expanding steel industry.
>
> Maturity of the loan is five years, and the spread over the interbank rate, which is not disclosed, is believed to be 1 per cent.

Following Soviet agreement to enter Western shipping cartels, thus softening their cut-rate war, there has been agreement between US and Soviet shipping companies to set up joint offices in San Francisco and New York. The Reefer Express Line of New York is also chartering a Soviet refrigerator ship for use on a banana run between Australia and the USA. Most significant, however, is the acceptance of mortgages on

Soviet ships for loan and credit backing by American financial companies. In one such deal, a group of Euromarket banks, led by First Chicago, has forwarded a $20 million, five-year loan to the state-owned Polish Steamship Company in return for a first mortgage on the two cargo vessels which the Poles are to purchase with the loan. The precedent of allowing a capitalist link on socialist property is an awesome prospect for ideologists.

Licensing is another form of limited but ideologically significant socialist activity in the Western market economies. Trade circles report nearly 800 Eastern licences sold to the West. The largest number (nearly 75%) was sold by Czechoslovakia and the USSR. Several Western firms specialize in commercializing Communist licenses which are bought for the most part by smaller firms as a means of cheaply obtaining a product which they could not themselves develop or procure. The Soviet Union's special FTO for licensing the sales of Soviet licenses to the USA claims that this traffic has grown by about 30% per annum, and indicates recent purchases of coal, gas plant and share oil processes as evidence of the rising penetration of Western markets. Nearly thirty licensing agreements have been reached with American firms alone.

Licensing between Western firms and the state trading organizations lends itself to widespread manipulation and regurgitation of Western technology which is almost impossible to control. Books and records of Eastern firms are not open to examination by licensers under existing legislation. Reports of sales and products under licence must, therefore, be accepted at face value—a practice which would never be accepted in the West. One major problem is the possible pirating of original Western licences and technology which may be repatented in the East as an original socialist innovation. As the licensing agreement is reached between a Western firm and a State-wide or COMECON-wide organization, naturally no recourse is available should marginal or minor improvements on an original Western licence be registered and offered for sale in the West. Such a misrepresentation appears to have taken place, for example, in respect of a joint Soviet–East German process for producing low-density polyethylene called "polymer 50." This process had been sold to the West German firm Salzgitter whose earlier BASF-derived licence lapsed in early 1976. Salzgitter has built six large turn-key plants in the Soviet Union to produce low-density polyethylene. Salzgitter has admitted that the technology, claimed to be "new" and "highly advanced," marked no great change over the BASF process it had previously used (London *Financial Times*, April 30, 1976). One West German technologist explains that "it has come to the point that if you merely tighten a screw a bit it is described as a wholly new process." Western firms confirm that virtually all of the engineering and technology (up to 80% for the first Soviet plant using Polymer 50) stems from the West. Though the Soviet and East German licensers claim a "three to fivefold increase" in labour productivity from the equipment compared to similar equipment purchased from capitalist countries, West German industry sources say that they are at a loss to understand how such results can be attained, using virtually identical processes and equipment imported from the West. The threat of wholesale and massive pirating of original licences through Eastern pseudo-patents will be difficult to prevent. The Soviet Union, for example, would never permit a socialist licence to be challenged in a neutral court once it had been registered. No laws of precedence or applicable rules of conduct are available to protect original Western licensers of the basic technology. As such modifications are made by the Eastern State body, no charge of illegality can be brought against the pirates.

Dumping socially necessary labour time

The rapidly growing criticism and scepticism in Western countries about claims that East–West trade parallels an inherently positive political convergence is eliciting a packaged Eastern counter-response. Fundamentally, the Agit-Prop campaign centers on three major themes:

1. That capitalist investment and technology is good for socialism whilst remaining completely under the proprietary and legal control of the state organizations.
2. That détente represents a victory for the forces of peace and socialism over the imperialist-revanchist monopolists who prefer cold war and armaments to trade and peaceful coexistence.
3. That while trade in the form of technology transfer aids socialism, it is also beneficial for the workers in the West because of the "2,000,000 jobs" such trade helps create.

Officially, the line is that the "crisis of capitalism" has entered its final and agonizing phase. Brezhnev and all Communist party factotums of both East and West profess to have diagnosed the beginning of the demise in the pervasive capitalist inflation and unemployment of the 1970s. East–West cohabitation, it is claimed, provides capitalist multinational manufacturers of machine tools, chemicals and transportation equipment with support for 2,000,000 jobs. Thus co-production deals become ideologically ethical as protecting the jobs of oppressed workers who would otherwise be unemployed. The figure of 2,000,000 was obviously chosen for its aesthetic and public relations symmetry. It is, after all, a round and pleasant figure. Certainly a better soft-sell chiffre than such odd and unaesthetic numbers as 2,129,069 or 1,937,965, for example. The modesty of the claim gains further credibility than such a number as 10,000,000 or 20,000,000 which could equally have been "researched" by such methods of economic investigation as are utilized by the Agit-Prop statistics departments.

Counter-charges and increasing protests in the West against alleged "détente-dumping" give the lie to this transparent fiction, however. Given that the entire cooperation system hinges on the combination of cheap, rigorously controlled, no-strike labour with Western technology and know-how, dumping is inherently and unavoidably a parameter of détente. Without the cheap labour component the loop could not produce the profits surge necessary to close the circuit and turn it into an integrated operating whole. The cheap-wage incorporated-labour element in the end-products of counter-purchase, co-production and joint ventures is the fundamental "comparative advantage" in the commitment of capitalist technology to Eastern Europe. Without this advantage and the credits, industrial cooperation would not take place. Cyrus Eaton, the renowned Cleveland millionaire-capitalist, President of Yale & Town Co. and an intimate and long-standing friend and colleague of the Rockefellers and the Soviet rulers, put it succinctly in 1970. Commenting upon his negotiation of a $40 million 50/50 joint venture tyre plant in the East, he explained that the Communist state partner would "own and operate the plant, supplying the operational management and labour." His own Western half would be located in tax-haven Switzerland which would market the tyres everywhere in the West. "This enabled the Eastern country to earn hard currency and," as he explains further, "because of lower labour costs the venture can sell tyres cheaper than Western companies can." "The plant in the East sells the tyres to the marketing subsidiary at cost—thus leaving profits to the joint marketing subsidiary." (*Capital, Inflation and the Multinationals*, p. 114.) As a pioneer of détente and an initiator of the Pugwash Conference to promote disarmament through dialogue between East and West, Cyrus Eaton is an eminently qualified expert on the subject. Détente, or Vodka-Colanization, could not be described more succinctly or accurately.

Under any existing national or international set of laws, rules, regulations, customs and practices in the West, such a system is clearly détente-dumping. Unduly low wages are rejected everywhere as an unacceptable competitive advantage in Western foreign trade. In every industrialized country protection is granted against unfair competition, low-price imports and the undercutting of prices in national markets and industry whenever excessively low wages can be proven. Admittedly, proving low-wage dumping in practice is not simple, even between Western countries. Calculating fair domestic prices and costs as well as the myriad other forms of "unfair competition" (export subsidies, tax rebates, privileged financing, preferential raw material prices, etc.) is almost impossible. There is no conceivable end to the possible impingements on "fair trade," which in practice is a virtually indefinable concept. Industry claims that even low tariffs lead to discrimination. But the rising volume of imports, especially of industrial goods from low-cost regions such as the Far-East (Hong Kong, Taiwan, South Korea, Singapore) as well as from Latin America and elsewhere has created serious market dislocations in North America and Europe. Demands are increasing for protection against TV sets, television tubes, radios and electronic equipment, textiles, knitted goods, clothing, acrylic yarns, chemicals and even ships, bulk steel and automobiles. Industry is claiming that preferential tariffs for raw materials and semi-finished goods from developing Third-World countries are undermining domestic high-wage, high-cost industry sectors, forcing closures and unemployment.

Multinational companies which are able to transfer production to low wage, weak union, and minimum tax sites on a global basis have aggravated the disruption of world trade. Increasing monopolization of markets and trading systems by cartels, ententes and joint ventures is an inescapable consequence of the growth of multinational enterprise and the newly emerging global economy. Traditional market forces have virtually vanished from the principal Western trading systems and in their stead a new form of foreign trade is gestating. It is trade in which quotas, prices and markets are negotiated on a voluntary basis between governments, importers and exporters. As in collective bargaining, temporary agreements are negotiated for different products or product lines. For example, in the face of threats by the Americans and the Common Market countries to impose dumping regulations, Japan agreed voluntarily to limit annual increases in the export of textiles, TVs and other goods to the USA, UK, Belgium, Holland, etc. Similarly negotiated agreements currently cover most of the critical low-cost exports from South-East Asia and certain Latin American countries. Even between Europe and the USA, negotiated agreements limiting exports of certain European steel products, coal, chemicals, and even food products have become extensive. In this way mass closures of less modern plants and much higher unemployment levels have been delayed, if not prevented.

As the leading multinationals increasingly dominate whole industries, making current technology, know-how and management a common factor around the world, the sole variable allowing comparative advantage in costs and prices as between South-East Asia, the USA and Europe is labour costs—especially salaries. Dumping has, therefore, become an integral phenomenon of modern foreign trade. The paradox is that high-cost, high-wage markets provide the only outlet for sale of low-cost exports. Given the ability to shelter overseas profits from taxes by transferring sales revenues through subsidiaries located in hospitable tax havens, wage differentials have become the key comparative advantage in foreign trade.

Difficulties of comparison

But if it is difficult to prove dumping in the West, where private exports are subject to public supervision and where details of prices and costs are at least officially available, building up a case against dumping from the East is almost impossible from a legal and technical standpoint. In the first place, wages in the socialist economies are centrally fixed for all categories of skills as are differentials (which are large by Western standards) between categories of workers and different industrial branches. These and other incentive systems are all incorporated in the overall economic Plan. There is, therefore, little margin available to the industry or enterprise for wage-setting. Low wages are a national economic parameter and cannot be differentiated as between various industrial sectors. If charges of low-wage dumping are raised about Eastern goods they can only be directed at the level of wages generally prevailing in the economy and not at the labour cost of the products, which is an unknown quantity.

The structures, levels and functions of pricing in the East are extremely divergent and varied despite their broadly similar basic socialist economic systems. Such extreme divergencies exist not only as between the different countries, but even between entire product groups and individual items within those countries. Prices and money are essentially accounting units, as we have already indicated, and they do no relate meaningfully to the value of production or commodity exchanges within the economy which are steered administratively according to quantitative aggregates of the central Plan. The differences in prices both within the COMECON area and within each country are so great that no foreign price influence upon local markets can be allowed because it would cause profound disruption. The differences also mean that currencies cannot be made convertible, lest foreign holders of convertible currencies should lay claim to local goods at local prices, which bear no relation to their relative or real value.

Exchange values of the different COMECON currencies are fixed arbitrarily *vis-à-vis* the ruble for purposes of comparing them with the dollar. But this so-called "transferable ruble" used for bilateral clearing of trade balances between the countries, in no way corresponds to the actual purchasing power of national currencies nor to the value of goods in the home markets. Prices in this context, therefore, have absolutely no validity in estimating the cost or value of products nationally and internationally. They are of no use in estimating fair prices for exports according to prevailing domestic prices because both prices and exchange rates are set arbitrarily and can be legally modified at will.

Foreign trade in all East European countries is the monopoly of the state. It is carried out through foreign trade organizations which have monopoly powers to trade in specific products with Western multinationals and banks. These bodies are separate and distinct from the productive enterprises, however. This means that joint co-production deals are effected between an administrative Eastern organization and the Western enterprise which is actually in the business of manufacturing end-products. All of the rights and authority of foreign trade organizations are delegated by the central authority of the prevailing economic Plan. Each Western firm, therefore, deals from a nationally and internationally competitive position of weakness with a central authority—a relationship which facilitates playing off national firms (and, indeed, their respective governments) against each other.

The bargaining strength of the Western firm is further weakened by the refusal of any access to the records, books, costs or pricing data of the Eastern production unit. Indeed,

it is not usual for such details to be made available even to the foreign trade organization itself. As a result, it is quite impossible to determine the real level of wages,
protection, subsidies or preferential prices which the state has accorded the Eastern
factory. Legally, therefore, it is not possible to charge dumping pursuant to Western
criteria.

Unemployment in the West

East European governments, therefore, summarily dismiss charges of low-wage dumping as an affront to their socialist integrity. They also insist that, though they do not
directly employ wage and salary employees, the foreign trade organizations are *bona
fide* firms which act autonomously according to normal commercial practices and competitive conditions. But the fact remains that the foreign trade organizations exercise a
monopoly over all buying and selling on behalf of the country within the sector of their
industrial jurisdiction outside their national borders and are administrative organs of
the central authority. They are not enterprises which actually employ labour and produce goods. All of the contracts concluded by a foreign trade organization on behalf of its
home production units are based upon nationally prevailing wage rates which are secret
and unavailable to the Western partner. In fact, wages can be fixed as high or as low as
the Eastern partner wishes in order to secure the project and optimize returns from it.
The Western partner is completely ignorant of the real situation in the enterprise which
is doing the actual production. In some COMECON countries, disclosure of production
figures, costs, accounting records or other data are treated as a criminal offence or even
as espionage.

Because of the pressure upon all Eastern countries to boost hard currency exports
through cooperation deals and counterpurchase arrangements, Eastern governments
will "sweeten the pot" by offering larger wage differentials to increase West-side profits.
With no capital, no convertible currency and few acceptable exports to offer from an
under-equipped domestic base, this incentive is all the Eastern cooperators have to
offer. For themselves, of course, it is merely an accounting or book-keeping figure with
no impact upon the real economic conditions. The net result is a wholesale foreign trade
system based upon low wages in the East (both in real terms and in wages of account),
which amounts clearly to institutionalized dumping.

The result can only be growing unemployment in the West and the accelerated closure of marginal and less modern plants whose production will be replaced through
Eastern cooperation deals. Just as the massive transfers of capital credits to the dizzy
amounts of 80, 90 and 100 billion dollars will reduce capital liquidity in the West, drive
up interest rates and help kindle inflation, so the counter-transfer of goods produced
upon Western machines by cheap Eastern labour will undercut national prices and
contribute to higher unemployment. The result will be that East–West "stagflation" in
which rising prices and increasing unemployment go hand in hand.

The Agit-Prop argument that cooperation deals are creating jobs is at best a half-
truth. At the early stage of producing the original equipment and machine tools within
the capital goods industries of the West, some increase in employment could occur to the
extent that idle capacity is not available and that important numbers of additional
workers are needed to man new machines, which is seldom the case. The Western
machine tool firms sometimes divert fully used capacity from other customers because of
the higher prices offered in Eastern deals. But since the production of advanced machine
tools often requires custom-made equipment and a highly-skilled labour force with a
very long lead-time on training, there is little flexibility in recruitment. Such skilled

workers are seldom unemployed, but guarded zealously by the firm even during down turns.

Taking the example of a one-shot project such as manufacturing a complete turn-key plant for delivery to Eastern Europe, we may estimate that such a contract could provide up to 100,000 hours work for a large Western machine-tool enterprise. Once this turn-key plant goes on stream, however, or once the process installed and operating in an Eastern co-production project starts up, with good maintenance it continues to turn out products for up to ten, fifteen or twenty years before replacement. During all this time, goods will continue to be exported to Western markets in substitution for locally manufactured ones. It is not possible, of course, to predict accurately the net relative increment or decrement in working hours induced by the export of the original capital goods and the import of the resulting manufactured products. This depends on a great many indeterminate factors, not the least being the overall state of the economy and the existing levels of employment. However, it is a widely recognized truism that current problems of rising structural unemployment are today decisively influenced by the multinational transfer of production to the more favourable locations in the global economy, especially from regions of high wages and strong unions to those of lower wages and weak unions with facilities for tax-haven money management. A massive move into Eastern Europe to establish a production base for the sale of low-cost products in Western markets must, therefore, inevitably mean more unemployment.

There are already impressive indications that more and more cheap East European products are being sold in the West. Dumping charges are proliferating with reports of more and more plant closures due to Eastern dumping.

Charges against Eastern dumping

UK
* Czechoslovak, Rumanian and Polish agreement to restrict shoe exports to the UK to 1975 levels declared ineffective as 1976 levels rose 17%. British-made sandals hold 10% of home market, Polish and Czech share, 80%.
* Rumanian polyester fibre subject to anti-dumping duty following industry protests led by ICI.
* Rumanian, Czech, Polish, Hungarian, GDR import quotas for men's wool suits of 350,000 per annum exceeded. Further government action demanded by industry and unions following loss of nearly 10,000 jobs in the UK trade.
* COMECON imports of men's overalls swamp British market at dumped prices.
* Czech, Hungarian and Polish light bulbs selling in the UK at prices below cost of materials.
* Hungarians and Yugoslavs claimed to be dumping knitted polyethylene textile products.
* COMECON imports of TV tubes and cathodes cause worsening of recession in the UK industry.
* Hungary selling PVC coated fabrics to UK at dumping prices.
* Czechoslovakia dumping sugarbeet harvesters in UK.
* GDR selling men's suits of artificial fiber in UK at about one-third of normal UK price.
* Poland and Czechoslovakia allegedly selling wood fiber insulating board in UK at dumping prices.
* Polish Fiat 125s selling for about 500 rubles less than comparable Western models in the UK market.

* Britain's Department of Trade imposed provisional anti-dumping charges on alarm clocks from Czechoslovakia, the GDR, Hungary, Poland, Rumania and the USSR, pending investigation by the Department of Trade.

West Germany
* Polish coal imports alleged to be made at below-cost price.
* West German authorities threaten to take action against GDR for selling textiles, women's stockings, clothing and other items in West Germany at dumping prices. The GDR is selling men's summer sport suits in West Germany for DM 12.50, while the same suit sells in the GDR for M 150 (M 1 = DM 1 at the official rate). For the 1977 summer season the GDR delivered 480,000 men's summer shirts to West Germany priced at DM 65–400.
* West Germany's textile and clothing industry has been severely "dumped" out of over 150,000 jobs for the most part by cheap East European imports. An article published in *Der Spiegel* (No. 39/75) stated that the industry, once the third-largest in the world, "now falls on uncertain future" not because of "accepting cheap goods from developing countries but because of the Eastern-bloc textiles supplied at prices far below West German prices—often far below their own production costs too." The Soviet Union is not involved to any great extent as the traffic is from all the other Eastern-bloc countries which export more cheap textile goods to Western Germany than all the developing countries including South Korea, Taiwan and the city enclaves in the Far East.
  The West German market "is being flooded with quality hose from East Germany, clothes from Bulgaria, underpants from Rumania, suits from Czechoslovakia, women's overcoats from Poland and brassieres from Budapest." One half of all the men's and boys' underwear come from Poland, Czechoslovakia and Rumania, one third of all imported jackets and trousers, one third of all women's coats and dresses, most women's work clothing, and most cheap men's shirts come from the Balkans and East Germany. At least 100,000 unemployed persons in Western Germany have socialist dumping tactics to thank for their condition ... The creation of new jobs for these people in other branches would require investments totalling some 10 billion DM," the article claimed.
* The GDR delivered 450 tons of knitting yarn to West Germany at prices of DM 4–12 per kilo, versus DM 20 for the same quality from West German production. The price charged in the GDR for the same yarn is M 77–95 per kilo.
* West German industry accuses the GDR of selling steel in West Germany at less than cost. The *European Chemical News*, a trade journal, reported 12 May 1978 that "Thinly disguised German threats of anti-dumping action against Soviet low-density polyethylene (ldPE) imports appear to have had their desired effect. Following the start of investigations in January [of 1978], Soviet ldPE exports to Germany have decreased in volume, while prices have been increased slightly.
  "In September-November 1977, Soviet ldPE shipments were entering the West German market at a rate of around 4-5 000 ton over the period at prices 35-40 per cent below the prevailing market levels of DM 1.35–1.40/kg for general purpose pipe grade. Since the beginning of 1978, imports have slipped to below 3 000 ton and although figures for March-April have not been released, observers suggest that they will be nearer the 2 000 ton mark.
  "The USSR has also increased its prices and although they are still by far the lowest obtaining on the West German market they have risen from the previous cut-throat levels.

"The initial impetus behind the investigation undertaken by the West German Verband der Chemischen Industrie (VCI) came from market leaders BASF, Hoechst and Bayer. BASF is heavily committed to the ldPE business with a 200 000 ton/year capacity at its Ludwigshafen complex, plus its 50 per cent share in ROW's 740 000 ton/year Wesseling plant, in partnership with Shell. Bayer's interest stems from its own 50:50 joint venture with BP in the 140 000 ton/year Erdölchemie plant, which is scheduled to boost capacity by 200 000 ton/year.

"The flow of ldPE imports from the USSR is largely the result of a deal signed between West German contractor Salzgitter and the USSR. It covered the construction by Salzgitter of a 120 000 ton/year ldPE plant at Kazan valued at DM 126m. with repayments by the Soviets taking the form of some 150–250 000 ton of ldPE in 1971–1983. In a similar deal, Salzgitter has contracted to build a DM 174m. 240 000 ton/year ldPE plant at Severodonetsk, due onstream this year. Repayment will involve exports of 250–350 000 ton between 1978 and 1986.

"The Germans and the Swiss seem particularly concerned about the long term implications of contracts for cooperation both on employment and on their own markets, and they are less prepared to accept the sometimes very tight conditions their counterparts impose. The most recent project to be discussed between the Germans and the Russians is the construction of an oil refinery at Tomsk, which is to have a capacity of 10 million tons a year.

"The Soviets want to pay the entire cost of the project [. . .] in deliveries of oil. 'It is unrealistic at a time when the West's oil requirements are reduced,' observes Lutz Mann, the head of Hoechst's 'East bloc' department in Germany. 'A project paid entirely in kind – that has only happened once – with the French. It is a bad example that the German chemical industry is determined not to follow.' "

This has been followed by a similar "unrealistic" deal: "West Germany's Krupp-Koppers has signed a DM 250m. contract with Techmashimport for the construction in the Soviet Union of a 120 000 ton/year dimethyl terephthalate (DMT) plant. The contract was signed in Moscow before the visit to Germany by Soviet president Leonid Brezhnev in May 1978.

"The plant, based on Dynamit Nobel technology, will be built at Mogilev in Byelorussia—the centre of Soviet polyester fibres production. It will be installed as part of the general agreement signed in 1976 between the USSR and a number of West German firms headed by Hoechst. This agreement covers the installation in the Soviet Union of a total of 230000 ton/year of polyester fibres capacity and is based entirely on compensation.

"After intensive negotiations with the Soviet Union, Krupp-Koppers, in association with a number of German-based firms, managed to secure the repayment for this project in petroleum products (believed to be naphtha), benzene, paraxylene and DMT. Krupp engaged other firms to market the products because 'it is too heavy a burden to carry alone.' "

France
* French manufacturers have protested Polish exports of children's shoes for 16–20 francs. Also women's stockings and men's underwear from Eastern Europe at prices 50–75% below the French average.
* East European electric motors are being brought in at prices 30% under those for French products, and machine tools from the Soviet Union and the GDR are priced 50% lower than those made in France.
* Soviet tractor exports to France expanded in 1977, following new contracts signed by

Actif-Avto, a branch of the Union des Cooperatives Agricoles du Sud-Ouest (UCASO), run by Jean-Baptiste Doumeng, France's leading East–West trader in farm produce and machinery, a French Communist Party company. Actif-Avto, a joint venture of Doumeng and Tractoroexport, has signed a 50 million francs contract to import some 2,970 Soviet tractors of varying sizes. Actif-Avto says that Soviet tractor sales had been rising steadily since 1965. The company runs a center near Paris for receiving the tractors, adapting them to the French market, and for storing spare parts. Soviet tractors undersell French models due to lower wage costs in the USSR. The French Communist Party also imports tractors from Czechoslovakia which have been selling at a rate of up to 2,000 a year in France since 1947, as well as Rumanian and Bulgarian tractors.

* Svoboda Perfumery is manufacturing five tints of a dye shampoo in cooperation with l'Oréal SA of France. L'Oréal is working with similar agreements in Rumania, Yugoslavia and Bulgaria. All these arrangements provide for counterpurchase exports to l'Oréal's domestic market.

* "The Soviet Union will ship ammonia to France under a 10-year agreement beginning in 1979 or 1980. Overall value of the contract amounts to $200 million. Intsel France, the international metals and chemicals trading arm of Péchiney-Ugine-Kuhlmann, has negotiated the arrangement with Sojuschimexport. The purchase will be a form of compensation payment for four major ammonia-producing units that France's Creusot-Loire Entreprises is supplying to the Soviet Union based on Pullman Kellogg technology" (*C & FN*, 22 Aug 1977).

Italy

* Italian manufacturers have protested against imports of East European electric light bulbs, electric motors and TV picture tubes whose import prices, they say, are 35–50% below the Italian manufacturing costs. East European TV picture tubes have captured 50% of the Italian market.

* Russian "Lada" and Polish "Polski" Fiat 124 models claimed to infringe market agreements by dumping in Italian market—claimant, Fiat.

US

* "Barter [and Nixon] brought Pepsi Cola to the Soviet Union and Russian vodka to the United States. The agreement of 1972, is a classical counter-trade deal. Pepsi Co. has exclusive distribution rights for Stolichnaya vodka in the US, which reached 200,000 cases worth $20 million [in 1977] while Moscow's Soyuzplodoimport plows its profit back into the purchase of Pepsi concentrate and the expansion of bottling facilities in the USSR. Under the barter agreement, Pepsi oversees quality and packaging and controls the use of its logo in the Soviet Union. The two plants now in operation turn out 6 million cases of Pepsi annually. Five additional plants, each with a 3 million case capacity, are to be operating by 1980. Pepsi expects to boost its US vodka sales to $100 million."

* US Cargo Insurers have protested to the American government against the Soviet rates which they claimed were state subsidized and too low. US rates could not compete and marine insurance was being lost to the USSR both in US–USSR shipping and Third Country shipping.

* Levi Strauss of San Francisco, the world famous blue-jeans firm, in April 1977 signed an agreement with Hungary for the manufacture of its blue jeans. Under the terms of the agreement, Levi Strauss will deliver material to Hungary and receive the finished garments at lower production costs because of the lower Hungarian wages. It

will therefore be "dumped" on its Western markets. Previously, Hungarians purchased jeans on the black market at $80–100 a pair. Domestically manufactured
jeans were impossible to sell because of their inferior quality. Now they will get real
"Levis," though their price will still be much higher than those sold in the West. And
later Levi Strauss concluded a deal with East Germany.
* Another novel dumping case concerns Polish golf-carts in the US. Exports which dump
workers out of jobs are against the law in the US. But when earning hard currency
profits are the criteria it is simply impossible to assess East European exports as to
fair prices. One of the thorniest legal tests of such dumping involved of all things
golf-carts manufactured in Poland, a country which has not a single golf-course. The
case has dragged on for years, an indication of the technical difficulties and practical
pressures involved. Distributed under the brand name Melex, low prices quickly took
nearly a quarter of the "country-club" golf-cart fleets. In 1974 Outboard Marine—a
firm that has since gone out of the golf-cart business—filed a dumping complaint. The
Poles argued that they were not selling for less in the US than at home if Poland has
no golf courses; Melex was manufactured efficiently, just for export, and was not sold
domestically. This touchy economic issue drew the personal attention of President
Ford and Polish leader Edward Gierek when the two met in the fall of that year.
Based on cost comparisons with a Canadian manufacturer, the US Treasury Department found that Melex was imported at $150 less than "fair value."

Multinational
* Western shippers accuse East European merchant fleets of "aggressive price dumping" in the international freight business. Soviet lines are cited as offering rates
20–25% below usual Western line rates, with rates as much as 40% lower between the
US West Coast and the Far East.
* The French shipowners' Central Commission has accused the Communist countries
of "opportunism" in having transferred over 200 ships to the Panamanian flag of
convenience. As a result, half of the commercial fleets of COMECON countries operate under conditions of "dumping," a spokesman for the Commission charged on
March 23 1977. It further accused the Soviet Union of violating international agreements concerning norms of safety and salary and economic conditions for crews. Thus
the COMECON pursues the same policies as private capitalist shipowners in using
Panamanian registrations to evade Western trade union and government standards
in commercial shipping.
* On November 21 Poland signed the biggest single order for merchant ships ever
placed in Britain: twenty-four vessels worth £115 million.
    Secretary of State for Industry Eric Varley justified it as a deal "of vital impor-
tance" to the publicly-owned British shipbuilding industry. He said it would provide
years of work, which was of special importance during a period of depression in the
world shipping market.
    The deal, which is for twenty-two bulk carrier cargo ships and two floating cranes,
has been partly subsidized by the UK government under a £65 million shipbuilding
intervention fund. Mr Varley, declined, however, to reveal the size of the subsidy.
Actually the credit is 100% of cost.
    Gerald Kaufman, a Minister of State for Industry, said the deal was part of a
continuing improvement in the British shipbuilding industry since it was nationalized. The boats will belong to a British-Polish joint venture holding company who
would be owner of the boats which are "leased to Polish operations." Also what Varley
did not report was that the deal was based upon 100% British credit, a condition that

no other country originally bidding on the project, including Japan, Germany and the US, would accord and upon a secret understanding that the cargo ships could be used in traditional British shipping lanes and would carry British and Polish cargoes presently being shipped on British bottoms. As the critics point out, such a total subsidy-credit could obviously have been accorded the British yards directly to build British ships to carry British goods. This would have assured work both for shipyard workers and the British merchant marine and not put a drain on reserves and export earnings. Also not reported was that major parts like the screw would be manufactured in Poland under earlier license agreement. The British licenser thus lost the business.

* A wave of Soviet-made sewing machines, heading for the Common Market, has provoked sharp protests and complaints of dumping of the low price, low cost products by manufacturers of Italy, France, Great Britain and West Germany. The EEC sewing machine companies, many of whom are strongly implanted in Eastern Europe, express concern at the Soviet Union's firm intention to double or even triple its exports to West Europe by 1980. Coming after a wave of Japanese exports which have taken over 20% of the market, Soviet sewing machines could mean the end of employment for Western workers in capitalist sewing machine factories.

* EEC fertilizer producers approached the Brussels authorities, with a view to a European anti-dumping plan. West German manufacturers have asked their government for measures to combat East-bloc dumping. The EEC Commission has also undertaken investigations into the alleged dumping of ammonium nitrate and NPK fertilizers from Yugoslavia. The Commission has stated that proof has been received of "dumping, premiums of subsidies" being paid in connection with certain Yugoslav nitrogen fertilizer exports to EEC members. The commission has already announced that a strict watch is being kept on all the area's imports from Yugoslavia.

* In May 1978 "definitive anti-dumping duties [were] imposed by the European Commission, replacing provisional charges to duty, on imports into the EEC of various iron and steel products from ... Bulgaria, Rumania and the German Democratic Republic. The products subject to definitive duties [were]: ... sheets and plates of iron or steel, other than electrical sheets and plates not further worked than hot-rolled, of a thickness of 2 mm or more originating in Bulgaria, Rumania and the German Democratic Republic [Hungary, Czechoslovakia, and Poland]".

* The European chemical industry has asked for fixing of a European price standard to control Eastern dumping prices. Under pressure of dumping charges in October, the European Commission announced its intention to consider ways of monitoring the growing number of compensation trading deals with COMECON countries. The deals, in which more and more of the large plants being built by West European, US and Japanese contractors in the Eastern bloc are to be paid for in products or other goods rather than currency, are causing mounting disquiet, particularly in the chemicals industry, because of the damage they could do to West European markets. The chemicals industry has already set up its own machinery for monitoring these deals through CEFIC, the European industry association.

  Mr Fernand Braun, the EEC Commission's Director-General of Industrial Affairs, has told industry leaders that monitoring the compensation deals should be considered on a Community basis, but the Commission gave no support to industry demands for the fixing of a European selling price as a yardstick for judging whether dumping is occurring. Its lack of real authority over industry rules out such action.

* By no means all dumping charges are of recent date. In 1957–1958 British firms complained of the dumping of aluminium and tin from the Soviet Union. In the early

sixties, similar dumping complaints were lodged against Soviet lathes, oil and related products and against more than two dozen other product lines, including complete industrial plants. As is customary in these cases, the evidence of dumping was entirely based upon the very low prices as little legal proof could be adduced for the reasons already outlined.

As the nature of Western transfer of industry grew, so did the complaints about dumping from those who felt the impact on their markets. In the sixties entire export industries began to switch to the East: Swedish furniture exports began to be produced in Poland; Dutch clothing and shirt manufacturers moved to Rumania and Yugoslavia respectively; the German printing industry shifted heavily to Czechoslovakia; the Italian Fiat 124 was to be manufactured in Poland and the USSR along with Pirelli tyres. The list of affected export products included: Olivetti typewriters, Montedison fibres, fertilizers and plastics exports; French auto parts, chemicals and aluminium products; German food processing and construction. Hosts of others were to follow as IBM, ITT, Ericsson, Dow Chemicals, Dupont, ICI and the rest of the multinational crew joined the migration.

The European Chemical Manufacturers' Association warned against the consequences of Eastern manufacturing, deliberately ignoring the fact that its own members were leading the parade. The British plastics industry, led by ICI who were deeply engaged in Vodka-Cola deals, demanded protection against East European dumping of plastics. In 1970, the Canadian government unsuccessfully sought to overturn a decision of the Anti-Dumping Tribunal to impose a duty on glass shipments from Eastern Europe on the grounds of conflict of interest. It felt that dumping charges by the Canadian subsidiary of the UK's Pilkington Company and the American Pittsburg Plate Glass Industries were insupportable in view of the extensive licensing deals and investments of these firms in Eastern Europe. It is possible that their complaints related to low-wage dumping of goods produced on their own equipment, just as, five years later, Umberto Agnelli, co-owner of Fiat, demanded tariff protection in Western Europe against the dumping of Lada and Polski autos which were the Russian and Polish siblings of the Fiat 124. Besides West German textile industry protests have been made against the dumping of textiles from the GDR; Austrian, British, American, French and Belgian trade unions against glass dumping from East Germany, Poland and Hungary; Dutch and Belgian industry against dumping of clothing and textiles; British industry and unions have charged dumping of TV tubes, automobiles, electric lamps, knitwear, textiles, suits, footwear and leather goods. It is particularly significant that, just as British multinational firms have been among the earliest East European cooperators, so the volume of complaints against COMECON dumping has been greater than from other countries.

Plant closures, especially in textile and artificial fibres, are growing in France, Great Britain, Holland, Belgium, the United States and Italy. Most of the larger firms, who are now carrying out far-reaching restructuring of their operations and laying off workers, have important cooperative activities in Eastern Europe from which they import products.

"A 'plague' is what scores of West German businessmen are currently calling [a recent] barter deal by which Volkswagen will deliver 10,000 of its Rabbit models to East Germany this year. To the dismay of other West German manufacturers and suppliers who are trying to force the East Germans to scale down their compensation and counter-purchase demands, VW agreed to accept 100% payment in the form of counter-deliveries. These will include lignite, heating oil, bicycles, machine tools and automotive parts for use on other VWs. A spokesman for the West German machine tool and automotive supply industries calls the deal 'a scandal.' He [said], "There has never been a barter deal of this magnitude, nor has anyone before caved in so completely to East German demands. It sets a precedent that will have catastrophic consequences."

"Krupp chairman Berthold Beitz says that 'East-West trade is starting to become like the barter trade of the Stone Age: wooden clubs in exchange for bone tools, bones for pelts, and pelts as payment for flint axes.' This is an ironic twist, for bartering is what got East-West trade off dead center in the first place when men like Beitz—whom diplomats have described as West Germany's 'most imaginative businessman' and whom other businessmen have called 'a frustrated diplomat'—first began dealing with the Communist countries in the late 1950s and early 1960s."

Blithely ignoring its own practices relative to co-production deals in other products as well as the fact that most of the dumping was taking place within the framework of cooperation agreements, Mr M. E. Werner, a leading official of Royal Dutch/Shell, during a meeting of financial experts in Paris in June 1977 complained that "the sales of chemical products at 'political prices' by the Eastern European countries were increasingly alarming the Western chemical industry."

Referring to the general concern in the industry about the incidence of massive dumping of fertilizer on Western markets, Mr Werner cited further examples of East European dumping worrying West European producers such as synthetic rubber which already had 20% of the market in France and over 30% of the market of the Netherlands. Deftly ignoring or pretending not to know about the system under which such dumping was taking place, Mr Werner stated that the difficulties did not arise out of the commercial exchanges themselves but from the practice of reducing prices to any level necessary to conclude transactions on the Western markets. He did acknowledge, however, that the problem was further aggravated by the fact that certain engineering companies in the Common Market when they sold chemical installations and equipment to Eastern countries often accept payments under the form of products produced by these new installations. "I admit that it is not an easy thing to remedy this. Dumping, or the distortion of the market, are contraventions difficult to establish in the case of centrally planned economies. The market prices in the countries of origin can be fixed at no matter what level desired by the government. Further, the legislation of the Common Market on the subject presents certain loopholes and anomalies, notably in regard to the GDR and Rumania, two countries where chemical production is very large," he stated. Royal Dutch/Shell companies, he warned, may profoundly re-examine their investment projects in the case where actual dumping could become a permanent characteristic of the West European market.

The cynicism of Mr Werner is impressive in face of Shell's own direct involvement in co-production deals.

Directly and indirectly, co-production and counterpurchase, the dynamic of East-West trade, will extend the dumping of low-wage, low-price goods throughout Western markets. Though the fact will continue to be denied and remain ultimately unprovable for the practical reasons outlined above, many factories and industries will feel the impact of its truth and will be forced to close—especially small and medium-size plants. The large firms will also accelerate closure of their less profitable plants in the home markets, despite protests and strikes, in order to make way for the products of their socialist co-production and joint ventures in Eastern Europe.

Besides dumping charges, the COMECON countries are regularly accused of unethical and distinctly anti-Marxist behaviour in dealings with reactionary régimes. Extensive dealings are carried out with Brazil, Argentina, Peru, and other military régimes in Latin America. A particularly shocking allegation was the British accusation contained in four British notes to the UN that Bulgaria, Russia, East Germany, Rumania and Czechoslovakia had engaged in "regular trade" with Rhodesia in violation of UN sanctions. The notes accused the COMECON countries of having dealt with Rhodesia in chrome and tobacco through Swiss intermediary companies such as Geneva-based Intarex, Centrex and Comaisa SA, the latter a Panama-incorporated firm with a long history in trading with the Soviet Union. The companies, of course, denied the allegations as well as to being front-companies for East-bloc deals, as did the COMECON countries and the USSR who accused the journalists reporting the charges as "guilty of a campaign of slander." The allegations were, of course, valid and factual—but, as is the custom in the UN, no investigation was carried out.

4

Multilateral Co-production with Third Countries

Parallel to the increase in East–West economic co-production based upon credit and technology transfer from capitalist to Communist countries repaid in counter-purchase and production sharing, there have developed similar relations between Communist countries and certain developing countries. Despite the massive accumulated debt owed to the West, according to the Economic Commission for Europe of the UN, East European countries and the Soviet Union have granted some 15 billion rubles of credits to support trade and cooperation with developing countries. The ECE reported that the number of intergovernmental cooperation agreements reached sixty-five at the beginning of 1976, which opened the way to cooperation contracts in investments and production. These number nearly 200 today covering specialization, joint participation in construction of enterprises, joint ventures, etc.

Specialization projects, for example, include the setting up by the GDR and Poland of textile factories in Egypt and Iran, which will import an important part of the future production. The Soviet Union and India envisage a major program of exchange of component parts in textiles, electronics and motor vehicles and the investment in an aluminium project, which projects the buy-back or counter-purchase of 500,000 tons of the future production. An agreement between Poland and Egypt envisages exchange of motor car components.

Often these deals are on a multilateral basis: Soviet, Czech and East German Foreign Trade Organizations are jointly participating in the construction of iron and steel plants in Algeria, India and Iran. FTOs of the GDR, Hungary, Czechoslovakia, the USSR and Bulgaria are setting up cement factories in Syria. Soviet and Rumania enterprises are involved in construction of oil refineries in several developing countries. Other examples of East European co-production or plant construction in developing countries are steel, electricity and engineering works built by the Soviet Union in Iran: cement, engineering works, refineries and petrochemical plants built by Rumania in Iraq, etc.

To the extent that the technology involved in these transfers is not obsolete and uneconomical, there is reason to suppose that Western technology and know-how, received through East–West cooperation, figure in such deals. And similar to the complete divorce between ideology and politics from trade in relations between capitalist and Communist economic systems, there is often a similar divorce in Communist co-production deals with developing countries. Recently, East-bloc countries have intensified their cooperation with oil-exporting countries which have aggressively anti-Communist régimes: Iran, Egypt, Kuwait, Libya, etc. It is another demonstration of the superficiality of ideological and political postures compared to the substantiality of credits and counterpurchase today. The Soviet Union proclaims unconditional support of the so-called South against the West both direct and indirect, as for example through Cuba in Angola, Zaire, Rhodesia, etc. Open and official commitment to liberation movements in Black Africa was announced by Podgorny during a swing through the region in March 1977. The USSR, GDR, and Czechoslovakia have announced full coordinating of anti-imperialist support for Black Africa. In the UN, the Soviet Union exercises rights of leadership in attacking capitalist imperialism in the developing countries, especially multinational companies' exploitation of their raw materials and basic resources.

This aggressive ideological offensive makes all the more striking the contradictions of a new development taking place, which involves international tripartite and multipartite cooperation between Communist and capitalist enterprises in the Third World and even in the West. This movement is a natural extension of the East–West bilateral economic cooperation. It permits capitalist firms' entry in pro-Communist or pro-Soviet developing countries otherwise closed to them. Above all, less modern, nearly out-of-date and long amortized Western technology can be first transferred to Eastern Europe and then to less industrialized countries under "socialist" patronage. A non-negligible advantage for Western firms is that they can use tripartite ventures to benefit from Communist ruble credits accorded under Communist cooperation agreements in Asia and Africa. And, of course, the cost and prices of the buy-back and counter-purchase products received are even lower than in Eastern Europe, given the much lower prevailing wages and other costs. For the Eastern partner the advantages are especially numerous. Politically it permits the Eastern partner, as consortium leader, to maintain a Communist imprint on multipartite projects. Lacking the technology itself, the Communist country is able to secure and divert imported Western capital to further operations in the developing countries. Many exports of the trilateral and multilateral ventures situated in the developing countries have access to Western markets under more favourable tariff schedules. The fact that one or more of the associates of such ventures is a capitalist monopoly multinational, continuously under attack in the United Nations, in North-South Economic Conferences, etc., is seldom a consideration. It is further confirmation that promotion of unlinking or separation of economic relations from politics and ideology has penetrated North–South as it has East–West relations.

President Carter and Party Secretary Brezhnev both proclaim their opposition to linkage between the various components of their international policies. Economics are economics and are to be kept separated from other issues of political intercourse, cultural exchanges, civil rights, freedom, disarmament, etc.—Marx and Lenin ideology and capitalist commonsense notwithstanding. The fact that in most cases the majority of the associates in trilateral deals are state-owned enterprises subordinated to state political policy makes the contractions even sharper. How can state-owned enterprises be unlinked from the political policies of the owner?

However, long before tripartite cooperation took place in the West, it was expanding in the developing regions. The ECE cites the example of tripartite cooperation in the food industry between a Hungarian–United States enterprise established in Switzerland which has negotiated a cooperation deal with an official organization in Kenya. In 1972, under the Colonels' dictatorship, the Greek Public Power Corporation contracted a partnership with Polish and Yugoslav enterprises. A major US multinational is negotiating a proposal for a joint project with the Soviet Union for Third World expansion using equipment from the American firm's subsidiary plants in North America, Brazil and the United Kingdom. Vöest-Alpine AG of Austria and the Polish Iron and Steel FTO have a project for joint exploration, bidding, planning and construction at home and abroad but especially in developing countries.

A leading chemical company of the Federal Republic of Germany and the Polish Chemical FTO are jointly constructing a chemical plant in Morocco. Under the arrangement the Polish firm will provide raw materials, the West German firm the capital and technology against payment by the Moroccan associate in the resulting intermediate chemicals. A major petrochemical joint project in Venezuela is being implemented with the cooperation of Hungarian and Austrian and British firms. A road vehicle production facility in Iraq involves a Hungarian partner along with French and Swedish ones.

An example of a complex long-term, five-way venture is the establishment of an aluminium plant in India with a Hungarian firm and Indian firms as prime partners and a Czechoslovak supplier of equipment based upon licenses and know-how from Swedish and Hungarian firms. A similar project includes cooperative deliveries by Austrian and Polish enterprises of US-licensed equipment to a Congo petroleum refinery. An illustration of growing capitalist equity sharing in trilateral ventures is a pharmaceutical joint venture established in Nigeria with Hungarian and Swiss partners. The private Nigerian and Hungarian state firms hold 40% each, the private Swiss firm 20%. The Hungarian partner is responsible for providing the managing director and production manager, with the other firms providing directors.

There are a number of general agreements between Eastern and Western companies which provide for seeking of projects with third-country partners on a world-wide basis. In 1974 a Pakistani firm and the Polish State Sugar Organization established a joint enterprise for the construction of sugar factories with local third parties on a world-wide basis.

Sub-contracting and incorporation of major components supplied by a co-production associate in final products are frequent in trilateral deals. For example, Bulgaria exports automobiles to developing countries under a French Renault license. In exchange for 1,500 Fiat-Polskas, Pakistan exchanges countervalue in textiles with Poland. A British company supplies the engine, fuel-injection system, and electrical gear for a Polish tractor being promoted in developing countries. In another case, capitalist enterprises share production of tractors assembled in India with Hungarian interests. Joint bidding by multinationals and Communist state enterprises constitutes a simple variant of "Vodka-Cola imperialism." An example is the expansion of Argentina's state-owned steel works on which tenders were jointly submitted by Soviet and American steel enterprises. More extensively, Brazil and Paraguay have associated the Soviet Union in a vast hydro-electric project valued at $3 billion, along with private Brazilian and Paraguayan firms—part of a United Kingdom–Sweden–Swiss construction consortium. An example of a specially complex multipartite East–West–North nationalist–socialist–capitalist monopoly venture is the Mauritian Refinery in Novadhibou: Austrian and East German enterprises are prime contractors with Belgian and British firms acting as sub-contractors; crude oil will be supplied by Algeria and the products marketed by Western oil companies in Africa and West Germany.

Péchiney-Saint Gobain, the French firm, and the Yugoslav firm Pragues Invest have created a joint venture to construct chemical plants in the developing countries, with or without partners. The Italian Castor of Milan and Yugoslavia have a co-production venture for manufacturing and selling Castor Washing Machines. As early as 1971, under the Franco régime, Polish, Rumanian and even Soviet firms cooperated with Western multinationals in Spanish trilateral projects in various industries: fishing, shipping, sugar refineries, coal, etc.

Recent multilateral projects in third countries

Polish, GDR and Yugoslav firms are participating in a consortium led by the Austrian Vöest-Alpine AG and local firms in building a cellulose plant in Cameroon. The plant will have a capacity of 122,000 tons annually and will be the largest of its kind in Africa.

Coal deposits in Colombia will be developed by Sederbros Brazil's steel holding company, Capex Poland's state coal enterprise and local Colombian interests. Other projects being discussed include liquification and gasification of Brazilian coal and construction of a sulphuric acid plant in Brazil using technology derived from US–Polish joint ventures.

The French electronic company Thompson CSF and the Polish electronic industry are carrying out joint production of TV picture tubes in Poland and marketing in cooperation with third country firms.

The giant Dutch multinational Akzo and the Dutch Sallast Nedam have created joint companies with Polish FTOs in the chemical and energy industries to promote business in third countries involving local participations. Soviet FTOs and the Austrian Elin-Union together with local partners will promote the sale and eventual manufacture of power installations including transformers and generators in third countries. Hungarian, Polish and Turkish interests have formed a vegetable oil company in Turkey. Péchiney-Saint Gobain and the Yugoslavian firm Pragues Invest along with local participants are constructing chemical plants in countries of the Third World as well as in Yugoslavia. The Polish Polimex-Cekop and the Belgian Sybetra through the Polish-Belgian partnership Bepolma together with Iraqi interests are constructing a $40 million fertilizer complex at Al-Khain in Iraq. Metrimpex, the Hungarian trading company and Langschwert of Vienna cooperate in the production and marketing of small office calculators both in their respective countries and in Third World markets through local partners. A Soviet–Italian venture (USSR–IRI) will prospect for engineering multilateral textiles in Third Countries. The Polish government has officially proposed the creation of joint ventures to American firms for the purpose of developing multilateral enterprises in the Third World in electrical power, chemicals, food processing and rolling stock.

Crvena Zastava, Yugoslavia, a joint venture producer of Fiat cars under license, has concluded a cooperation agreement with Colombiana Automotoriz of Bogota, Colombia, under which the Zastava 750 car will be manufactured in Colombia. The agreement provides for the manufacture of at least 2,000 cars annually and for an increase in deliveries of Yugoslav Fiat to some 5,000 units per year. In 1977, some 2,300 Zastava–Fiat cars will be imported. Yugoslavia will also deliver machinery worth over $100,000 and spare parts worth nearly $200,000. It will also supervise the start-up of production in Colombia.

A US–Soviet fishing company (Sovrybflot) has been formed. The USSR's fishing fleet has been forming joint ventures in Europe, Asia and Africa with local companies. The US edition is called US–USSR Marine Resources Inc. The American partner is Bellingham Cold Storage Co. of Bellingham, WA. Hakefish, popular in Europe, will be caught by American vessels and processed aboard Soviet floating fish factories.

The Hungarian Chemolimpex and two Italian companies have signed agreements to market Hungarian chemical goods internationally. The first agreement, for a period of four years, was signed between Montedison and Chemolimpex. It provides for Chemolimpex to supply an annual 7 million dollars-worth of olefins and aromatic compounds, while Montedison will furnish annually 20 million dollars-worth of synthetic raw materials and organic and inorganic chemicals for international marketing. The second, with Snia Viscosa, calls for the Italian company to supply Chemolimpex with 2 million dollars-worth of organic chemical industry products per year in return for an annual 8–9 million dollars-worth of aromatic compounds and petrochemical materials.

A joint Hungarian–Swedish company has been established to promote the sale of

Hungarian fruits and vegetables on the Scandinavian market. This follows the creation of similar ventures in 1976 with the FRG and UK. In 1976, Hungarofruct, the Hungarian foreign trading company, exported 8,500 million forints-worth of goods, with 6,500 forints-worth going to socialist countries and the remainder to capitalist countries. Hungarofruct's exports to socialist countries include apples, watermelons, peas, cucumbers and peaches, while capitalist countries bought red onions, tomatoes and tomato puree, apples and paprika.

The Swedish Asea and Poland's Mera-Metronex have signed an agreement for cooperation in the field of *industrial robots*. Asea will deliver a number of robots to Poland of handling capacities of 6 and 60 kg. Poland will manufacture the robots domestically under license, as well as deliver certain electronics and automation system components. Eventually it will be extended to third-country markets and multilateral ventures.

East and West German companies announced at the 1978 Leipzig Trade Fair their first "third market cooperation" contract to construct and equip a factory jointly in a third country. Krupp of Essen and the East German foreign trade enterprise Unitechna have agreed to build a cotton spinning mill in Ethiopia. It is seen as an example of East Germany combining its considerable political influence in Communist-aligned Ethiopia with Krupp's industrial reputation to produce a deal that would hardly have been possible a few years ago. The project is described as a large turnkey plant worth "somewhat less than DM 100m." East Germany has been seeking such a joint project with several Western companies but until now West German businesses were more interested in collaborating inside East Germany.

Tripartite industrial co-production and other cooperation projects are difficult to enumerate and quantify. The United Nations agencies dealing with this subject are under government pressures not to specify companies and projects in detail nor list names of participants. Multinationals claim secrecy is necessary to protect their commercial and competitive interests. National Communist enterprises maintain explicit project data to be internal state information and not for public disclosure. Dependable figures are therefore difficult to come by. Certain "official" estimates, for example, of the UNCTAD Secretariat put the number of tripartite or multipartite projects at between 100 and 200. The number is probably much higher, for many projects among thirty-five developing countries reporting such ventures have not been identified. The UNCTAD Secretariat indicates that the overall cost of the tripartite industrial cooperation projects it identified exceeded $21,000 million in real value at the time of implementation, and over $30,000 million in 1975 value. It amounted to slightly more than one-eighth of the total imports of investment goods by developing countries during the period 1964–1973.

Russian FTOs are reported pressing multinationals more and more into trilateral co-production in developing regions as a condition of conducting important bilateral East–West projects. This has been particularly true of pressure upon West German firms by the USSR and Poland, which accounts for the fact that the Federal Republic of Germany is with France the country with by far the largest number of trilateral deals among Western countries.

As to the industrialized countries involved, UNCTAD lists countries and participation in projects as follows:

From the breakdown of country involvement several characteristics of trilateral East–West cooperation stand out:

1) Deals do not discriminate in respect to countries' social systems and political ideologies; any régime and social system is acceptable for trilateral ventures. Communist state enterprises have extensive links with capitalist multinationals and

Countries involved	Number of identified [a] cases or projects completed or under implementation
Venezuela	1
Yugoslavia	23
Zaire	1
(not specified)	3
Sub-total of participation in projects by individual countries	28
Bulgaria	6
Czechoslovakia	19
German Democratic Republic	11
Hungary	39
Poland	40
Rumania	16
USSR	21
(not specified)	1
Sub-total of participation in projects by individual countries	153
Austria	20
Belgium	8
Federal Republic of Germany	36
France	33
Greece	2
Ireland	1
Italy	18
Japan	4
Spain	5
Sweden	6
Switzerland	6
United Kingdom	9
United States of America	15
(not specified)	5
Sub-total of participation in projects by individual countries	168
Total participation by individual countries	453

[a]   Identified at mid-September 1975 by or on behalf of the UNCTAD secretariat. The sub-totals for each group are not necessarily equated because (a) several projects involve more than three countries; and (b) in a few cases the information is still insufficient with respect to the exact origin, within a specific group, of one of the partners.

régimes declared to be ideological and political adversaries. For example, in joint USSR and US deals in such undemocratic and "officially" reactionary countries as Kuwait, Brazil, Argentina, Egypt, Saudi Arabia, Morocco, etc., trade and cooperation has been totally unlinked from ideology and political policy.

2) The authoritarian systems of the developing countries like Eastern Europe recognize that acquiring and utilizing the technology of the Western multinationals is crucial to effective development. But increasingly they are awakening to the fact that such technology is the most valuable asset and most "noble" property of multinationals, who will not sell it, export it, or transfer it without adequate proprietary rights and controls. Hence multinationals are being accepted and sought after as full partners with equity ownership and management authority in the joint ventures. The country of origin of the partner—whether capitalist, socialist or feudalist—is of necessity overlooked and divorced from the proclaimed political and ideological value systems.

3) The political and economic élitists of all sectors of the global economy are, consequently, integrating and converging their increasingly interdependent interests behind the façade of national and regional principles and morality. As the trend accentuates, the cleavage between the élitist Overworld of both the developed and developing regions (North and South or Third and Fourth World groupings, etc.) and the workers and people will spread. This evolution is transforming the terms of conflict from the traditional political distinctions between adversaries of the right and the left to confrontation between the "aboves and belows."

4) As in the case of bilateral co-production, the viability of trilateral co-production rests entirely on the even lower wages and unionized work forces which offer lower costs and higher profits for products sold ultimately on hard currency markets. As it requires forms of co-production and Western credits and depends upon capitalist technology and know-how, the result must be the dumping of low-wage industrial production on Western markets along with East European dumping.

The dilemma of how to assimilate this hybrid system ideologically will intensify as trilateral co-production deals increase in number and importance. Presenting the modern capitalist firm as an "associate" or junior partner in a "socialist" project is one rhetorical generalization frequently employed. Another is to assimilate capitalist technology within a Soviet or East European joint venture in a developing country and present it as a completely socialist project despite the capitalist silent partner.

Doctrinal gimmicks are being hurriedly elaborated to provide the rationalization for such self-evident negations of principles: claiming that technology transfer is totally distinct from multinational imperialism: presenting tripartite cooperation as a "socialist" alternative to establishment of wholly-owned capitalist subsidiaries; holding that socialist domestic policies based upon nationalized industry can neutralize the intrinsically negative features of multinational capitalist corporations; asserting that co-production will enable socialism to grow stronger and diminish capitalism's threat to its progress, etc.

Such concocted rationalizations will grow in numbers and sophistication as the pressure rises to explain away the Vodka-Recolonization of Africa, Asia, and Latin America. But, ultimately, all the "unlinking" in the world will be unable to prevent more and more people from preceiving and reacting to such multilateral integration of élitist vested interests of which the Kadhafi–Brezhnev–Agnelli–Berlinguer–Rockefeller–Lazare Frères interlink in the Libyan Fiat association is a recent clamorous demonstration (see Part V, ch. 2).

COMECON—Multinationals

The East European countries have not advanced very far towards the integration or coordination of their economies compared to the West, where the multinationals have overrun national boundaries and economic sovereignties. Altogether only fifty to sixty cooperation ventures have been established between Eastern enterprises in two or more different countries, in contrast to the several thousand industrial cooperation ventures with Western multinationals. Forms of joint undertakings which can be compared to Western multinationals number fewer than ten and are mostly concerned with improving coordination and specialization in the power and extractive industries. The most important are: Interatomenergo covering atomic nuclear energy and equipment; Adriatika Oil Pipeline and Friendship Oil Pipelines (construction of 1,000 km pipeline from the Yugoslavian Adriatic Coast to Czechoslovakia and Hungary with eventual linkage into the Friendship Oil Pipeline); the unification of energy supply providing for a region-wide integrated grid for generating and transmitting electricity as well as for production of fuels and equipment. Interatominstrument seeks to coordinate multilateral Research and Development in nuclear energy and production of apparatus and appliances for nuclear physics and medicine. Several coordinating councils for various branches of industry have been established such as Interelectron, Interchem, Intermetal, and Intertextilmash, which cover the sectors of electrical equipment, chemicals, iron and steel, textile-machinery. Others exist for chemical fibres, rail transport, shipping, ball bearings, etc., but practical planning coordination at the regional level is not yet achieved outside of the power and mining sectors. In response to the pressing needs for further integration of their economies, the East-bloc members adopted in 1971 the "Comprehensive Program of Integration and Specialization," which set forth broad guidelines for economic integration consistent with protection of socialist principles of the inviolability of national sovereignty and including proscription of any supranational authority or compulsory participation. The comprehensive contract proposes, for the first time, creating a new system of unified prices within the COMECON region and eventually a common convertible currency. Should this aim be realized, it would be the major step towards world convertibility of Eastern currencies and fuller integration with Western market economies. However, the prospects are that it will remain mostly jargon with little practical effect for a long time to come.

An example of the gap between proclamation and practical effect is provided by the hundreds of agreements among COMECON countries which have been concluded for industrial specialization. Despite the large number on paper, little activity has resulted. Many of these specialization agreements involve only two members who, in practice, are disinclined to forgo national development of their industries in the interests of regional specialization. But bilateral agreements in themselves are inconsistent with multilateral industrial specialization. Some fifty multilateral agreements have been signed between three or more countries. Recent ones are for specialization in COMECON-produced computers, agricultural implements, chemicals, herbicides and pesticides, and the regional specialization of some 300 types of building and construction equipment.

But like much of the East bloc's planning documents and official protocols, these agreements are largely verbalized declarations of intent with little direct application in industry. Much more progress will be made in bilateral and multilateral cooperation projects with Western multinationals. It is obviously more sensible to receive capitalist technological riches than to share COMECON economic poverty. When COMECON was created in 1949 its primary aim was to strengthen the bloc's economic autarky through the exchange of technical assistance and the development of national resources. It was

not intended to become a supranational institution nor a factor in economic development. The *de facto* centralizing, due to the overwhelming dominance of the Soviet
Union, made a statutory community unnecessary and, from the Soviets' point of view,
undesirable.

Nor was COMECON planned as a free-trade area or customs union as was the European Common Market, for example. Administrative control over foreign trade, non-
convertible currencies, exclusively bilateral trading practices and totally diverse and
incompatible price systems make free trade impossible. The relative political independence of Rumania and the departure of Yugoslavia (which currently has observer status
with COMECON) reduced its effective influence still further. COMECON has consequently remained an organization of "coordinating bodies" between voluntary participants with their economic and political sovereignty as organs of their respective
nation-states basically subject to national administrative and political direction. The
influence of COMECON international economic organization is, therefore, only marginal and essentially oriented towards non-operational information and research
activities. Hence there are obvious advantages to joint projects between state organizations based upon physical and technological investments and product-sharing of end
results on a multilateral basis. Several major joint projects have been agreed upon. An
especially intriguing one—held up by COMECON as an example of multinational
cooperation—is the Soviet Fiat, known in the West as the "Lada" and in the Soviet
Union as the "Zhiguli." Four other COMECON countries and Yugoslavia produce and
deliver components under Fiat license for incorporation into the final assembly at Togliattigrad as well as for Fiat in Europe. The Lada is the East's fastest growing export
product.

In 1972 a wood-pulp complex at Ust-Llimsk was agreed to in which all COMECON
members except Czechoslovakia are to participate. The USSR provides 60% of total
costs in machinery and equipment plus 100% of labour which, on the average, is the
lowest paid in COMECON, except perhaps for Bulgaria, and the undertaking is reckoned to be an advance model for further joint projects. For their 40% of capital investments the associates will get 50,000 tons of cellulose annually over a twelve-year period.

COMECON partners are to supply a part of the capital equipment for a huge metallurgical complex at Kursk. But the irony is that the USSR is accepting consumer goods
as part of its investment because of the low level of its technology. In exchange, the
participants will receive deliveries of the metals produced. A large part of the Soviet
equipment is being purchased from West Germany, especially iron-ore dressing plants
and steel alloy production units. Though the deal is a co-production venture for the West
German companies, the Soviet Union is paying cash in hard currency for a lot of the
equipment because of the high 9% interest rate demanded for German credits. An
earlier threat that the West Germans would lose the contract turned out to be bluff. As
usual, the high interest rate has been buried in the prices.

The Kiyambayev asbestos combine agreement was signed in 1973 and involves the
participation of all COMECON members except Czechoslovakia. The plant is rated at
500,000 tons per annum capacity and all the participating countries will be repaid in
asbestos products over a twelve-year period. Though the partners are supposed to contribute equipment, the USSR is forced to take some of the contributions in consumer
goods because of the inferior technical quality of the capital goods preferred. As in the
Kursk metallurgical complex, Western technology is being purchased by the USSR from
indispensable Western co-production partners. Western asbestos firms are to purchase
large annual supplies from the plant. The world's largest asbestos cement company,
Eternit, is reported as seeking to purchase 40,000 tons a year of the output. This raises a

COMECON joint undertakings

	Sector	Location
OSSD	Railway networks	Warsaw
OSS	Telecommunications	—
ZDU	Electronic power grid	Prague
OPW	Railway freight car pool	Prague
Interpodschipnik	Ball Bearings	Warsaw
Intermetal	Iron & steel	Budapest
Agromash	Agricultural machinery	Budapest
Metunion	Medical instruments	East Berlin
Interchim	Light chemicals	Halle
Eser	Computer technology	Moscow
Insa	Maritime transport	Gdynia
Intersputnik	Satellite telecommunications	Moscow
Intertalonpribor	Weighing & measuring equipment	Moscow
*Interatominstrument	Nuclear instruments & equipment	Warsaw
*Interatomenergo	Nuclear power stations	Moscow
Interelectro	Electrical equipment	Moscow
*Intertextilmash	Textile machinery	Moscow
*Assofoto	Photochemicals	Moscow
Interport	Seaports	Szczecin
*Interchimvolokno	Chemical fibers	Bucharest
*Interprisadka	Petrochemicals	Sofia
Intergeotechnika	Geological prospecting	Moscow
*Interkomponent	Electronic components	Warsaw

*international economic associations.

vital issue since asbestos has been proven a very hazardous material and a carcinogen. Not only does it produce asbestosis, a dreaded lung disease caused by asbestos dust, but in 1975 it was also confirmed as producing lung cancer and mesothelioma, a cancer of the abdomen lining. Two 0.05 micron fibrils, so small that they can only be seen through an electron microscope, are sufficient to induce such cancers. Hundreds of thousands of asbestos workers are being condemned to contracting cancer. Asbestos consumer products, asbestos in air conditioning and insulating installations and asbestos-cement in construction are proven hazards. At such a high level of risk, there is no "safe" exposure possible to asbestos. Western unions in Sweden, Holland, the United Kingdom, Canada, France and Germany, for example, are pressing for immediate introduction of adequate safety standards, i.e. of "no detectable level" or "nil parts per million of air." They are insisting upon the production of substitute products which are available. Where this is impossible they are demanding that production be stopped. Consumer exposure to asbestos is extensive and dangerous. The discovery of high levels of asbestos fibres in numerous French wines which were simply passed through asbestos filters sent shudders throughout the world. It would be interesting to know the safety standards operated in the Kiyambayev combine. Western producers insist that even the most advanced technology cannot provide a "no detectable" level protection from asbestos fibres in the work environment. Have the Eastern bosses found methods of worker protection unknown in the West, or is it the very lack of concern about this problem that has attracted the interest of Western firms?

It would also be interesting to learn whether the Western firms intend to replace their Western production with Kiyambayev products rather than go over to more costly substitute materials. There are good reasons for anxiety. Given the enormous gap in the COMECON bloc between official standards and effective application, the Western multinationals appear to be looking to co-production deals to replace production which is in danger of being curtailed in the West because of proven dangers to workers' health and frequently also to the health of consumers—as has also occurred in the case of vinyl chloride, polyvinyl chloride, styrene-benzene, epichlorohydrin, acrylonitrite and a number of other suspects.

A vexing problem has arisen between Eastern partners over what nationality a joint COMECON venture is considered to be, especially in the case of subsidiaries in the different countries. Given the closed national structure of the central plans and the freedom of prices and costs from any relationship with foreign trade, the question of determining legal status becomes very complex. One proposal being considered is share equity ownership which would allocate parts of the undertaking to the participating national countries. But would this not mean that a parent or subsidiary would be owned by "stockholders" as in the case of capitalist stock corporations rather than the state? Also that a subsidiary would functionally and legally have to respond to the directives of the executive top management from outside the country? These aspects would surely impinge upon the integrity of the socialist national economy and its central plan.

One such joint-stock company, Haldex, is located in Katowice, Poland, which extracts coal and building materials from slag, utilizing a Hungarian process. A Polish–East German spinning mill, Przyjazv, considered one of the first joint production ventures, was established in Zawiercie in Poland. The questions of exchange rates, valuation of sales, and wages for the East German technicians have caused considerable perplexity. But the issue of how a sovereign Marxist–Leninist state can permit foreign ownership of the means of production on its territory was baffling and has been pigeon-holed as insoluble. Thus another small retreat from the principles of a socialist autarchical centrally planned system is sounded. Both joint ventures within COMECON and between Eastern enterprises and Western firms will comprise the next inevitable phase. State ownership of the means of production will slowly give way to corporate or enterprise ownership and controls thus converging to Western structures and practices. While perhaps not yet conclusive proof of a trend towards the capitalization of Communism (such as already occurs in respect of Communist firms in the West) these pragmatic adaptations of doctrine within the COMECON bloc to the exigencies of multinational Vodka-Cola development can certainly be considered as significant portents of future trends.

Part II

Behind the façade of trade and barter, new relationships are being woven between the select authoritarian élites. The individuals who comprise the élite nucleus operate within an 'Overworld' of organized conspiracy, which is a mirror image of the 'Underworld' of organized crime. Very often these two entities coincide and act together. Such a confluence of the two is illustrated in the case of Richard Nixon. This man could reckon on two protectors: Donald M. Kendall, president of Pepsi Cola, for whom he exchanged a capitalist beverage for Brezhnev's Vodka, and Meyer Lansky, financial boss of the Mafia. This phase of his career seems to have been conveniently forgotten by the propagandists for 'Vodka-Colanization.' However, let us dwell a moment on the tragic irony of this strange, unfinished political fate. Rejoicing in the admiration of both Mao and Brezhnev, there is no doubt that without the unhappy accident of Watergate this primarily anti-Communist figure would have remained in the eyes of history the symbol and instigator of the policy of détente. Conspiracy, fraud and the smell of plots are the basis of the Vodka-Colanizers' action plan.

This part brings together three different examples which illustrate the double standards in practice. The link between the three incidents rests in the active complicity of the Communists operating secretly with the capitalist multinationals.

Thus, the negotiations over the sale of American wheat to the USSR went ahead without the knowledge of the government and the farmers. From the first meeting in Canada in 1963, up to the New York negotiations at the Hilton Hotel in 1972, the big wheat deals and the manipulation of hundreds of millions of dollars were the sole result of secret discussions between big company speculators and Russian agents belonging to the State machine.

At first sight the Sindona and Rosenbaum affairs may seem remote from Nixon and the policy of collaboration with the East. In fact, the operations of these financiers illustrate the extreme flexibility of the Vodka-Cola power molecule, which uses the system's multiple resources to obtain agreements and illegally to manipulate vast sums. The clients and intermediaries of this system are equally the Moscow-Narodny Bank (the Soviet bank in London), the Vatican or the Italian Communist Party, which participated in the construction firm belonging to the Vatican which owned the Watergate office block. Throughout these scandals, the multiple links between these businessmen and the main protagonists of Vodka-Colanization should not be forgotten.

1.

The Rise and Fall of a Vodka-Cola Pioneer

By the evening of 22 October 1962 it seemed a foregone conclusion that Richard Milhouse Nixon was about to become a vague shadow of a political has-been, a conservative counterpart to Adlai Stevenson and Nelson Rockefeller in the museum of eternal losers. After a harsh lesson in the presidential elections against John F. Kennedy, he had just suffered a humiliating defeat in the race for the governorship of California. As a pillar of the cold war and a fierce anti-Communist, he had worked energetically alongside Senator McCarthy during the fifties' witchhunts, but now looked merely bilious and bad-tempered as he stuck rigidly to outmoded attitudes which appeared increasingly divorced from the reality and demands of international political strategy. American intellectuals could only hope that 'this man from nowhere,' who reflected a social phenomenon rather than a political class, would return to the oblivion from which he had come.

Six years later, at the Republican Party convention in Miami, that home for the idle, rich and retired, he swept away all opposition and won the party nomination with a large majority. A further five months of effective campaigning brought him out in front of his Democratic rival Hubert Humphrey in November 1968 to become the 37th President of the United States.

From the beginning, it was obvious that some extraordinary regeneration of the brain cells had taken place. He had overcome the mental blocks, the prejudices and misunderstandings of his previous stance on foreign policy. The one-time crusader against Communism had become the champion of 'cooperation and collaboration with the Eastern countries.' With the support of his adviser Kissinger, who could juggle concepts in a way that only Harvard-Rockefeller intellectuals know how, he launched the idea of 'détente.' This formula was sufficiently vague to calm the anxieties of his allies and to reassure the media men and the professors of political science who together form that connective fabric necessary to win over public opinion. It was to be a two-tier operation.

The first stage was marked by a presidential visit to Europe in 1968. A speech at NATO headquarters in Brussels clearly indicated an 'end to the cold war.' A new page of history had been turned for the United States, and increased cooperation with the East was to become one of the major preoccupations of the American Executive.

The second stage included visits to Moscow, the Chinese campaign and an end to the Vietnamese débâcle. Nixon choreographed a whole diplomatic ballet of triumphant travels and effusive embraces and appears to have formed friendships so firm that Watergate left Mao and Brezhnev standing like two furious orphans deprived of their playmate. Equally naïve specialists saw Watergate and the loss of the San Clemente hermit as a series of body blows to détente: evidence of the religious, almost superstitious belief that national policy is always created in government offices. Evidence, too, of that taste for fragile and delicate conceptualizations which fall to pieces when they are put to the test. But before being entered in the profit and loss columns of history,

Richard Nixon is worth a last, sidelong glance, for he was one of the most flexible of those puppets so skilfully manipulated over six to seven years. The men pulling the strings changed the political, economic and social realities of our time with each tug. Their activism was on a scale commensurate with what was at stake. For they hoped to sweep away ideologies, to infiltrate, control and dismiss national governments in order to complete the formation of a new world power.

In 1962 Nixon had a simple outlook on life. His ambition was to find the most financially rewarding career and New York looked like the ideal place for a political coming of age. He had managed to remain close friends with several of the big industrialists who sponsor the Republican Party. Chief of these was Elmer Bobst, who started out as a $30-a-week drugstore salesman before becoming director of the Warner Lambert Pharmaceutical Company and one of the richest men in America. The two men liked each other and had a close relationship. Nixon's daughters called Bobst "Uncle Elmer" and the two families regularly spent Christmas together. Bobst suggested to the former Vice-President that he should join the important New York law office of Mudge, Rose, Stern, Baldwin and Todd. On 1 June 1963, after several weeks of negotiations, Nixon signed a contract in his suite at the Waldorf Astoria to the effect that six months after being admitted to the New York bar he would become a partner in the firm with an annual salary of $150,000. Both sides stood to benefit. Mudge and Stern was generally reckoned to be a rundown, old-fashioned firm. The arrival of a well known figure like Nixon would surely improve things. "As my lawyer Richard Nixon was saying to me the other day ..." is the kind of thing every manager would like to be able to let slip during conversation. And close collaboration with a possible presidential candidate would have its attractions for every business man in the tangled corridors of power. It was a fair deal. Mudge, Rose was to make Nixon a rich man and Nixon was to rebuild the ailing reputation of Mudge, Rose. And nobody was fooled. Six months after his arrival, the firm became "Nixon, Mudge and Rose." It did not really matter that Nixon had only very limited experience in legal affairs. He had had his own tiny office above a garage in the Los Angeles suburb of Whittier between 1937 and 1942.

It was not long before the advantages of the situation became clear also to another Republican big-wig, Donald Kendall, president of Pepsi Cola. This dynamic, baby-faced fifty-year-old had evolved an extremely aggressive and diversified marketing policy to combat his eternal rival Coca-Cola. It was an odd battle considering that, apart from the name and a negligible difference in taste, there is nothing to distinguish the two products, though both companies keep the composition of their beverages a closely guarded secret.

The countries where these two firms operate build factories under licence and are given machinery to do the bottling. But the actual drink is made in the United States and arrives in special planes which are immediately placed under armed guard. This is patently ridiculous and show just how far companies like Pepsi and Coke will go to sell their brand name. It also points out the amorality of a business world which is interested only in new markets and increased cash flow. The two firms share the same world-wide intoxication strategy. They sell the same drink which is based on caffeine and colouring and reputed to be toxic. In 1956, after detailed work on the subject, an American senate commission of enquiry issued a report concluding that the product was injurious to health. Needless to say the report was immediately classified.

With a firm commitment to world wide trade, Kendall was on close terms with the big groups which control and direct American international policy, like the International Washington Council and David Rockefeller's "Dortmund Group." The members of both these organizations have one thing in common, as we shall see throughout this section.

Whether politicians, businessmen or academics, they have all abandoned the most intransigent hard core of anti-Communist ideology in the United States to become total converts to the cause of détente.

Some years later Kendall held a key post as co-chairman of the US–USSR Trade and Economic Council alongside Kosygin's son-in-law, German Vishiani, a Georgian technocrat with a weakness for luxurious living and the efficiency of Western capitalism. This institution, with offices in Washington and New York, was sponsored by a large number of State Department and Ministry of Trade officials and leaders of the business world. It actively organized talks, meetings and seminars on an increasing scale and opened the way to integration between the élites on both sides, apparently unimpeded.

In 1963, like many capitalist managers, the president of Pepsi was well aware of the importance and potential of the Communist markets. And Nixon's previous political office made him first choice as a trade representative. Accordingly Kendall agreed that Pepsi's interests should be handled by Mudge, Rose, and more particularly by Nixon who had become the life and soul of the firm. So, between two musical evenings in the home of John Mitchell, a colleague from Mudge, Rose and later Nixon's Attorney-General, the former outcast of American politics stepped up his journeys abroad, formed new contacts and relationships with political leaders, gave himself a smoother, more refined image and prepared his comeback—talking a great deal all the while about Pepsi Cola. An ardent defender of Formosa, he got Chiang Kai-Chek to agree to an exclusive deal with Kendall's company, just five years before recognizing the People's Republic of China. He had meetings in Moscow with Kruschev; and when Kruschev had been ousted he saw Kosygin and Brezhnev. It was a lengthy and delicate business.

Kendall's rivals, Coca-Cola, who had begun negotiations with Czechoslovakia before the Dubček era, reached an agreement after "normalization" without ever thinking to break off discussions during the invasion by Warsaw Pact troops. Business, after all, is business ... But a similar deal for Pepsi in the USSR required more delicate handling. The Western Communist parties' propaganda campaigns against American imperialism, Coca-Colanization and the "Coca-Cola Fascists" during the cold war were still fresh in people's minds. It would be difficult to justify the existence of a capitalist establishment on the sacred soil of the socialist motherland. Finally Nixon carried off the contract which he initialled during an official visit as US President in 1972. But the fact that the party comrades had thus won the right to poison themselves with Kendall's sugary, capitalist syrup was actually the result of a brilliant discovery made shortly before which demonstrates how ingenious the human mind can be when stimulated by the prospect of earning billions of dollars. This discovery was a specific example of capitalist invention and its ability to solve problems in a concrete way, leaving political and philosophical aspirations almost totally aside. The dialectic of international trade made it possible to effect a quite extraordinary synthesis by which Pepsi's supremacy over Vodka resulted in the appearance of a new product, the Vodka-Cola enterprise. The appearance of this ideqlogically hybrid and theoretically improbable creation opened the way in the East to the reintroduction of hateful capitalist concepts like profit, gains and surplus value which Marx had roundly condemned as the bases of man's exploitation by man.

It was a simple transaction, like all such business deals. Mr Kendall and his experts signed a contract for the building of a plant in the USSR designed to produce 74 million bottles a year. As in hundreds of other such cases throughout the world, Pepsi supplied all the technology, know how, engineers and technicians under licence. But since the Russians could not settle the account in rubles and wanted to keep their gold to buy wheat, they paid Pepsi in Vodka and by making the company sole agents for Soviet wines in the United States. A trading company was set up specifically for the purpose, with the interesting name of "Henri Wines."

This deal has a political significance far and above the purely commercial aspect. It contains the broad outlines of new trade relations between East and West based on cooperation and co-production rather than import–export deals. It would take more than the subtlest dialectic to justify this. There is no doubt that the privileged few on both sides will benefit from these new forms of cooperation, but it seems unlikely that the Western worker will profit in any way from a détente which may, on the contrary, cost him his job. Clearly the capitalist managers are attracted to the East because of the low wages there and the fact that strikes are prohibited.

None of this prevented Kendall from demonstrating a flexible sense of democracy in his comments on the Soviet leader Leonid Brezhnev, whom he had just met in Moscow. He described Brezhnev as "a man profoundly concerned about the wellbeing, liberties and happiness of his people."

Despite his apparent concern about morality, the president of Pepsi never worries about the dangers engendered by the product he manufactures. Perhaps he imagines that most of his sins in the East will be offset by the terrible effects of Vodka consumption among the Soviet people. The authorities there continually condemn alcoholism as a socio–economic scourge and an industrial embarrassment. The precepts of grandpa Marx and uncle Lenin seem to melt away in an alcoholic haze, a shortlived rejection of an otherwise dismal and restrictive life. Absenteeism and work-shyness, the gut reactions to repetitive and piece-rated factory work, are morally unacceptable in a socialist state and severely punished by law as hooliganism and parasitism. So, at a time when there is general agreement in the West that company structure should be changed and production lines humanized, any similar ideas in the East, however quietly expressed, are regarded as inadmissible acts of insubordination. Lenin's successors, in their respect for party dogma, remember his admiration for that great slave-driver and captain of industry, Taylor.

A concern for secrecy is one of the basic characteristics of all the circuits of power. There must be no public, legal or democratic control whatever over their activities if they are to operate efficiently. We should stop being hypercritically high-minded in this respect. No government or political party, however left wing, could change the existing situation without provoking immediate condemnation. Nixon's character qualified him to play the elliptical rules of power like a virtuoso and he involved himself in a daring mixture of activities. Throughout his career in the forefront of the political, moral and business worlds, he operated in the two interconnecting and equally rewarding areas of the Pepsi *Overworld* in which he became a missionary for multinational capitalism, and the *Underworld* of multinational crime. Thus, the man who came to symbolize the dangerous and original balancing act of détente with the East never let go his connections with the criminal syndicate. He actually strengthened the cooperation between those two different hemispheres of power, money and corruption. The man responsible for this collaboration was a puny weakling, whose waxy complexion and tired, self-effacing manner made him indistinguishable from the tens of thousands of wage earners who pour out of their offices onto the New York sidewalks at hamburger time. Meyer Lansky, apparently so inoffensive, has been regarded for more than thirty years as the undisputed boss of the Mafia. A financial genius, he survived Capone, Dillinger, Lucky Luciano and Frank Nitti, and brilliantly reorganized the Cosa Nostra to meet the economic realities of our time. He runs banks and business companies and invests the syndicate's money in large-scale, impeccable financial and industrial operations. By this change of tactics he has made the Mafia a fully paid-up member of the American economy. Lansky operates skilfully within the sealed systems and secretive dealings of banking, and his investments are important to the overall economic picture. He created Las Vegas and the technique of "laundering." Every evening, at closing time, a figure known as the bagman leaves each of the Mafia-run casinos for the airport with a bag containing a large proportion of the receipts. This money is deposited in numbered accounts in the Bahamas, Puerto Rico, Switzerland or in one of the other tax havens which lie dotted round the American coast. Mysterious banking circuits then swallow up the deposits which pass unchecked through the tax havens and out the other side. The money laundered in this way can be reused at any time to buy companies or finance political activities, because Meyer Lansky is a good citizen with a close interest in "public affairs." He has made considerable contributions to the electoral campaigns of candidates like Roosevelt, Truman, Eisenhower and Nixon.

His relationship with Nixon goes back some years. In 1940, Nixon was an introvert law student at Duke University who read romantic novels and dreamt of becoming an FBI agent. When this particular ambition came to nothing he opened a small office as a legal consultant and immediately started working for Bugsy Siegel, Lansky's West Coast partner.

In 1941, at Siegel's suggestion, Nixon went on a mysterious trip to Havana. He later said, "I used my trip to look into the possibilities of opening an office there." He stayed in a Mafia-owned hotel and his local contacts were mostly working with Lansky. For, with remarkable foresight, Lansky, the Paganini of tax evasion and immoral earnings, had seen all the possible advantages accruing to the Mafia from well founded and diversified operations in the West Indies. Casinos, prostitution and drug rackets provided the amenable petty tyrants of the area with financial comforts denied them by the severities of local economic underdevelopment. Coupled with this favourable political climate was a laxity in tax affairs which guaranteed the criminal syndicate every prospect of great wealth. At the time of Nixon's first trip to Cuba, Lansky was already a close friend and right-hand man to dictator Fulgencio Batista; he ran Batista's police force and managed his personal fortune. But these activities needed a reputable front, some kind of political justification. A lobby was created and swelled over the years to receive various malleable figures familiar with administrative procedure and the pathways of federal power. By 1946 they had evolved a specific strategy, "The Defense of the Caribbean, the last bulwark of the free world before the reds rush onto the American coastline." This succinct argument, a few basic words cleverly fitted to the prevailing atmosphere, made George Smathers, senator for Florida and a member of the Finance Commission, the most active of the anti-Communist, pro-Mafia group. A college companion of John Kennedy, he played poker with Truman, golf with Eisenhower, and was quick to form a friendship with future President Nixon.

An ardent defender of the Duvalier, Batista and Trujillo régimes in the American senate, this ostentatiously elegant man was anxious to be where the power and money were and obsessed with denouncing "the international Communist conspiracy." Elected on a Democratic ticket, he destroyed his liberal political opponent, Claude Pepper, in the 1950 elections by saddling him with the dubious nickname "Red Pepper." The young Richard Nixon used the same smear tactics during his first electoral campaign against the Democrat Helene Douglas. He knew the harmful effect of words like "traitor" and "communist," and with surprising sensitivity to shades of meaning, he nicknamed his unfortunate opponent the "Pink Lady."

Mickey Cohen, Siegel's successor in California, lent considerable financial support to each of Nixon's campaigns. And very soon Nixon was taken in hand by Murray Chotiner, a Los Angeles lawyer, who played Pygmalion to his Galatea. Between 1949 and 1952 Chotiner took on the defense of 221 cases of gangsterism, some of them concerning leading members of the Cosa Nostra. It was he who fashioned Nixon for the political world and pushed him up the ladder of the fringe meritocracy. He was also the only man to whom Nixon continued to show his gratitude. During his first term of office the President even alloted his "second father" an office in the White House.

But this did not change Chotiner's basic needs. Before, during and after his period as the Rasputin of the American Executive, he pursued his untiring quest for justice and his stubborn defense of social cases mishandled by a meddling magistrature. It was thus that he became interested in Jimmy Hoffa, the well known union leader who was sentenced to twenty years of cellular, monastic meditation for "embezzlement and extortion of funds and continued collaboration with criminal organizations." This particular legal episode owed a great deal to the tenacity of the then Attorney-General Bobby Kennedy who appears to have harboured a curious prejudice against the Mafia when he was not trying to enlist its help in destroying ominous political figures like Fidel Castro.

Both gangland bosses and Overworld leaders share the same love of business and the same lack of scruples. Their efficiency depends on their ability to buy political influence and corrupt administrations and constituted bodies. In fact, the kingpins of the criminal world today are just like the great captains of industry, and equally immoral in their activities.

Adlai Stevenson, who failed to win the presidential election on the Democratic ticket despite his years as the *prima donna* of the American liberals, owed his career as governor of Illinois to Jack Harvey who worked with Al Capone on all the West Side operations in Chicago. Harvey's most active protégé, Paul Ziffren, moved to California where he led the Democratic State Committee before supporting the Johnson–Humphrey ticket and the Humphrey–Muski ticket four years later.

In 1952, Nixon was appointed Vice-President to Eisenhower, partly through Thomas Dewey, twice a presidential candidate, a former governor of New York and an influential member of the Republican electoral committee. Two interesting facts emerge from Dewey's career. Firstly, it was he who freed Lucky Luciano from prison so that he could go to Sicily in 1943 and rally the *maffiosi* to form strategic support for the American landings. Secondly, and more importantly, Dewey, together with former CIA director Allen Dulles, had a large holding in the Mary Carter Paint Company, a curious enterprise owned by Meyer Lansky. Another important shareholder in the company was Charles "Baby" Rebozo who remained a close and trusted friend of Richard Nixon, his beach neighbour in California. While out hunting swordfish or playing gin rummy the two men discussed their mutual dislike for "intellectuals, liberals, scruples and the climate of moral defeatism", which they reckoned to be undermining the United States. A small, fat, vulgar, jovial man, Cuban-born "Baby" Rebozo had met Nixon through George Smathers during a trip to Havana. He had made his first million during the Second World War by "recycling" tyres at a time when rubber was rationed. Now the wealthy president of the Key Biscane Bank of Florida, "Baby" Rebozo was still attracted by the idea of any kind of business or investment in the paradise islands of the Caribbean.

Like Smathers, he was an ardent defender of the Trujillo, "Papa Doc" and Batista régimes and appeared to believe that Communist infiltration could be contained most effectively by increasing the number of gaming tables and organized brothels. Fidel Castro's accession to power in 1960 forced Lansky to shift his activities to the Bahamas where the white politicians were open to bribery. He went into partnership with Max Orowitz, a multimillionaire with interests in Florida and New York. Orowitz also owned two banks which received regular deposits from the syndicate and specialized in the transfer of illegal funds to Switzerland.

In one year, the Bahamanian Minister of Finance and Tourism, Sir Stafford Sands, received $2 million from Lansky and Orowitz. The money was deposited in a numbered account in Zurich, and, in exchange, the politician authorized the construction and opening of further casinos, hotels and night clubs. The United Bahamanian Party to which he belonged received $350,000 from a bank belonging to Max Orowitz in 1961.

In 1962, just after his defeat in California, and a few months before his return to business, Nixon visited Paradise Island, a luxury resort off Nassau. He had been invited by the owner, H. Hartford, who was trying desperately to get a certificate of exemption so that he could set up a casino. Stafford Sands, who had not forgiven him for contributing to the funds of the main black opposition Liberal Party, was obstinately refusing to grant such a certificate.

In 1966 Hartford transferred most of his shares to the Mary Carter Paint Company. Nixon negotiated the deal which was carried through by the Exchange and Investment Bank of Switzerland. This Geneva establishment was run by Ed Levinson, the Mafia's business manager in Las Vegas and Batista's Cuba, Benjamin Siegelbaum, a fellow-worker of Lansky with wide banking experience, and Lou Poller, a friend of the union leader Jimmy Hoffa and former president of the Miami National Bank owned by Samuel Cohen. The Exchange and Investment Bank formed the last link on one of the chains used by the syndicate to transfer profits to the European tax havens.

It was not, however, Lansky's only banking outlet in Switzerland. Through his henchmen John Pullman and Tibor Rosenbaum, in particular, he also controlled the International Credit Bank, whose clients ranged from the Rothschild family to the State of Israel to Prince Bernhardt of the Netherlands, before being forced into bankruptcy.

In February 1967, Stafford Sands received $750,000 for his signature on a curious document making Paradise Island part of the Bahamanian Club of Nassau, the only establishment in the area with a gaming licence.

In January 1968, a hotel and a casino valued at $15 million were opened on the little island. The whole complex was run by Eddie Cellini, Lansky's man in Havana and a former casino owner in Kentucky, whose brother Dino handled syndicate business in London. A $2 million bridge was built to link Paradise Island with Nassau.

All the members of the jet set came to the opening, but conversation revolved round just one of the guests, Richard Nixon, who was generally recognized as having a good chance of winning the Republican Party's vote for that year's election. Some months later Nixon and his team moved into the Americana hotel in Miami to take part in the Grand Old Party convention. Two days after his arrival, the Mary Carter Paint Company's yacht, which had been graciously lent to the future President together with its crew as Nixon's communication center, moored in front of the hotel.

Nixon had planned a last visit to Paradise Island for the end of November 1968, but this was prudently cancelled after a speedy enquiry on the part of the secret services had revealed the Mafia's involvement in the area. Fearing the bad impression such a presidential visit might make just two weeks after his election, they managed to dissuade him from publicizing friendships which, however longlasting, ought nevertheless to continue behind a veil of discretion.

Soon after, the Mary Carter Paint Company sold part of its property, renamed itself Resorts International and concentrated on casinos. It also acquired the services of its fiercest opponent, Robert Peloquin, a close friend of Bobby Kennedy, who was appointed vice-president of Paradise Enterprise after leading the anti-Mafia counter-agency at the Ministry of Justice.

In 1970 Lansky demonstrated his exceptional talent for exploiting the existing tangle of enforceable legal provisions. Through Resorts International he invested $2 million in a new company managed by Peloquin which offered advice and assistance to American and foreign businessmen on how to combat Mafia infiltration within their firms. The consultants Peloquin recruited were all former high-ranking federal investigators who had helped to inculcate the popular myth that there was still an incorruptible column soldiering tirelessly on against a secret and far-reaching criminal brotherhood. It was only logical that they should now make their living from an organization which they had done so much to spotlight.

In January 1969 Resorts International, now quoted on the American Stock Exchange, bought 900,000 shares in Pan Am from Gulf Western. A month later Lansky's company held top secret negotiations with David Rockefeller's Chase Manhattan for the transfer of another million and a half shares. Resorts International were trying to acquire a 10% holding in the airline company.[1] In March the Civil Aeronautic Board blocked the deal.

Being unable to reach such national institutions as Lansky and Rockefeller, Robert Morgenthau, director of the antifraud service of the IRS indicted one of their accessories, Max Orowitz. Lanksy's former partner in the Paradise Island business was building up a series of large scale, flamboyant real estate deals in Florida. The money accumulated by his company, the General Development Corporation, was transferred to numbered accounts in the International Credit Bank.

Orowitz's jail sentence was subsequently commuted for reasons of ill-health by Justice Minister John Mitchell. Morgenthau's zealous perseverance in showing up the inadequacy of existing legislation and the gutlessness of the authorities greatly irritated the President's men, and in under a year Richard Nixon had replaced him and reorganized the IRS.

Some months after his election Richard Nixon sent Nelson Rockefeller on a study trip to Latin America. It was a wise choice. Rockefeller knew the continent well. His family had been administering a shrewd dose of paternalistic charity and relentless opportunism there for decades, recovering in dollars what it paid out in cents.

This two-way process relied on two Rockefeller-run organizations. The AIA, of which Nelson was president until 1958, pursued a health and education policy which was actually a coverup for the activities of the IBEC (International Basic Economic Corporation). The economic expansion and financial successes of the IBEC can be measured in direct proportion to the level of political oppression and human suffering in the countries where it operates. From Bogota to Rio, from La Paz to Guatemala City, the IBEC bolsters the faltering economies of authoritarian régimes, many of them nationalistic military dictatorships. The Rockefellers' strategy in Latin America is a fine illustration of big business attitudes generally. They are only too glad to leave the local flunkeys, whose political awareness stops at the edge of their peaked caps, labouring under the delusion that they are safeguarding national independence. The childish pleasures of politics make their activities morally justifiable, and the Latin American dictators can trip round their playgrounds burbling nursery rhymes about the Marxist bogeyman. For, paradoxically, the only way to keep the continent stable and depoliticize the people, so that the big companies can chase after profits, is by maintaining the illusion of a Communist threat.

Peoples deprived of their democratic rights, in many countries for several years,

---

[1]In November 1976, the directors of Resorts International scored a major hit when their campaign to permit Las Vegas-type gambling casinos in Atlantic City, New Jersey succeeded. Some years before, a Lansky-organized campaign to legalize gambling at Miami Beach had failed.

responded spontaneously, unequivocally and massively to Rockefeller's visit. In Honduras a student was killed by the police during demonstrations. In the Dominican Republic, refineries belonging to Standard Oil were blown up. In Costa Rica 2,500 students demonstrated. In Panama the National Guard was overwhelmed. Riots forced the Venezuelan government to cancel the visit. In Bogota 20,000 men of the Colombian special security forces put down strikes. In Ecuador, Rockefeller's car was stoned and ten demonstrators were killed by the police. In Bolivia his twenty-four-hour visit was reduced to three hours inside the airport after bombs had exploded on the motorway leading to La Paz. In Chile Salvador Allende's government had to cancel the visit after the announcement of a national strike. The Brazilian military government put hundreds of opposition members into preventive detention and censored the press. In Buenos Aires, following the death of a demonstrator, a national strike was declared and nine IBEC supermarkets were bombed.

On the few occasions when he could make himself heard Rockefeller spoke to the crowd of the "necessity for social reforms which would ensure the future wellbeing of individuals." He promised the politicians increased economic aid and American military support in the continued struggle against "the communist conspiracy." He stressed the integral role which the IBEC would play in this policy, but omitted to mention that his organization had been doing business for more than a year in the Eastern countries thought to be behind the waves of subversion. In fact, in a 50% partnership with Tower International Inc., which belonged to Cyrus Eaton, the Cleveland industrial millionaire and friend of Kruschev, the IBEC was developing luxury hotels in Warsaw, Belgrade, Prague, Sofia and Bucharest. It was also building a rubber plant worth more than $200 million in Russia, a $50 million aluminium plant in Yugoslavia and a glass factory in Rumania. Altogether these deals amounted to several billion dollars, with extremely profitable terms for the Western capitalists. Like Stroessner's Paraguay and Somoza's Nicaragua, Ceausescu's Rumania and Brezhnev's Russia were supplying the Rockefeller interests with a cheap and manageable labour force at a time when American intervention in Vietnam was at its height. Rockefeller's only lengthy stopover was at Haiti. After a welcome from his old friend "Papa Doc," whom he publicly embraced, Rockefeller recalled the "stabilizing" role played by the voodoo dictator in an area prone to social eruptions. Since 1964 there had been positive and productive relations between the crime syndicate and Duvalier and his entourage. Lansky, who had staked everything on Nixon's winning in 1960, had to wait till the end of the Kennedy era to make his move. The Democratic President's neo-reformist initiatives in relations with the South American continent hindered the progress of any semi-clandestine deals. But when Johnson was elected in 1964, the new President appointed Bobby Gene Baker, a close relative of Lansky, as his personal adviser, Baker being secretary of the Democratic majority in the senate before he foundered in a financial scandal. The obligatory George Smathers, former senator in Florida and now a lawyer, joined the duo. And by 1968 Meyer Lansky could rejoice in Nixon's election quite disinterestedly since he no longer needed his help in Haiti. He ran the prostitution, drugs and gambling rackets there and owned the international casino in Port-au-Prince. He even gave Mike McLaney, one of his Cleveland colleagues, the job of promoting tourism to the island. Whole charter flights of pressmen were invited to Haiti to be taken around and looked after on condition that they waxed lyrical about the beauty of the island, the stability of the régime and the luxuriousness of the tourist infrastructure.

On 8 January 1969, while Nelson Rockefeller was sitting down to a last lunch with "Papa Doc" and the chubby-cheeked baby who succeeded him, the federal police intercepted a Haiti-bound plane at Miami international airport. The plane's cargo was enough to deter hardened gamblers for life. There was a complete set of tables and roulette wheels all fitted with remote-controlled electronic equipment so that even the most determined player had no hope of winning. This was the Mafia's way of modernizing Haiti. The whole incident illustrates the principle that technological imports should be suited to local demands. But all such schemes, whether they involved "fixing" tables in Haiti or exporting vast quantities of IBM computers to Moscow, were soon to prove that new products are worthless unless the local social and economic environment is completely ready for them.

2.

The Wheat Negotiations

When Nikolai Baibakov stepped down from the rostrum of the Supreme Soviet on 6 December 1966, after taking two hours to deliver his annual report on the present state and future prospects of the Soviet economy, the 1,300 dozing delegates duly responded with restrained applause. He had succeeded in pulling the wool not only over their eyes, but also over the eyes of all the foreign observers. The Kremlinologists had sieved carefully through every phrase, every metaphor, every loose word in the Gosplan chairman's speech in the hope of finding some indication as to the health of the Soviet economy, but to no avail. The most they had been able to gather was that although the growth in heavy industry had been 4.9%, consumer goods and food industries had grown only by 2.7%—apparently the lowest rate of increase since the end of the Second World War. But this was merely one more indication of the exhaustion of the Communist economy, to be added to a stack of existing conjectures.

It seemed that in an atmosphere of carefully distilled tedium the parliamentary session must draw to a peaceful close, after hours of deliberately vague and naively apologetic speeches.

Gregori Vashenko was virtually an unknown when his turn came to speak on the morning of 7 December. As chairman of the Planning and Budget commission of the Supreme Soviet he was just one of those legions of nameless, faceless and politically ineffectual deputies to be found in any parliament.

But when his speech, which he delivered extremely slowly, turned to agricultural matters, his audience became unusually attentive. The average harvest during the period of the 1970–1975 plan would be 8% less than the average planned for.

Rapid calculations on the part of everybody present made it look as if sober-voiced comrade Vashenko had just disclosed the worst Soviet agricultural figures since the disastrous harvest of 1963 which had cost Kruschev his post as First Secretary the following year. With a crop of 165 million tons instead of the necessary 215 million predicted in the plan, the Soviet authorities had no choice but to engage in a classic operation which illustrates the full extent of Vodka-Colanization. They had to purchase American grain, or, more accurately, to purchase grain from the all-powerful monopoly companies over which the American government has no control—not that it wishes to. If it is true, as Brillat-Savarin said, that "the fate of a nation depends on the way its rulers feed it," then the fate of the Soviet people looked black indeed.

Since 1917 Russian agriculture has been distinguished by a high degree of inefficiency. Exaggerated stress on industrialization and the revolutionary role of the working class had led Soviet leaders to look on the peasants as a large social group whose very existence was harmful since it left the October Revolution looking incomplete and unfinished. For the security of the new régime, the members of this forgotten class would have to start thinking as a proletariat and, if necessary, be forced into urbanization.

In 1921 famine killed three millions in the Urals. Lenin's subsequent desperate appeal for American aid made the fortune of a young émigré doctor and founder member of the American Communist Party. Armand Hammer chartered a vessel and shipped $1,000,000's worth of wheat to the Bolshevik régime. The insolvent leaders let him take his pick from the splendid art collections of the Tsarist régime. The Goyas, Rubens, Malevitchs and Van Dycks Hammer chose gave him one of the finest private collections in the world. He was a shrewd man and managed to establish warm and friendly relations with Lenin and Anastasius Mikoyan, though ideological agreement never dulled his sense of reality. He opened a pen factory in Moscow. He helped the Allied Drug and Chemical Corporation to fertilize Russian fields and thirty-eight foreign companies to win the right to contribute to Lenin's NEP, that intermission in the Revolution. Hammer's clients included Parker Pens, Underwood Typewriters and the very anti-Communist Henry Ford. Now an octogenarian billionaire, Hammer continues to make regular visits to the USSR, like a faithful widower visiting his wife's grave.

Every month he leaves Los Angeles in his two billion franc Gulf Stream jet for Leonid Brezhnev's office in Moscow. In April 1973, fifty-two years after his first business deal, he successfully negotiated an $8 billion, twenty-year contract for the exploitation of Soviet gas and oil on behalf of his company Occidental Petroleum, up to that point almost insolvent and under considerable pressure from creditor banks.

For an aging businessman this was a very good deal. Lenin lay embalmed in Red Square, the American Communist Party was non-existent. All that Hammer was gambling on was the stability of a régime very different in its nature and aims from Lenin's picture of a bright tomorrow when golden urinals would be built, a vision which had attracted the young émigré in 1920.

Under Stalin, mass deportations, forced collectivization, priority treatment for heavy industry and an abortive attempt to acclimatize wheat in Siberia made malnutrition and famine two facts of everyday life in the Soviet Union. Artistic socialist realism and the building of a socialist state dictated that an electric pylon be more beautiful than a stalk of wheat. Kruschev tried to check this development and redirect priorities. Nobody who saw it could ever forget the romantic picture of the First Secretary delicately holding an ear of corn between his fingers. In his famous speech at the 20th Party Congress in 1956, Kruschev recognized the lamentable condition of Soviet agriculture and revealed that production in 1952 had scarcely exceeded that in 1916, the last year of the Tsarist régime. But although he tried to make Russia the world's leading manufacturer of tractors, although he appreciably increased the peasants' income and launched a vast campaign for the clearing and cultivation of more than 100 million acres of virgin land in Kazakhstan and Siberia, Soviet agriculture continued to fail.

No matter how energetic the program, there are two factors which will always make it difficult for the Soviet Union to be self-sufficient in grain.

The first is climatic. As much as 70% of the wheat fields lie between the 49th parallel and the Arctic circle, a region of heavy rainfall, insufficient sunshine and an extremely short growth season. In Siberia frost begins to hit large areas of cultivated land from the beginning of September. The managers of farms in these districts report that favourable meteorological conditions occur only once every four years.

The 1975 disaster resulted from a combination of adverse circumstances. First an abnormally mild winter meant that the snow which protects the wheat never fell. Then, after the spring thaw, an extremely dry June scorched the fields and production fell.

The second factor arises from the large number of blockages, counter-orders and deficiencies inherent in the system. Basically, the life of the Russian agricultural worker can be viewed as a kind of obstacle race in which he has to dodge between the various administrative hurdles set up by the central authorities. A journalist from

Pravda visiting a collective farm during the last harvest, noted that the workers were buried under a stream of contradictory orders telling them to stop work in the middle of harvesting and wait for further orders, or summoning them to meetings at regional headquarters in the middle of threshing.

In a five month period that particular farm had received 778 telephone calls and a continual flow of directives which either duplicated, invalidated or contradicted each other. The journalist then went to the district agricultural office which had unleashed this flood of roneod paper. Frightened officials evasively suggested that he go to the provincial office. Like a character out of Gogol climbing up the hierarchy one step at a time, the stubborn journalist finally learnt that in the space of four months the regional officials had received more than 6,000 memoranda from ministries in Moscow, many of them from agencies directly connected with the Kremlin.

The agricultural sector still employs one third of all Soviet workers, but production is not high enough to support a total population of 252 million. This fact is a bitter pill for the Communist leaders to swallow, especially when they can look out of the corner of their eyes at the plains of the American Middle West where, admittedly in ideal climatic conditions, 4% of the American working population produces 80% of world cereal production.

In the USSR only 676,000 of the 2,762,200 tractors produced between 1966 and 1974 are in working order. According to *Pravda* (September 1975) production of a new model of harvester began in 1964, but of the 10,000 ordered only about 30% have been delivered. Since the Central Committee meeting in March 1965 investment in the agricultural sector has noticeably increased. A provision of 131 million roubles in the last Five Year Plan has risen to 171 million ($227 million) for the next five years. But conditions of life remain hard and precarious and the majority of young people prefer to move into the towns. The lack of skilled labour becomes more acute every season. Newspapers carry reports of hundreds of cases in which farm machinery has not been repaired in time for the harvest. Equipment is old and unmodernized, production costs have increased by 45% and the quantity of fertilizer used on the fields is only one third as high as the level used by European, Canadian or US farmers.

Until recently very little of the harvest was stored because no provision had ever been made in central planning for building silos. Experts estimate that 20% of the 220 million tons harvested in 1973 was lost in this way. Productivity goals and the need to mobilize resources fade when confronted with the trials of everyday existence.

More than ten of the large conurbations are suffering from an acute bread shortage. Queues wait resignedly for several hours as they did in the worst days of the Second World War. In a crisis like this, the peasants prefer to keep their corn to try and feed their livestock for a little while longer.

Unless massive quantities of feed grain are imported very soon, a large proportion of Soviet cattle will have to be slaughtered. There is no knowing the effect this will have on the health of the average citizen. The prolonged absence of protein from the diet which may result from no bread and little meat today, followed by no meat tomorrow, is a serious threat to the physiological future of people forced to perform hard manual labour. The long-term genetic health of the Soviet people may suffer as a consequence.

Faced with this situation, the Soviet rulers' only hope is to turn once more to America, the only country whose agricultural wealth is great enough to cope with their problems.

The rationing in 1963, when Kruschev's mistakes unluckily coincided with the worst vagaries of the Soviet climate, forced the heirs of Lenin to go down into their gold reserves. The money raised was converted into American currency to make $1 billion set aside for buying Australian and Canadian wheat, the much larger and more diversified

American market being avoided for the sake of doctrinal intransigency and a sense of appearances. It was only one year since the Cuban Missile Crisis, only two years since the Berlin crisis had demonstrated the evident superiority of Stakhanovism over East German building methods. At such a time starving people would find it hard to take the spectacle of their leaders gambolling over the fields of Iowa and somersaulting over the sacrosanct principles of Marxism by eating American bread.

Such tactical qualms no longer appeared to worry the American grain lobby formed by the six private companies which control the world market in cereal products. This cartel, which makes OPEC look like a gang of hooligans unable to do more than break a few windows with their catapults, began to pressurize the Kennedy administration. It hoped to open the way to negotiations with the Russians, despite the arsenal of legislation left over from the Foster Dulles days which imposed draconian limitations on trade with the Communist world. One by one, the citadels of the Executive fell. Finally, Orville Freeman, Secretary of State for Agriculture and closely linked to the grain companies let the project through.

Dean Rusk, Secretary of State and former president of the Rockefeller Foundation, who played a decisive role in the development and consolidation of trade relations with the East, approved the plan. "On condition," he added, "that the Soviet Union undertakes not to send any of the grain delivered to Cuba."

Representatives from each company came together to form a consortium. It was decided, in order to avoid indiscretions and diplomatic tensions, that talks with the Communists should take place in Canada at the Chateau Laurier Hotel in Ottawa.

The President voiced a note of caution during a press conference on 10 October. John Kennedy's argument took on a premonitory tone. "If we do not sell to the Russians," he said, "the Soviet propagandists will use our lack of concern to reduce tension and allay suffering against us among the other nations."

It looked as if cold war corn was already well into the millwheels of détente.

Forty-two days later a volley of shots in Dallas put an abrupt end to the President's career, but not to the negotiations. Johnson buried his predecessor, took over the relevant documents and, on 29 November, seven days after Kennedy's assassination, signed an amendment granting him discretionary power to approve loan guarantees to the Export–Import Bank. Soviet representatives were officially authorized to buy 350,000 tons of durum wheat for $78.5 million to be paid in cash, plus $11.5 million for freight charges and transporting the corn to the Black Sea ports in American boats.

In fact the actual figures behind this window dressing were 4 million tons of wheat worth more than $200 million, and these figures were negotiated in the utmost secrecy. Even they represented less than half of what the grain company directors had hoped for. They must have had to face the joint opposition of such disparate but fiercely intransigent elements as the arms syndicate and the right wing of the American Senate led by Barry Goldwater.

Throughout the deals, however, the most energetic and articulate opposition came from one man who had been totally abandoned by the political classes. Richard Nixon, that wise man among wise men, fulminated like Spengler against "those who peddle the cause of freedom." In an interview he gave to the ABC Television Network he even went so far as to predict that these sales would "constitute the worst error in foreign policy made by the American government, and a greater disaster than the Bay of Pigs incident."

And yet it was under the Nixon administration that the most important trade deal involving the sale of American wheat to the Communists was to take place.

In June 1969, shortly before his meeting with Mao Tse Tung, the other Nixon ended the seventeen-year trade embargo on exports to China brought in by Truman at the beginning of the Korean War. In the heat of the moment he also abolished the regulations governing "the granting of special licences" for all trade with the USSR and the Eastern European Communist countries. This meant that only an ordinary licence was required and that no notification or specification of exports need be made until they left the country.

When Earl Butz, American Minister of Agriculture, went to Moscow in the spring of 1972, the cold war was buried for ever under millions of bushels of grain and Soviet food problems promised a rosy future for the Big Six of the Middle West. The only difficulty was that until then the Communists had settled their accounts straight away: an effort which did them credit, but which they confessed themselves totally incapable of continuing. Negotiations, conducted for the Russians by Minister for Foreign Trade Nikolai S. Patolichev and two deputies, Mikael Kuzmin and Zoltan Golodobenko, ended on 8 July with an announcement from Nixon at his San Clemente home, that financial aid would be granted to the USSR for the purchase of wheat grain in the shape of $750 million's credit.

So, with the Johnson Act in 1934, the last legal obstacle was removed to an "official" increase in Soviet–American economic relations which actually covered a wide area of operations already.

In fact the American Executive had no control whatever over the situation. All it ever did was to put up tax payers' money to help a purely commercial deal, the full details of which it never knew.

It all started ten days before in total secrecy. On 1 July 1972 two men crossed the tourist-filled lobby of the Regency Hotel in New York on their way to their $180-a-night room. These two were the heads of Exportkhleb, the Soviet government agency handling foreign grain deals.

They had been sent to buy 20 million tons of wheat from the United States at the best possible price, without incurring any publicity. They were to talk to the six companies whose profits together exceed those of the oil companies.

While Patolichev, the Minister, operated on the political level by trying to obtain credit, these two were to act on the level of hard facts by playing the companies off against one another and by using against them the secretiveness basic to their activities. The chief of Exportkhleb was Nikolai Belusov, a tall, thin man in his fifties, who spoke English with a slight accent and appeared to be an old hand at international negotiations—he had played a decisive part in the 1963 discussions in Ottawa. His assistant on this occasion was Leonid Kalitenko, aged forty-two. The two men were soon joined by Paul Sakun, one of the leading officials in the Ministry of Foreign Trade.

Every year the grain companies shuffled round billions of dollars to dominate the world market and 90% of American exports. Earl Butz, Minister of Agriculture, summed it all up when, with innocent cynicism he said in August 1974 "Starving men listen only to those who have a piece of bread to give them."

Throughout the discussions both sides remained admirably pragmatic. The Russians continued to negotiate while Nixon mined the harbour of Haiphong and while the grain companies to whom they were talking shared out the $204 million profit they had made from food sent as aid to Thieu's Vietnam and Lon Nol's Cambodia. The global strategy of the big companies takes on many forms. They crammed Allende's Socialist–Communist Chile with food by exporting 261 million and 383 million dollars-worth of wheat to Santiago in 1971 and 1972 respectively. Then in 1973 the Chilean government found itself unable to pursue a similar import policy due to lack of credit. Today it is quite clear that food shortages exacerbated the discontent of the middle classes whose break with the régime accelerated the fall of Allende.

These firms are involved in an extremely wide range of activities and maintain control over ryefields, storage, road and river transport, elevators in the ports and foreign markets.

They operate with the big freight companies which dominate merchant shipping all over the world. In many countries they even have their own harbour facilities.

A carefully interconnected network of local offices, political contacts and hidden pressures in many countries of the world supplies them with sources of information so accurate and reliable that the now overstrained CIA uses them.

Using the most sophisticated methods of contemporary speculative capitalism, they manipulate the market with the complicity of the big banks, and are infiltrating the offices of political power.

Before joining the Nixon administration in 1971, Earl Butz sat on the boards of three companies, Ralston Purina, Stokely Van Camp and International Minerals and Chemicals, all connected with agricultural affairs and all notorious for their intransigence in negotiations with the farmers. At sixty-six a true crusader for a return to free enterprise and a free market, he was working towards one specific, if limited end, "to keep the government out of agricultural problems." A stiff and charmless figure, Butz was like one of those doormen who are employed to keep out gate-crashers without shutting the door on their fingers.

In the morning of 2 July Belusov called the luxury Manhattan offices of Michael Fribourg, owner of the Continental Grain Company. This company handles 25% of the world cereal market, owns dozens of cargo planes and at least a hundred associated companies responsible for a variety of activities from baking bread to the manufacture and sale of frozen dinners to chicken breeding. Continental also controls wheat fields and mills in Venezuela, Puerto Rico, Ecuador, Guadeloupe and Zaire, beef-rearing in the Argentine and winter sports resorts in Spain.

Founded in Arlon, Belgium, by a French exile from Metz, Continental Grain has always been wholly owned by the Fribourg family. The company finally put down roots in the US in 1922 and its present president, Michael Fribourg, took American citizenship in 1944 after spending the war in the secret service. A man without any real cultural home, Mr Fribourg happily cultivates his image as a refined and aristocratic lover of rare furniture, fine wines and old masters. But his company's annual sales figures of $3 billion are not enough for him. Fribourg is an idealist (or so he would have us believe) with a recurrent dream of strengthening Soviet–American relations through increased trade between the two sides.

On close terms with the apostles of détente, but also with Franco, Fribourg made frequent trips to Moscow and was well acquainted with Soviet politicians, some of whom he entertained on his yacht at Cannes in 1961 and in his chalet at Crans-sur-Sierre in 1962. Belusov was one of the men he had talked to at Ottowa during the palaeolithic 1963 negotiations which preceded the happy days of détente.

On that morning, however, Belusov was out of luck. Fribourg was attending working meetings in Paris and when his New York office tried to reach him he had already left the French capital for a long trip to Spain. But Bernard Steinweg, Fribourg's brother-in-law and a member of the Continental management, was still in Paris. As soon as he heard about Belusov's call, he chartered a plane and flew back to New York with Gregor Ziv, the firm's Russian-born foreign relations manager. The two men were met at the airport by Clarence Palmby, one of the vice-chairmen of Continental. Palmby's career shows just how weak the partitions supposedly separating the private sector from the federal administration really are. A former dairyman, he began working for the US Feed Grain Council, an organization controlled by the big companies for the purpose of developing American grain exports. Soon after he was appointed assistant to the Minister of Agriculture with the title of Under-Secretary of State, while his son Tom went to work for the Cargill Company, the most important member of the grain lobby.

At the ministry Clarence Palmby held a key position as director of the USDA which determined and awarded the volume of governmental subsidies to exporters as fluctuations in the world price demanded.

In March 1972 Palmby was offered a job by Mr Fribourg. At the end of April he bought a $100,000 apartment on Sutton Place South on credit, giving guarantees from the directors of Continental as personal security. On 23 May he resigned from the administration to join Fribourg's company on 8 June as vice-chairman in charge of planning and development, with a salary of $110,000 a year, three times the figure he earned in the government.

While Palmby and Gregor Ziv were meeting Leonid Kalitenko at the bar of the Madison Hotel, Belusov put through a call to the Minneapolis district of Wazyata where Cargill Inc. have their headquarters in a 63-roomed replica of a French chateau. Owned by two families, the Cargills and the MacMillans, Cargill Inc. is the largest private company in the US. With annual sales amounting to $5,027 million in 1972 and 9 billion in 1975, the strength of this firm reflects the digestive capacity of the American consumer. Cargill leads the world market not only in terms of its sales, but also in the wide diversification of its activities which range from Peruvian anchovy factories to insurance companies. At the present time, the company has information sources in thirty-four countries, and its foreign operations are handled by a Swiss subsidiary, Tradax, in Geneva. The leading exporter of Argentine wheat, maize and barley, Cargill in association with Continental has controlled practically all Canadian wheat exports since 1935. A real conglomerate with soya-processing plants in Spain, East Germany, Belgium and France, the Minnesota company is also quick to exploit political situations, which it does with consummate skill. In 1968 Cargill announced that it was prepared to open a vast elevator in dictator Park Chung Hee's South Korea, and obtained 95% of the necessary finance from the American government. The local director of Korea Cargill, Seung Man Park, had been closely connected with the American forces during the Korean War. Myung Chon Chang, who handled construction and engineering, had worked in South Vietnam from 1966 to 1968. A large proportion of the employees were veterans of the Korean War and all of them received a military-style training which, according to Edwin Fuller, vice-chairman of Cargill for Asia, "makes them into perfect workers."

Because of the size of its financial dealings and its need for liquid cash, Cargill Inc. has credit facilities with forty banks, including eight of the ten biggest American banking establishments, though like the whole grain industry, it has a preferential relationship with the Chase Manhattan Bank. Cargill's directors refer to the Rockefeller establishment as the "leader of the banking world" and coordination between the two goes back to 1983 when John Peterson left the Chase board to manage Cargill's financial operations. In 1945, the Minnesota firm issued a report indicating that "of a number of creditors, the largest is the biggest banking establishment in the world, the Chase Manhattan Bank."

The grain company always consults the New York bank before engaging in any large financial deals, and this common economic and financial strategy also applies on the political level. Although the owners and directors of Cargill are as conservative in their attitudes as the diehard members of the Republican Party, the company itself is free from any such ideological bias and nets any fish which may prove most useful to it from the common political pond, without worrying about labels. Thus the late Democratic senators for Minnesota, Hubert Humphrey (mayor of Minneapolis) and Walter Mondale (Jimmy Carter's Vice-President) and their law-offices always did benefit from the generosity of the company. Humphrey made frequent visits to the Cargill headquarters and in 1972 the Congressional Record listed the contributions Walter Mondale had received from the firm while one of the heirs of that cauliflower empire was working on the senator's staff.

Although it has brushed shoulders with all the US presidential candidates, Cargill has never hidden its commitment to Richard Nixon. Relations date back a long way and were probably based in the beginning on more than just political opportunism. The stern anti-Communist attitudes of Eisenhower's Vice-President, his Savonaro-like intransigence on behalf of the middle classes obviously endeared him to the plutocrats of the Middle West who sat delightedly recording Communist losses in the days before they thought to exploit them.

After his political thrashing, when Nixon had altered course to provide legal assistance for small companies, he made contact with Cargill, which was one of the clients of Mudge, Rose. In the spring of 1964 he went to Minneapolis where the company organized a press conference for him at the Minneapolis Press Club. Nixon's success at this, his first public appearance since the California defeat, promised well for his future career and brought him to the eyes of those businessmen looking for a presidential candidate.

In 1970 Cargill established a toehold in the White House through William Pearce, one of its vice-chairmen, whom Nixon appointed special adviser for trade questions with the rank of ambassador. Pearce used his time in the administration to skilfully change existing congressional attitudes, to ensure that legislation was amended to favour the companies even further and, chiefly, to extend trade relations with the Soviet Union. To complete its strategy Cargill also became a member of the US–USSR Trade and Economic Council, the nerve center and temple of East–West economic détente. And in a last shrewd move, the firm placed Fred Seed, its honorary chairman, on the board of the National Council for Sino–American trade.

It therefore came as no surprise to Erwin Kelm, chairman of Cargill, that Belusov should call him. Sales to the Soviet Union formed part of the program of trading possibilities which his company had been considering for several years.

It was 2.30 in the afternoon. Four hours later the firm's Lockheed "Tristar" with Kelm, his assistant Barry Saunders and section managers for wheat, barley and maize aboard, landed at New York's La Guardia airport. One hour later Belusov and Sakun met the Cargill managers at the Regency. Discussions were strained. The Russians appeared uninterested in buying barley and maize and obstinately refused to touch on the question of wheat. After dinner Kelm and his team suggested that they should stay in New York and resume discussions the following day. "No," said the Soviets. "It is not necessary to prolong this meeting, we will call you again." Three days later Saunders called the Regency Hotel to learn that Belusov, Kalitenko and Sakun had left without leaving any message.

On the morning of 3 July, Bernard Steinweg of Continental took the first plane to Washington to meet Carol Brunthaver, Palmby's successor at the USDA. Like his predecessor, Brunthaver came from the grain companies. He had been an economist with Cook Industry of Memphis, another company to become involved in the Russian deals. But Brunthaver could not have been less like the quietly cynical Palmby. An active and deeply patriotic man, he liked to remind people that he had served his country as a fighter-pilot during the Korean War. He was a mixture of meticulousness and administrative caution. The business Steinweg had come to discuss with him was crucial for the rest of the negotiations.

At that time the world price of wheat was lower than the American price. The Russians had decided to buy large quantities from the United States. Steinweg wanted to know what government policy on export subsidies was to be. Had the Minister of Agriculture decided to keep the previous year's price of $60 per ton, or $1.63 a bushel of wheat, since this was the only way in which the American companies could remain competitive while the domestic price was $2.70 per bushel?

Brunthaver, who had been in office for less than two weeks, showed little interest in the finer detail of the deals, the quantities of wheat being negotiated, the total sums involved and, more especially, the possible effect on domestic prices.

Some 382 days later, before a Senate sub-committee, Steinweg confirmed that he had met Brunthaver in the company of James Good, vice-chairman of Continental, and Samuel Sabin, the company's Washington representative. Steinweg even said that he had told the USDA director that the Soviets wanted to buy 4 million tons of milling, 5 million tons of durum wheat and possibly 2 million tons of maize. These figures represented the largest private grain deal ever negotiated in the history of the United States. Carol Brunthaver denied having received any such information from Steinweg. All he had done was to restate the traditional position of his department, namely that the usual subsidies would be available for exports however large. Brunthaver did not suspect that his decision would open the gates to a wave of political and public reaction so strong that no such secret and profitable deal could ever be put through again.

Reassured, Steinweg returned to New York to find Fribourg, who had rushed back from Spain, and to continue discussions with the Soviet delegation. On the morning of 5 July, comrade Belusov announced that Exportkhleb wished to buy 5 million tons of milling, 500,000 tons of durum wheat and 4.5 million tons of feed grain.

Ironically a large proportion of the winter durum wheat had come originally from Russian fields and had been acclimatized in Kansas by refugee farmers from the Crimea.

Continental's contracts stipulated that the deliveries should be paid for in cash on presentation of freight documents certifying that the cargoes were ready to be shipped from American ports. But these sales would not be allocated according to the $750 million credit obtained by the Russians, which was announced to the public on 8 July.

In the evening of 5 July, the successful completion of the deal was celebrated in Vodka at Fribourg's Manhattan home. Everyone was pleased that a settlement had been reached so quickly and discreetly and agreed that the whole deal must be kept completely secret. In this way Fribourg would avoid any sudden rush of speculation on wheat and the Soviet mission would leave the Continental management blithely supposing that they were the only American businessmen involved in the negotiations.

On the morning of 6 July Belusov and his team left the Regency and went to the Hilton where they took three rooms at $95 a night. That afternoon the telephone rang in the Memphis office of Ned Cook whose company handles between 10 and 18% of American cereal exports. Tennessee-based Cook Industry acquired its wealth from the cotton trade and is a comparative newcomer to the grain market. With the Cook family holding 40% of the shares, it is the only company among the big six which sells its shares directly to the public. The extremely efficient management of its present boss Ned, a graduate of Yale, has made it one of the most vigorously expanding firms in the US. A meeting was arranged for 9.30 a.m. the next day at the Hilton.

Belusov then immediately called Philip McCaull, executive vice-chairman of the

Louis-Dreyfus Corporation, the least known of the big companies, which handles 10% of the American grain trade. It belongs to the Dreyfus family who live in Paris and who have interests in a wide variety of enterprises including glass factories, two merchant shipping companies in London and France, and the Louis-Dreyfus Bank, a supplier of considerable finance for deals with the Communist East. The Dreyfus family also controls the European Mortgage Bank (the fifth largest mortgage house in Europe) and seems to be developing a morbid sense of apprehension. The New York office recently refused to confirm to a journalist that Gerald Louis-Dreyfus was head of the group.

Belusov suggested that McCaull should meet him two days later. The following day Patrick Gardner, vice-chairman of Louis-Dreyfus, met Brunthaver in Washington. Their meeting followed exactly the same course as before. Still equally uncurious, Brunthaver assured him that the government would stick to its policy on subsidies and do everything it could to keep American wheat at the world price of $1.63 per bushel.

That same day, Ned Cook and William Sparks, director of the grain section, left Memphis international airport at five in the morning on board one of Cook Industry's luxury jets. At 8.30 the two men called the Hilton from New York airport but Belusov and Kalitenko claimed to be too busy to see them until 3.30 that afternoon.

In fact the Exportkhleb chiefs were waiting for Barry Saunders of Cargill Inc. whom they had refused to see four days before, but had called back the previous night. At 10 o'clock Saunders arrived, flanked by Melvin Middents, Cargill's wheat specialist, and Tom Connally, director of the New York office.

Over the previous two days Saunders had received a series of intriguing reports all mentioning abnormal activity in Continental Grain which was shipping exceptionally large amounts to the Russian ports. Brunthaver, whom he had seen that morning before going to the hotel, had told him nothing. At 2 o'clock Belusov signed an agreement to buy 1 million tons of red winter durum wheat from Cargill Inc. "This is the biggest contract I have ever negotiated in my life," Saunders said later.

At 2.30 Saunders left the hotel, and at 3.15 it was Ned Cook's turn to knock on the door of suite 4201. He left with an agreement from the Russians that they would buy 300,000 tons of grain and spend a couple of days with him in Memphis.

On the morning of 7 July Gerald Louis-Dreyfus and his two vice-chairmen, Theo Joseph and Patrick Gardner, made their way to the Hilton. They left again at lunch time with a contract for 750,000 tons. The same day the Soviet delegation called Karl Brasmer, vice-chairman of the Bunge Corporation, a New York subsidiary of the Bunge and Born families' Latin-American financial empire. Over the previous two years this firm had had all kinds of problems. There was an enquiry into its financial activities in the US and shortly before two of the Born brothers had been kidnapped by Argentinian guerillas and released for a ransom of $6 million. Since then the firm had transferred its headquarters to Brazil where the directors had several firm friends among the leading officers of the military régime. After word from Brasmer, Walter Klein, chairman of Bunge, arrived that evening from Sao Paulo. At 10.30 the two men met the Exportkhleb contingent and by the small hours they were signing a contract for 600,000 tons.

We have now reached 8 July. By midday Belusov, Kalitenko and Sakun were on their way to Memphis in Ned Cook's plane for a well deserved spell of relaxation. At that very moment the White House officially announced that $750 million credit would be granted to the USSR for the purchase of wheat. In theory this credit was to extend over a period of five years, but in fact the Russians used the whole sum in one year. It was at this point that the first indication of the grand operation which had begun some weeks earlier hit observers and the public.

On the morning of 9 July the Russians sailed down the Mississippi on Cook's 58-foot yacht and signed a contract for another 300,000 tons of wheat. Cook also agreed not to deliver damaged corn and to have technical experts examine the Russia-bound cargoes.

At 1 p.m. the Chicago Stock Exchange, which reflects any trends in the cereal world, quoted a bushel of wheat at $2.44. This meant that the USDA had to provide 81 cents per bushel in export subsidies.

On 11 July the economic services of the White House asked Brunthaver for a report on the size and details of the deals, but he was unable to give them anything more than vague indications, with no specific tonnage. On 12 July, after a detour to Florida where Cook owns a villa at Palm Beach, the Russians returned to New York. On 13 July, convinced that they had succeeded in their mission by exploiting the deficiencies in the market economy to the full, they left the United States for Moscow via Amsterdam.

In fact their activities, though admirable from the point of view of trade tactics, dealt a serious blow to the American working classes who found themselves having to pay for the deals.

However, the clever machinations of Belusov and his companions lost some of their sting when they arrived back in Moscow to learn that the Soviet experts' estimates had been exceedingly over-optimistic. The total amount of grain needed to feed the nation was actually 60 million tons, far more than the sum contracted for in the United States.

On 29 July Belusov and Kalitenko returned to the New York Hilton by way of Canada where they had bought 3.5 million tons. In the space of three days they purchased a further 300,000 tons from Cook Industry, 1.5 million tons from the Dreyfus Company, 1 million tons from Cargill and 550,000 tons from the Swiss group Garnac Grain Company.

The whole business was like a bedroom farce. Each company went through a series of delicate manoeuvres to obtain the necessary grain without threatening the stability of the market, while blissfully ignorant of the amounts being sold by its competitors and of the total sum of Soviet purchases. This time the part of the deceived husband was played by Peter Petersen, the American Secretary of State for Trade. On 31 July in Moscow he announced that his talks with the Kremlin leaders on prospects for widening Soviet–American trade had reached a stalemate. Petersen and his ministry had been told nothing at all about the negotiations which ended the same day in New York.

Altogether more than 19 million tons were to be removed from the American market.

But George Schultz, Herbert Stein and Gaspar Weinberger, Nixon's economic three musketeers, were nervous. News of the deals was beginning to leak out and they were worried about the effect on national politics. The total amount of export subsidies looked suspiciously like a raid on the Ministry of Finance. Arthur Burns, President of the Federal Bank, stressed the possible inflationary repercussions. The Bakers Union had already expressed fears of a rise in the price of flour which would have to be recovered in increased bread costs.

The farmers were indignant. Despite their apparent wealth, they bitterly reaffirmed their dependence on the grain companies—deals made at the Chicago Stock Exchange are always concluded in advance, while the crop is still standing.

Obviously the price fixed at the time of agreement is based on the crop; but it is even more dependent on the likelihood of market sales and only the big companies have access to all the relevant information. Thus the uninformed farmers of Texas and Oklahoma had sold in June at $1.40 a bushel and lost millions of dollars. In any case, the companies can pressurize recalcitrant farmers into surrender in a wide variety of ways. Agreements with the transport firms have given them total control over road and rail transport. Unless he is prepared to see his harvest rotting in the fields, the small farmer has no option but to accept price cuts of 20, 30 and sometimes even 50 cents on every bushel of wheat sold.

Minister of Agriculture, Earl Butz, and Minister of the Economy, William Simon, who made his fortune in Salomon Brothers office, tended towards a passive, optimistic attitude. They maintained that, whatever the total figure, these sales would have very little impact on domestic prices. But on 22 August the final decision was made. On 24 August, Charles Pence, one of the directors of the USDA, called the managers of the big companies and summoned them to a meeting in Washington the next day. On 25 August Carol Brunthaver set out the new governmental policy on exports.

The companies were to have one week to clear up all contracts made before 23 August for which subsidies of up to 47 cents a bushel would be available. After that time the government would refuse to peg the price at $1.63 any longer. This administrative measure was actually a legal dodge intended to calm the ruffled US farmers, many of whom had voted for Richard Nixon.

In fact the Agriculture Ministry decision was a waste of effort. Practically all the contracts had already been cleared and the Soviets had embarked on the second stage of their operations, having swelled the grain companies' coffers by more than a billion dollars. The wait-and-see policy adopted by the government had cost the American tax payers nearly $210 million in export subsidies.

In September Soviet experts made an equally discreet trip to London where they made contact with the shipping companies of the Baltic Exchange which handles two thirds of world sea transport.

These negotiations were held in total secrecy. Even Pim Junior and Co., an English subsidiary of Continental Grain, never knew how much grain Michael Fribourg had sold. From this point, however, things began to go downhill for the Russians. Their careful plans were continually foiled by the harsh facts. The New York agreements had allowed for one third of the grain to be shipped to Soviet ports by American boats, one third by Soviet boats and the remainder by independent companies. The Russians soon realized that there were not enough boats suitable for this kind of freight available. They would have to go to Amsterdam or Oslo to find more ships. The news leaked out and gathered strength as it spread. Within three days the freight charges quoted in the Baltic Exchange rose from $9 to $13 a ton.

Added to these financial difficulties was a series of logistical problems. The supertankers initially chartered had to be ruled out when it transpired that Soviet ports could not handle any shipping with a greater capacity than 100,000 tons.

At the end of December 1972 the first boats reached Odessa, Riga and Leningrad to find overcrowded ports with ancient, out-dated equipment. Some boats had to wait more than a month before being unloaded, which meant increased freight costs for the Russians. There were not enough storage silos in the ports and no facilities for drying the grain as must be done to prevent it rotting. All the necessary machinery was in Siberia. Central planning turned to pathetic improvization. Departing trains were emptied and goods dumped on the quays to deteriorate. Every available railcar, however antiquated or dilapidated, was requisitioned to take the precious grain to the Northern plains and bring it back to the ports after drying.

There was worse to come, however. As a number of holds were opened the stench of rotting and damaged cargoes rose to the noses of the swindled Communists. The maritime administration had increased the subsidies traditionally granted to American shipowners so that they remain competitive on the world market. Since this assistance was given per round trip the owners had connived with the port authorities to send their boats out half empty and thus increase the number of sailings. During the year 1973 they received $55 million from the American government.

More than anything else, the misfortunes suffered by the Soviets illustrate the efficiency of the system set up by the companies to keep their operations secret. In some ports, like New Orleans, they endeavour to work round the inspectors who perform quality checks on the grain. Whole cargoes of broken, crushed and sour-smelling grain are shipped fraudulently out of the port. Bunge Corporation admits to having spent more than $3 million in two years on bribing controllers to sign false certificates and turn a blind eye to poor products when quality checking. Twenty-one employees of the Swiss Garnac Grain Corporation's US subsidiary have been charged in the courts with fraud. Cook Industry has been accused of "falsifying the transport, nature and load of several cargoes" in cahoots with the Mississippi River Grain Elevator Company of New Orleans. Embezzlement of this kind cost the Soviet Union hundreds of thousands of dollars. Two officials from the Ministry of Agriculture went to Odessa to examine the cargoes. The wheat delivered was of inferior quality to that ordered and in certain cases whole boatloads had perished and were infested with weevil.

The French Louis-Dreyfus company refused to reply to a Senate commission of enquiry and appointed Nathaniel Samuels, Nixon's Under-Secretary of State at the Treasury and a former banker with Kuhn and Co., head of its American subsidiary.

The Big Five based their defense on the theme of "baffled honesty." "We have the general interest at heart," said Erwin Kelm, president of Cargill, for example, "but we realize that the public does not seem to understand the services we render. It is very frustrating."

The ineffable Clarence Palmby, vice-chairman of Continental Grain, went one step further. "Our bankers put their heads in their hands when they see the small profit margins we sometimes make."

The results from Cook Industry, the only company whose operations are known in detail, give us a pretty accurate picture of the impact Soviet purchases made on the grain companies' profits. For the tax year ending 31 May 1972 (before the Soviet contracts were signed) the company's net profits were $7.9 million, rising to $53.6 million in 1973 and $91.1 million in 1974.

Faced with the market verdict the firms have adopted a defensive strategy. They know that consumers hold them responsible for much of the inflation and the increased price of foodstuffs which has more than doubled in four years. The farmers find their protectionism increasingly harder to bear. The present price quoted on the Chicago Stock Exchange is around $3.80 a bushel, not including any government subsidy.

Like every political power, the Executive has lagged behind public opinion. A five-year agreement with the USSR allows for 8 million tons of grain a year to be sold without government interference. But this is a pure formality since the government controls neither agriculture nor exports. Even so, the Department of State felt obliged to dispel any misunderstandings. "There is no question of trying to use these grain sales to obtain concessions from the USSR in areas such as the field of individual liberties. Wheat should not be used as a political weapon while the ink on the Helsinki documents is still wet."

The directors of the grain companies are like those shy men who become awkward when too much attention is directed their way. They know that their position is only temporary and that when the present political guerrilla warfare is over they will return to the anonymity which guarantees their efficiency. They can already comfort themselves with thoughts of the faithful USSR which steadfastly continues through all the double-crossing and fiddles to sell its stocks of gold and borrow to buy American grain. Presumably the Kremlin leaders think that resignation to these humiliations will keep them in power. The 25th Party Congress concerned itself with damaged potatoes. Failures in this particular area of rural production cost Dimitri Polianski, a friend of Chelepin, his job as Minister of Agriculture and his place in the Soviet Politburo's club for decrepit old dodderers. In this way the faults of the system as a whole could be attributed to the policy of one man.

By 5 July 1975, a few weeks before the Helsinki conference and seven months before the opening of the Moscow Congress, Soviet sales of gold in Zurich had reached $100 million. At the same time the foreign trade bank of the USSR effected a medium term loan of 350 millions on the highly speculative Eurodollar market through the Soviet Moscow Narodny Bank in London. On 20 July Cook Industry sold 2 million tons of wheat and Cargill Inc. 1.2 million tons, together worth more than $460 million. Some days later the Russians bought 1 million tons from Cook, then another million in Canada and 750,000 tons in Australia. Soon after, details of the agreement made on 16 July with Continental Grain for 4.5 million tons of maize and 1.1 million tons of barley began to leak out.

It is generally estimated that the Russians will have bought 30 million tons on the world market during 1977.

Since the 1974 Jackson Amendment made it impossible for the Soviet Union to benefit from special conditions of sale and long term credit, Moscow has been forced to use its gold mines and oil wells to pay for its purchases. Although Soviet manufacture of hydrocarbides has increased by 150%, sales to satellite countries have been reduced, and accounts have to be settled in dollars for the sake of proletarian internationalism. This extraordinary regression to a system of barter more suited to the most backward countries bodes ill for the agricultural future of the Communist State which may well find itself on a level with India in a few years.

However, some credit is due to the Soviet leaders for their remarkable understanding towards countries of dubious political morality. Podgorny, Kosygin and Brezhnev can teach the whole world a lesson in tolerance. After discussion with Franco's Spain and the colonels' Greece, they have now turned their sights to the South African régime. On 20 February 1976 they bought 3 million tons of maize in Pretoria to feed Soviet livestock, a deal which could hardly be further from the Party cell's feverish discussions on the best methods of destroying "racist, Fascist and imperialist states."

Soviet officials may not be very farsighted but they do have a well developed self-preservation instinct and are well aware that they can still go a lot further along the road to compromise. They have invited Western businessmen, the brief-case pioneers, to collaborate in the creation of a coherent environment designed to check the present sliding into an endemic state of penury.

Jarvis International Construction and Butler Corp. of Kansas City are building several vast grain silos. Large quantities of pesticides and herbicides have been bought from the Stauffer Chemical Company of Westport and from Rohem and Haas of Philadelphia. Triple "F" Feed of Texas, of Brenwood, is about to conclude a $25 million deal for the production of concentrated protein for animal feedstuffs, while the FMC Corporation of Chicago is working on acclimatizing new varieties of tomato and improving harvesting systems in Moldavia, the only Soviet Republic partly governed by members of the KGB.

The Minister for Chemical Affairs, Leonid Kostandov, has signed contracts involving more than $600 million with PPG, Union Carbide, Du Pont and Dow Chemical. A huge complex for the production of ammonia fertilizers is to be built in the Kuybyshev region in cooperation with Arnold Hammer's Occidental Petroleum. The Russians will pay for this by exporting part of their product to the United States. The Export–Import Bank recently agreed to a loan of $180 million to help this project go through.

Furthermore, on 18 December 1976 the Soviet Union asked for the use of American reconnaissance satellites to obtain an exact analysis of their 1977 harvest—an interesting point when one considers that the two "Landsats" in question have been used as spy satellites for some years by the CIA.

3.

The Financial Web of Vodka-Cola

When the cracks began to appear in Michele Sindona's financial empire, first in the United States and then in Italy, they revealed a fantastic web of tax evasion, corruption and bribery of political staffs which grew more comprehensive with each revelation. The Sindona file now provides a perfect microcosmic cross-section through which to examine the activities of that multinational organization of stateless financiers who form a bridge between the big companies and the tax havens.

It all began in New York in the office of French-born André Meyer, the "wise man of Wall Street." Forty years as American president of Lazard Frères et Cie had given Meyer a reputation for levelheadedness and shrewdness which enabled him to amass a personal fortune valued at more than $200 million.

The Lazard Frères Bank played a very active part in the transfer of low-interest capitalist credits to the Eastern countries.

Meyer provided a link between the Rockefeller family and the French banks. To take one example, Lazard Frères was the largest shareholder in the Banque de Paris et des Pays-Bas, which opened a branch in New York called Parisbas Corporation, and directed by Robert Craft, vice-president of the Chase International. This important branch of the Chase Manhattan numbered André Meyer, David Rockefeller and John McCloy, former president of the World Bank, among its directors.

André Meyer had a seat on the managerial boards of about sixty multinationals. He handled the personal fortunes of the Rockefellers, Giovanni Agnelli and the Kennedys and looked after the interests of such disparate clients at the Vatican and ITT.

Harold Geneen, the ITT boss, and Meyer had an open and efficient working relationship. Meyer's right hand man, Felix Rohaytn, the infant prodigy of high finance, was on the ITT board and played an outstanding part in the firm's diversification program and its strategy of buying up lame ducks. In 1965 Rohaytn negotiated ITT's take-over of the Avis carhire company for $52 million. In 1969 the young master of the joint-stock company turned his steely gaze to the insurance sector.

To commercial empires continually on the look-out for new sources of liquid assets, the insurance companies offer the advantages of regular receipts of cash through premium collection and enormous portfolios of shares.

In 1969 negotiations began to buy the Connecticut-based Hartford company, the fifth largest US insurance company, with assets of $2 billion. This deal would bring ITT the richest morsel it had ever consumed. Eugene Black, former president of the World Bank and then manager of ITT and director of the Chase Manhattan, had to reassure the Hartford board. "You'll see," he told them, "I know no other company with a better looking management than ITT."

The director of the antitrust division, Richard McLaren, a former Chicago lawyer specializing in the defense of the big companies, did not appear to share Black's views. Since taking up office he had considered it an urgent necessity to stop conglomerates merging because, as he said, "this concentration leads to a dangerous disruption of the economic and social order." He therefore stepped up the number of objections to and counter-enquiries into ITT's appropriation deals.

On 7 August 1970, Ned Gerrity Sr, vice-president of ITT and director of the company's external relations, sent a short letter to his friend, the then Vice-President Spiro Agnew, expressing concern about McLaren's independence of tone and action. Soon after Harold Geneen met with John Mitchell, the Justice Minister. During their cordial exchange of views, Geneen, a generous Republican, recalled the high price of a presidential electoral campaign and Mitchell assured him that Richard Nixon saw no reason why the acquisition of Hartford should not go through.

On 24 August Trade Minister Maurice Stans received John Ryan, a Washington lawyer described as ITT's ear to the ground in the federal capital. Ryan then reported to William R. Merriman, vice-president of ITT that "Stans and Mitchell are going to ask Kleindienst [deputy Justice Minister convicted in the Watergate affair] to do something about McLaren. There was a rhetorical question raised: "How will McLaren react, or if you like, how good a Republican will he be?"

At the same time Rohaytn and Geneen were bringing off their coup. In violation of all existing antitrust legislation, and despite the suspicions of the commission on Stock Exchange operations, ITT secretly bought 1,700,000 Hartford shares for $30 million, thereby acquiring a controlling majority. It was a shrewd tactical move which blocked any hope of retreat for the anxious, scrupulous or reticent Hartford men.

This kind of manipulation demanded great discretion. The shares had to remain frozen until the Nixon administration had completed its impending legalization of the deal. Selling might give rise to speculation and force ITT to buy back at a higher price than the figure it had unofficially paid.

André Meyer, who was totally at home in the international financial scene, got the Central Bank of Italy to agree that he might discuss depositing the shares in the Mediobanca which handled some of the Vatican interests. The director of the Mediobanca, Michele Sindona, a slim and active fifty-year-old Sicilian, had acquired a reputation as a live wire over the previous few years. While waiting for the merger to be agreed, the Mediobanca agreed to keep the shares as if they owned them, for a commission of $1,300,000. The shares were transferred through the Zurich branch of the Dreyfus bank. Enrico Cuccia, one of the directors of the Mediobanca and a close friend of Ugo La Malfa, the chairman of the Italian Republican Party, obtained the necessary authorization for this deal from the Trade Minister.

Sindona later claimed that Enrico Cuccia had cooked the books at the Mediobanca and that he, Sindona, knew nothing about the details of the Hartford–ITT deal.

Finally the story had a happy ending. McLaren, the antitrust man who had made the mistake of believing himself useful, was dismissed. In 1972 ITT was busy making detailed preparations for the Republican convention at San Diego and donated $400,000 to the committee for the re-election of Nixon. No sooner had the nice President been returned to office than all the nasty things happening to the poor ITT management stopped as if by magic.

The Hartford–ITT deal was authorized. In two years the insurance company grew from fifth to third largest in the US. Its profits increased by 60% and in no time it was accounting for one quarter of ITT's profits.

But the most important thing to emerge from this episode was the willingness and malleability of the Italian financier Sindona, a man committed to creating an empire based on holding companies.

In 1974, the year of his downfall, Sindona controlled 146 companies dotted round such tax shelters as Liechtenstein, Luxemburg, Switzerland, Panama and Liberia. Sindona's semi-public activities began in 1953 when he joined in preparations for the American landings in Sicily orchestrated by the gangster Lucky Luciano. In 1946 he joined the triumphant and all-pervasive Christian Democrat Party, to which he remained closely attached. His sociable manner won him friends across the whole spectrum of Italian politicians from a former General Secretary of the center right party to the present President of the Council, Giulio Andreotti, though none among them were Communists. Within a few years he had moved on from Christian Democrat headquarters to the Pope's chambers of audience. Sindona impressed the Vatican officials as a responsible man at a time when they were concerned about the need to internationalize their affairs and find more profitable sources of income.

There is a joke which could be applied to the Holy See. Suppose that the Vatican officials are planning to reorganize their business. They ask the US McKinsey study center to compile an in-depth investigation to assess the profitability of their various activities. After months of minute examination a report lands on the Pope's desk. It says "Give up religion and devote yourself to your share portfolio."

Despite its harsh words about capitalism, the Vatican is actually involved in such capitalist institutions as the Rothschild Bank in France, the Crédit Suisse in Zurich and London, the Chase Manhattan, the Banker Trust and the Morgan Bank in the United States. In the US alone the Vatican has large share holdings in General Motors, Shell, Gulf Oil, General Electric, Bethlehem Steel, IBM and TWA.

Before the arrival of Sindona, the Vatican had interests in the Italian IANA (Italo–American Nuovi Alberghi) which owns the Rome Hilton and the CIGA (Compagnia Italiana Grandi Alberghi) which controls most of the Italian luxury hotels. One of the Vatican's reliable friends, Massimo Spada was chairman of Lancia, vice-president of the powerful Banco di Roma, the Italian banking institute (with 10 billion lire capital), and on the board of the Société Méridionale Financière (122 billion lire capital), of the Central Financial Institute (150 billion lire capital). Massimo Spada and the Vatican were both on the board of Finsider, a state-owned group with a capital of 195 million lire, which produces 90% of all Italian steel through twenty-four companies. Finsider was one part of the very powerful IRI, a state body formed under the Fascist régime which controls, among others, the Italian shipping companies, Alitalia, the Autostrade del Sol, the telephone system and Alfa Romeo, a firm in which the Vatican was also a shareholder. IRI also had a 90% interest in the Santo Spirito bank, but its chairman, the Marchese Giovanni Battista Sacchetti, and its director, Luigi Mennini, were two of the best known Vatican bigwigs. Similarly, Vittorino Veronese and professor Silvio Golzio, chairmen respectively of the Banco di Roma and the Italian Credit Bank, two extremely important Italian financial establishments, were members of the wealthy "Pius XII Foundation for the lay apostleship" created in 1953. This institution, of which Massimo Spada was chairman until 1969, is now run by Cardinal Villot, a close collaborator of Paul VI.

Another member of this pious business world in the pre-Sindona days was Count Enrico Galeazzi, a trusted friend of Pius XII. Nicknamed the lay pope, for a number of years Galeazzi held the decisive post of "governor of the State and City of the Vatican," a job usually reserved for members of the clergy. His aristocratic origins and cosmopolitan education soon enabled him to interest a number of American businessmen in the investment policy of the Holy See. A close friend of the ultra-conservative Cardinal Spellman of New York, Galeazzi also had a long-standing friendship with Joseph Kennedy, the father of the clan. Galeazzi was a director of Invest, an investment and credit company with 25 billion lire capital.

In 1968 he moved to the management of the Generale Immobiliare, one of the world's largest construction companies which was owned by the Vatican. In 1958 the company had sold a large part of the 102 million square feet of land it owned in the Rome area to the Italian Olympic Committee for the Games at a speculative rate. It also obtained exclusive rights to build some of the Olympic fittings, the motorway linking them to Rome and fifteen sport complexes. In France the Vatican company controlled the Société Immobilière des Champs Elysées which built the Pan Am offices, and in 1968 it bought 70% of the shares in Watergate Improvement Inc. of Washington. This enabled the Generale Immobiliare to build and own the luxury building complex on the banks of the Potomac which housed the Democratic electoral headquarters in 1972.

In accord with the principles of economic prosperity, the Vatican could prove extremely accommodating towards atheistic materialism. One of its companies, Ceramica Pozzi, with 23 billion lire capital, supplies Italy with sanitary equipment, taps and bidets. In 1967, while Cardinal Mindszenty, the archbishop of Hungary was kicking his heels inside the US embassy in Budapest where he had taken refuge after the 1956 uprising, the Vatican, through its "Foreign Affairs Minister" Mgr Casaroli, was reaching an agreement with the Communist government for Ceramica Pozzi to build a factory there.

In early 1969 Sindona entered the financial world of the Vatican. The Holy See held a large share in Snias Viscosa, a chemical group specializing in the manufacture of synthetic fibres and textiles. Snias Viscosa had always used the powerful Hambro's banking group as its financial agent in London and Hambro's had a partnership in Italy with the Banca Privata Finanziara owned by Sindona. Sindona also worked as a consultant to Hambro's investment company, Westminster Hambro's Trust Ltd, owned jointly by Hambro's and the Westminster Bank.

Born in Patti, near Messina, Michele Sindona studied law before setting up a tax consultant's office in Milan which was much used by representatives of the multinationals seeking to invest in Italy. Many of these companies settled their accounts with Sindona in shares. By 1957–1958 he had more than fifty foreign clients and soon found himself with a considerable personal fortune which he prudently transferred to a fictitious company called Fasco AG in Liechtenstein. This nominal company was to remain Sindona's advance base while he built his financial empire. In 1959 Fasco AG obtained a majority interest in the Banca Privata Finanziara, which apart from its connections with Hambro's Bank, had also formed a preferential partnership with the Continental Illinois Bank of Chicago, whose owner-president David Kennedy became Nixon's Finance Minister in 1969. Sindona's activities on both sides of the Atlantic suited the large tax payers' long felt need for a means of evading tax.

In June 1969 a waltz of portfolios began. The Vatican sold some of its shares in the Generale Immobiliare to the Paribas Transcompany of Luxemburg, which was connected with the Rothschilds and controlled by the powerful Banque de Paris et des Pays-Bas. A month earlier Sindona had bought a package representing 3.5% of all the shares in the Vatican construction company from the Italian general insurance group. This gave him a seat on the firm's board on 14 June 1969. Seven months later he used the Luxembourg holding company to buy a one third share in the Generale Immobiliare.

It was then that the Holy See began using him as its chief financial consultant. He imported into Italy a typically Anglo-Saxon institution known in the US as an "investment" bank and in England as a "merchant" bank. In a world where mutual interests are interwoven through personal relationships, the little Sicilian made full use of his gratifyingly distinguished image and of an extraordinary coincidence. His friend Graham Martin, the anti-Communist American ambassador to Rome, named him "man of the year." Two years later *Time Magazine* described him as "the greatest Italian since

Mussolini." Through David Kennedy Sindona met Paul Marcinkus, an American pre-
late of fifty-one with the athletic physique of a playboy and a reputation for being an
excellent golfer and something of an adventurer. Marcinkus and Kennedy both came
from the same town of Cicero, Illinois, and had known each other for years.

Working as foreign travels organizer for Paul VI, the American bishop soon found
favour with the Holy Father. In that closed world where personal rivalry and conflict of
ideas are just as fierce and exaggerated as in the Kremlin and the White House, the
clever Marcinkus looked like "a man on the way up." Supported by Mgr Pasquale
Macchi, the pope's personal secretary, in 1969 Marcinkus was appointed head of the
Institute for Religious Works, the Vatican bank. At first sight the Catholic banking
house appeared commendably austere. It handled 10,500 accounts on behalf of individuals and religious orders. The pope's account was number 16.16.

In fact Marcinkus was in charge of a vast, diversified, construction and property
empire scattered over a dozen countries. He also had control of the Vatican's secret
funds, its gold reserves at Fort Knox, and totally bypassed Mgr Giuseppe Caprio, the
sixty-year-old administrative secretary of the Vatican's patrimony who had been in
charge of the Holy See's investment policy until then.

In a few months Marcinkus's managerial methods, his contempt of prerogatives and
the way he trod on official toes had won him a fine body of enemies within the change-
less world of the Roman Curia. He also had opponents among the laity, including figures
like the Marchese Sacchetti and Luigi Mennini who were worried about Sindona's
influence. In fact Marcinkus and Sindona had come up against the eternal problem,
faced by all property owners: how to shift currency and assets out of the country without
encountering national government controls.

Since 1963 the Vatican had been living under a delayed sentence. The influence of the
more permissive Christian Democrats had allowed it to remain exempt from the tax on
dividends, or *cedolare*, instituted in 1962 by the center left cabinet. Over the years
various sectors of public opinion had found the annual renewal of this non-liability
increasingly intolerable. In 1967 the weekly *Espresso* described the Vatican as "the
biggest tax evader in post-war Italy."

In 1968 the government of Giovanni Leone, later President of the Republic,
announced that this measure might be subject to reexamination over the course of the
next two years and that the Vatican might then be obliged to settle its arrears. Marcinkus was given the task of extricating the Vatican from its foreign financial commitments and steering the resultant capital through a series of transnational wanderings.
The broadness of Sindona's organization suited this kind of operation perfectly. The sale
of the Generale Immobiliare was only the first phase.

In 1971 Sindona opened a public bid to try and take control of Bastogi, the largest
Italian holding company with assets estimated at more than $200 million. Bastogi
controlled a large share of Montedison, the state-owned chemical giant. Hambro's
Bank, the Continental Illinois and the American Morgan Bank which had always had
connections with the Vatican all supported Sindona in this effort.

The government was quick to react. Guido Carli, then governor of the Bank of Italy
and who seemed the only rational and stable figure in a political world punctuated by
continual governmental crises, blocked the manoeuvre. In fact there was a systematic
distrust of Sindona among the various political and administrative groups which
remembered his early activities and blamed him for having helped American and other
foreign companies acquire control over various sectors of the Italian economy.

In the face of this obstacle Sindona made a complete about-turn. His activities were
confined within narrow limits. His Liechtenstein-based holding company Fasco AG

controlled his Italian interests (the Banca Privata Finanziara, the Banca Unione and the Generale Immobiliare); his Swiss bank, the Geneva "finance bank"; the Wolf Bank in Federal Germany; a finance company based in the Bahamas (Edilcentro) and the Rome newspaper *Daily American*.

Another holding company, Fasco International SA, also set up in a tax haven, Luxemburg, controlled his American interests. And it was towards America that he now directed his offensive.

In 1972 he bought 21.6% of the shares of the Franklin National Bank from a holding company for $40 million. The Franklin, with assets of over $5 billion and 104 branches in Manhattan and Long Island, was the twenty-first largest bank in America. At that time speculation on the dollar was in full spate. Marcinkus transferred a considerable proportion of Vatican funds into Sindona's new set up in the hope of making a quick killing. A publicity campaign was launched to attract small investors. "$2.50 a month," read the ridiculous billboards, "makes you an owner of the Franklin National."

In fact, to compete with his more powerful rivals, Sindona had evolved a policy of lending to businesses at extremely generous interest rates. Unable to finance these activities solely through over-the-counter deposits, he borrowed continually on the highly speculative Eurodollar market, a source of hot currency over which the government had no control. $500 billion exempt from any credit restrictions lay waiting for businesses and banks looking for short term liquid capital. This particular water-hole for the thirsty pachyderms of high finance was haunted by the Communist banks which had been the first to draw water there.

The revolutionary comrades' interest in capitalist finance dated back to their political infancy. In 1919 the Soviets set up the Moscow Narodny Bank in London; it now stands at 24–32 King William Street and is still owned entirely by the USSR. In 1921 they opened the commercial Bank for Northern Europe at 79–81 boulevard Haussmann, Paris. The Eurobank, so called from its telegraphic address, was behind the creation of the Eurodollar market.

Over the last six years the wind of détente has blown a number of Communist banking houses towards the artificial tax havens of the bourgeois world, including the Comecon Bank, the East–West United Bank in Luxembourg.

But the Moscow Narodny Bank and the Eurobank still do most to further the policy of close and all-embracing collaboration with the West. At the present time the Eurobank, which belongs to the USSR State Bank and the Foreign Trade Bank, is the largest foreign banking house in Paris. Two and a half times larger than its nearest rival the Bank of America, the Eurobank has regular dealings with such important capitalist establishments as the Chase Manhattan, the Swiss Bank Corporation, the Canadian Imperial Bank of Commerce, the Morgan Guaranty Trust and the First National Bank of Chicago, to name but a few. It acts as a depository for the funds of the French Communist Party and handles the Party's financial interests. The Eurobank also plays a vital part in the expansion of trade to the Communist bloc. 40% of its business consists of import–export transactions, most of them concerning the USSR. Only 15% of its activities are connected with France. 45% of its dealings are based on various Eurodollar market operations, which has given it a name as "the bankers' bank."

So, a bank belonging to a Communist world where moral arguments still run very high is devoting most of its energies to speculation and defrauding national governments. No amount of legalistic formalism or jargon will change this state of affairs. The Eurobank is officially entered on the register of the Paris Chamber of Commerce. But attempts to argue that this makes it a French bank are no more valid than saying that the Crédit Lyonnais is Spanish because it has a branch in Madrid, or that opening offices in Moscow has made the Chase Manhattan Russian.

The hard facts are staring all of us in the face, even those of us who still believe the Kremlin leaders' revolutionary verbiage about the imminent fall of capitalism. The fact that Communist banks work in close symbiosis with the great capitalists makes any such eventuality highly unlikely. The relations forged by their transactions permit access to a certain amount of confidential and top secret information about the economic health and prospects of the West. Until now the Communist banks do not appear to have used such sources to undermine their so-called ideological opponents. The continued confidence placed in them by Stock Exchanges and financial establishments does not say much for their revolutionary faith.

This permits speculative coups like that carried out by the Soviet banking network in Switzerland late in December 1976. In less than half an hour the Zurich Wochzod Bank by careful telephone sales managed to unload between 300 million and 500 million dollars against Swiss Francs. Sold in "small" packets of 10 to 20 million each to different Swiss banks, the dollar fell from 2.45 to 2.42 providing the Soviets with a huge speculative profit before vigorous intervention by the Swiss National Bank stabilized the price at around 2.437. It was the biggest operation of its kind in Swiss history. Profits could have been from 12 to 15 million capitalist Swiss Francs.

The history of the Moscow Narodny, with which the violently anti-Communist Sindona carried through various deals, also raises some interesting points. It is owned by fifteen shareholders, all of them Soviet state organizations, and yet permissive legislation magically transforms it into a London-based British bank, subject to English law and to the control of the Bank of England. After opening a first branch in Beirut, in 1971 the Moscow Narodny set up another in Singapore where President Lee Kwan Yew pursues a dual policy of harsh anti-Communist repression and encouragingly lax fiscal laws. In 1975 the Moscow Narodny was involved, within a consortium, in twenty-one medium term credit deals together amounting to more than $2,645 million. This gives a fairly clear picture of its vitality. But its connections with various highly suspicious characters finally led to difficulties for its South East Asia base. Since 1971 the Singapore branch had conducted a very efficient offensive strategy. With net assets of $400 million, by late 1974 it could claim assets of over $1,100 million, far exceeding all its American rivals including the First National City Bank and the Chase Manhattan. It was actively involved in the property speculation boom not only in Singapore but also in Hong Kong, Thailand and Indonesia.

One of the bank's most faithful clients was the Mosbert Holding Ltd, a conglomerate registered in Hong Kong and directed by Amos Dawe, a Sino-Canadian. Over the previous ten years Dawe had acquired more than 200 industrial, trading and financial companies scattered round South East Asia and Australia, with a total value of more than $380 million. In 1974 Dawe negotiated the purchase of three Californian banks. He bought a majority share holding in the Peninsular National Bank of Burlingame, by paying $3 million to the Central Banking System Inc. of Oakland. The following summer he spent $9 million on two more West Coast banks. Soon after this he went bankrupt and investigations revealed that the Moscow Narodny Bank alone had advanced him more than $40 million for various highly illegal operations. To avoid any crisis of confidence, Gosbank (the Soviet State Bank) and the Vneshtorgbank (the Foreign Trade Bank), both chief shareholders, decided to give the Moscow Narodny Bank a capital injection of $16 million. It has lost huge amounts to speculating brokers and real estate plungers in the UK in the last few years.

The Moscow Narodny Bank was burned again in 1977 when its claim to two pieces of property in Hong Kong that were collateral for a loan went sour. The Russian bank filed a writ claiming that Hong Kong real estate developer Edward Wong Wing-Cheung owed it $7.6 million for a 1973 loan. The loan came to light when Wong's $430 million scheme to develop a resort suddenly collapsed. The troubled loan is embarrassing to Moscow Narodny because the bank is a prime target of Peking, which is worried about Soviet attempts to "infiltrate" the colony's economy from its very anti-communist base in Singapore.

At the same time the Soviets reduced the activities of the Donau Bank in Vienna, set up to help finance trade with the East. The manager, Vasili Morsin, had lent $102 million in one year, including $9 million to Austrian companies so unhealthy that they soon went bankrupt.

It would be only fair to wish the Moscow Narodny better luck in its future choice of customers and investments. It recently opened an office in Moscow to finance capitalist deals for multinationals. It remains to be seen whether misfortune will dog it there.

In November 1972 Harold Gleason, a former public relations man, set up a meeting between David Kennedy, then a banker, Sindona and Maurice Stans. Sindona told Stans that he was considering offering $1 million to the campaign for Nixon's re-election. His previous generosity to sections of the Italian Christian Democratic Party was well known. Sindona was hoping that the International Revue Service's enquiry into his financing and capital transfer methods would come to nothing.

A month earlier Sindona and his partner Carlo Bordoni had invested $15 million of Franklin capital on the Eurodollar market. Compared with the bank's total assets of $5 billion this figure might seem modest. But the Franklin's net domestic capital only amounted to $19 million. The $15 million was transferred in two stages. It went first on 10 and 24 October 1972 to Interbanca, a Milanese banking house of which Sindona was both director and shareholder. It was then divided between the Amincor Bank AG based in Switzerland and the Banca Unione of Milan, both owned by Sindona, to be invested in the Eurodollar market for a short period renewable every six months.

In early 1973 the future of the Franklin looked doubtful. The losses resulting from prolonged and unlucky speculation appeared vast. James E. Smith, the "currency controller," who belonged to a body independent of the Treasury, was told to examine the bank's future prospects. But Smith was basically an ambitious young man, working to make the brand image of the Association of American Bankers more attractive to the Capitol élite. He was a protégé of David Kennedy, to whom he owed his job. His short report on the Franklin was exaggeratedly optimistic.

In early May, however, the bank suffered a voltage reduction which many interpreted as the beginning of the end. Its losses over the previous four months amounted to $40.4 million. One weekend Paul Luftig, then president of the Franklin, suggested to Sindona that he agrees to the recovery scheme put forward by the Manufacturer's Hanover Trust whereby they would grant a loan of $30 million for an interest in the bank. With Smith's support, Sindona refused, sacked Luftig and appointed Harold Gleason manager of the bank. Sindona was hoping for a $50 million injection of capital which would benefit the 20,000 shareholders and restore confidence in the bank, or so he thought. He also hoped to increase his own 21.6% holding to a controlling majority of the bank.

This scheme produced exactly the opposite effect. Rumours of decline and bankruptcy spread from the closed world of Wall Street to a wider public. A number of depositors rushed to the bank's branches to recover their money. In one day $325 million, or 11% of the total deposits, were withdrawn.

David Kennedy went to London to meet the directors of the National Westminster, one of the big British clearing banks. He asked them to buy the Franklin or at least to invest the $50 million promised by Sindona. In the face of such a serious situation the

National Westminster cautiously refused to commit itself. While in London, Kennedy also met Marcinkus who had come specially from Rome on hearing of the dangers of a crash. The two men met in the Grosvenor House Hotel. Rumours concerning the Franklin affair had reached Italy and had put Marcinkus in an awkward position with regard to the agents of the Roman Curia. His main fear was that the losses recorded might have repercussions beyond the United States and affect the various "Sindona operations" in which the Vatican had large investments.

On his return Kennedy met Sindona in his New York home at the Pierre Hotel near Park Avenue. The two men asked James Smith, Joseph Barr, former Secretary of State at the Treasury for Johnson, and Morris Shapiro, director of a lawyers office in Wall Street with a sizeable interest in the Franklin, to try and work out a plan which would keep the bank autonomous. They all knew that they could count on support, and secret support at that, from the Federal Reserve Bank of New York. Between May and July the Federal Reserve granted the Franklin loans totalling an extraordinary $1 billion, at exremely low interest rates. Obviously the New York money dealers' corporation had no desire to see the kinds of activities which formed party of their daily grind exposed to the public. Smith, Barr and Shapiro hoped to redevelop the Franklin on a regional basis, while restricting its Long Island activities. But this scheme never got off the ground.

Arthur Burns, president of the Federal Reserve, was prepared to abandon Sindona. In the presence of Finance Minister William Simon, he spoke vehemently to James Smith. "What will you do if the bad figures continue and lead to a run on your bank? Any loss of faith would destroy our whole financial system."

In July the Franklin was virtually declared insolvent and the whole business was put into the hands of the Federal Deposit Insurance (the FDI), the government agency which guarantees bank deposits up to $40,000 on an individual account, for all the banks within the Federal Reserve System.

During the summer Frank Wille, president of the FDI had talks with representatives of the seventeen big banks most likely to refloat the Franklin, or buy it outright. By the end of August there were only two potential buyers left: the Manufacturers Hanover Trust and the Rockefeller-owned Chemical Bank of New York. The Chase is one of the largest shareholders in the Chemical Bank which is co-owned by the financier Kuhn Loeb and once belonged to Franklin Delano Roosevelt.

In a last minute manoeuvre, David Kennedy managed to persuade the European–American Bank and Trust Company to enter the ranks. This consortium was set up in 1968 to bring together several banking houses with total assets of more than $90 billion. The banks involved were:

the Midland Bank (GB)
the Deutsche Bank (W. Germany)
the Société Générale (France)
the Société Générale de Banque (Belgium)
the Amsterdam–Rotterdam Bank (Holland)
the Creditanstalt (Austria).

At the end of September Sindona announced that he was leaving his job at the head of the Franklin and disappeared. He turned up two weeks later in his luxury villa in Geneva, from where he tried to restore confidence in his Italian affairs which had been threatened by publication of the Franklin scandal.

On leaving New York he had apparently taken great care to cover his tracks. On 2 October 1974 the New York Federal Reserve wrote to James Smith that "it is no longer possible in the public interest to continue lending money to the Franklin Bank." Without the help of the Federal Reserve and its intravenous injection of $1.7 billion, the Long Island bank was doomed.

However, James Smith tried one last throw. On 6 October he sent a telex to Interbanca announcing that the deposit of $15 million made by Sindona and Bordoni would not be extended and asking for the money to be repatriated by the end of the month.

On 7 October Interbanca informed Smith and the directors of the Franklin that the sum could not be repaid because it had passed out of the bank.

Sindona had had the last laugh at his former shareholders' expense. On 8 October 1974, at 3 p.m. Smith declared the Franklin bankrupt in the Brooklyn Federal Court. The Federal Deposit Insurance immediately opened an auction sale. At 5 o'clock it was announced that the European–American Bank had bought the Franklin, thereby ending the biggest banking crash in US history. For $125 million, 2 millions more than the Manufacturers Hanover Trust Co., the European group had strengthened its foothold in America and acquired the chain of branches it had lacked until them.

The Sindona saga, however, had only just begun. The Italian financier had tried to counter-attack while defending a marginal but strategically important position. But many people who had previously trusted him now found him a dangerous accomplice whose own instability threatened to topple them into the stagnant waters of notoriety. Although the Italian public had few illusions about its politicians, any further revelations concerning certain figures might be disastrous. This was especially true of some of the Christian Democrats. Their party in particular had benefited from the operations of Sindona who, according to several reports, had contributed $1.5 million a month since 1972 to party funds through the Party secretary Philippi Miceli. Moreover, at a time when the Italian cabinet was stressing the need to oppose speculation on the lire, Sindona organized vast safaris of capital belonging to various parties and more than 500 names of eminent persons. He had a special relationship with Giulio Andreotti, often Prime Minister and almost continually Minister since 1947. Andreotti had always appeared to be the Vatican's man in the Christian Democrat Party and this had helped him to become Finance Minister on several occasions. Sindona had known him for about twenty years and had acted as his consultant on the development of an extraordinary tax on inherited wealth which never became law.

In fact Sindona's basic mistake was to threaten a politico–industrial balance which the ruling parties had taken great pains to construct. The fact that his dealings brought considerable power and influence to the Christian Democrats and the Vatican had not passed unobserved by a group of laymen connected with the business world which had formed round the Republicans Ugo la Malfa and his friend Guido Carli,[1] the all-powerful governor of the Bank of Italy.

In late 1973 Sindona was nursing a grandiose scheme to merge his Italian interests into a single holding company whose total assets would then exceed those of Fiat. He obtained permission to merge two of his banks, the Banca Unione and the Banca Privata Finanziara into a new firm, the Banca Privata, with assets of $2 billion. Fasco AG held 51% of the capital and the Vatican 15%. Sindona then intended to combine the Banca Privata and the Generale Immobiliare into a single holding, Finambro, whose only asset until then had been a small bank in Milan. His plan was a simple one, to increase Finambro's capital from $770,000 to $30 million in one step and to $245 million in a second move. He then hoped to bring off the final coup of transferring control of Finambro to the Liechtens-

[1]In the June 1976 elections, Carli was elected deputy for the Republican Party which had been led for years by La Malfa. Carli was then made president of Confindustria by Agnelli's men, Agnelli being the owner of Fiat.

tein Fasco AG holding, thus juggling a considerable part of Italian wealth first into his own pocket and then out of the country.

But ministerial leapfrog was against him. Sindona's opponent Ugo La Malfa then held the vital post of Finance Minister. Only he could authorize the capital increase asked for and he knew that Sindona had rashly anticipated any official decision by asking many investors for funds already. He had only to wait for the right moment when the money had begun to flow into Sindona's companies in Vaduz, Luxembourg and Geneva, and then to announce that permission for the operation had been refused for panic to set in.[1] There was a gathering of the clan of hardliners who wanted to banish Sindona completely from the politico–economic world so that it could resume its former petty quarrels. And while the clan prepared the gallows, their apparently unsuspecting victim continued his multinational activities.

Thus in the space of two years Eugenio Céfis, then chairman of the powerful, state-owned Montedison group, transferred 250 million lire to Luigi d'Amato, a newspaper owner. D'Amato, a former Christian Democrat deputy and close friend of the ex-President of the Republic Segni, ran a publishing company called Esedra which published an economic daily *Il Fiorino* and an evening paper *Vita*. These two organs of the press were then obliged to print discreet but effective defense of the management methods of Céfis, who had already bought control of three big Italian dailies, *Il Mondo*, *Il Tempo* and *Il Corriere della Sera* from the Agnelli family. D'Amato appears to have been something of an opportunist, for he had also been connected since 1970 with Finmeccania, one of the largest companies in the IRI group, Montedison's competitor. Camillo Crociani, president of Finmeccanica, was a former Fascist condemned to death in 1945 who turned up again in 1976 as a supporter of the Italian Communist Party. Crociani had a reliable collaborator in the Esedra board in the shape of Certo Puggioni. D'Amato received his money through Prope (the company for research and commercial penetration), an IRI firm dealing with "subsidiary" financing. On further investigation it transpires that Sindona had a large shareholding in Esedra, which made him the referee in any conflicts of interest between Céfis and Crociani. Moreover Sindona used his Finabank in Geneva to effect illegal capital transfers for Céfis. Regular deposits were made into a numbered account at the Moscow Narodny Bank in London. Sindona's partner Carlo Bordoni handled these particular transactions with sureties from the leaders of the Italian CP which had close links with its country's "capitalist monopolies."

In May 1975 La Malfa announced his refusal to authorize the capital increase Sindona had asked for on the foreseeable, but nonetheless convincing, grounds that such permission might lead to capital being transferred abroad. The threat of an impending crash for the Franklin made his decision easier. The Stock Exchange was reacting badly to these rumours. In Milan shares in Generale Immobiliare plummeted from 800 to 450 lire in one month.

The Bank of Italy then intervened, effectively cutting off every line of retreat for Sindona. An enquiry revealed that two separate accounts had been kept and that the Banca Privata had lost about $260 million in foreign deals and transactions between various companies within the group.

The IRI, and through it the Christian Democrat Party, persuaded the state-owned Banco di Roma to grant Sindona's bank a supportive loan of $100 million. On 10 June three representatives of the state bank met the Sicilian in New York. The three men

---

[1] Sindona later accused La Malfa of never having called a meeting of the credit committee which was supposed to make judgments on operations of this kind.

were Giovanni Guidi, Ferdinando Ventriglia, since appointed Director General of the Treasury, and Mario Barone, a childhood friend of Sindona, who had succeeded in fighting his case on the Banco di Roma's board.

Indeed, Sindona had paid 2 billion lire for this appointment. But it would have taken a brilliant mind and a good will, which Barone did not possess, to save him now. The discussions lasted several days. On 17 June in exchange for a loan of $100 million Sindona agreed to transfer to the Banco di Roma 51% of the shares in the Banca Privata and 120 million of the 229 million shares he held in the Generale Immobiliare. This agreement left Sindona looking like a gambler who walks out of the casino at three in the morning over a carpet of cigarette butts with his pockets empty.

The four men then planned a deal so glaringly obvious in its implications that it was clear for ever after that tax fraud was part of everyday management methods in big companies, including state-owned firms.

For it was agreed that the loan granted to Sindona should be paid into his Generale Immobiliare Banking Corporation of Nassau through the Banco di Roma's subsidiary in the Bahamas. The US Congress commission of enquiry into Watergate later revealed that Nixon himself had had a secret account for the transfer of personal interests in the Bahamas since 1972.

The directors of the state-owned IRI group to which the bank belonged hoped to make it look as though the Banco di Roma itself was not involved by idiotically claiming that the Bahamas subsidiary was a foreign bank and therefore not subject to Italian law. But there were wider issues involved. Firstly, there was the fact that a deal of this size should be taking place not only outside Italy but in a tax haven as well. Then there was the way in which the IRI, a symbol of public ownership, had proved that it could exploit the international banking routes in a bid to escape the legislative and fiscal "inclemencies" of Italy.

It is interesting to note Sindona's ironic comments on such deals in an interview he gave to *Newsweek* on 28 April 1975, a year after his collapse. "All the big American banks have branches in the Bahamas, Luxembourg or Liechtenstein, where they deposit their funds. The money never reaches America but is entered in the account books of the American banks. The same principle applies to the major European banks. Banking rules are much too 'lenient'!"

On 20 July the agreement was signed. On 1 August $50 million, half the total sum, was transferred to the Bahamas. The shareholders, now aware that the Franklin was about to fold, panicked. Deposits at the Banca Privata fell from 900,000 million lire (£600 million) to 400,000 million lire (£260 million). The directors of the Banco di Roma then decided to freeze the second $50 million. But for this decision to be implemented, Guido Carli had personally to agree; and although this secretive and arrogant man hated Sindona, he wished to "preserve the credibility of the Italian banking system abroad."

This particular moral argument has its points, but seems rather weak when one considers that a few months later the scrupulously honest Carli resigned his office to work in the private sector for Agnelli. In any case the last shreds of the Sindona empire looked none too healthy. By the beginning of September the Banca Unione of Milan, one of the two banks merged into the Banca Privata, had lost 30 billion lire in exchange deals, 18 billion lire in "non-demandable credits" paid into the Herstatt Bank of Frankfurt which fell a few months later, and 104 billion lire mysteriously swallowed up by fictitious subdivisions of Sindona's Swiss and Luxemburg companies like the Gadena, the Mella, the Kilda, the Nabusa and the Queriso.

Carli decided to put the Banca Privata into the hands of the receiver. To save some of the losses, several other state banks, like the Italian Credit Bank and the Banca Commerciale, were asked to take part in operations.

In early October, abandoned by all his former friends and threatened with prosecution, Sindona sent a letter to Geneva announcing his resignation from the Generale Immobiliare and its foreign subsidiaries. Soon after, he flew to the United States. On 9 January 1975 the Swiss authorities ordered the finance bank in Geneva to close down. According to Daniel Bodmer, Secretary of the Federal Banking Commission, this decision was motivated by the "losses resulting from excessive speculation following transactions made with Edilcentra International Ltd of the Bahamas," a company owned by Generale Immobiliare of Rome. According to the Swiss authorities, the bank had suffered losses amounting to $19.6 million in excess of its assets.

This was a loss of both money and prestige. It was a hard blow for the Vatican which held a 49% share in the Swiss bank. Now considerably poorer and discredited, the clerical leaders found an ideal scapegoat in Mgr Marcinkus, who was criticized for his relaxed life style and his misappropriation of funds. Mgr Benelli, an important ecclesiastical dignitary and deputy Secretary of the Vatican State, who had always been worried by the growing influence of the American bishop, led the attack. "The judiciary enquiry," said Benelli, "will enable us to find out exactly how our financial affairs operate. It is intolerable!" Soon after, Marcinkus was dismissed, but his intimate knowledge of the Vatican's most secret affairs protected him to a certain extent and he was given a diplomatic post.

According to Massimo Spada, the Vatican lost 24 billion francs from its 15% share holding in the Banca Unione and £43 million from Sindona's illegal operations through the Swiss bank. Whether or not these figures are accurate, Paul VI rejected the proposed budget for 1975 on the grounds of the "excessive expenditure involved." How thrifty!

The Sindona affair was a pantomime, with Sindona as the poor clown who comes out onto the stage hoping to entertain the audience single-handed for four acts with his improvisations about money only to find the bored public booing him off after a few minutes.

Even so, it is possible that Sindona accomplished the ultimate ecumenical achievement. The Vatican's share in Generale Immobiliare, which included the Watergate complex in particular, was later bought by Fiat and by a mysterious consortium. And it soon transpired that a third share in this consortium was owned by someone connected with the Italian Communist Party.

Several apparently impeccable banking houses had worked with Sindona. In the same way, the Banca Privata is said to have acted as an agent for the National Westminster Bank in its massive foreign speculation on the dollar, which placed the bank in a difficult position when the convertibility of the dollar was suspended.

In 1974 another rogue of the numbered account came to a bad end. Tibor Rosenbaum was the banker who had links with both the Mafia and Prince Bernhardt of the Netherlands. Manager of the International Credit Bank of Geneva, Rosenbaum was born in Hungary and had been a hero of Jewish resistance during the Second World War. An ardent Zionist, he had supported the creation of the State of Israel from the beginning.

In 1949 he was director of the Helvis Management Corporation which handled trade between Switzerland and Israel. As early as 1959 his company was involved in a financial scandal after contributing funds to an ultra-religious Israeli nationalist party in order to win contracts from the Ministry of Health.

Rosenbaum was a close friend of Pinhas Sapir, the Labour Party financier who had developed the policy of economic support for Israel from the Diaspora. In 1960 Rosenbaum became director of the bank and made it a staging post for the Cosa Nostra. There funds from the Las Vegas casinos mingled with the money deposited by Edmond de Rothschild.

Before long Rosenbaum had formed a partnership with Bernie Cornfeld, who was then setting up the IOS. Rosenbaum, who was also Liberian ambassador to Austria, had a number of contacts among West African governmental circles. The two jobs complemented each other. Accounts could be settled through Rosenbaum's Swiss bank, but customers could also pay by buying shares in IOS in Switzerland.

The two partners could not have been more different. Cornfeld was an eccentric, an adventurer and a visionary; Rosenbaum was a finickety pietist who attended the synagogue regularly and was so obsessed with the need for secrecy that he used the service entrance of his bank to go to work every morning. But Rosenbaum was so successful financially that in 1968 the Israeli government entrusted him with the purchase of military equipment. On one occasion Shimon Peres, the then Prime Minister of Israel, even appealed for his help in raising $7 million in twenty-four hours for reasons of "national security." Rosenbaum got the money and a commission of $500,000 for his pains. Although the International Credit Bank was on the list of Jewish banking houses boycotted by the Arab States, he managed to buy oil for Israel from Middle Eastern companies in Lausanne. Naturally there were some blots on the escutcheon. In 1968 *Life* revealed that Sylvain Ferdman, Rosenbaum's assistant and a collaborator with Lansky, had carried $350,000 from Miami to place it in the "Maral 2818" account at the Geneva bank. But, generally speaking, International Credit enjoyed a good reputation in banking circles.

In 1966 Rosenbaum and Cornfeld started planning a vast-scale speculative operation in Rome, based on Tenuta di Copocotta, a 1,200 acre parcel of land West of the capital which had belonged to the Italian royal family. Rosenbaum hoped to turn it into a housing estate and is alleged to have paid $22 million on the land, with plans to spend up to $150 million on the construction program. Cornfeld was ready to sell shares in Tenuta through the IOS and Generale Immobiliare were to handle most of the building work. In the space of two years Rosenbaum spent $6 million on roads, drainage and the construction of "show" houses. He then learnt that the authorizations necessary for the rest of his scheme would not be granted. He immediately arranged for his German associates, the Hessiche Landesbank to contact its Polish correspondent, the Polska Handlowska Bank, and ask it to bring pressure on the Italian CP.

Giorgio Napolitano and Eugenio Peggio, the two CP leaders contacted, who had used Rosenbaum's bank for trade deals with the East on several occasions, reacted cautiously to the Polish request. Rosenbaum made several trips to Rome and lunched with Napolitano, apparently without success. The Communists were committed to a wary journey to power for which they had to appear incorruptible and were therefore unwilling to associate with a man who steered so close to the edge of the law.

Rosenbaum then turned to his contacts within the German Social Democratic Party, men like Willy Brandt's friend Egon Bahr, hoping that they would influence the Socialist minority within the Italian center left government. This, too, failed. In 1970 the 1,200-acre plot was declared a "green belt."

From then on the path led downhill for Rosenbaum. His situation was aggravated still further by the liquidation of the Frankfurt Herstatt Bank in which he had a number of interests. Like the dishonest accountant who fiddles the company to pay his gambling debts, Rosenbaum now turned to the Israel Corporation, which was owned and directed by Edmond de Rothschild. This organization had one simple aim: to collect money from Zionist circles and invest it in public and semi-public sector Israeli companies such as the Zim shipping company.

Rosenbaum's friend Michael Tsur, former Director General of the Israeli Ministry of Trade and Industry and now manager of the Israel Corporation, advanced him $8.5 million drawn from corporation funds. In fact Tsur embezzled a total of $14.5 million not only from the Israel Corporation but also from Zim Navigation and a third Israeli company, Oil Refineries. The money was transferred to the International Credit Bank of Vaduz in Lichtenstein which also belonged to Rosenbaum. The existence of the two tax havens of Luxemburg and Liechtenstein considerably hampered investigations.

The International Credit of Geneva held six major investments in Israel: 100% ownership of Lodzia Textiles; 22% of Ata Textiles, with 51% of the voting rights; 51% of the big electronics firm Rapac; 33% of the Gallery of Modern Art in Jaffa; $1 million in Israel Corporation and an apartment in the Plaza Hotel in Jerusalem which actually belonged to the International Credit Trust of Vaduz and was bought with the interest on the $1 million deposited in the Israel Corporation.

Rosenbaum was equally unlucky in his investments in 1972. His Italo–American Corporation owned the 500-room Du Lac Hotel in Rome. Rosenbaum sold the company to his brother-in-lw William Stern.

In 1974 Stern, now affected by the collapse of the International Credit Bank, received an extraordinary proposition from Rosenbaum. Apparently a buyer was ready to take the Du Lac and Stern would receive $50,000 commission. When the deal was settled soon after, the buyer turned out to be Horn Holding of Vaduz, a company controlled by Rosenbaum himself.

It was Rosenbaum, too, who handled the sale of Warmelo Castle which belonged to the late mother of Prince Bernhardt of the Netherlands. Evlyna Trust, a Liechtenstein company connected with International Credit, bought the property for $400,000. The deal was arranged by Herbert Batliner, a Vaduz lawyer and consultant to the multinationals and wealthy individuals.

Because of this deal, Bernhardt asked Edmond de Rothschild, his Bildeberg Club friend, not to prosecute Rosenbaum, especially as Rosenbaum had just negotiated the construction of a Club Méditarranée (in which Rothschild is a major shareholder) on the Russian Black Sea coast. Michael Tsur, for his part, was tried in 1975 in Jerusalem and condemned to fifteen years in prison.

Part III

Effective power is increasingly eluding the reach of the democratic process and its controllers appear to be absolutely indifferent to changes of régime which might take place within national borders. This is perfectly reflected in the cooperation which has been instituted since the October Revolution between the large capitalist firms and the Bolshevik powers, despite radical changes in the system.

Before the appearance of the "Vodka-Cola" phenomenon, the political and ideological cold war was controlled, directed and initiated by all sectors of the Overworld while in the East non-convertibility and national autarchy preceded the "capitalization of Communism."

The military-industrial complex, the ideology-mongers at the universities and the financial power controlling the big foundations, all had a major influence in the process of East–West confrontation with the disastrous results known to everyone.

Since Communism has been reinterpreted from the perspective of profit via the co-production system, the strategy has switched from one of confrontation to cooperation between the élites of the two sides. This change is founded on a convergence of economic interests between political systems which are different, even implacably opposed, in ideology and social systems.

Russian workers and citizens will not benefit from the advantages of respect for individual liberty or the application of the most elementary human rights; for their part, American workers and citizens will not gain any of the benefits which may spring from a right of ownership in the enterprise, economic planning or industrial democracy.

Only the economic interests of the members of the Vodka-Cola club will be taken into consideration.

Today, governments are losing control of their economies because of the growth in the global power and extreme mobility of the multinationals which can no longer be controlled at the level of national policy.

Real power over investment, credit, employment or overseas trade has been transferred directly from the elected government into the power of the monopolies. There are many private institutions which coordinate this transfer.

In the USA, for example, the Business Round Table lobby brings together 160 presidents from the largest multinationals whose job it is to influence government policy. Their president, Irving Shapiro, is one of the front-runners of Vodka-Cola colonization. Managing Director of Du Pont, director of IBM, he is also a member of the Trilateral Commission, of the US–USSR Trade Council, of the Bildeberg Club and of the Council for Foreign Relations, all of which are agencies of the Overworld, maintaining control over economic affairs. This molecule of power dominates similar functions in many other capitalist countries of the West.

Centralized agencies of this kind exercise control over the most important branches of the global economy, rather than governments or servants of the body corporate of the state, both of which are already quite obsolete.

It is logical that these dominant forces have been led to mould and supplant the political power of official, democratically elected institutions in order to insure the protection and expansion of their economic interests. In the East, of course, this change was not necessary, since the formal institutions (government or parliament) have never been more than a screen for authoritarian conspiracy and shady Party schemes.

As it happened, the organizations which were the high priests of cold war found themselves at the head of the crusade for economic détente. Since the aims of the authoritarian Overworld had switched from conflict to profit, it was logical that the people and institutions who were dependent on its patronage underwent reprogramming.

At the present time, Ford, Rockefeller, Agnelli and numerous other giants of industry are creating, via their foundations, all sorts of clubs, study centers and commissions whose job it is to strengthen the bonds of tacit complicity between the intellectual community and the directors of super power.

The apotheosis has been illustrated by the example of the Trilateral Commission, which emphasizes the hold over American institutions exercised by the Vodka-Cola corporations. In fact, Carter, his Vice-President Walter Mondale, and thirty leading members of the new Democratic administration, originate from this private chamber of world power.

The Trilateral Commission is the creature of the ubiquitous David Rockefeller. The symbol and the hyphen between the Vodka-Cola polarities, he controls the Rockefeller Foundation, the Rockefeller Brothers Fund, the Council for Foreign Relations, the Bildeberg Society. Associated with the banks and the oil companies, he also holds sway with overwhelming influence, amid other Vodka-Cola organizations: the Ford Foundation, the Brookings Institute, MIT, Harvard University, Stanford University, Hudson Institute, Rand Corporation and the Russian Studies Institute. All the programs of meetings and discussions drawn up by these bodies include growing numbers of Voda-Colanizers from Eastern Europe.

The following chapters reveal many of the facts of this Overworld and list the personalities and the agencies behind them. But despite all these glimpses, there is no doubt we have only exposed the tip of the iceberg.

1.

The Foundations and Clubs of the Community

There is no doubt that if Max Weber were alive today, he would be writing his essay on the morality of capitalism with the help of a generous study grant from the Ford or Rockefeller Foundations. The lasting strength of the big companies is not based solely on a capacity for economic development which enables them to reshape as they will the social landscape and the parasitical political playground. For the multinational power base is also working to buy information and direct aspirations. It demonstrates the same capacity for innovation and foresight in its manipulation of the intellectual as of the economic and financial spheres. Precision of thought and adherence to opinion have become extremely relative and negotiable concepts. In this respect the big foundations have fully adapted to the contours of the human mind and will exploit a whole range of thinking from recognized idiocy and dozy naivety to cynical opportunism. Blessed be the men of wealth for theirs is the kingdom of tax havens, and it is fitting that the just man should be sitting on the right hand of the deified Dollar. There are 25,000 foundations in the United States, which together control tax-free funds of $20 billion. Wealth is concentrated into the hands of philanthropic institutions. The income of the 596 largest foundations is more than twice the net profits of the fifty largest commercial banks in the country. The present income of the Ford Foundation, *primus inter pares*, is greater than that of the largest world banks at $2 billion for the last thirty years.

In 1973 this mammoth of graduated generosity kept its vast heart beating at an annual pulse rate of $3 billion in net assets, a figure greater than the GNP of many of the member states of UNO. The Rockefellers have two institutions: the Rockefeller Foundation, which had net assets of $980 million in 1973, and the Rockefeller Brothers Fund, which has assets of about $200 million, though its exact financial situation has never been disclosed. Indeed, we should emphasize the extreme modesty shown by the directors of these philanthropic conglomerates. There is nothing ostentatious about their dealings. Two thirds of them have never published an annual report of their activities. What information can be gleaned from the few details they spare us concerns only those operations which they wish to make public. There are still vast areas of half-light.

The foundations can only exist and function as they do on a basis of legislative ambiguity and fiscal indulgence which can be summarized as follows:
1 They can use their capital to lend money or buy areas of activity.
2 The income obtained in this way can be kept within the family.
3 The legatee appoints the directors of the foundation and retains control over the investments made. Every company can make a 20% charity deduction by donating funds or transferring a large part of its property to a foundation, thereby avoiding any tax on profits.

These organizations have always been more like international banks than benevolent societies, and their supposed independence from their generous donors is no more than soft soap.

Henry Ford transferred 90% of the shares in the Ford Company to his foundation
without losing any of the economic influence involved in the deal. This prudent move
permitted nine tenths of the assets of the third largest company in the world to become
tax exempt and enabled the heirs of the Detroit empire to avoid paying estate duty.

This kind of conjuring trick, which puts nothing in the hands and everything in the
pockets is unacceptable to anyone still labouring under rigid ideas such as the division
of powers and the virtues of state control.

Adapting to any change in attitudes, the Ford Foundation has managed over the
years to cram its vaults in far too defiant a fashion by selling, lending or investing 92.7
million shares in the Ford Motors Company worth $4 billion.

During this same period, it has acquired interests in Time Inc., Magnovox General
Mills, Pepsi Cola, American Motors, Exxon, Gulf Oil, IBM, Lockheed, Boeing and Dow
Chemical. Between 1950 and 1962 it lent more than $300 million to commercial com-
panies. Although its charter declares that "all its actions must answer charitable ends
and nothing else," the Ford Foundation has bought control of Philco Corporation with 1
million shares in Ford Motors, which it undervalued by $4 per share compared with the
market price, thereby making a total cost reduction of $4 million. Since the market
price was itself double the value entered on the foundation's ledgers, the foundation
more than doubled its profits from this deal; non-taxable profits of course.

It is easy to see why this kind of institution has attracted various capitalists who are
busy building industrial empires in which the twin arches of business and charity meet
in the topmost keystone of power.

John MacCloy, former American High Commissioner in Germany, was director of the
Ford Foundation from 1953 to 1965. On the advice of MacCloy and his assistant Shepard
Stone, the Essen gun merchants created Krupp Stiftung, a DM 159 million foundation
modelled on its glorious American elder brother. This shift of assets enabled Krupp to
regain control of their steelworks which had been placed under allied management. In
one year the foundation received DM 2 million from the industrial empire. Arndt
Krupp, the last of the line, even stated: "Our family has always been extremely
interested in the Fords' relations with their venture, and we have always admired the
decisions they took."

The Ford Foundation, with over $2 billion in its portfolio, is the largest institutional
investor in the US stock market. Some 80% of its investments were in equities in 1976.
Taking only the portion of the institution's equity investments which are managed by
an inhouse staff of 25 people, the largest holding was 257,000 shares of IBM worth $72.5
million over the year ended September 30, 1976. Exxon, the second largest holding, was
worth $55.5 million at year-end. AT&T was in third place in 1976, with the Foundation
staff adding 188,704 shares during the year for a total market value of $47.42 million.

The Foundation also has some $83 million of its equity and fixed-income investments
out with five domestic, three Canadian and four European money managers. These
firms were chosen for specialized investments.

The Foundation, which once received its income from Ford Motor stock only but no
longer owns any, has over the years been diversifying. The portfolio is now rather
heavily weighted toward energy-oriented companies. At the end of fiscal '76 the
internally-managed portfolio held $119.4 million in domestic oil and gas stocks, $106.3
million in international oil and gas issues, $84.24 million in oil and gas machinery and
service companies, $3.7 million of Santa Fe International, an offshore drilling outfit,
and $46.56 million of oil and gas producers stocks. These totals represented 25 issues.

Some of the Foundation's larger holdings in this category were: Atlantic Richfield,

$20 million; Philips Petroleum, $25.7 million; Gulf $32.9 million; and Schlumberger, $40 million. Its smallest oil and gas investments were in Mobil, $615,000; Murphy Oil, $2.7 million; and British Petroleum, $3.39 million. Most of these are companies with dominant Rockefeller interests.

On the other side, the Foundation continued to cut expenditures relative to assets. During fiscal 1976, expenditures were 8% of assets, or $184 million, and this represented a percentage which had been reduced from 10% in 1975 and 17% in 1974. This will be decreased further this year, a Foundation spokesman said, bringing it down to 6% of assets. But despite these reductions, long-term commitments totalling $272 million still represent a substantial portion of current expenditures, the annual report cautioned, "so for some years to come, expenditures will continue to exceed annual budgets and the Foundation will be expending more than its dividend and interest income." This income totalled $95 million in fiscal '76, slightly less than in 1975, the annual report said.

The Rockefellers demonstrate the same ability to jump gracefully through the hoops of strict legality, while keeping property, power and capacity for control intact.

The Rockefeller Foundation was created in 1913 with the basic aim of maintaining family control over its oil empire which had been cut down two years earlier into seven separate companies, following a Supreme Court ruling dividing Standard Oil for monopolistic activities. Today the foundation is the largest shareholder in Standard Oil Company (Exxon) of New Jersey, with 4,300,000 shares, worth several hundreds of millions of dollars. It also owns 2 million shares in Standard Oil of California, 300,000 in Mobil Oil and 300,000 in Continental Oil. Other smaller Rockefeller Foundations own another 3 million shares in Exxon, 300,000 in Mobil and 450,000 in Standard of Ohio.

The assets of these companies, in which the Rockefellers are majority shareholders, amount to more than $50 billion. So the family can keep their oil pool united, unruffled and intact as they dip their nibs in it to sign their benevolent checks.

Other Rockefeller interests within the foundation include the Chase Manhattan Bank (third largest bank in the world with $18 billion), Metropolitan and Equitable (second and third largest insurance companies, with $25 and 13 billion respectively), Eastern Airlines ($830 million), Consolidated Natural Gas ($1 billion) and the Rockefeller Center ($300 million). The total assets of these companies is $58 billion.

In fact the Rockefeller and Ford Foundations exercise a decisive influence over political and social affairs. They direct and, if necessary, modify the development of morals, ideas, values and institutions. These private agencies take the place of public bodies and government and form an administration of their own with extensive means of pressure and ways of influencing public opinion. The fact that they represent the source of real power goes a long way to explaining why they are tolerated by politicians. Since 1945 virtually every man or woman to hold an important political office has at some time been employed by or otherwise benefited from one of these two foundations. This section will show their continued influence on the shape of American foreign policy. They make the State Department look like a transit lounge.

Further analysis points up the indissoluble links between a screen of philanthropy, the exercise of power and the management of wealth.

The Rockefellers do more than even the Mellons and the Du Ponts to feed and reinforce their family mystique and the myth of their identification with the American power base. The total fortune of the dynasty is divided among more than 200 companies. This figure includes six of the ten biggest American industrial firms, six of the ten biggest banks, five of the ten largest insurance companies and three of the biggest companies involved in the four other branches of activities listed by the magazine *Fortune*. These twenty economic and financial Titans have total assets of $640 billion.

Outside the commercial sphere, the chorale "Rockefeller is good" can be heard echoing from vast organs with stops labelled Rockefeller University, Rockefeller Center, Colonial Williamsburg, Rockefeller Family Fund, the Museums of Modern and Primitive Art in New York and Chicago University, as well as the Foundation and the Rockefeller Brothers Fund.

Coordination between these philanthropic, tax-exempt activities and strictly economic concerns is handled by the Rockefeller Family and Associates. This informal organization, which is little known even by the experts, was created by John D. Rockefeller Jr, son of the founder of the empire and father of Nelson, David, Laurence and Winthrop. The association holds regular meetings on the 56th floor of 30 Rockefeller Plaza for members of the family and their chief employees. While the White House and the Western leaders exchange memoranda, marginal comments and loud words, the Rockefeller Family and Associates sit in peaceful seclusion, planning and deciding on any questions of law, management, investment, loans and philanthropy raised within the various organizations of the empire. According to one member, Charles B. Smith, the aims of the group are simple: "To earn more and yet more money for the family."

The following extract from *Probing the Rockefeller Fortune, A Report Prepared for Members of the United States Congress, November 1974*, by G. William Domhoff and Charles L. Schwartz, gives some indication of the Rockefellers' corporate linkage.

During some recent investigations by a Senate subcommittee which was looking into the ownership and control of the airline industries the name "Rockefeller Family and Associates" came up. (Harper Woodward of R.F. & A. is a director of Eastern Airlines.) The Committee's Counsel, whose staff had been unable to find this organization listed in any reference books, asked,

"Do you have any way of telling us what ownership Rockefeller Family and Associates have and how they interlock with other companies in the United States?"

The witness, an official of the Civil Aeronautics Board, replied, "We do not have that information."

With the list given in Part I of this report, showing a large number of corporations on whose boards of directors there sits an identified representative of R.F. & A., it is now possible to tabulate their interlocks with other companies. The task is a tedious one but we have done it, focusing our attention on the most recent year for which reference books are available—nominally 1973.... For each company with an R.F. & A. representative on the board, each other director was looked up in these reference books (and sometimes in *Who's Who* as well) and a record was made of every other corporation on whose board of directors he also sat at that same time.

The gross result of this research is a list of over 1,000 corporate interlocks for Rockefeller Family and Associates. The list is so huge that we refrain from publishing it in its full form for fear of simply drowning the reader. We sought, instead, some way of choosing and presenting the essence of this tabulation without all of its detail.

It is, of course, arguable just what a corporate interlock, or a list of corporate interlocks means. It certainly doesn't mean that Rockefeller owns or controls some company just because of an interlock with it. At a minimum, it probably does mean that Rockefeller agents are in effective communication with those businesses interlocked with them. The hard question ... concerns measuring the degree of influence which the collective Rockefeller financial network, acting through R.F. & A., and possibly with other more submerged allies, exerts on these other companies it is interlocked with.

We have chosen the simple formula of selecting out only those companies for which we found more than one interlock with R.F. & A.... The resulting list of multiple interlocking companies was further distilled by selecting only the larger companies....

The following table contains the results of this tabulation. The companies are ranked in the order given by *Fortune* and the numbers in parentheses give the number of interlocks which each company has with representatives of the Rockefeller Family sitting on boards of directors.

For example, the first entry in the table reads "General Motors (2)." This means that we have found two cases of a director of General Motors Corp. who is also a director of a company that has a Rockefeller Family representative on its board.

Industrials
General Motors (2)
Exxon (3)
Chrysler (R.F. & A. + 1)
General Electric (2)
Mobil Oil (3)
I.B.M. (R.F. & A. + 4)
U.S. Steel (3)
R.C.A. (2)
Eastman Kodak (2)
Union Carbide (2)
Caterpillar Tractor (2)
Xerox (4)
W. R. Grace (4)
General Foods (5)
Singer (2)
Ralston Purina (2)
Honeywell (2)
Bendix (R.F. & A. + 2)
Colgate–Palmolive (4)
American Can (2)
T.R.W. (3)
National Steel (2)
Uniroyal (4)
Republic Steel (2)
American Motors (R.F. & A.)
F.M.C. (2)
Warner–Lambert (2)

Industrials (cont.)
Allied Chemical (2)
U.S. Industries (3)
Raytheon (2)
Eaton (2)
Standard Oil, Ohio (2)
Teledyne (2)
Nabisco (2)
Kennecott–Copper (4)
Bristol–Myers (2)
Burroughs (2)
Illinois Central Inds (2)
Studebaker–Worthington (2)
Amer. Smelting & Refining (2)
Eli Lilly (2)
Corning Glass (3)
Emerson Electric (2)
Scott Paper (4)
Carrier (3)
Avco (2)
Hewlett–Packard (2)
Diamond Shamrock (R.F. & A.)
Cerro (2)
Universal Oil Products (2)
Airco (2)
Int'l Mineral & Chem. (R.F. & A.)
Cluett, Peabody (3)
Harris-Intertype (2)
Carborundum (2)
Sybron (4)
Texasgulf (2)
Gannett (3)
Ceco (2)

Commercial Banking companies
First National City Corp. (3)
Chase Manhattan Corp. (David + R.F.
    & A. + 3)
Manufacturers Hanover Corp. (5)
Chemical New York Corp. (4)
Bankers Trust New York Corp. (4)
First Chicago Corp. (3)
Marine Midland Banks Inc. (3)
Wells Fargo & Co. (2)
Charter New York Corp. (2)
Mellon National Corp. (3)
First National Boston Corp. (3)

National Detroit Corp. (5)
Bank of New York Co. (2)
Cleveland Trust Co. (2)
Detroitbank Corp. (3)
Lincoln First Banks, Inc. (R.F. & A.)
Southeast Banking Corp. (3)

Life-Insurance Companies
Prudential (5)
Metropolitan (5)
Equitable Life Assurance (3)
New York Life (2)
Massachusetts Mutual (2)
New England Mutual (2)
Mutual Benefit (2)

Diversified Financial Companies
American Express (6)
Continental Corp. (4)
C.I.T. Financial (R.F. & A.)
Crum & Forster (R.F. & A.)

Utilities
American Tel. & Tel. (5)
Consolidated Edison (2)
Detroit Edison (3)

Transportation Companies
Pan American World Airways (4)
Eastern Air Lines (R.F. & A. + 3)

Retailing Companies
Great Atlantic and Pacific Tea (2)
S. S. Kresge (R.F. & A. + 1)
Federated Department Stores (3)
Winn–Dixie Stores (2)
May Department Stores (2)
R. H. Macy (R.F. & A. + 4)
Marriott (2) (R.F. & A. + 4)

The following are sizeable companies not included in the listing by *Fortune*:

U.S. Trust Co., New York (5)
Fidelity Union Bankcorp, N.J. (4)
J. Henry Schroder Banking Corp. (3)
Bowery Savings Bank (3)
Greenwich Savings Bank (R.F. & A. + 3)
Maccabees Mutual Life (2)
Liberty Mutual Life (2)
Reliance Insurance (2)

Canadian Corporations
Investors Group (R.F. & A.)
Royal Bank of Canada (3)
Investors Growth Fund (3)
Investors Mutual of Canada (3)
Great–Western Life Assurance (4)
Montreal Trust Co. (2)
Canadian Pacific Ltd. (2)
International Nickel (2)

Fifteen members of the Rockefeller Family and Associates alone hold 118 director-ships in 97 different companies. The combined assets of all the companies listed add up to $640,000,000,000.

Other organizations to benefit from Rockefeller generosity include the United Nations and the Organization of American States. By ensuring that certain people hold office, sometimes as experts, by spending a certain amount of "seed" money for projects and by establishing study programs in which the foundation or the institute cooperate with the agencies of these international organizations, the Rockefellers can maintain considerable influence in these bodies.

The least paying proposition, however, probably remains the Republican Party which, according to Theodore White, is "as financially dependent on the Rockefeller family as the foundation or the university." The family has made up every deficit, and Nelson Rockefeller keeps a little piece of blue paper in his inside pocket reminding him exactly how much the party has cost his family over the years.

But this is only apparently a paradox. Nelson has never succeeded in making an impression on the political shadow theatre. In his almost heart-rending tenacity he is like those mercurial producers who are not content to finance the play but must take the leading part as well.

The purely political aspect of Nelson's career has never reached beyond the bound-aries of New York State where he was governor from 1958 to 1974. But through his career as governor we can see how shamelessly pressure of various kinds was brought to bear on the situation.

Most reactions to recent cases of corruption show a total misunderstanding of the methods used in the contemporary exercise of economic influence. Lockheed is just a detail. It is force of circumstance which corrupts politicians, and this includes the Communists who would have us believe that they form the last bastion of integrity. Power always corrupts. Absolute power corrupts absolutely. Corporate corruption is virtually legal in many countries including Great Britain, Italy, Poland and the USSR. In West Germany it is even tax-deductible. Here philanthropy is used as an excuse. Bribes are the surest means of calming scruples and winning approval. But a little verbal conjuring will change them into gifts, loans or patronage and these empty euphemisms embrace such antithetical concepts as dedication and tax-exemption. Nelson Rockefeller's gross earnings over the last twenty years have amounted to more than $130 million. But the careful use of exemptions and allowances has meant that he pays tax at the same rate as someone earning little more than £6,000 a year.

Contempt for the letter of the law and the sure knowledge of being able to act with total impunity inbues certain of the Rockefellers' activities with an aroma of cynicism which can also be traced to various Communist leaders.

On 1 September 1961, an addition was made to the Penal Code of New York State in the shape of article 200 35. The new law, ratified by governor Rockefeller's signature, imposed a year's prison sentence or a $1,000 fine on "any person found guilty of offering ... gifts to an officer, an employee of the public services or any individual occupying an official position." Between 1967 and 1974 Nelson distributed more than $3 million and made other generous gifts, but only half of this sum went to the foundations. Between 1961 and 1964 he donated $310,469.49 to the Business Foundation of the Government of Albany, a charitable organization which paid not one dollar in taxes. This dodge enabled Rockefeller to secretly pay the salary of Frank Moore, former Lieutenant-Governor of New York. To win black votes he promised in 1970 to build a huge hospital complex costing more than $1 billion in West Harlem, to be financed solely by the Rockefeller Brothers Fund.

Charitable organizations are also used to take control of commercial companies. In 1974 the founder-president of Bio-Medical Sciences Inc. was sacked by a majority coalition of five shareholders: the Rockefeller University, the Rockefeller Center, the Rockefeller Brothers Fund and Colonial Williamsburg.

Since 1962 the Rockefeller Brothers Fund has been the largest shareholder on Chrysler with 80,000 shares, and more than $1.6 million's worth of debentures in Chrysler Financial and Realty Corporation. J. R. Dillworth, president of the Rockefeller Foundation, was also a director of the automobile company from 1962 to 1970.

The Rockefeller Brothers Fund also finances the Council of Foreign Relations, the true seat of American foreign policy-making, whose president David Rockefeller is also the boss of the Chase Manhattan Bank.

Henry Diamond, an employee of Nelson Rockefeller, was in charge of New York State's Department for the Preservation of the Environment from 1970 to 1973. In 1973 Nixon appointed him a member of the "citizens' committee for the quality of the environment," a federal study group which received a quarter of its finances from Congress and the remainder from the American Conservation Association, an offshoot of the Rockefeller Brothers Fund. In mid-December 1973, Diamond succeeded Laurence Rockefeller as chairman of this "committee". Six months later he received a gift of $100,000 from Nelson and left his New York job to become executive director of "the national commission on the critical choices of America." The rapid proliferation of such study groups makes it possible to short circuit the ministries and the traditional forms of administration, and gives the men of influence a guarantee that every important decision will be referred to them. The Commission on Critical Choices, "the real center of government planning and social analyses", was financed by Nelson and Laurence Rockefeller, who each donated a tax-free $1 million. The vice-chairman of the organization, appointed by Nelson, was Gerald Ford.

The few odd enquiries there have been into the activities of the foundations have always come up against obstructive and fervent officials who are serving two masters. In 1963, Stabley Surrey left Harvard University to join the Kennedy administration as a tax expert in the Finance Ministry. A few months later, when faced with the task of creating a commission to examine the workings of the charitable, tax-exempt organizations, he chose fourteen men, six of whom were directly linked with the big foundations. Two other members of the group were consultants receiving regular salaries from other "philanthropic" organizations.

The whole business was brought into the open by Wight Patman, a stubborn and honest senator, who had devoted his latter years to hunting down the excesses of big business. "The attitude of the big foundations," he said, "is patently arrogant and contemptuous towards Congress and the public." The aristocratic Rockefeller Foundation president, Douglas Dillon, who had worked in high finance all his life, was quick to respond. His argument is a piece of incoherent tub-thumping, which reasons that the few unfortunate mistakes made by big capital are offset by their virtues and achievements.

Dillon Read and Company, the large investment bank, had always had special connections with the oil companies. Dillon's importance in the post-war era is a matter of historical fact. A high-ranking politician, he and his associate James Forrestal between them held eighteen ministerial posts, ranging from Defense to Finance by way of the Navy and chairmanship of the State Department Planning Committee.

Mac George Bundy has been president of the Ford Foundation since 1966. Now aged about fifty, he affects total faith in his intellectual superiority, which keeps him safe from disillusionment. Bundy is a scion of the United Fruit Company, a multinational company which established itself in Central America in the fifties and became a symbol of the most authoritarian colonization. The Banana Republics were so many orchards for United Fruit, which could make or break their governments. Young Mac George grew up like his brother William, sure in the knowledge that he belonged to a chosen class.

Mac George Bundy's political godfather was Henry Stimson, an influential member of the Council of Foreign Relations, and Defense Minister during the Second World War. In 1957 he directed the Harvard Center for Foreign Affairs, an anti-Communist institution financed by the CIA and the Ford and Carnegie Foundations, which was given the job of developing a "defense policy for the free world." The leading members of the center were John Foster Dulles, former president of the Rockefeller Foundation and Secretary of State, Dean Rusk, his successor at the Rockefeller Foundation from 1952 to 1960 who replaced him at the State Department three years later; James Perkins of the Carnegie Corporation, who later became president of Cornell University and a director of the Chase Manhattan Bank, and Don Price, vice-president of the Ford Foundation and former director of the Harvard Business School. Bundy's hardworking assistant at the Center was his deputy director Henry Kissinger.

Eleven years later, when Kissinger was summoned to advise Nixon, he had become director of the Center which still appeared equally anti-Communist in its leanings.

From 1960 to 1966, Bundy worked as special foreign policy adviser to Kennedy and Johnson. More particularly, he acted as a go-between for the White House and the CIA. The head of the intelligence service then was Allen Dulles, John's brother, and legal adviser to the Rockefellers' Standard Oil company and Bundy's United Fruit, as well as being a director of the Carnegie Foundation.

Bundy was behind such memorable resolutions as the assassination attempt on Castro in 1961, the Invasion of the Bay of Pigs in 1963, the crushing of the San Domingo revolution in 1965 and the escalation of the war effort against North Vietnam at the time when Hanoi was first bombed. Support for this show of strength against Communist and Progressive forces came from Defense Secretary Robert McNamara, who had developed such matchstick models as the theory of graduated reprisal which allowed for the use of nuclear weapons against the USSR in cases of aggression. Today, McNamara has passed through the board of the Ford Foundation to become president of the World Bank, where he plays lady bountiful to the Third World. By granting or refusing credits to developing countries the World Bank can, in fact, keep the Southern hemisphere in total dependence on the big multinationals. There are very good reasons why McNamara's predecessors as president should have included John MacCloy and Eugene Black, director of the Chase Manhattan and president of the Ford Foundation.

In retrospect, the most striking aspect of Bundy's and McNamara's views in the sixties is their extreme inadequacy. Their attitudes were merely more sophisticated versions of the ideas of MacArthur, who wanted to destroy China in the fifties, or the opinions of the former Chief of Strategic Air Command who hoped to "put Vietnam back in the Stone Age." Today, like Dillon, Bundy has had these previous episodes in his career glossed over; and the Ford and Rockefeller Foundations, with one foot firmly in the Eastern countries, can negotiate with Communist leaders free from any governmental control, looking for all the world like paragons of philanthropy in the service of détente. William Bundy, Mac George's brother, is now manager of *Foreign Affairs*, the Council of Foreign Relation's highly influential review, after working at the CIA from 1951 to 1961 and at the Pentagon from 1964 to 1969. His editorials and numerous articles by Euro-Communists are hymns to the advantages of peace and cooperation with the Communist world, although the *Pentagon Reports* published in 1971 described him as "planner in chief" of the aggressive raids over North Vietnam, which culminated in the adoption of the Gulf of Tonkin resolution.

The big foundations are the dressing rooms of the government. John Foster Dulles (the Dulleses were relatives of the Rockefellers) was president of the Carnegie Endowment and then of the Rockefeller Foundation, before he became Secretary of State and high priest of the Cold War. Dean Rusk was president of the Rockefeller Foundation from 1953 to 1960 before becoming Secretary of State from 1961 to 1969, since when he has been special adviser to Nelson Rockefeller. John Gardner, Minister of Health, Education and Welfare, was president of the Carnegie Corporation of New York from 1955 to 1965. Dwight Eisenhower was a director of the Ford and Carnegie Foundations. Robert McNamara, Defense Secretary from 1961 to 1968 and now president of the World Bank, has been a director of the Ford Foundation and piously manages both the Robert Kennedy Memorial Foundation and his own institution.

Among other things, Henry Kissinger has been director of the "Special Studies Project" attached to the Rockefeller Brothers Fund. Douglas Dillon and Robert Roosa, Finance Minister between 1960 and 1965, are directors of the Rockefeller Foundation. David Bell, vice-president of the Ford Foundation, spent six years at the White House, first as budget director for Kennedy and then as manager of the International Development Agency. Ralph Bunche was secretary of the Rockefeller Brothers Fund. Cyrus Vance, Jimmy Carter's Secretary of State, sat on the boards of several Rockefeller Foundations. Paul Hoffman, former president of the Ford Foundation was American delegate to the United Nations. Max Millikan, a colleague of Nelson Rockefeller, was joint-director of the CIA. John Connally, Nixon's Finance Minister, former governor of Texas and close associate of Sindona, was a director of the Sid W. Richardson Foundation. Arthur Schlesinger and John K. Galbraith, two of Kennedy's advisers, are on the board of the Twentieth Century Fund. John MacCloy and Eugene Black, former presidents of the World Bank, have been directors of the Ford and Rockefeller Foundations. At least four members of the Nixon cabinet had their own foundations. These were Maurice Stans, Trade Minister; John Volpe, Transport Minister; George Romney, Social Affairs Minister; and David Packard, Under-Secretary of State for Defense.

Real coordination between these institutions actually takes place within the Council of Foreign Relations, where representatives of the various foundations, the big business élites and the political, financial, University and press worlds regularly meet together. Every single important decision affecting American policy has been developed and proposed by the Council, which is now chaired by David Rockefeller and financed by the Rockefeller Brothers Fund and the Ford and Carnegie Foundations. This select clique has 1,400 members, more than half of whom have belonged since 1946 and have therefore had plenty of time to prove their anti-Communism. And yet it was at the home of the Council, at Harold Pratt House, a four-storey New York building on the corner of Park Avenue and 68th Street that détente sprang joyfully to life. It is fascinating to see how this particular religious institution has brought its ideas up to date, leaving behind its precepts of total chastity to encourage caresses with the Communists.

To take just one example of the Council's influence, sixty-four of the eighty-two people chosen by John F. Kennedy to staff the State Department, whether Democrat or Republican, were members of the Council. His Secretary of State Dean Rusk (a Democrat) and his Finance Minister Douglas Dillon (a Republican) both belonged to the Council and to the Rockefeller Foundation. Seven of the assistants and under-secretaries, four of the Pentagon officials (the deputy Secretary of State, the comptroller, the assistant for foreign security affairs and the personnel assistant) were connected with the organization. So, too, were two of Kennedy's personal advisers, Mac George Bundy (a Republican) and James Schlesinger (a Democrat). Schlesinger later became director of the CIA and the Defense Ministry, (where he was replaced by Gerald Ford) before returning to the Carter government as Energy Minister.

The Council's influence on governmental action has never been denied. In 1939 Secretary of State Cordell Hull and War Minister Henry Stimson, member and president of the Council respectively, used Rockefeller money to set up study groups on economic, strategic and political problems connected with the war. According to the influential American journalist Joseph Kraft (a member of the Council), the American Executive in 1942 had access to "a collection of proposals and analyses applicable to the postwar period." In 1942 MacCloy (a member of the Council) was appointed Stimson's assistant at the War Ministry. In 1945 the Council's plans resulted in the creation of the United Nations, the World Bank and the International Monetary Fund, three contrivances designed as a sop to dreamers and, more especially, as a way of institutionalizing the existing economic power. Forty-seven of the American delegation to the inaugural session of the UN belonged to the Council. Among them were Edward R. Stettinius, director of the Morgan Bank and Secretary of State; Nelson Rockefeller, Secretary of State for Latin American Affairs; John Foster Dulles, Republican spokesman on foreign policy; and John MacCloy, Under-Secretary for War.

In 1946 the Council was chaired by Allen Dulles, a lawyer connected with the Rockefellers and future director of the CIA.

In 1947, another member of the Council, George Kennan, director of the State Department's Political Planning Service, and later ambassador to Moscow, published an article in *Foreign Affairs* which was taken as an official justification for cold war policies. This resoundingly successful analysis, which he signed "X," set out Kennan's opinions on the Communist threat and ways of containing it. By taking the article literally, American diplomacy was spared the necessity of considering the matter for the next twenty years.

The importance which the Chase Manhattan Bank of David Rockefeller accords to the Council on Foreign Relations was clearly spelled out in one of the Bank's bulletins devoted to East–West trade (*East–West Markets*, May 16, 1977). In an article devoted to a CFR staff-man, Zygmunt Nagorski, Chase states:

> Although Mr Nagorski has not been directly involved in the shaping of US foreign policy, for the past eight years he has been working in the "kitchen of ideas that go into the implementation of American policy" at the Council on Foreign Relations, which is still the real home of the US foreign policy establishment. In this environment he has argued that East European countries should be viewed and treated more as individual, national entities by the US, despite their dependence on the Soviet Union. For instance, "the long-term credit policy of the US toward these countries should not be based on purely financial considerations but aimed at maintaining political stability."

In other words, the foreign policy establishment believes Rockefeller credits should become the underpinning of the Communist élite in power and the buttress of the status quo against destabilizing forces such as dissidents and proponents of freedoms of speech, strikes and voting.

The members of the Council oligarchy are also remarkable manipulators. Since 1945 there has been no reason why this state of affairs should cease. The whole of the American and Western intellectual establishment is as quick to defend and justify the minority's decisions and vacillations as the Muscovite Agit-prop officials.

Leaving aside certain inherent human tendencies to subservience, this suspension of the critical faculty can best be explained by the hold which the economic and financial power base has over universities and research institutes.

In 1975, 107 of the 191 most important academic centers in the United States were dependent for basic finance on the Ford Foundation. Eighteen were financially controlled by the Rockefeller Foundation. Eleven of the twelve most prestigious American universities with institutes for foreign studies are reliant on the generosity of the Ford Foundation. These are Columbia, Harvard, Chicago, Berkeley, UCLA, Cornell, Indiana, MIT, Michigan State, Stanford and Wisconsin.

These institutions also act as umbrellas for ninety-five research centers, eighty-three of which are financed by Ford and five by the Carnegie Foundation.

The universities provide a privileged setting for the symbiosis between the intellectual, military and business worlds.

In 1945 the Rockefeller Foundation set up the first institute for Russian Studies at Columbia. This academic body had direct links with the Military School and with the University's Center for Naval Warfare, whose director, Schyler Wallace, obtained a seat on the Ford Foundation board some years later. The founder and first director of the institute was G. Robinson, head of the "research and analysis" division of the Soviet Section at the OSS, forebear to the CIA. Joseph Wilits, director of Social Sciences at the

Rockefeller Foundation, donated $1,250,000 to the institute over five years. Wilits, like Robinson and Schyler Wallace, was a member of the Council on Foreign Relations. The aim of the Russian Institute is to train students for technical and directorial posts in those government agencies handling foreign activities. In 1960, students at the school published a pamphlet entitled *Employment Opportunities for Students Trained in Foreign Affairs*. The most frequently listed jobs, in order of priority, were with the CIA, the State Department, the International Development Agency, the American Information Agency, the National Security Agency. Then came the Chase Manhattan Bank, the First National City Bank, Mobil and Standard Oil of New Jersey. Last of all, despised and rejected, were the United Nations and other international organizations. In 1968, the institute's director, Andrew Cordier, who was also an adviser to the State Department and the Ford Foundation, revealed the unsurprising news that 40% of the graduates went into government services, and 30% were divided between the big banks and the international business world.

On its creation, four of the institute's five directors were members of the State Department, the OSS and the Council on Foreign Relations. In 1947 the Rockefeller Foundation donated $75,000 in bursaries to various students. Between 1947 and 1953 the Carnegie Foundation granted study prizes to students at the institute who also benefited from regular scholarships from the University of Columbia.

Robinson was succeeded as head of the institute by Philip Mosely, president of the Joint Committee of Slavic Studies and director of the World Research Committee of the Social Sciences Research Council, an organization financed by the foundations and the CIA.

In 1947 there were also plans to set up a Russian Studies Center at Harvard. The initial idea came from John Gardner, a graduate of the OSS who later became Health Minister and president of the Carnegie Corporation. Gardner was also a partner of the important Wall Street lawyer, Deverdeaux Josephs, who was reputed to be one of the four best informed experts on American economic questions, together with the bankers Robert Lovett, John MacCloy and Douglas Dillon. Josephs was a director of several nerve centers of American finance, including the New York Life Insurance Company, the Rockefeller Center, and the American Smelting and Refining Company. During the spring of 1947, Gardner and the Harvard board were actively engaged in setting up the study program, which was seen as an inter-university organization. It was envisaged that the post of president would go to Clyde Kluckholm, a Harvard professor who had previously worked for the OSS.

After two meetings in mid-October between Gardner, Kluckholm, the president of Harvard and Charles Dollard of the Carnegie Corporation, a former colleague of Deverdeaux Josephs, the center was born. Financial support came from the Carnegie Foundation in the form of $750,000 to be spread over five years. In 1953 it was the Ford Foundation's turn to contribute to the center's expenses. In 1949 the center embarked on the *Refugee Interview Project*, a large-scale study of the Russian social system based on intensive interrogation of numerous Soviet refugees. This project was financed by the US Air Force Institute of Research into Human Resources. All information acquired was to go to the Pentagon and the CIA to fuel the anti-Communist propaganda machine. Various Navy, Army and Air Force personnel and members of the College of War and Industry worked at the Russian center as professors or experts.

Between 1950 and 1960, Harvard University became an inner sanctum for the spokesmen of anti-Communist ideology in the United States. One of the finest fruits to grow from this early grafting was Henry Kissinger, a perfect symbol of all the compromises which may beset the humble man's career prospects.

From 1954 he directed the International Seminary at Harvard, which was entirely financed by the CIA and was frequented every summer by entertaining personalities such as Raymond Aron from France, Bertrand Russell from England, Olof Palme from Sweden and Socialist leader Bulent Ečevit from Turkey.

In 1956 Kissinger coordinated the Rockefeller Brothers Fund "Special Studies" and became Nelson's adviser on foreign policy. Basically he devoted his mind to serving his employer's own hobby-horses, sticking as closely to them as he could. He betrayed no independence of mind whatever, no pride in his own opinions. Nelson Rockefeller has always had a passion for information; in this respect, Gerald Ford's appointment of him as leader of a commission on the activities of the CIA in 1975 was rather like asking a criminal to lead enquiries into the whereabouts of his stolen loot. In many countries Rockefeller interests and CIA networks appear to be one and the same.

The size and diversity of the Rockefeller empire explain why Nelson has been associated with important resolutions concerning espionage, whatever the government in office. Under Nixon he sat on the Foreign Intelligence Advisory Board set up to monitor the various para-diplomatic activities of the CIA and the National Security Agency. Rockefeller's assistant and staff officer there was Nancy Maginess, who became Kissinger's second wife in 1973.

But Kissinger had many more paths to cross before he reached the heights of notoriety. In 1955 Rockefeller gave the impression of being a hardliner. He supported an increase in the military budget, the development of exotic and varied forms of tactical nuclear warfare and the establishment of a massive civil defense program. In 1957 Kissinger published a book entitled *Nuclear Weapons and Foreign Policy* which recommended a hardening of already rigid attitudes towards the Communists and the use of tactical nuclear weapons. The spectacle of Kissinger outdoing Eisenhower's Vice-President Nixon in the fervour of his anti-Communism and of the two men then coupling to produce an infant peace-strategy must have been a morally comforting sight. Kissinger's book was the product of observations made by a study group set up by the Council on Foreign Relations. The members of this group included a former CIA chief, two former Pentagon officials, the president of the Carnegie Institution of Washington, Mac George Bundy, William A. M. Burden, director of Lockheed and of the Manufacturers' Trust Company and David Rockefeller. Some months later the Pentagon hired Kissinger as an adviser.

In 1961 he enthusiastically welcomed the start of American intervention in Vietnam. In 1968, the year of the presidential election, he became deeply involved in the campaign for Republican investiture. Tirelessly brandishing a machete, he attempted to hack out a path towards the supreme office for Nelson Rockefeller. But no matter how Kissinger redoubled his attacks on Nixon, no matter how loud he voiced his doubts as to whether Eisenhower's Vice-President had it in him to make a good President, the governor of New York advanced too slowly and laboriously. Once the lanterns of the electoral carnival had gone out, the actors removed their make up and found themselves back where they had started. Nixon had beaten Rockefeller, but Kissinger had demonstrated his efficiency. Warmly supported by Nelson, he became the new President's foreign policy adviser, thus proving that for the truly cynical the American dream of social success could still be more than a myth.

Every deviation from the orthodox was rapidly brought into line. In 1966 Stanley K. Sheinbaum was sacked from Michigan State University and could find no work thereafter, because he was the first man to expose the cooperation between that university and the CIA in South Vietnam. At Stanford, Ronald Hilton was director of one of the oldest Latin American institutes and had been publishing the *Hispano–American Report* since 1948. This was the only university publication to criticize the policy of the big companies in the Southern hemisphere. In 1960, David Packard, as spokesman for Stanford's financial backers, demanded that the university control the contents of Hilton's publication. Some months later the Ford Foundation assigned $42 million for the creation of a Hispanic Studies Committee intended to compete with Hilton's. This new center was directed by the distinguished academic Dean Carl Spaeth, whose only recommendation was that he had been Nelson Rockefeller's assistant for Latin American questions and director of Overseas Activities at the Ford Foundation. In 1963, under severe pressure, Hilton was forced to leave both his post and his journal. Two weeks after his resignation, the Ford Foundation donated $550,000 to Stanford to be used solely for the study of Latin American problems.

In 1960 the Hoover Institute underwent a similar change of orientation at the whim of its founder and patron. The director, a liberal, was sacked and replaced by the conservative economist Wesley Glen Campbell, who had previously worked with the Pentagon, the American Chamber of Commerce and the American Business Institute, an organization notorious for its extreme rightwing attitude. The former president Herbert Hoover redefined the priorities of the institute which had until then been dealing with apolitical archive material. Its aim, he declared, "must be to demonstrate through research and publications, the disastrous consequences of the doctrines of Karl Marx, of Communism and Socialism, of the materialist economy and atheism, and to reaffirm the validity of the American system." Campbell constructed his staff to suit his reactionary attitudes. His assistant had previously worked with Edgar Hoover, the fervent anti-Communist who ran the FBI for forty years. Ronald Regan, governor of California, named Campbell "regent" of the University of California. Packard, Standard Oil, Gulf Oil, Union Carbide and Lockheed, the center's main sources of financial support, showed their pleasure at this rightwing backlash by increasing their contributions. A year after Campbell's arrival, the annual budget was $2 million as opposed to a previous $400,000. The Hoover Institute supplied the Nixon administration with a large number of experts appointed to the Bureau of Foreign Security Affairs at the Defense Department which was in charge of coordinating foreign policy and military activity. These men had every opportunity to demonstrate their flexibility by implementing a policy of détente totally at variance with the criteria governing their initial ideological training.

It does not always take tanks to scratch trivial graffiti on the public urinals still waiting for Lenin's promised transmutation into gold. The most efficient method, which incidentally maintains a superficial appearance of democracy, is more like the work of a taxidermist, or the manufacture of lifesize, inflatable dolls designed to satisfy basic physiological needs. Usually these dummies are given an intellectual exterior sufficiently suggestive to satisfy the erotic dreams of the customer. The Herbert Marcuse model was very successful. This German export persists in believing that no philosophical work will be taken seriously unless it is as heavy and unreadable as Hegel.

A university mandarin with revolutionary ideals, he emphasizes the American working class's capacity for revolution, while addressing the most abstract and hypersophisticated fringe of Western intelligentsia. His book, the *One-dimensional Man*, the disenchanted analysis of a capitalist system and culture which he suggests should be destroyed, was totally financed by the Rockefeller Foundation.

Noam Chomsky, the linguist of international repute, plunged into the Vietnam conflict like a bad swimmer diving into the sea, with a lifebelt. Over the years he contributed to an increasing number of enquiries, books and conferences. To further his case against the "Fascist" tendencies of the US he pored over the effects of napalm bombing with all the frenzy of a medical student discovering the dissecting table. And yet this spokesman for a courageous and Kleenex-clean America never thought to resign from his post at MIT, the Pentagon's real factory, nor to break off relations with the US Air Force which generously financed his linguistic studies.

These two examples of the lengths to which intellectual abnegation can go are by no means isolated.

Anyone who criticizes the "American State" or the "Capitalist system" is clinging onto absurdly abstract and theoretical terms which only serve to reinforce the real powers sitting smugly behind their screen of tattered concepts.

The whole of the Overworld power base will remain equally pragmatic and equally adept at mixing the missal with the account book. James B. Duke, the tobacco magnate, was modelling himself on John Rockefeller when he created his foundation. Today, with more than $600 million in net assets, the Duke Endowment is the fourth largest charitable institution in the United States. Through the Methodist Church, which it finances, it exercises total control over the souls of North Carolina, the home of Duke's tobacco plantations. The efficiency of the operation manifests itself on two levels: for this kind of mental imprisonment keeps the whole state shut off from social and economic reality. Even now North Carolina is about as sensitive in its perception of the outside world as Albania. No trade union has ever managed to establish a foothold there or to influence a population manipulated by their pastors in the services of great interests. For European employers like Michelin, ICI, Hoechst and Akzo, which feel that their belief in free enterprise is being increasingly attacked by their social partners, the Southern States are becoming a New Amsterdam. At the same time the Duke Endowment has no trouble in adapting to the realities of contemporary finance. Its president belongs to the board of the Morgan Bank and is a director of General Motors and of the Penn Central Railroad Company.

Two thirds of Exxon's net income comes from the company's operations in fifty-two different countries. This means that the Rockefeller has to achieve on a global scale what the Duke Endowment succeeds in doing on the one-state level. In many cases, gifts are parachuted down directly over derricks and pipe-lines. In 1966 the Foundation spent $1 million on education and training for the Nigerian élites and only $1,000 on Kentucky. Obviously a country which is bound to become the biggest oil producer in the African Continent and is transfused with ethnic conflicts and nationalistic tendencies is worth more attention than a single American state, unless of course it is about to secede.

The same year, for similar reasons, Colombia received $2 million, again from the Rockefeller Foundation, which continued to ignore the existence of South Carolina, Wyoming, Maine and Delaware.

Outside America, US government policy and the programs of the big foundations are often inextricably bound together. Over the last thirteen years, three of the Rockefeller's charitable organizations have obtained $18 million from the International Development Agency.

In 1973, the Ford Foundation employed 850 people in the United States and 920 in other countries. In 1975 its favourite causes were India, Indonesia and Brazil, three countries well known for their affable and tolerant régimes. A couple of rural hospitals in the Punjab or sterilization experiments in Singapore should not blind us to the realities of the situation. The foundations do not bring comfort to the suffering masses of the Third World, only peace of mind to their rulers. And they are true political crossbreeds, closer in their outlook to the New York or Parisian middle classes than to the people living in the shanty towns around their capitals.

The fact that there are some admirable people with indisputably humanitarian ideals involved in these charity sales does nothing to alter the foundations' position as vehicles of a political system designed to uphold the economic domination of the Overworld.

Think-tanks, military centers, etc.

In 1968 the new American left was reinforced by the creation of the Institute for Political Studies. With offices in Washington, this new center aspired not only to become an organ of opinion but also to establish a close involvement in active politics. Its co-director, the writer Marcus Ruskin, was also president of a committee for the formation of a new party, and in 1968 the institute supported the presidential campaign of the black comedian Dick Gregory who opposed the Vietnam war. Ruskin later figured as co-defendant in the suit brought against pediatrician Benjamin Spock who was accused of encouraging draft-dodging. In 1969 the other director of the Institute, Richard Kauffman, demonstrated his outstanding awareness of American realities when he sent Congress a report predicting the nationalization of the arms industry.

This Park Avenue radicalism, which transforms the law courts into fashionable drawing-rooms, is financed by the clearly willing Ford, Samuel Rabin and Milbank foundations.

The tendency of leftwing brains to become hypertrophied in self-admiration is brilliantly exploited at the Center for the Study of Democratic Institutions. This intellectual gymnasium is situated near the Pacific beaches in Santa Barbara, in a position which lends itself to soul-searching about the future of the alienated working classes. It was created and financed by the Ford Foundation. In 1970 the Albert-Parvin Foundation also began to contribute support and put in one of its employees, Justice Douglas, as president of the center's management board. Through Parvin and Douglas the organization came under the influence of Lansky and the Mafia.

Before entering the field of philanthropy, Albert Parvin owned the casino hotel Flamingo in Las Vegas. Since its opening in 1946, several of the owners of this establishment had come to an untimely end. First there was the *maffioso* Bugsy Siegel, killed in 1953. His successor, Gus Greenbaum, met a similar fate in 1955. Parvin bought the business, remained alive, and on 12 May 1960, signed a contract with Meyer Lansky. Lansky negotiated the sale of the Flamingo, so as to bring Parvin a handsome profit and himself a commission of $200,000. In November 1960, again on the advice of Lansky and his assistant Ed Levinson, Parvin placed the $10.5 million received from the sale in a foundation set up in his name a few weeks before. This meant that, like all the great American professional bodies, the crime syndicate now had its own charitable, tax-exempt organization. Since 1954 Parvin had been high on the Justice Ministry's list of organized crime leaders. In 1961, the lawyer William J. Douglas was appointed head of the foundation. The other members of the board were Robert Hutchin, former president of the Ford Foundation, Robert Gooheen, president of Princeton University, William Campbell, leading judge of the Chicago district bench and Henry Ashmore, a progressive journalist and director for the Center for the Study of Democratic Institutions. The foundation's legal adviser was Carolyn Agger who worked for Arnold and Porter. She was married to Abe Fortas who later became a Supreme Court judge before being dismissed from office in 1969 because of his involvement in various financial scandals.

In December 1962, Bobby Baker, a friend of Lansky and a close colleague of Lyndon Johnson, met the Liberal leader Juan Bosch in New York. Bosch was a candidate in the approaching presidential elections in the Domincan Republic. In January 1963, the Parvin Foundation decided to concentrate its Latin-American acitivities on this particular Caribbean state. Justice Douglas made Juan Bosch out to be one of his old friends. On 2 February, Bobby Baker and Ed Levinson flew from Miami to meet Lansky, who already had a firm foothold in San Domingo, as he had done in Batista's Cuba twenty years before. His protégé dictator Trujillo's bloody and brutal end had taught him the urgent necessity of playing the cautious, reformist hand. Bosch was by now totally under Mafia control. The Parvin Foundation financed his campaign, while the members of the syndicate exploited his weakness of character. On 27 February 1963, the American Air Force plane taking the official delegation to the investiture ceremonies landed at San Domingo. Down the gangway came Lyndon Johnson, then Vice-President, followed by Hubert Humphrey, two Under-Secretaries, Mr and Mrs Jack Valenti, Mrs Elisabeth Carpenter, Bobby Baker and Ed Levinson. A few weeks after the election, the Parvin Foundation offered to finance an educational television project in the Domincan Republic, while Douglas was seconded as adviser to Bosch in his efforts to produce a new constitution.

The Mafia was also busy protecting its many investments in the island. In the spring of 1963, there was a meeting in the Dominican capital between important "family" leaders like Angelo Bruno, John Simone, Joseph Sicarelli, Eugene Pozo, Santos Trafficante Jr, Louis "Sleep Out" Levinson (Ed's brother), Leslie E. Kruse, Killer Kane and Sam Giancana, the Chicago Mafia boss. Bobby Baker and Abe Fortas were negotiating the sale of fruit machines for the Serv. U. Corporation. Finally on 26 August, during a conversation with Clifford Jones, former Lieutenant Governor of Nevada and associate of Baker, who had worked with Lansky, Bosch confirmed that the concessions and gambling licences which his predecessor Trujillo had granted to the Cosa Nostra would continue to be honoured.

Between 1966 and 1969, the Parvin Dorhman Company bought the Aladdin, Fremont and Stardust gambling hotels in Las Vegas. Their partners in this deal were the FOF Proprietary Fund Ltd. of Geneva, an offshoot of speculator Bernie Cornfeld's multinational financial empire.

Much of the European left wing, which claims to be intellectual and responsible, betrays a basic misunderstanding of American problems, which is all the more disturbing when one realizes that such people bring the same lack of fundamental awareness to bear on analyses of their own countries. Their tendency to use the word to suit some personal ambition or to remould reality to suit some ideological argument may have serious consequences. While these few, non-Communist, leftwing featherweights pirouette about, the field is free for all kinds of totalitarianism to come to power.

These people tend to see everything in black and white terms. They rightly applaud the just and heroic "struggle" of the Vietnamese people and lambast "American imperialism," while hailing the work of organizations like the Massachusetts Institute of Technology, which is totally bound up in the military–industrial complex nurturing the South-East Asia conflict. It is in this appendix of the Defense Ministry that the arms industry, through its connections with the foundations, becomes inextricably linked with the research centers. And MIT succeeds in allaying the fears of the idle, progressive politicians who will take the odd pause in their parliamentary activities to pore respectfully over 300-page, computer-written essays on the ill effects of pollution in Uganda.

On a more serious level, the activities of MIT have been summarized by its spokesman

Edward Hanify as follows : "We are among the top scientific forces engaged in research considered vital to national defense by the government. We are a scientific arsenal of democracy, designed to secure our survival. "Of the seventy-five leading arms manufacturers, nineteen have representatives on the MIT Corporation management board. The Rand Corporation is still the best known of these intellectual institutions carefully moulded to the advantage of the arms industry. Created in 1946, it is financed by the Ford Foundation and keeps 1,100 people, 600 of them professional research scientists, hard at work in its Santa Monica home. Contracts with the US Air Force account for two thirds of the Rand's annual budget. It has worked on rocket propulsion, on putting space stations into orbit and on improving ballistic missiles. More recently a number of military services have asked the Rand to compile interdisciplinary studies on "foreign aid" and "anti-guerilla warfare." Recent Rand reports have been entitled "Vietcong, Motivation and Morale," "The Support of Guerilla Systems and Limited Warfare," "Politics and Economic Growth in India."

Chairman of the board, David Shepard, has been executive vice-president of the Rockefellers' Standard Oil of New Jersey. His fellow board members include Michael Ference, vice-president of Ford Motors, William Hewlett, an associate of David Packard and former Under-Secretary of State for Defense, Philip Mosely, director of the European Institute at Columbia, Lauris Norstadt, former Commander in Chief of NATO and president and managing director of Owens-Corning Fiberglass Corporation, James Perkins, president of Cornell University, and Don Price, former director of Harvard and of the Rockefeller Foundation.

During the summer of 1950, a Center for Foreign Studies was set up at MIT as an extension to the Harvard Russian Institute, to research into "the means of ensuring a penetration of ideas beyond the Iron Curtain" for the military establishment. Financial support came from the CIA and the Carnegie and Rockefeller foundations, and Pr Walt Rostow was given the job of organizing the creation of the Center. A former secret-service official, Rostow later directed the State Department's Political Planning Service under Kennedy and Johnson, before succeeding Mac George Bundy as chief presidential adviser on foreign policy in 1965. Rostow was also a distinguished member of the American academic and bureaucratic establishment, who, as an economist, had evolved a theory of underdevelopment without ever setting foot in the Third World. His ideas are about as consistent and weighty as comic strips when compared to real literature. When first founded, the center's board members included Allen Dulles, the CIA boss, Charles Bolhen of the State Department and later ambassador to Moscow and Paris, Philip Mosely of the Russian Institute at Columbia and Leslie O'Steven, retired vice-admiral. The first director of the center, Max Milikan, left his post in 1952 to become joint director of the CIA.

In 1951, at the request of the Army, Navy and Air Force, the Lincoln Laboratory was set up at MIT to work in the electronics field. This agency developed the SAGE system, the DEW and the BMEWS, three defense and anti-missile warning systems presently in use in the US. In 1968 the Air Force spent $66 million on the laboratory, a sum representing roughly two thirds of MIT's income from defense contracts. With financial support from the Pentagon's Agency for Projects and Advanced Research, the laboratory also conceived the PRESS project. On the Pacific atoll of Kivajaleim, its researchers worked on offensive and defensive programs designed to make American intercontinental ballistic missiles capable of increased penetration into enemy air space.

The Laboratory of Instrumentation was also a totally separate unit of the Massachusetts Institute. Until 1969, there were 1,100 scientists and technicians working there, with an annual budget of more than $30 million from contracts for the Defense

Department. This center devoted special attention to automatic aircraft controls, modules, nuclear submarines and ballistic missiles. Recent projects have provided for the development of guidance systems for Polaris submarines and Poseidon missiles. In 1970, following a number of student demonstrations, the Laboratory of Instrumentation was renamed the Charles Stark Draper Laboratory, a company theoretically independent of MIT. This was actually a pure legality: the laboratory worked in closer collaboration than ever with the MIT board and the value of contracts undertaken has risen to $60 million.

Its researchers have applied their talents to the Apollo program, the US Air Force SABRE System and Poseidon missiles. The verges of Highway 128 which links Boston to its suburbs have become the setting for a vast picnic. Over the last fifteen years, more than 160 companies established by former employees have grown up around MIT. Some of these firms, such as the Itek Corporation and Teledyne Inc., have become giant multinational ventures with several thousand employees and annual sales of hundreds of millions of dollars. Three quarters of them are military research organizations which continue to work in total symbiosis with the institute. The president of one such company, Mitre Corporation, which works on aerial defense systems for the Pentagon, is James Kilian, director in chief of MIT.

It was inevitable that such a confusion of interests should have ended in Vietnam, a perfect medium for the interested parties. The companies could sell and replace extraordinarily sophisticated and expensive equipment. The military men could win medals by conducting a technological war which involved few risks, cost few lives and which they could not lose. The only people to see Vietnam for the fiasco it was were the sacrificed population and the tens of thousands of ordinary men who acted out their bloody roles in a nightly soap opera dished up to Western television viewers. With all due deference to the good souls who like to believe that the causes which they consider right will triumph, the big arms companies would have been only too delighted to carry on their involvement in South East Asia, had the necessity of trade with the East not forced them to cut short their fruitful mail-order business there.

David Packard provides us with a typical example. Nixon's Under-Secretary for Defense was a former garage owner who had made a fortune manufacturing electronics systems and contributing to the American war effort between 1942 and 1945. Now an industrial giant with annual sales of more than $1 billion, his firm has always maintained its loyal adherence to the interests of the military–industrial complex. Packard's company achieved record profits in Vietnam, while at the same time signing important contracts with the USSR and the Eastern countries.

One of the most important facets of a hypersophisticated industry like arms manufacture, where technical innovation now counts for everything, is the training of skilled and qualified personnel. Packard and his partner Hewlett lurk on the board of the venerable university of Stanford near San Francisco Bay, from where they can help to administer and finance the Stanford Research Institute. This center for industrial studies, built around the university, is working in the fields of electronics and physics. Assisting Hewlett and Packard in their burdensome task are John Gardner, former president of the Carnegie Foundation and present director of the Urban Coalition Foundation which is co-financed by the Rockefeller and Carnegie Foundations, and Stephen Bechtel, president of the largest construction company in the world. The Bechtel Corporation is responsible for such varied proofs of man's creative genius as the American bases in Vietnam, Thailand, Cambodia and the Philippines, and the construction and laying of the giant Alaskan and Middle Eastern oil pipe-lines. Today Bechtel has acquired the services of George Schultz, former Finance Minister to Nixon, and has shifted a large part of his business, as Packard did, towards the Communist markets. Over the twenty-two years of its existence, Bechtel, Packard and Hewlett have made the Stanford Research Institute one of the largest American research centers, with a staff of more than 2,000 and an annual income of $60 million, half of which comes from defense contracts.

The SRI acts as an umbrella for centers for "naval warfare," "the experimentation and development of combat" and "strategic studies." But its finest flower is the chemical and bacteriological warfare program financed by big business and the Pentagon, which calls itself "Studies and Research on the Dissemination of Solid and Liquid Agents in case of Bacteriological and Chemical War." A number of researchers from SRI worked in South Vietnam and Thailand. The Stanford Electronics Laboratory, attached to the university's Electronic Engineering department, developed a system to detect, warp and destroy enemy radar which was used by American airmen over North Vietnam.

Michigan State University worked with the CIA on drawing up the 1961 South Vietnamese constitution, which was intended to legalize and affirm the Diem régime. The Michigan State also trained the South Vietnamese police force. This spontaneous devotion to American foreign policy was largely the responsibility of John Hanah, president of the university and former poultry breeder. After initial obscurity, Hanah entered politics in 1949. He worked under Nelson Rockefeller on a presidential commission set up to develop "Point 4" of the foreign aid program during the cold war. Hanah made Michigan State University "one of the largest providers of services and educational programs throughout the world," and as the university developed, so Hanah rose. He left his chicken houses for a post as assistant in the Defense Ministry and then became president of the Chicago Federal Reserve Bank, director of the Michigan Bell Telephone and more recently president of the American Council on Education, the largest university lobby in Washington.

In 1960, one of his companies, the Hanah Mining Company, which owned several iron ore concessions in Brazil, fell foul of president João Goulart's nationalistic whims. Four years later the indiscreet politician was wiped out by a military group composed of model pupils of the Pentagon training centers.

At the same time, the ubiquitous John MacCloy left the board of the Chase Manhattan Bank to become the chief shareholder in the lawyers' office of Milbank, Tweed and Hardley which had connections with the Rockefellers. There Hanah's threatened interests became MacCloy's concern. Given Hanah's business to handle he negotiated directly with the leader of the Brazilian military dictatorship, general Castelo Branco. The new president received him several times. From all appearances he scattered his scintillating conversation with a few subtle arguments to the effect that any American aid depended on the return of concessions to Hanah. This is a typical example of a private person taking the place of a government body in political talks for purely economic interests. But Hanah's attraction to the Third World doubtless explains why Nixon appointed him head of the International Development Agency where he took over from David Bell, vice-president of the Ford Foundation.

If the CIA has now come to replace the Scout movement as a home for naive, malleable and idealistic youth, then Hanah can be regarded as a new Baden-Powell. A puritanical Protestant, he wanders like McNamara, Bundy, Rostow and many others, across the peaks of the business world, his only provision for the journey being a moral sense of the general interest which allows him to justify the unjustifiable. The way in which the interests of such men overlap and intermingle creates economic and financial blood ties which grow stronger from one generation to another. In 1889, after he had just spent $35 million on the creation of Chicago University, John Rockefeller met Frederick

Gates, director of the American Society for Baptist Education. This meeting opened up new paths for Rockefeller. Though his language was pretentious, Gates had all the fire of the itinerant preacher. Thus, when Rockefeller in all innocence hired this servant of God to help him plan and justify his philanthropic policy, Gates, a severe critic and a shrewd speculator, turned on him, "Your fortune is growing, growing like an avalanche; you must distribute more and more as it increases. If you do not do so, it will bury you, you and your children and your children's children."

Frederick Gates's son was recently American ambassador in Peking. Philanthropy moves in mysterious ways.

J. Edgar Hoover will doubtless remain one of the most solid but least known edifices of American socio-political architecture. In his forty years as the irremovable director of the FBI he managed to identify the activities of the federal police with the maintenance of a moral order in which respect for traditional values like the Bible or the army meant being systematically anti-Communist in outlook. But Hoover was actually a more complex figure: a St George who had been tamed by the dragon. His best friend, Lewis Rosenthiel made and trafficked in whisky and was known for his connections with the racketeers. He also owned Schenley Industries Inc., whose subsidiaries in Massachusetts, California and Florida experienced some difficulties in coexisting with the local police.

A third of these Hollywood gangster movie figures was Roy Cohn, a close friend of both Hoover and Rosenthiel. Cohn spent many years "red-hunting" in the service of governor McCarthy. Schenley is now one of the Vodka-Cola companies with a joint venture in the USSR. Seagram's Whisky, another company with origins in the racket also has "distilled" relations with the Soviet Union.

On 10 June 1965, Hoover inaugurated his foundation, which stands like a blockhouse hermetically sealed against "totalitarian" radiation in a distant suburb of Philadelphia. Its president, Louis B. Nichols, was until 1957 Hoover's closest assistant at the FBI before becoming vice-president of Schenley. The foundation's first officers were responsible for storing pernicious Soviet publications bought directly from Moscow for a dollar a copy, and most of them came from the police force. One of the vice-presidents, Donald Parsons, for example, left the FBI, to become president of the Parsons Paper Company. Similarly, the secretary, Deke De Loach, left the police force and the foundation in 1970 to join Donald Kendall, Pepsi Cola and the sulfurous shores of those forbidden pleasures practised beyond the Iron Curtain.

But it is William Simon who deserves our special attention. This ambitious young cop was director of the Bureau's Los Angeles office before becoming vice-president of the foundation. In 1967 he set off up the slippery slopes of the business world which he climbed with disconcerting speed. He entered Salomon Brothers, the largest American investment banker brokering billions of dollar loans to multinational business, housed in an ultramodern $8 million building at 1 New York Plaza. In 1975 the annual total of the deals and placements carried out by the company exceeded $250 billion.

Partnered by John Mitchell and Nixon's office of Mudge, Rose and Stern, Salomon Brothers also led the field in matters connected with negotiating and placing municipal and federal loans. Simon proved exceptionally incisive. Less than three years after entering the firm he became one of the seven members of Salomon's executive management committee in October 1970. In 1972 his detailed knowledge of Wall Street and his sharp sense of profitable investments brought him an annual income of $2 million. Simon was clearly ready to take up public service. In the same year, seventeen directors of Salomon Brothers gave $100,000 to the committee for the reelection of Nixon. Simon himself contributed $15,000, the price of a first-class ticket for a political cruise. In

December 1972 Nixon appointed him assistant to Finance Minister George Schultz, leader of the liberal Chicago school of economics which later advised the Chilean junta. A year later the Yom Kippur War and the resultant oil crisis made Simon "tsar of energy." His warm personal relations with the directors of the major companies made him an ideal choice as negotiator with the OPEC leaders.

In 1974, at the age of forty-six, his hair still worn with a clear-cut parting, his spectacles severe-looking, and with even less charisma than a combination on a safe, Simon became Minister of Finance. His predecessor, Schultz, had returned to the private sector to work for Stephen Bechtel, the construction king and a fervent supporter of economic integration with the East. For all these people came in and out of the same club by the one revolving door.

Politicians who become businessmen and businessmen who have sunk to political office are all actively pursuing their number one strategy of economic expansion towards the East. To this end there must be total control of the political adminstrative machine. So it was that Gerald Ford, still reeling from his election, added to Simon's ministerial duties by making him director of a "Bureau of Economic Policy." In this fourteen-member mini-government the New York businessman kept an amicable but nonetheless real rein on his government colleagues, as well as on Arthur Burns, president of the Federal Bank, William Eberle, managing director of the Council on International Economic Policy and Alan Greenspan, chief of the White House economic advisers.

Appointed controller of the vast areas of "great multinational capital" Simon could dream of bringing the virgin lands of Siberia and Kazakhstan under one management, and dwell on his ironic transformation from a would-be exorcist of Communism into a participant in frequent working breakfasts with the Kremlin leaders.

The creation, financing and use of clubs, universities and foundations represent so many weapons in the hands of the Vodka-Cola movement. When the upkeep of reputable minds costs so little and that pittance tax-deductible, then the holders of economic power can afford to neutralize and take over the intellectual fabric of the country as part of their daily activities.

Through Simon, Salomon Brothers gave New York University $3 million for the creation of a study and research center linked with the financial organizations.

George Murphy, former president of Irving Trust, the fourteenth largest banking house in America, and a client of Nixon the lawyer, was on the board of this venerable institution. So, too, was Elmer Bobst, president of Warner Lambert Pharmaceutical and a close friend of the defeated president. Uncle Elmer donated $30 million to the university for the creation of the "Bobst Library". Cleverly manipulated by its benefactors, New York University, a cold store for all kinds of outdated thinking, had become an important element in the consolidation of the breakthrough to the East. It has opened branches within the Karl Marx University of Budapest and offers after-sales service in the USSR designed to promote the use of conventional concepts likely to bring the élites of both sides closer together. According to Jean Monnet, Europe is closely involved in this movement. The fall of the Nazis left their manufacturing company, Krupp Industries, friendless and desolate. But with the help of Berthold Beitz, the company achieved a second breakthrough into the East which was far more successful than Hitler's had been. Since the days of the Cold War Krupp has had a firm foothold in Poland and the USSR and has thereby been able to continue its peaceful growth in the shadow of another totalitarian régime. In June 1974, Beitz met Derek Bok, president of Harvard, and donated $1 million to the university in the name of the Krupp foundation, in order to further the development of " European Studies." Both meeting and money were

negotiated by Guido Goldman, director of Harvard and an early freedom fighter in the
struggle against Communist advancement, who has since turned to reaping the golden
harvests of détente. The creation of these non-governmental superstructures enables
the members of the Overworld to avoid distressing and useless confrontations with a
debilitated and tongue-tied political power, while continuing to camp in the smoking
ruins of what was the traditional, institutional framework. Milton Rose, Nixon's partner and associate in the New York law office, was director of the Farfield Foundation, an
organization totally infiltrated by the CIA. He was also in charge of Accion Inter-
nacionale, an institution financed by the big companies to promote a program of urban
development in Latin America in the fight against Marxist influence. And yet, in the
midst of this anti-Marxist militancy, Rose continued to work with threequarters of his
clients on profitable deals with the Eastern bloc.

We shall have more to say about the activities and financial manipulations of Nixon's
accountant, Maurice Stans, later. However, when faced with the task in 1972 of amas-
sing funds for the presidential campaign, he managed to collect a record $60 million.
This sum perfectly illustrates the efficacy of certain methods which can be applied
within the electoral framework. All the companies wanting governmental authorizations for business in Eastern Europe had to put 1% of such a turnover into the moneybox
Stans was preparing to offer Nixon. Moreover, in order to ensure that no source of
American wealth was overlooked, Stans lent his support to the creation and development of hundreds of tin-pot committees with names like "The Active Friends of a
Balanced Society," or "The Committee for the Preservation of the American Dream."
Safely anonymous behind these prefabricated collecting boxes, generous donors could
make out cheques for the candidate of their choice. Donations came in this way from
Leonard, Harvey and Ray Firestone, heirs of the rubber empire. Leonard Firestone was
one of the twenty-six board members of the Richard Nixon Foundation and at the same
time a director of the Wells Fargo Bank (a Rockefeller interest) and the Western Airlines aviation company, as well as the Firestone Tire and Rubber Company. On social
evenings at the Bohemian Club, he could meet with fellow Californians such as John
McCone, former director of the CIA and ITT director, known for his discreet but effective
"support" of Allende's régime; Henry Kaiser, managing director and president of Kaiser
Industries; Stephen Bechtel and George Ducommon of Ducommon Engineers.

These five men, hardliners in political and social matters, could sit looking at the
Pacific while they dreamt of the banks of the Volga.

In 1971, Stans, then Trade Minister, was the first member of the Nixon administration to stand shivering on the frozen airport of the Soviet capital. He had come as a
commercial traveller to collect the first of the treaties signed by the Russian *nouveau
riches* in the hope of modernizing their industrial plant and machine tools. Stans had
left Washington for Moscow with half his mind on Bangkok. The Stans Foundation,
created in 1945, had several interests in anti-communist Thailand, notably in Thai
Industrial Estates, a company with numerous connections in those South Eastern capitals involved in the Indo–Chinese conflict. Stans had formed close relationships with the
local oligarchies involved in Washington's containment policy. His partner in South
East Asia was Henry Kearns, who had long represented the right wing of the Republican party and accompanied Nixon on several business trips to the Far East during the
sixties.

A former member of the Hoover commission of information services, Kearns became
director of Firestone for Thailand, after working as assistant Trade Minister for Foreign
Affairs under Eisenhower. Stans and Kearns found it all the more easy to manipulate
government funds because Kearns had previously worked for Nixon as director of the

Export–Import Bank which provides federal export credits, particularly for deals with the East. When the two accomplices ceased their profitable collaboration in 1972, the Stans Foundation received shares in the Siam Kraft Paper Company, a firm set up by Kearns with no other backing than $14 million from the Export–Import Bank. Blessed be the American tax-payers!

Another of these minor, Macchiavellian Medicis, Gustav L. Levy, was director of Goldman Sachs, one of the most powerful Wall Street banks. In 1972 he contributed $70,000 to Nixon's reelection campaign. Working as financial consultant to various organizations and to governments like the Panamanian, in 1974 Levy joined forces with Henry Fowler, Johnson's Treasury Secretary and President of the US Atlantic Council. This unofficial body was founded in 1961 by former Secretary of State Christian Herter, a member of the Council on Foreign Relations and heir to one of John Rockefeller's partners in Standard Oil. Its informal gatherings are attended by Henry Kissinger, Douglas Dillon, the banker and president of the Rockefeller Foundation, John MacCloy, the late former Vice-President Hubert Humphrey, former Secretary of State William Rogers and Jacob Javits, a Republican senator and influential lawyer to several multi-nationals. Like all clubs of this kind, the Atlantic Council was a meeting place for the men of real power who share the same taste for efficiency and an identical cult of the secret. But here it is not just the headmen of the business world who contribute to the discussions on the future of economic man. The most important of the men who make their mark on the military policy of the US and of the Western world also attend. Lauris Norstadt, former NATO chief and his successor William Leimnitzer meet with Lock-heed boss William Burden, the man with the ready cheque book. Industrialist David Packard, former Under-Secretary for Defense, who makes his money from contracts with the Pentagon and the East, can swap reminiscences with former ambassador in Saigon, Henry Cabot Lodge, or with Andrew J. Goodpaster, commander of the American troops in Vietnam. Through intensive reeducation, all these members of the old guard, rigged out in their starched uniforms, are being converted to the commercial priorities of arms production, and have long since accepted that testing nuclear warheads by sending a few samples to Leningrad or Peking would result in no more than a shortlived statistical estimate of their efficiency.

The military are no longer a rebellious social group prepared to threaten the peace which the businessmen have worked so hard to create. All the big guns are now on the same side as big business and will accept the new attitudes provided they are given new gadgets for their tanks from time to time.

So while Fowler and his friends keep up their superficial, belligerent rhetoric to justify the preservation of cracked old relics like NATO, they are actually accustoming the twilight figures stuck in ministerial and civil service offices to the idea of ever-increasing collaboration between the US arms industry and the members of the Warsaw Pact. The arrest of James Settler on 8 April 1976, however, emphasized the danger of entrusting private organizations with almost governmental authority in matters of foreign policy. Settler, an adviser to the Atlantic Council, had been involved in espion-age activities for East Germany and the Warsaw Pact nations since 1967. He had passed on microfilm of confidential documents from NATO and from Western government offices or agencies.

If we unravel the threads of the tangled profit-based knot a little further, we find the firm of Northrop, a competitor of Lockheed and, like it, a specialist in bribery. North-rop's lawyer, the Californian Herbert Kalmbach, worked for five years as legal adviser to Nixon and secretary to the board of his foundation. Kalmbach was also one of the twenty-six members of the Lincoln Club of Newport Beach. This club has been a meeting place over the last twenty-five years for several important West Coast backers of the Republican Party who continued to believe in the presidential vocation of Richard Nixon.

In 1969 Kalmbach was asked to handle the legal interests of the Atlantic Richfield Oil Company, one of whose directors, Donald Kendall, is president of Pepsi Cola and stand-off-half in the push towards the Kremlin. When Kalmbach went to help Maurice Stans rake in the dollars in 1972, he obtained $60,000 from Kendall in the name of Atlantic Richfield.

The oil company is also a member of the US–USSR Trade and Economic Council, the forum for all those American companies who believe that the multinationals have a mission to bring civilization to Lenin's successors.

Two years later, in 1974, president of Atlantic Richfield Robert Anderson, former Treasury Secretary and adviser to Nelson Rockefeller on his Commission on Critical Choices, was involved in a financial scandal in London and could applaud from a distance while Kalmbach and Stans tumbled into the gutters of legal indictment after slipping on a fraudulent cheque for $200,000 made out to Nixon by the international financier Robert Vesco. Obviously Vesco did not intend to put his money in just anybody's pockets, not even the large and accommodating pockets of Prince Bernhardt of the Netherlands, the right-hand man of big capital. The Prince of Lippe had something in common with all Lockheed's middle men who took it upon themselves to praise the American aviation company's finish and futuristic lines. Like Crociani in Italy and Yoche Kodome in Japan, Bernhardt worked with the totalitarian régimes of the day. His career was simple enough. As an impoverished and ambitious country squire, he agreed to join the National Socialist Party. In 1934 he was given a job at the Paris headquarters of the Nazi chemical empire IG Farben, a position where tokens of trust were demanded of him. Like many other employees of IG Farben in its numerous subsidiaries throughout the world, Bernhardt received his orders directly from Berlin, from an agency called HW7. The man in charge of this information office, Dr. Max Ilgner, was indicted at the Nuremberg Trials in 1945. It was he who revealed the coordination and symbiosis between the chemical giant and the supreme command of the German army, and he, too, who revealed that one of the many informers working for him was a certain Prince Bernhardt of Lippe Biesterfeld. In 1936 the Prince crossed the first bridge on the way to the eden of high finance by joining the Kruger Bank of Amsterdam, whose owner, Gerhard Fritze, worked closely with IG Farben. The rest of the story belongs to women's magazines. During the war years Bernhardt donned an RAF uniform more appealing in its colour, cut and nationality to a newly-wed heiress.

To do him justice, Bernhardt's career betrayed great skill and extraordinary farsightedness. He never wandered into the dead-end streets of political games. He never stopped in the lobby to talk to the doorman but went straight up in the elevator. Aiming high and accurately, he formed connections with the few dozen people who controlled world banking and industry and therefore held the real power.

Bernhardt arranged a calm haven for all these wanderers, irritated by the inefficiency of governments and imbued with a sense of the global responsibilities they apparently desired to assume. There they could go between two board meetings and indulge in cocktail chatter about the future of the world as they saw it and as they wished it to be.

The first gathering took place in 1954. The efficient butler Bernhardt and his friend Paul Ryskens, president of the multinational Unilever Group, organized a meeting for Western European and North American businessmen to discuss the problems of the Atlantic world. This first party was held at the Bildeberg Hotel which stands in a park near the Dutch town of Haarlem. Thus it was that the Bildeberg Club was born. Twice a year, in October and January, the Prince and his secretary Ernst Van der Beugel, director of Rank Xerox, invite the world managers and lesser leaders from the news media, politics and academics, to luxurious and isolated palaces, protected from the rumours and humours of the outside world by troops of police beyond the wildest dreams of even the vainest head of state. Among the "associates", as members are called, are Giovanni Agnelli, the boss of Fiat and of Italian Industry; Marcus Wallenburg, the most powerful Swedish banker and industrialist; Edmond de Rothschild of the French bank; Douglas Dillon; Robert McNamara, former president of the Ford Foundation and of the World Bank; George Ball, former American foreign policy adviser, director of the Lehmann Brothers financial group and adviser to Jimmy Carter; Wilfred Baumgartner, former president and managing director of the French multinational Rhône–Poulenc and former governor of the Bank of France; Emilio Collado, vice-president of Exxon; Sir Eric Roll of the English Warburg Bank and former governor of the Bank of England; former Secretary of State Dean Rusk, and, of course, David Rockefeller. Bernhardt is also a shrewd businessman who sits on the boards of more than three hundred official and commercial organizations including Fokker aircraft and Royal Dutch Shell, and he has 12 million dollars' worth of shares in Exxon. Details of this kind create links. While we are subjected to puerile television programs pontificating about the duties and responsibilities of the statesman, the members of the Bildeberg Club go their separate ways in total secrecy, never publishing the smallest communiqué. On 23 April 1971, for example, Kissinger attended one of the club's meetings at the Woodstock Inn Hotel in Vermont which belongs to Laurence Rockefeller. Some weeks later he flew to Peking to bring Mao's obscurantist and exhausted China back into the great family of trading and dispensing nations.

Bernhardt has never hidden the fact that the aim of the Bildeberg, where the Western élites coordinate their thoughts and attitudes, is to create a "world government." This age-old ambition has been frequently expressed by David Rockefeller, a leading Bildeberger and original financial angel of the heavenly venture. There is no denying that people of this kind may feel rather restricted in their living space when the only entrance hall they have access to is as tiny as Japan, when they keep barking their shins on Europe and when they are confined to small spaces like the USA. Even their extra half a room in the USSR and their garage in the Southern hemisphere does not really add much. In this respect men like Rosenbaum and Vesco were probably objects of envy for those elegant figures in their sober, well-cut suits, condemned as they are to keeping up an appearance of respectability. Tibor Rosenbaum must have symbolized the kind of unrestricted, financial vitality dreamed of by all the men of power. And though they regarded the suspect international financier Robert Vesco as a kind of black sheep who was bound to come to a bad end eventually, his independence and freedom of movement fascinated them in the meantime. These two men, the ultimate examples of their kind, were regular guests at the royal palace in the Hague, and members of the Bildeberg demonstrated an affectionate indulgence towards them. It was not until Vesco fled to Guatemala to escape prosecution and arrest for fraud that Bernhardt decided to expel him from the club.

Clearly we are not implying that some extravagant plot is being hatched in shadowy secrecy by a handful of ambitious and powerful individuals. Otherwise we should have to assume that the empire bosses kept James Bond as their bedside reading. No, the truth is more subtle but no less disturbing in its possible implications. Every day the nation state loses a little more of its power and its substance. In the face of this decline, which partly explains the current crisis, the Overworld sees itself as the only force still capable of producing results. The capitalists' profession and the workings of management produce specific mentalities, attitudes and values. Wilson's famous statement that "what is good for General Motors is good for America" is not the product of a mean or vicious mind. His identification between the two is a real and sincere one.

The people who build up the big businesses and increase their capital, hope to shine through their capitalistic activities as the benefactors from whom any improvement in the standard of living will flow.

The interpenetration between their interests and those of humanity in general is achieved by the use of ideas as rationalized and artificial as their actions. The human factor in such ideas is of course totally hypothetical and abstracted.

In their manipulative and pragmatic way, they put over a particular line of argument. But just as their profit and losses are reflected in the trade figures of 30, 50 or 76 nations rather than just the one, so, too, their ideas are constructed in sufficiently amoral a way to appeal to rival political systems. They all invest in South Africa and Chile, but also in Czechoslovakia and the USSR. Tomorrow they will be in Cambodia or in China, as well as in Haiti and Spain.

The Helsinki summit on European cooperation and security was so much moon-shine, in which East and West were prepared to agree that all men had the right to breathe in the same way or to stick their stamps on their envelopes in an identical fashion. But beyond that Western politicians demonstrated a conspicuous lack of valour. For, on the grounds of non-interference in political systems, they agreed to jettison all human, social questions and abandon the defense of those values which underlie our dignity as free men. As a result of the Helsinki meeting, the Communist régimes are now accepted as a *fait accompli*, and any criticism, opposition and comment on the situation and tensions in Eastern countries is gradually dying out. Fortunately, however, this contemptible and foreseeable defeat in the political sphere will bring victory to the business world. Western technology has not capitulated. Too modern, complex and sophisticated to be halted by traditional, economic and politcal barriers, it is winning great triumphs in an area characterized by organizational deficiency. Sheltered from prying eyes by a restrictive political and police system, Western managers can force the desperate Communist leaders to modify their economic set-up so as to provide the multinationals with a larger income. Men and institutions on both sides are very similar. In the West the dictates of efficiency demand that the business enterprise be pyramidal, hierarchical, authoritarian and anti-democratic. Information circulates from top to bottom, participation is purely a formality. Power is concentrated in the hands of a few small groups. The Politburo and the ruling élites of the satellite countries function in an identical way. It is therefore easy for those who are connected with these organizations to work together. They are not trying to establish an ideal ownership structure, nor to debate the grounds for a market economy, but solely to keep the factory wheels turning and to optimize production while keeping human or union nuisance to a minimum. Businesses who have eliminated democracy from their structure are forced to look for stability and for trade with régimes which have abolished "effervescence and uncertainty" in their political and social dealings.

Today the leaders on both sides confront each other with the same worries, and the same tendency to dismiss ideology as part of the simple fare better reserved for those inhabiting the vast swamps of public opinion.

At the present time, however, the non-governmental power base accepts that highly centralized control can only be maintained if integration is structured and bureaucratized. The ideology developed and the terms of reference transmitted will have to be strong to resist the frictions and variations so often present in our pitiable democracies. There must therefore be an institutionalized world government in which traditional values can be more effectively controlled and directed. The proliferation of councils and committees obviously results from the élite's desire to remain in control of operations by influencing attitudes through propaganda. The Italian operation, which we shall discuss more fully later, forms an essential part of this Vodka-Cola approach. Berlinguer and his pals were successfully launched by a bourgeois press which had grown lethargic in the face of those "good Communists" with their independence from Russia. (In fact the whole business would never have got off the ground without the agreement of Moscow.)

When the Italian Communist Party acquires even partial control of the state machine, it becomes possible to begin the second phase in which Italian Marxism can be brought back into line with traditional Communism. In this way the world managers will be able to rely on a strong and effective CP to destroy any opposition to a totalitarian régime and its restrictive structures, especially the opposition of trade unions. As this program evolves, it will become possible to painlessly eradicate the basic difference between left and right, which is a respect for individual human values rather than a stress of economic and financial power. In an international code stripped of these factors, everything will become progressively more banal. The transition from Vodka-Cola to Vodka-Espresso provides the perfect cocktail mixture. The futility and opportunism of the Western left wing will be overwhelmingly responsible for the advent of this new form of alcoholism. Academic arguments and articles in fashionable magazines flirting behind the fan of "realism" are sure evidence of a decadent and moribund world. It is not the capitalist bourgeoisie which is to blame, but the aesthetes of the limited circulation new idea, who make their careers out of just and comfortable causes, and who have continued to lead us astray over the last thirty years. It is they who are the modern counterparts of Lampedusa's characters in the *Leopard*. But, though there can be no place for these clowns in the world looming ahead of us, some of them are past masters of the art of contortion and will always have the chance of twisting themselves into the new official line.

The Fifth International Industrial Conference held in California from 17 to 21 September 1973 was a perfect illustration of the accession of post-political power. The Stanford Research Institute played host to the 650 guests attending the conference's UN-type business assembly. Western managers, representatives of openly Fascist states and Communist officials could be found sunbathing on the same private beach or lunching side by side in fashionable restaurants, demonstrating how successful integration can be on the level of élites fused by common interests and a shared love of power. Chief among the American delegates were the industrialist David Packard, David Rockefeller, John McCone of ITT, George Ball, Stephen Bechtel, Karl Klausen, president of the Bank of America (the largest bank in the world), and Walter Wriston, president of the First National City Bank (second largest). Germany was represented by Hermann Abs, a former collaborator with Hitler and honorary president of the Deutsche Bank (the largest German bank), and the Social-Democrat politician Helmut Schmidt, then Minister of Finance. Under the eye of his older friend, the future Chancellor uttered a vigorous and well-received defense of "increased multinationalization among the big firms." The two men were accompanied by Bernhard Plettener, president of Siemens, who said "The desire to put off any increase in East–West trade manifested by certain people is as unrealistic as the hope that the Soviet economic and political system will change after increased exchanges with the West." The group of cold war financiers who had been converted to détente after touching the Russian icon also included Sir Ernest Woodroofe, president of Unilever, John Loudon, chairman of Royal Dutch Shell who met Sheik Yamani, the Saudi oil minister, James Parker, vice-president of General Electric and Edgar Kaiser of Kaiser Industries. In a statement to the *San Francisco Chronicle*, Kaiser said "Business men like this kind of meeting very much. This assembly will enable us to exchange views and information on various questions and make contact with people who may become partners in the future. Thus, at the opening session, I met the Indian delegates and we talked about their problems in aluminum production. Today we signed a $60 million contract with them for cement and aluminum operations in their country." Whilst the ruins of the Moneda palace were still smoking and the body of Salvador Allende lay still warm in the grave, several representatives of the Pinochet junta, including the president and vice-president of the daily *El Mercurio*, attended these meetings. And there they were able to hold long and agreeable conversations with Kosygin's son-in-law German Vishiani, a highranking official in the KGB and president of the State Committee for Science and Technology in the USSR, who was wandering about the Californian coast while his father-in-law and his old card-playing friends sat in Moscow mourning the death of the Chilean president and the irreparable outrage committed by "North American Fascism and imperialism." A few haggard zombies haunted the gates of the Stanford Institute protesting against the part played by certain multinational companies in Allende's fall.

The demonstrators were aiming particularly at Peter Petersen, president of Lehmann Brothers. As Nixon's Minister of Trade and leader of the Council on Foreign Economic Policy, he had been one of the most active promoters of détente, making frequent visits to Moscow and increasing trade cooperation with the East, while at the same time organizing the economic blockade on Chile. When challenged by the demonstrators, Petersen shrugged his shoulders and said "This conference has nothing to do with politics." Shortly afterwards, a five-year cooperation contract was agreed between the Stanford Institute and the Russian State Committee for Science and Technology. This agreement, the first of its kind to be concluded with a Western research center, was signed in Moscow by Vishiani and president of Stanford Charles Anderson.

According to Tass, this initiative was concerned with "the study of possibilities for increased trade, the organization of international industrial conferences, the application of science and technology to economic development and the study of various sectors of cooperation between the Soviets and international business ventures."

While European political leaders organize summit conferences solely to evaluate the extent of their differences, the business world has achieved total integration and a flowing two-way traffic in information. National and ideological barriers have become a faded screen, used only to conceal the idle chatter of a few fops still fascinated by outward show like red carpets, official cars and handshaking for the cameras.

Umberto Colombo is president of the Scientific and Technological Policy Committee of the OECD (Organization for Economic Cooperation and Development). He is also the new president of the discreet European Association for Management and Industrial Research, founded in 1966 with its headquarters in Paris. The 155 members of the Committee represent two thirds of European industrial potential. This managers' club takes a special interest in sales and transfers of technology to the East and works in close coordination with American and Japanese officials. Colombo's firm, Montedison, is very active in the Communist states, as are Fiat, Olivetti, Pirelli, Finmeccanica, Finsider and ENI, which make up the bulk of the Italian mob within the organization. The way in which an international body like the OECD is being engulfed by private interests is a recent phenomenon and belongs to the global power strategy.

Last November, for example, FAO, the United Nations Food and Agricultural Organization, set up a World Food Council composed of representatives from forty-two countries, whose former director-general was none other than Nelson Rockefeller's man

John Hanah, a former director of the CIA university of Michigan and an industrialist whose interests are spread among states as sensitive to the human consequences of under-development as Brazil and South Africa.

Once again business was taking the place of exhausted nation states in the costly financial transfusions intended to keep these international organizations alive. The multinationals practise Trotsky's theory of entryism. If we accept in Marxist terms that an "infrastructure" however rusty determines the "superstructure," then these brain-less, global skeletons become commercial and political bases of the greatest importance for the private sector. The days of buying a few delegates or infiltrating the leadership have gone. Today multinational companies have a decisive influence on FAO, which has agreed to yield some of its areas of responsibility to them. The ICP (Industry Coopera-tion Program) aims to "establish top level liaison and direct dialogue between Third World governments and industrial leaders." The most crafty of the companies have rightly seen this as a perfect path to expansion. The idea of ICP members going on "humanitarian" missions to developing countries was launched by Enrico Bignami, director of Nestlé's world operations.

Just like the World Bank, the ICP bases its strategy on keeping developing countries in a state of "underdevelopment" and totally dependent on private capital. A recent ICP mission to Pakistan included directors of Shell Chemical International, and Mitsubishi, Oswaldo Ballarin, director of Nestlé Brazil, led an ICP mission to Dahomey. Discussions with the Socialist government of Sri Lanka on increased foreign investment in the agricultural and industrial sector were led by the directors of Philips and the Policy company Polimex Cekop. In fact, although the USSR contributes no funds to FAO, the Italian organization and the ICP furnish a preferential area of cooperation for the Vodka-Colanizers. After their round trips between Moscow and Washington, they all return to the via della Terma di Caracalla; and this includes the Hungarian directors of Agripp Agrober and the Poles of Polservice. Cargill, the world's largest cereal company, which sells damaged grain to the Soviets, is represented by its vice-president William Pearce, the man Nixon appointed in 1969 to dismantle the existing legislation which imposed too many restrictions on trade with the East. The ICP is a splendid catalogue of Soviet agricultural dreams, from John Deere tractors and Caterpillar harvesters to Akzo fertilizers. And then there is the IBEC which belongs to the Rockefeller family and Cyrus Eaton, the pioneers of simultaneous economic dealings in the usually weak, totalitarian and anti-Marxist Third World states and in the inefficient Communist régimes. To complete the family tree, ICP's consultants and advisers are the Business International Corporation, a company based in Geneva, whose president, Orville Free-man, was Kennedy's Minister for Agriculture and a director of several large companies connected with food production. Business International, which is heavily involved in activities in the East, publishes a regular, confidential, house bulletin entitled *Business Eastern Report*, giving Western businessmen information about their present progress into the Communist markets.

The international organizations' commissions of enquiry into the activities of the big companies have about as much effect as their debates on respect for human rights in Chile. Kissinger suggested to the OECD that they should work out an umpteenth code of practice, just as in 1973 the United Nations consulted the directors of IBM, Shell, Du Pont, Nestlé and General Motors for their enquiry into the role of the big companies in developing countries.

Naturally, there is always room in this rash of discussion conferences for repre-sentatives of the leftwing political parties and trades unions, who are invited to emphas-ize the organizations' liberalism and their willingness to hear both sides. And these

ideal sparring partners, their faces scarred by their many previous bouts, leap around
the ring for a few rounds, counter-punching in such a way that the fight looks to be all
fair and square. The conspicuous weakness of the left wing lies in its vanity and its lack
of realism. It is all high-flown words and unrealistic attitudes to facts. Its use of the
abstract conceptualized word is a gift to the Overworld leaders who can implicate it in a
falsely global approach and thereby avoid the real socio–economic issues.

How can European leftwing politicians speak of "American hegemony"? What have
Henry Ford's America and the America of the black ghettoes in common? Do they
imagine that the Vanderbilts, Astors and Du Ponts share the same preoccupations as
Wallace's constituents? Would they allow any foreign observer to make equally sweep-
ing statements about France or England? Their analysis of the problems is a function of
strictly nationalistic, short-term political objectives which makes them as incompetent
as their opposite numbers in power. Each one brandishes the great book of his religion
without ever having succeeded in suppressing sin. How dare they evoke the necessity
for full employment in the name of human dignity, when millions of workers are condemned to an early death from mentally and physically debilitating labour? In their
theorizing they overlook the essence of the problem which is the power connections
within the company and the economic system. They are the real collaborators in the
Vodka-Cola strategy. As career politicians, they cannot allow the bourgeois capitalists
the privilege of good relations with the Communist élites, but must claim for themselves
the honour of having made the hitherto backward and unpresentable Marxist leaders fit
to be seen by the middle classes. Vulnerable to all forms of seduction, understanding
nothing of structural and industrial economic realities, they conceptualize everything
in the name of world plans.

If Mac George Bundy, the man responsible for American escalation in Vietnam and
for coordination between the CIA and the White House, goes to Moscow as president of
the Ford Foundation to negotiate an agreement with Brezhnev on environmental problems on behalf of the US, his visit becomes an important contribution to the peace effort.
And yet the Ford Foundation, a private, capitalist organization, has taken the place of
the State Department in an official, international negotiation. Besides, agreements on
the environment and interplanetary cooperation do nothing to alter the status quo.
Since man forms no part of these topics, it is possible to build up any number of general
statements while avoiding any reference to individual liberties, the Gulag, or social
injustice. The joint Soyuz–Apollo mission, which was sold as the symbol of a new era of
cooperation, has been reduced to a few puffs of smoke. An agreement signed in 1974 by
Philip Morris director Ross R. Milhiser and the Soviet State Committee for Science and
Technology, gave the American company the chance to sell a cigarette called Soyuz–
Apollo in the USSR. This is the only tangible result of the joint mission. Philip Morris
negotiated the deal from its European headquarters in Lausanne.

Another such piece of dehumanized nonsense, the environmental question, was put
together by those unrepentant polluters, the oilmen. It was Rockefeller's man, Robert B.
Anderson, the president of Atlantic Richfield, who founded the Agency for the Environment with a $40 million grant from Nixon and $60 million more than the United
Nations. His staff were recruited from the State Department, and his leading board
members included Aurelio Peccei of the Club of Rome and a former director of Fiat and
Olivetti. In 1974, the first director of the agency, the Canadian Maurice Strong, a
member of the Rockefeller Foundation board and a close friend of Nixon, returned to his
previous job as director of an oil company. Strong was also appointed director of the
Canadian Federal Energy Agency by Prime Minister Pierre Trudeau, while he was still
active on the boards of the Chase Manhattan Bank and the Rockefeller Foundation.

However, the world conference on ecological problems which took palce in Stockholm in 1972 was a remarkable success, since it occupied several progressive minds in a skilful remould of reality.

What this agency did was to pose the problem of responsibility for pollution in planetary rather than business terms. So, by appealing to the planetary emotion we are all bound to feel at the growth of a blade of grass or the prosecution of litter bugs in any part of the world, the real culprits were able to go to ground without ever touching on the real problems of pollution: man in general and no oil company in particular was indicted for the pollution of the seas and the atmosphere by hydrocarbon particulates.

The same thing has happened with the Club of Rome. This think-tank assembled round Italian industrialist Aurelio Peccei has also developed a two-pronged abstract and post-political line of reasoning. Its members are a shrewd mixture of big company directors and representatives of the Eastern block, like the official Polish thinker Adam Shaff or the ubiquitous Vishiani. Peccei's arguments are based on a Darwinian view of mankind as a homogeneous blend in which it is possible to talk about "the common future of humanity and the interdependence of peoples." The KGB prisoner committed to a psychiatric hospital and the black South African from Soweto gunned down by the police must be thrilled to think that they are both part of the one earth. Under pretext of going right to the heart of the problem, the Club of Rome is able to glue disparate realities together and to make cooperation and integration between the élites of both sides look like a form of progress. Its first bulletin entitled *Predicament Mankind* was produced by a team from MIT and financed by the Volkswagen Foundation which collected the money from several oil companies.

Following the same principles, the Center for the Study of Democratic Institutions, a satellite of the Ford Foundation, organized an important international conference called *Pacem in Maribus* in the laws of the sea. This indirectly resulted in the recent meeting on the subject in Caracas under the aegis of the United Nations. Assembled round a bowl of plankton, all the leading minds reached agreement that a common patrimony should not be poisoned.

There, too, they remained happily distant from the banal problems affecting man, that animal so obstinately rebellious to certain forms of political training.

Cyrus Eaton, the Cleveland billionaire industrialist, began his career as secretary to John Rockefeller. He then built his fortune by developing friendly relations with Kruschev and trading relations with the USSR, before leaving active life for some years suffering from an infractus. From his prolonged convalescence and tactical, political meditations, the "Pugwash movement" was born in the late fifties. A first, flimsy rope bridge had been slung between the two sides, obsessed as they were by the strictures of the cold war. Some years later Eaton became a partner of the Rockefellers in the IBEC, but by then the brothers were already helping to finance the symposium which held its first sittings in 1957 at the village of Pugwash, Eaton's birthplace in New Caledonia. The basic idea was to bring the realities imposed by big business's desire to break into the Eastern markets and the ivory-towers of the intellectual and political leaders closer together. The first aim of Pugwash was to achieve integration between scientific researchers, the life-blood of what was to become the Vodka-Cola animal. The creation of a trans-ideological community of scientists was a simple and profitable proposition for various reasons.

First, such people represent the future prosperity of technological power. Second, basic to their relations are a high degree of linguistic abstraction and various common professional interests. They are as indifferent to their surroundings as the solo musicians who can play Tchaikowsky with a change of orchestra in Paris, Rome or Moscow.

Thirdly, three quarters of them reject politics as despicable, derisible or heart-breaking, which means that they can be presented as the enlightened *avant-garde* of the global project stripped of any national or partisan references.

Before long, the American side of Eaton's operations became involved in a joint seminar for the leading lights of Harvard and MIT which gave all the anti-communist academics an opportunity to get to know the Soviet delegates paraded before them during the various sessions. In 1960 Walter Rostow made a long speech to the Communist representatives on the necessity for an arms control policy. Five years later, however, a Lyssenko-type hybridization turned the Rostow dove sitting on the Pugwash perch into a Vietnamese hawk, a species then common to the White House birdcages which have since been cleaned with the detergent of détente.

At the end of a Pugwash party held in London, Bertrand Russell declared "In a new world war nuclear weapons will certainly be used. We insist that the governments of the world realise and publicly recognize that their objectives cannot be achieved through world war." He had not long to wait for a response. Thirteen years later, Howard Riffai, director of the International Institute of Applied Studies, unwittingly answered the English philosopher when he admitted "Here, we do not believe for an instant in thermonuclear war."

Here was Laxenberg, the former summer residence of the Austrian imperial family, a stone's throw from Vienna, where the Vodka-Cola scientists entered the second phase of their passage into orbit after Pugwash's initial launching. There, in a country virtually surrounded by the people's democracies, an hundred or so egg-heads sit planning and controlling our future, all ideological barriers down. Chancellor Bruno Kreisky's Social–Democrat government had encouraged the creation of this institute, which was originally conceived and negotiated in Moscow in 1966 by Mac George Bundy, then foreign policy adviser to Johnson. In October 1972 the final agreement was initialled by Vishiani, for the Soviets, and by Bundy, for the Americans; Bundy had in the meanwhile become president of the Ford Foundation in yet another interesting conjunction of public and private activities. According to Vishiani, Laxenberg, the symbolic evidence of détente, was "the first multinational, non-governmental, scientific institution."

American financial support in the shape of just over $3 million a year actually comes from the Ford Foundation, and through it from the high priests of economic penetration into the East. The Volkswagen and Agnelli Foundations also contribute. The researchers working in Laxenberg's curious combination of the snack-bar and the convent are all products of the university compost heap, carefully treated with frequent feeds of high finance. The director, Riffai, came straight from Harvard, as did his successor Roger Levien, who spent more than ten years in the Rand Corporation, the Pentagon's study bureau, and a place renowned for the generous-spirited minds it fosters.

Naturally, the institute works on a global level and tends to emanate a specific methodology, a new and common mode of thought. Levien has explicitly stated: "The differences between East and West are not nearly as great as is thought." As one might expect, the Communist Warsaw Pact states are also involved. Indeed, the institute chose to arrange its first international meeting on 22 October 1975 in Varna, Bulgaria.

The scientists all wander round in their shirt sleeves and lunch together off the same tin plates. They also all manifest an intense horror of futility. In an interview with a journalist who was trying to raise the question of political contradictions which he considered an inevitable result of such cooperation, one Laxenberg scientist furiously retorted, "Here we are scientists, we are interested in serious things, not in ideology." Understandably, the human sciences, which give rise to subjective discussions where the quality of argument tends to deteriorate, play no part in the curriculum of this intellectual club.

Laxenberg's researchers have also made their way into UNO which has placed contracts with the institute amounting to a quarter of its budget. Some people have already raised the possibility of giving the institute executive powers in specific areas, such as food and energy, to be controlled by the world authorities there. Already, some of the studies made there are seeking to supplant national programs, on such specific subjects as the effects of pests in Canadian forests, the protection of Pacific salmon, the pollution of the waters of the Rhine, or comparative analyses of management methods in big industrial complexes in the United States and the Soviet Union.

The basic idea is that government should refer to them and thereby forfeit what little critical faculties and desire to think for themselves they still have. "Let us do your thinking for you." The Hudson Institute already does, and is about as accurate in its predictions as *Old Moore's Almanac*. No matter, the important thing is to take over the area and promote one's own objectives.

Cooperation between the Communist rulers and the global managers in attempts to institute a new Platonic republic on a world scale, with an élitist government unbalanced by any democratic counterweight, has considerably accelerated. Time is money. Laxenberg was set up just after Nixon and Brezhnev had signed the Soviet–American Treaty in Moscow in May 1972, and just before Pepsi Cola had signed its agreement with the USSR. Operations of this kind are always conducted with great discretion. During the spring of 1973, Nixon created the East–West Trade Policy Committee which was chaired by George Schultz, presidential economic adviser and Finance Minister. Other members of the committee included Henry Kissinger, his assistant Helmut Sonnenfeld, William Simon, Trade Minister Frederick Dent, and presidential adviser William Eberle. They were all supported by private firms involved in the operation, and all of them developed a policy of American trade exports unrestricted by any governmental control.

The Defense Ministry, which could have raised objections concerning possible strategic uses for some of the materials sold, was carefully excluded from the committee.

In June 1973 Brezhnev paid Nixon a visit during a neighbourly trip to Washington. After several hours in the cool of the Oval Office, the two heads of State decided to work out a protocol to be signed by George Schultz for the Americans and Foreign Trade Minister Nicolai Patolichev for the Russians. This memorandum accepted the necessity of creating "a specialist organization to permit the free circulation of trade and a stress of economic relations between the two systems" in a climate of mutual frankness and understanding.

In September 1973, Frederick Dent met with the directors of several big American companies. At the same time, Kendall arrived in Moscow. The man who had succeeded, with Nixon's help, in not only establishing Pepsi Cola in the USSR but also getting the Soviets to finance a vast television advertising campaign for his product, was met by Patolitchev and then went on to Yalta to see Brezhnev. According to the Novosti press agency the two men agreed that relations would have to be institutionalized by the creation of a common trade institute. The American manager was a firm believer in the impact of personal relations: "I have never seen a country where this phenomenon is as important as it is in the Soviet Union. The way in which we can influence the Soviets' policy, not only in matters of military détente, but also in their own attitudes to life, is by increasing contacts, not by isolating them."

On his return to the United States, Kendall went to San Clemente for a lengthy meeting with Nixon. A month later the US–USSR Trade and Economic Council was legally constituted. This organization is the real cathedral of the Vodka-Cola movement where détente is celebrated in its most glorious form.

There are fifty-two people on the management board. Half of them are Soviet officials representing government services and trade organizations. Foremost among the American delegates are Alden Clausen, president of the Bank of America; Armand Hammer, president of Occidental Petroleum; Michael Fribourg of Continental Grain; Howard L. Clark, president of American Express; Richard Gerstenberg, president of General Motors; Frank T. Carry, president of IBM; Irving Shapiro, president of Du Pont of Nemours; Willard Rockwell of the Rockwell International arms company; Edgar Kaiser of Kaiser Industries; Reginald H. Jones, president of General Electric: and, naturally, David Rockefeller. The co-chairmen are Kendall and Vladimir Alkhimov, Soviet Secretary for Foreign Trade. The two men have been old cronies since they spent eleven months negotiating the agreement which led to the Pepsi Cola factory being built in Novorossisk in May 1974.

It was not long before American Express (a Rockefeller interest) and Intourist decided to work more closely together on facilitating travel and hotel arrangements for the thousands of American businessmen expected in the USSR. A glance at the complete membership list reveals that the council represents the biggest firms in the US, and, through them, an essential element of present-day multinational power. On 26 December 1973, the US-USSR Trade Council opened a permanent office in New York, at 280 Park Avenue, and a month later, on 27 February, a branch office was set up in Washington near the White House. The man responsible for coordination between the two was Harold B. Scott, who had been assistant Minister of Trade under Maurice Stans and Peter Petersen. In the meanwhile the council had opened an office in Moscow in the National Hotel facing the Kremlin. The staff later moved to the Pullman Company offices before reaching their final and official resting place at 3 Shevchenko Embankment. The Russian office is directed by John Connor Jr, son of Eisenhower's and Nixon's Trade Secretary.

At the end of December the Council for Agriculture Market Development met in Moscow. There are sixty private American food and poultry breeding companies within this association, which works in symbiosis with USDA, the Agriculture Ministry office responsible for allotting export subsidies. The president of the Council for Agriculture, Darvin Stolte, is also president of the US Feed Gain Council, an official organization virtually controlled by the grain companies. This pilgrimage to Moscow coincided with the grain shortages in the USSR. In January 1974, despite opposition from the American Congress, a consortium of Occidental Petroleum, El Paso Natural Gas and Bechtel Construction obtained a loan of $49.5 million from the Export–Import Bank for preliminary studies with a view to exploiting Siberian gas.

Shortly afterwards the adoption of the Jackson Amendment (basically, American money in exchange for Soviet Jews) proved an embarrassment both to the American Vodka-Colanizers and to the Communist leaders who were relying on an abundant use of official credits to finance their economic expansion.

On 10 March, the US-USSR Trade Council organized a meeting between about forty American managers and Russian officials. Worried by the critical attitude of Congress, Patolichev went first to see Schultz and then Nixon. The two men assured him of their desire to "complete" the liberalization of trade relations in favour of the Russians which Brezhnev had been promised at the previous year's summit. In an attempt to change the situation, those two mainsprings of federal government, Kissinger and Schultz, entered the front-line and each took a turn in the task.

In a deposition to the Senate Finance Committee, the Secretary of State said that a refusal to grant the USSR most favoured nation status would "have essentially political rather than economic consequences." This clever representation of the facts was basically saying: "You Senators will bear the responsibility for any defeat suffered by our policy, since you have supported humanitarian claims at the wrong time."

Schultz took it upon himself to stress what he saw as the absurdity of connecting the pursuit of nation-to-nation economic relations with the defense of individual rights. And he was in a position to know, since as leader of the Chicago School of Economics he had played an essential part in planning the social policy of the Pinochet régime. He hoped that there would be no doubts cast on the prevailing political system in the USSR; he thought that Congress had made an "ill-considered" initiative and saw no reason why a general defense of "human rights" should hamper the development of more normal trade relations with countries which did not practise a market economy (for which read "undemocratic" by nature.) People like Schultz and Kissinger obviously have very mediocre views of life when one considers that all their acts are determined by a total absence of morality. For them the Communist world, that burial ground of all democratic hopes, is an oasis where they can secretly carry on activities now increasingly regarded as controversial in the West.

Not long after his resounding speech in defense of free enterprise, Schultz left the White House to resume working for the Californian Stephen Bechtel. No sooner had he started his new job than Schultz went to Moscow, not this time as an official US representative, but on Bechtel's orders, to negotiate with his old friends, the Soviets, the construction of a "giant international trade center." This $110 million complex is intended to provide offices for 400 American companies, apartments for 625 families and 600 hotel rooms for visitors. The plans include the most up-to-date communication services, a restaurant, entertainment and conference facilities, and even a golf course. Imagine the Western manager and his Soviet opposite number striding across the green from hole to hole, safely protected by police, barbed-wire and guard dogs from the "255 million fanatics" of the Communist faith. What a marvellous symbol it will be of mental colonization and of the moral superiority of the Western system!

The whole project, which is to be financed by a consortium of American banks directed by the Chase Manhattan, is due to be built with the cooperation and under the control of Armand Hammer's Occidental Petroleum.

To cover Schultz's departure, Nixon appointed his economic adviser Kenneth Rush, a former professor at Duke University, head of the East–West Policy Committee. Here, also, the two activities overlapped, and Rush gave all the signs of being both a resourceful diplomat and an experienced businessman. As Assistant Secretary of State under Kissinger, he had spent over fifteen years as director of the powerful chemical group Union Carbide, which devotes a large part of activities to trade with the Communist countries. In 1970 Rush was appointed ambassador to West Germany. He was on excellent terms with Herbert Wehner, the hidden power in German politics and the only man in the Social Democrat Party who could ensure that any one candidate became chancellor or that any statesman whom he regarded as outworn was coldly removed from office. While Nixon was consolidating his détente strategy, this friendship between the German Socialist veteran and the American anti-union capitalist coincided rather strangely with Willy Brandt's *Ostpolitik*, an act of devotion providing moral justification for German firms to cross paths with a different form of totalitarianism.

The management of the East–West Policy Committee was virtually in the hands of the Rockefellers, whether through Kissinger or through Peter Flanigan, Under-Secretary for Trade and director of Douglas Dillon's Dillon Read Bank.

The committee met five times in fifteen months. It has no operational ambitions but provides a forum for various reliable figures who all share a basic desire to keep the policy of trade with the East safe from outside interference. Their avowed aim is to defend the activities of the US-USSR Trade and Economic Council, a private organization which nevertheless appears totally free to determine US foreign trade policy. Kendall is right to say that his organization "is not a political element and cannot become involved in non-commercial activities in any country." Obviously it is nonsense to disassociate political factors and economic realities. But it is true that a private capitalist's deals with the leadership of militarily and ideologically rival powers are not part of politics: they *are* the actual foreign policy of the country, whatever the superficial rhetoric. Since 1968 the choice of governmental staff and the broad lines of American foreign policy have tended to justify and favour the strategy instigated by Kendall and his peers. Over recent years it has come to look as if the ultimate aim of the American presidential office, in all its solemnity, can be reduced to a mere desire to see more empty Pepsi cans littering the streets of East Berlin or Leningrad. Are we to suppose that in the near future the White House, the Elysée Palace, 10 Downing Street and the Quirinal will stop issuing laws and instead distribute guarantee certificates for the products they are given to promote?

The way in which Western firms use Communist countries is rather like the way the motorist uses his indicator and the side-road. Whenever the vehicle looks so dilapidated that it is likely to infringe the law, the capitalist takes to the woods to avoid indictment.

For example, we have ample proof that the PVC used in the chemical industry is carcinogenic. To avoid any restrictions on its use, the companies prefer to transfer this dirty and unhealthy section of production, which has caused union disputes, to the East. Naturally the CGT or the CGIL, who are so quick to denounce the injurious labour conditions in the capitalist monopoly industries have never mentioned this problem. In the United States various sectors of public opinion have expressed anxiety about the increases in the use of nuclear energy. And yet on 18 May 1974, American and Soviet engineers attended two important meetings on the common development of "technological power." The first, in Washington, was a session of the joint Soviet–American Commission on the Peaceful Use of Atomic Energy, which ended in the signing of a new protocol calling for common research into nuclear synthesis and neutron reactors. At the same time a Russo–American seminar was being held in Moscow on the fuels used in magneto-hydrodynamic power stations, an area in which Soviet technology is considerably advanced. Since then such meetings have occurred at more frequent intervals, in accordance with the Washington–Moscow nuclear directive. At the same time, a ten-day conference was organized in New York by the Carnegie Endowment, a foundation connected with the Overworld, and by the American Society for International Law, whose president, the financial lawyer William Rogers, is a friend of Nixon and once worked as his Secretary of State. At the conference sessions, American and Soviet legal experts studied the problems of copyright and the preparation of legislation which would make it possible to control international trade. The delegates also approached the question of publishing articles simultaneously in American and Soviet journals, a first step towards trivializing and controlling information on an international scale. The basic differences between Jdanov and Henry Luce, founder of *Time-Life*, lie in the choice of format each offers to the public. In their respective countries both men have run media empires in which news has been controlled to serve power. The Vodka-Colanizers' ideal journal, which they seek to promote, would undoubtedly be a mixture of *Pravda* "for the critical independence" of its articles, and *Playboy* for its selection of clichés.

The jaws of the vice are tightening all the time. Even so, Frederick Dent, Minister of

Trade, was still obliged to use outdated phrases in his evidence to Senator Church's Commission of Enquiry. "National Security," he declared, "is our first preoccupation in trade negotiations with the East." Is there any way in which Senators who have sat snoring for decades on the benches of the Capitol could solve the kind of algebraic equation posed by David Packard? How is it that this industrialist working for the Pentagon is given the job as assistant Defense Minister of deciding which materials sold to the East may be strategically dangerous, when his firm, a pillar of the US-USSR Trade Council, has long been working with the Communist countries?

Nowadays any opposition to détente is considered as discreditable as an admission of opposition to peace. Confusing the two is a shrewd manoeuvre, reminiscent of Communist peace campaigns in the fifties as symbolized by Picasso's dove. In both cases an attempt is being made to neutralize the critical faculty. In an opinion poll conducted by the Harris Institute (owned by the *NY Times*) for the Chicago Council on Foreign Relations, a Rockefeller organization financed also by the Ford Foundation and the Lily Endowment, revealed that 97% of American politicians, including two thirds of the Senate, were in favour of increased trade with Eastern countries. 93% of them and 83% of the public thought that such a state of affairs would permit an improvement in the energy situation.

The Overworld is amazingly adaptable. Frank Church, for example, has given government a remarkable face-lift. As president of a Commission of Enquiry into the activities of the multinationals, he has succeeded in winning over the fringe of citizens whose scepticism about the morality and efficiency of politicians has tended to increase over the years.

Careful attention to his "show" reveals that all the questions and answers could be taken in two ways. Church's good manners and grooming, his sharp air of formal respectability make him a kind of ideal son-in-law figure, an escort any man would be happy to see with his daughter: the product of an establishment all of whose conventions he has respectfully adopted.

An ambitious but cautious reformer, the senator from Idaho knows that any suspicious enquiries into the legality of business dealings is likely to produce expressions of pained astonishment and angry modesty from the men of the financial world. It is not the size of their wallets which Church is trying to control, rather their general presentation. He may have to deal with the odd outbreak of commercial acne, but that is only to be expected when the young things are growing at such a rate.

Top managers of Polish industry and experts of Polish Management Institutes together with ten scientists of well-known Business Schools of American Universities, such as the Carnegie-Mellon University, the New York University, the University of Illinois and other universities organized a Conference dealing with management of big economic organizations from 21st to 24th March, 1977 in Warsaw. Contacts between Poland and the U.S.A. in the era of company management were initiated in 1967. Since then three or four Polish experts were dispatched to the U.S.A. every year for training purposes as guests of the Ford Foundation. The Polish Institute for Management Organization and Cadre Training developed a teaching method using American computers which is supposed to be a happy mixture of "American technology" and "Polish ideas." Poland fully utilizes the management theories and methods of various countries, particularly western countries, but mainly those of the United States. One subject they need not study usually taught U.S.A. managers is how to prevent trade union organization and how to defeat strikes for wages and industrial democracy. Or, are the Polish "students" teaching their authoritarian methods to the U.S. Universities? Harvard Business School, of course, has been receiving Soviet management students for years under subsidized programmes. Here, too, strikes and collective bargaining with unions have never figured on the curriculum.

Marx was right in saying "The mental traditions of past generations weigh like a mountain on present generations." He allowed his own shameful admiration for modern capitalists to show through his *Communist Manifesto*. A few lines further on, of course, he sends them all down the drain-pipes of History with the help of the proletariat, the America to which all progressive thinkers come in the end.

But words have never made fiction into fact. Even placed in the context of capital, Zorro will always be a strip-cartoon character. The neo-Marxists Baran and Sweezy are bound to admit that they are too late to see whether their theories are right. In fact Western industrial workers, whose numbers are being reduced by automation, appear violently allergic to the concept of Communism. And on the other side of the coin, the would-be successors of Marx, even if they have altered his will, are seeking out the company of their class enemies. The rulers of allegedly Socialist states are amazingly frank about their activities when discoursing with capitalist leaders. They admit that their chief delight and ambition is not really to export and develop the revolutionary way, a process which might cause them great losses, but to remain in power for as long as possible, floating motionless among their colleagues. What interests them is social climbing and corporate responses.

In his monumental work, *The Rich and Super-rich*, Ferdinand Lundberg has pointed out how certain names, taken as symbols of capitalist success, have acquired mythical proportions for the Communist leaders. Rockefeller is way out in front of the favourite American cousins on the Kremlin hit parade.

"David is always lunching with an emperor, a shah, a king or a president," said S. J. Weimberg of Goldman Sachs Bank. "If I went to all the receptions he gives for these people, I would never have time to work." At the superbusiness rallies organized by the president of Chase Manhattan, where business deals and world government are jumbled together, the Communist leaders have become very special guests, even character witnesses. One June afternoon, when questioning Donald Kendall, Church was unable to suppress a reflex of vanity which can be taken as a yardstick for his credibility.

"The last time I went to the USSR I travelled with a group including David Rockefeller, and he was treated like a celebrity, just as splendidly as we treat him in his own country. I think American capitalists in the USSR have a special status, based on a strange reversal of principle, just as in our democratic society crowds turn out to cheer royalty. It's a strange psychological twist."

Kendall replied, "Mr President, I don't think there's much difference."

Then Charles Percy, senator from Illinois and an influential member of the Church committee who was once president of the large Bell and Howell company, spoke up. "I went to Moscow with my daughter, Sharon Rockefeller. Well, the officials treated her like a princess; they were falling over each other to see her."

Kendall then said "David Rockefeller was treated the same way when he went to People's China and the Middle East. He's a Rockefeller!"

Church is not alone. Like the European parliaments or the Japanese Diet, the Capitol is full of representatives of intermediary bodies so steeped in high finance that when it comes to the point they simply disintegrate.

To take an example, the Business Round Table is the largest existing lobby. First set up in 1972, this association brings together the presidents and managing directors of 170 companies, 37 of them among the 50 largest American companies on the magazine *Fortune*'s annual list. And those 37 include 9 of the 10 largest (the 3 biggest banks, the 7 biggest oil and steel companies). With an operational budget of $2 million and a policy committee of forty members, this group makes sure that the laws affecting economic liberalism are scrupulously respected.

Today the association has a dominating influence on the Federal Reserve Bank through its twelve district offices.

Five of the nine directors of the Federal Reserve Bank of New York, the most influential of the twelve, have direct links with these pressure groups. They are representatives of the Chase Manhattan Bank ($34 billion on deposit on 13 September 1975); J. C. Penney ($6,200 million in annual sales); Union Carbide ($5,320 million in annual sales) and Kennecott Copper ($1,664 million in annual sales).

The present president Paul Volcker was Assistant Finance Minister. In the same way, the board members of the Federal Reserve Bank of Cleveland include representatives of Westinghouse Electric ($5,799 million in annual sales); Federated Department Stores ($2,900 million in annual sales); TRW Inc. ($2,300 million in annual sales) and Heintz and Co. ($1,650 million in annual sales)—all members of the Business Round Table. So, too, are Exxon ($4,521 million annual sales); American Telegraph and Telephone ($23,560 million in annual sales) and Sears and Roebuck ($13,100 million in annual sales), whose directors sit on the board of the Federal Reserve Bank of Richmond.

There is no longer any point in raising the fiction of political authority. Politicians, caught as they are in the vast spider's web spun by economic forces, have long since lost the advantages of political influence. It now looks as though the public and private sectors are inextricably intertwined. According to a senate report, most of the big firms are effectively controlled by nine finance companies which hold a majority of their capital. Meanwhile the portfolio of federal government stocks—about 93 billion dollars' worth—is managed not by the Treasury, but by the Federal Reserve Bank of New York. The FRB has a special Federal Open Market Committee to administer the portfolio which brings in more than $6 billion in annual interest. And the Committee works in continual cooperation with a carefully selected list of security dealers who negotiate the buying and selling of bonds on the market. The four pillars of these lucrative operations are the Bank of America (the largest bank in the world with $57 billion on deposit), the First National City Bank (2nd largest with $45 billion on deposit), the Chase Manhattan ($34 billion on deposit), and Morgan Guaranty Trust. And it is these same establishments which carry on their monopolistic activities in the private sector through their interests in most big companies—David Rockefeller is also one of the forty members of the Business Round Table Policy Committee, along with A. W. Clausen, president of the Bank of America, who sits on the board of the Federal Reserve Bank of San Francisco.

3.

The Trilateral Commission

This austere family council has for some years been judging our democratic excesses with a severely critical eye. Two hundred men from the United States, Japan and Europe sit questioning our sense of responsibility, and wondering whether it would not be better to place us under their guidance.

The star turns of this particular melodrama are Alden Clausen, president of the Bank of America; J. P. Austin, president of Coca-Cola; Peter Petersen, president of Lehmann Brothers and his colleague George Ball, both ex-ministers; J. K. Jamieson, president of Exxon; Lee Morgan, president of Caterpillar; David Packard, president of Hewlett Packard; Robert Roosa, ex-Finance Minister and colleague of Averill Harriman; Michael Blumenthal, director of the Rockefeller Foundation and president of Bendix, and Cyrus Vance, director of the Rockefeller Foundation and partner of Simpson Thatcher.

The European members include Giovanni Agnelli, boss of Fiat; Kurt Birrenbach, West German deputy, former CDU minister and president of the Thyssen metal working group; Pierre Jouven, president of Péchiney–Ugine–Kuhlmann; baron Lambert, banker; John Loudon, president of Royal Dutch Shell; Sir Eric Roll, managing director of the Warburg Bank and former governor of the Bank of England; Hans Gunther Sohl, president of the German Federal Union of Industry; Sir Ready Geddey, president of Dunlop; Guiseppe Glisente, director of Rinascente; Jacques de Fouchier, president of Paribas; Sir Frank Roberts, president of Unilever and Lloyds; Edmond de Rothschild; Olivier Giscard d'Estaing, president of the Companie Financière; and Raymond Barre, French Prime Minister.

The Japanese *zaibutsu* are represented in full by Churiro Fujino, president of the Mitsubishi group; Sumio Hara, president of the Bank of Tokyo; Benichiro Komai, president of Hitachi; Akio Morita, president of Sony; Eji Toyota, president of Toyota and Takeshi Watamabe, president of Trident International Finances.

The operation known as the Trilateral Commission was developed, financed and inspired by David Rockefeller following his discussions in late 1972 with George Franklin and the Dutchman Marx Kohnstahm, former chairman of the Jean Monnet Committee and director of the European University Institute of Florence. Today Kohnstam and Franklin are the European and North American directors of the Trilateral, which brings together all those men who see themselves as the guardians and defenders of Western values against attacks from the left.

The journalists on the commission include several editors in chief, among them Arigo Levi (editor of Agnelli's *La Stampa*); Theo Sommer (*Die Zeit*); M. Fisher (*Financial Times*); Richard Holbrooke (*Foreign Policy*) and Hedley Donovan (*Time*). The mediamen include Shintaro Fukushima, president of Kyodo News Service, Kazuhige Hirasawa, TV commentator in Japan Broadcasting, and Arthur Taylor, president of CBS. The Netherlands are represented by Andre Kloos, chairman of the Socialist Dutch radio network and John Loudon, boss of Shell, director of the Chase Manhattan Bank, and, more particularly, president of the Atlantic Institute. This institute was set up in 1960 following a resolution adopted during a NATO conference, with the specific purpose of stimulating "the spirit of collaboration between the peoples of the Atlantic world and the reinforcement of Western cultural and spiritual values."

Loudon suggested to David Rockefeller that the institute should work together with the Trilateral and this proposal was put into effect in December 1975. But maintaining this court of ruling élites is an expensive business. Rockefeller spends nearly $1 million a year on arranging meetings throughout the world and commissioning studies from prominent experts like the Dutch Nobel prize winner Jan Tinbergen, complaining bitterly as he does so that he receives no kind of support. The academics involved range from Graham Allison and Robert Bowie, professors at Harvard, to Andrew Shonfield; Ralph Dahrendorf of the London School of Economics; Richard Cooper, professor at Yale; Paul McCracken, former presidential economic adviser and professor at the University of Michigan; Henry Owen, director of the Foreign Policy Studies program at the Brooking Institute; Edwin Reischauner, former ambassador to Japan and professor at Harvard; Charles M. Robinson, president of Marconi Corporation and director of the Stanford Institute; Elliot Richardson, former Trade Minister and member of the Woodrow Wilson International Center; Carol Wilson, professor at the School of Management; Alfred Sloan of MIT and Zbigniew Brzezinski. Brzezinski is a graduate of the Russian Institute of Communist Studies at Harvard and professor at the University of Columbia, after having worked for the State Department Planning Service under Johnson. Of Polish origin, he is one of those specialists in Soviet–American relations trained in the anti-Communist school. Having worked for David Rockefeller for some years, "Zbig" was appointed director of the Trilateral on its foundation in 1973. It was he who introduced to the Commission an obscure, self-effacing governor who knew little of international problems but who, with Brzezinski's help, began to meet European and Japanese leaders and travel more widely round the world. And now, with a veneer of cosmopolitanism, Jimmy Carter has become the 39th president of the United States, still followed by Brzezinski who is now his chief foreign policy adviser.

The Carter administration has, if conceivable, more corporate presence than any Republican administration in recent history. From the perspectives of the Vodka-Cola strategy, it clearly illustrates the consummate skill of the Overworld power brokers in promoting a Democratic President to replace a Republican President equally convinced and committed to Vodka-Colanization. For those inclined to a power-relations theory of history, generally discarded by establishment intellectuals and media-merchants as conspiracy-minded paranoiacs, the composition of the new administration lends elegant and rigorous support to theories of Overworld conspiracies. Even for those who just as dogmatically insist that history is largely a sequence of coincidences and uncontinued accidents acted out by individuals of essentially goodwill and integrity and who refute all suggestions of extensive collusion and continuance among media merchants, foundation functionaries and quasi-clandestine councils and commissions and power lobbies, the Vodka-Cola composition of the Carter administration is proving embarrassingly difficult to ignore.

In February 1977 *Newsweek* stated that the managers of Coca-Cola see their time as having come to take over the lead role from its arch-rival Pepsi, in the Vodka-Cola system. Just as the pay-off between Nixon and Kendall led to Pepsi's exclusive implantation and profitable expansion in the Soviet Union's soft drink market, Carter's analogous relationship to J. Paul Austin offers Coke a fabulous opening for its conglomerated East European operation, even if it cannot sell Coke to Soviets (except for an offer to officialize Coke for the Moscow Olympics). Coke's foreign representatives and subsidiaries back-stepped Carter's foreign trade program from Georgia headquarters in

Atlanta and it was natural that Georgia's largest multinational established strong ties to the state government administration and the governor's office. Along with IBM, Coca-Cola boasts the most company-associated members in the cabinet. Besides the Carter–Austin friendship, Charles Duncan, appointed Deputy Secretary of Defense and former high official of Coke, has been permitted to retain his $14 million-worth of Coca-Cola shares. Griffen Bell, Carter's choice for Attorney General, and Joseph Califano for Health, Education and Welfare Secretary were Coke's Atlanta and Washington lawyers, respectively. Both could conceivably be involved in a retrospective conflict of interest problem, in the event of US litigation on Coke's hazard to health such as has arisen in other countries (Belgium, Denmark, Portugal, etc.).

The prohibition of the sale of Coca-Cola in Portugal as a possible danger to health was lifted late in January 1977, coincidentally shortly after the new US administration opposed a critically needed emergency loan of $300 million to the Portuguese government of Mario Soares. The following editorial appeared in the *Wall Street Journal* of 4 January 1977:

> *Coca-Cola Diplomacy*
> For weeks the government of Portugal nervously waited word from Washington that its request for a $300 million emergency loan was approved and the money was on the way. Over the weekend the loan was finally authorized.
> But the loan was a long time coming. US Treasury officials would only say "technical reasons," all the while promising that the loan is still "on track."
> It may be only coincidental but shortly before the loan was approved Portugal ended its 50-year prohibition against Coca-Cola. A joint Swiss–Portuguese company within six months will begin bottling the stuff, which up to then was smuggled from Spain at about $2 a bottle for the large economy size.
> If we were hyper-imaginative types, we'd suspect some Lisbon bureaucrat got the idea that the $300 million loan was being delayed because of the ban on Coca-Cola. Isn't Coca-Cola based in Atlanta? Isn't President-elect Jimmy Carter from Atlanta? Wasn't it once rumored that Mr Carter might name his old friend, the chairman of Coke, the Secretary of State? Didn't Mr Carter in fact name his old friend, former Coke president Charles Duncan Jr, the Deputy Secretary of Defense? Didn't he name Atlanta Congressman Andrew Young his Ambassador to the United Nations, and hasn't Mr Young been saying nice things about Coca-Cola's compassion for the Third World?
> What does this mean to détente? Will a SALT agreement with the Soviets be delayed until Pepsi is booted out of Moscow? Will the GOP align itself with 7-Up? And what is Henry Kissinger drinking these days?

In addition to such first-degree kinships, second-degree relationships exist through common membership in several of the important umbrella organizations of the Vodka-Cola system. J. Paul Austin and Califano, like Carter and Mondale, are Trilateral Commission and CFR members, with the former holding the very influential chairmanship of the powerful Rand Corporation. With far-flung operations in most East European countries and further vast-scale new investments planned, Coca-Cola unconditionally supports Jimmy Carter's détente policy both within and on the outside of government.

IBM's relations to the Carter administration are, if anything, even more extensive than Coke's, as are its East European operations. IBM possesses a corporate presence in nearly every Communist country where its computers and equipment are increasingly being imported, leased and reexported. IBM logically is among the most rabid and unconditional protagonists of détente and military expansion at home, just as it was of National Socialism in Germany in the early days of Hitler. As Thomas Watson Sr, the founder of IBM, admired Hitler at his beginning, so his progeny, Thomas Watson Jr, seems an early admirer of post-Stalin Communist régimes. No opportunity is neglected to finance, promote, advocate or lobby the cause of East–West détente and US–USSR friendship and cooperation, just as it never loses an opportunity to remain clamorously silent in respect of protests, complaints or criticisms of Soviet and Czech oppression of human rights and cheap-wage dumping contrary to the terms of Helsinki. Just as silent, in fact, as it was over the Soviet invasion of Czechoslovakia in order not to jeopardize its negotiations with the Czech authorities.

An original sponsor and member of the American Committee on US–USSR relations lobby, Thomas Watson Jr sits on most important joint US–USSR and US–satellite country trade commissions and committees. IBM is a generous contributor to numerous clubs and cliques energetically promoting détente. With very large packets of IBM shares held by Rockefeller-associated banks and companies, IBM's interlocks and inter-links with the Overworld power centers are exceptionally numerous. Watson Jr himself is on Chase Manhattan's board of directors, a trustee of the Rockefeller Foundation, member of the Council of Foreign Relations and the Trilateral Commission, all of which are presided over by David Rockefeller as well as numerous other economical political clubs of the community (as the US foreign affairs establishment calls itself these days) to which both belong. The Carter administration's IBM computer connection is impressive. Four important government posts are filled by ex-IBM board members: Cyrus Vance (State) was on IBM's executive committee; Harold Brown (Defense) headed IBM's audit committee; Patricia Harris (HUD) dealt with executive compensation; Lewis Branscomb was the first choice for White House science adviser. Carter's first choice for Commerce Secretary was Jane Cahill Pfeiffer, IBM vice-president, who turned it down on IBM's urging out of fear of over-exposure, and his first choice as Treasury Secretary was Irvin Shapiro, Du Pont chairman, IBM board member and head of the most powerful Vodka-Cola lobby in Washington. IBM's General Systems Division moved its headquarters from New York to Atlanta at the time Carter became governor of Georgia and helped reorganize the Georgia administration, emphasizing central data processing using IBM's most modern hardware. Former Attorney-General, Ramsey Clark, has declared that the Carter administration has more "corporate involvement than in any administration since Ulysses Grant's second term, when most of the cabinet was connected with the Pennsylvania Railroad." Illustrative of corporate power's indifference to the incidental detail of which party heads the government, IBM replaced its outgoing "Democrat" board members with two incoming members who took a leave of absence from IBM to serve in the Republican cabinet: Scranton (Ambassador to the United Nations), CFR (Council of Foreign Relations) and Rand Corporation; William Coleman (Secretary of Transport), Trilateral Commission, CFR, Brookings Institute and Rand Corporation.

The strong IBM tone can be expected to heighten the green light to the policy of détente and turn Brezhnev's colouration a deeper pleasurable red. IBM's capitalist involvement in the Communist bloc countries is among the most massive and gaining rapidly, with a company presence in nearly every East European country: USSR, Poland, Rumania, Hungary, Czechoslovakia, East Germany and Bulgaria. It has hundreds of its computers and associated equipment operating in East European industries as well as in military and strategic planning defense establishments. The most modern and sophisticated computers and associated hardware are being taken off ban lists and being made available to help develop "theoretical" anti-American strategical and tactical strike models and scenarios. Lifting Congress restrictions on volume of credit and granting the USSR and others "most favoured nation" trading status will provide a windfall to IBM cash flow levels, and, of course, the IBM presence in the Justice Department will certainly not be detrimental to its interests in its eight-year-long multi-million-dollar anti-trust litigation.

Treasury Secretary, Michael Blumenthal, was a great success as president, chairman and general manager of Bendix, for which he made a lot of money, hence his motto "Everything has to make money to be successful." The principal stockholder in Bendix is the First National City Bank of the Rockefeller family. One of the ten largest armament firms, Bendix made huge profits in Vietnam and has very large Pentagon defense contracts. It has become a leading armament exporter with lucrative contracts to help make the armies of Saudi-Arabia, Iran and other countries stronger and more lethal, defensively, of course. Blumenthal's last major success before taking a leave of absence from Bendix (bound to make a lot of hard currency profits for the company) was signing a contract for a joint venture to make spark plugs in the Soviet Union. It calls for a $40 million plant with credits provided by Bendix-related US commercial banks, i.e. First National City, Chase Manhattan, etc., capable of producing 50 to 75 million spark plugs per year, 50% of which will be sold outside the Soviet Union by Bendix's international marketing network. A key feature of the deal is that it calls for Bendix personnel to be directly involved on site in managing the operation, for example in authority over quality control and power of decision in further investments and exports.

On leaving Bendix, where his salary and bonuses in 1975 exceeded $200,000 for the $65,000-a-year post, the Corporation promised Blumenthal $23,000-a-year consulting fees for life. Even if under the worst sort of conditions it is suspended during his term of office, it will be restored when he leaves the government. It is another example of corporate nepotism prevailing in high reaches of government and pervasive within the Carter administration, in contrast to the rules governing non-corporate nepotism in appointment to government jobs which forbids anyone appointing family members up to the degree of second cousin.

The Vodka-Cola strategy of creating and utilizing private commissions, foundations, clubs, etc. to orient and control political policies has gestated a degree of bureaucratic nepotism in support of détente and furthering the global design. In addition to the above examples, numerous other top and lower-level posts have been filled by members of the Trilateral Commission, CFR, Bildeberg, Atlantic Council, Carnegie Endowment, Rockefeller and Ford Foundations, etc. Out of a total of around sixty US members of the Trilateral Commission around twenty are now in the government and over thirty are members of the CFR. Continuing the tradition, the Secretaries of State and Defense are members of the CFR and the former, like most of his predecessors, is a close Rockefeller associate. Here are some of the appointees and their "community" Vodka-Cola membership previous to or at the time of that appointment:

Cabinet level
Carter, Trilateral, personal ties to heads of IBM, Coca-Cola and Rockefellers.
Walter M. Mondale (Vice-President), Trilateral, Council of Foreign Relations, Atlantic
    Council, Bildeberg Society.
Cyrus Vance (Secretary of State), Trilateral, CFR, Rockefeller Foundation, Atlantic
    Council, IBM, Law firm has important Rockefeller family accounts.

Richard N. Cooper (Under-Secretary of State), Trilateral, CFR.

Harold Brown (Secretary of Defense), Trilateral, CFR, IBM, Research institutes funded by foundation money.

Charles Duncan Jr (Deputy Secretary of Defense) Coca-Cola (keeps $14-million-worth of shares).

Griffin Bell (Attorney-General) Coca-Cola attorney in Atlanta.

Michael Blumenthal, Trilateral, CFR, Bendix, US–East European trade commissions.

Anthony M. Solomon (Under-Secretary of Treasury), Trilateral, CFR.

Kenneth S. Aelsan (Deputy Secretary of Treasury) CFR, Rockefeller Associates, New York banks, committees, etc.

C. Fred Bergsten, Brookings Institute, CFR.

Juanita Kreps (Secretary of Commerce) Eastman Kodak, New York Stock Exchange.

Joseph Califano (Secretary of Health, Education and Welfare), Trilateral, CFR, Washington attorney for Coca-Cola.

Patricia Roberts Harris (Secretary Housing and Urban Development), board of directors of Chase Manhattan Bank, IBM.

Presidential advisers and key appointments

Zbigniew Brzezinski (national security) Trilateral, CFR, Bildeberg, Russian Institute and Russian Studies Institute, Columbia University (Rockefeller and Ford Foundation funded).

Charles Schultz (economics) CFR, Brookings Institute.

Andrew Young (United Nations) Trilateral Commission.

James Schlesinger (energy), Rand Corporation, CFR.

Marshal (Soviet affairs), CFR, Director Russian Institute, Columbia University (Rockefeller and Ford Foundation funded).

Lewis Bascomb (science adviser) CFR, IBM, Rand Corporation.

Paul Warnke (Arms Control and Disarmament Agency) Trilateral, CFR.

Ellsworth Bunker (co-negotiator Panama Canal Treaty) CFR, last US ambassador to Vietnam.

Sol Linowitz (co-negotiator Panama Canal Treaty) CFR, Coudert Bros law firm closely associated with Rockefeller family.

Elliot Richardson (ambassador at large) Trilateral, CFR (ex-Republican ambassador to UK).

Richard Gardner (ambassador to Italy), CFR, American Committee on US–Soviet relations). Staunchly favours Italian Communist Party in government.

Samuel Huntington (White House Staff) Trilateral Commission, CFR. Author of Vietnam pacification program in Vietnam. Controversial papers for Trilateral Conference supporting authoritarian régimes.

Leslie Gibb (State Department) CFR, *New York Times, Carnegie Endowment* (foreign policy magazine).

Richard Holbrooke (State Department) Trilateral, *Carnegie Endowment* (foreign policy magazine).

Examples of foundation funding of some Vodka-Cola clubs

Rockefeller Foundation: Brookings Institute, Rand Corporation, New South Project (Carter).

Rockefeller Brothers Fund: Trilateral Commission, CFR, Bildeberg Club.

Ford Foundation: Trilateral Commission, CFR, Bildeberg Club, Rand Corporation, New South Project (Carter).

Elli Lilly Endowment (controlled by Rockefeller-owned Chemical Bank of New York):
Trilateral Commission, CFR, New South Project (Carter).

Apart from their links with US institutions, councils and businesses, certain of Carter's men can be seen to have connections with foreign governments.

When Paul Warnke received Senate confirmation as director of the Arms Control and Disarmament Agency and chief US negotiator at the Strategic Arms Limitation Talks (SALT), it was revealed that he was registered with the Justice Department as a foreign agent for the government of Algeria from 26 March 1975 until 23 February 1977.

Warnke, a general partner in the Washington-based law firm of Clifford, Warnke, Glass, McIlwain and Finney, which represents "commercial interests" of Algeria in the US, notified the US Justice Department in late February, after Carter offered him the job, that he was terminating his registration as a foreign agent.

Clark Clifford, former Secretary of Defense and currently on a special mission to Greece and Cyprus, is still registered as a foreign agent for the government of Algeria. A Justice Department official said that Clifford, who is a partner in the same law firm, retained the foreign agent's designation along with his new diplomatic role because of a State Department notification that qualified his presidential representative's position as being in the national interest.

In a related area, Sol M. Linowitz, former chairman of the board of Xerox Corp. and named by Carter chief US negotiator for the new Panama Canal Treaty, was registered as a foreign agent for the government of Chile in 1972, and also represented the government of Colombia from 7 March 1974 to 4 February 1977. The Justice Department official said that Linowitz, a senior partner in the New York Rockefeller-related law firm of Coudert Bros, interpreted federal and state laws for the government of Chile. In the case of Colombia, Linowitz represented both the government and a Colombian association of sugar growers in the US.

The Justice Department said that Warnke primarily represented the government of Algeria in its US dealings concerning Sonatrach, an enterprise of the Algerian government involved in the construction of a gas liquefaction plant. The issue of Warnke representing the Algerian government recently was raised by Republican Larry McDonald. Noting that Warnke had testified before the Senate Foreign Relations Committee on 6 October 1975, Republican McDonald accused Warnke of "possible conflict of interest" since he "urged limitation of American armaments to the Middle East without discussing the Soviet role in accelerating the Middle East arms race." McDonald charged that Warnke failed to tell the committee that he was registered as a foreign agent for the Algerian government, which has received Soviet support in the past.

Algeria is, of course, a leading Third World critic of the US, which constantly sides with East-bloc attacks against capitalism and American imperialism but at the same time maintains numerous joint ventures with leading "American imperialist monopolies" such as Bechtel, El Paso Gas and others.

Part IV

To get a glimpse of the future of détente, we must look at the past. This will give us a better chance of gauging the "credibility" of the claims of the Vodka-Colanizers.

The attitude of the Communist rulers, "the inhuman exploitation of their own humanity," to paraphrase a Marxist slogan, is amply demonstrated.

No echo of the Helsinki declarations has made them free the dissidents so carefully cherished in the Gulags, psychiatric hospitals and work camps. No belief in a creed of *mea culpa* will spring from the development of Euro-Communism to cast out the dogma that is at the heart of all these "sins." There is no incentive to place optimistic bets on the future when the companies who are today most committed to the East are the very same which cooperated with the Nazi system. The directors of the multinational giants like General Motors, Exxon, IBM, ITT, Du Pont, the Chase Manhattan Bank, collaborated with Krupp, IG Farben, Mannesman and the Deutsche Bank when they, in turn, collaborated with the Hitler régime.

Is this simply a question of individuals? Was National-Socialism only initiated by the few who were judged at Nuremberg? All the past examples argue against a democratic outcome. With operations in Greece, Spain, Chile, these companies reaped similar record profits from military intervention in Vietnam, whilst at the same time dealing with the Communist world. Soon after, the American arms industry moved from Indo-China to Eastern Europe, thanks to the co-production system.

But the case of ITT is the most dramatic. Anti- and pro-socialist at the same time, it encouraged the destabilization and overthrow of Allende, whilst extending its cooperative links with Communist régimes. The keepers of the tablets of the Communist law were perfectly adapted to the Vodka-Cola era and felt no contradiction in the fact that the vice-president of ITT, John McCone, had been the director of the CIA, nor that the president, Harold Geneen, had behaved like a "vulture crushing the people of Chile."

Basically the penetration of ITT into Eastern Europe is as tenable as the Mafia being asked to draft a new criminal code, whilst insisting on immunity for its own criminal activities. The Rockefeller arms companies defended Vietnam against Communism at a profit, while investing these profits in the enemy's economy.

The factories of Coca-Cola, symbol of American imperialism during the fifties, continue to proliferate throughout the Communist countries, whilst the GIs, defenders of the last bastions of the free world, continue to consume this "typically American" drink.

Cyrus Vance, Jimmy Carter's new Secretary of State, declared shortly after his nomination that "to link problems of trade to human rights issues is to try and mix apples with oranges." Arthur Goldberg confirmed that the complete rejection by the Soviets of any reference to human rights in the Helsinki follow-up in Belgrade would not endanger détente as the two "were not linked". On the other hand are the numerous statements of Brezhnev presenting the capitalists as no more than crass in the West but transformed to missionaries bringing peace, détente and a reduction in tension in the Soviet Union.

Naturally an alliance of this kind precludes any intervention in the internal affairs of each partner. That is why the Jackson Amendment, which we outline in this section, constituted in the Kremlin's eyes a hostile and anti-Helsinki interference. This opinion was shared on the capitalist side by the apostles of détente, usually linked to the American Jewish lobby, and who showed by embarrassed hesitation on this occasion that they too accorded a higher priority to profits than to human rights. Unlinking profits of détente from "indivisible freedoms" is the major aim of Carter's strategy, in order to permit profits amid protests, thus preserving both the support of the Overworld and of the voters. The entire human rights campaign of the Carter administration is a concocted endeavour to demonstrate its eternal theological opposition to the "values" and spiritual evils of Communism for Congress who will be asked in return to abrogate the Jackson Amendment. Thus the eternal and moral opposition will be inspired but unlinked from the prosaic and practical needs of détente in the form of unlimited credits, most favoured nation trading status, etc., so critically needed to support Vodka-Cola profiteering.

1.

Helsinki in the Light of Munich

On 31 July 1975 the Helsinki Summit Conference on European cooperation and security opened in a climate of universal indifference. Apart from expert commentators assigned to cover the summit and a flood of congratulatory, detailed or concerned articles, there was no indication of any interest from the public who seemed increasingly unimpressed by those public relations operations basic to political life today. Thirty-four people landed at Helsinki airport at precise, fifteen-minute intervals, in a tedious, repetitive sequence apparently designed to dull any curiosity and to make the serious, urgent-looking figures of the delegates as anonymous as possible.

Even Communist China, which had described the "beauty" contest as "a disgusting comedy," was represented in Helsinki shop-windows. Mao's heroic mill-workers had manufactured the T-shirts bearing the conference emblem, regardless of the reactionary states and revisionist governments represented there.

At the other end of town, the thirty-fifth delegate, and the only one with any real power, made his entrance at the train station. Leonid Brezhnev descended from his special train with the good-natured air of a local government official visiting one of the outlying spots of his region. For him this conference represented a successful outcome to twenty-one years of Soviet diplomatic efforts to manoeuvre his opposite numbers into a position of harrassed exhaustion. Leaning comfortably against the bulwark of his country, Brezhnev led his fellow delegates into a kind of Orwellian nightmare, totally cut off from reality. Helsinki was an extraordinary celebration of the word and the presence, its be-all and end-all. The speeches were interchangeable, the principles uttered, hoped for and commended had already been violated by the facts.

But none of that mattered. The important thing was that it happened, not that public reaction to it was stifled in the East or apathetic in the West. From the number of motions raised it became clear just how fragile and precarious the politician's position is. The only way he can keep himself in power is by abusing the spoken word. The 400 delegates had 1,800 journalists to celebrate their technique. They were to conceptualize and synthesize Helsinki. A hundred years after the first, the second Congress of Vienna was taking place with Metternich–Kissinger meeting Talleyrand–Brezhnev. This arbitrary but reassuring view allayed the doubts of public opinion and the worries of men of government by re-affirming the preeminence of politics in a totally artificial way. Not only were the Soviets present at this "happening," they even kept the ball moving with a few general principles sufficiently vague to keep the talks together and prolong discussion. But throughout they were clearly influenced by Stalin's rule for negotiation: "What's ours is ours, what's yours is negotiable." Leonid Brezhnev insisted that the number of troops stationed in Europe be reduced and won legal recognition for the status quo. On 1 August the final 400-page document was brought by special plane from Geneva. It was the result of two years of intensive negotiations between experts of the countries represented at Helsinki and was initialled by the political leaders of the thirty-five delegations attending the summit. The basis of this charter was "respect for an inviolability of existing frontiers." The Soviet Union had re-stated its adherence to détente by a few global formulae. The Western politicians had demonstrated their good will by acknowledging the legality of the Eastern European countries where minority, autocratic Communist parties maintain a system of coercion with their backs to the wall.

Not once during the summit or the long preparatory negotiations for it, did anyone raise the question of democracy in the Soviet Union and the other Communist states. This exemplifies Kissinger-style diplomacy; since his arrival in politics in 1968, the Secretary of State had based his whole strategy on a rhetoric of peace rather than of freedom.

There was, of course, a third package providing for the free circulation of men and of ideas, but it seemed highly unlikely that it would come to anything and it was dependent on the signing of bilateral agreements which the Kremlin appeared loath to start putting into practice. One clause in the final document prevailed upon governments to "grant accredited staff reporters entry and exit visas for specific periods." On 6 August the Soviet authorities turned down requests made by four American journalists for a permanent visa. Three days later *Pravda* rejected "demands for supposed liberalization of the régime." "Socialism will develop," continued the newspaper, "and nobody will be allowed to interfere in the internal affairs of socialist countries and, more especially, to impose foreign recipes for the solution of social problems. To impose inadmissible conditions on the movement towards peace can only be the act of those who do not want détente or social progress."

Giscard d'Estaing himself had proof of this intransigence when he went to the USSR in October 1975. His timid attempts at dialogue resulted only in his being left stamping his feet in a cold Red Square outside the door of the Kremlin apartments which Brezhnev had irritatedly slammed in his face.

As it was, the 2,850,000 words uttered during the Helsinki summit did not succeed in disguising the ambiguities and contradictions inherent in the very definition of détente. It is unlikely that the Soviets have ever taken a Western politician very seriously. They know just how shortlived his professional life may be and how insecure his political training ground really is. They may hold talks with "bourgeois politicians" for formal reasons, but they regard the signing of agreements or treaties as no more than a tactical, diplomatic concession, confined to a system of government which has only a very tiny slice of power. The only men to whom the Communist leaders can speak as equals have always been the bosses of capitalist industry, whose security of tenure provides a guarantee of profitable agreements. Kruschev summed this up in his brutally frank manner when he was receiving a delegation of Italian politicians and industrialists in 1958. He abruptly left the two ministers to whom he was chatting and advanced, pointing his finger, towards Giovanni Agnelli, the Fiat boss, who was standing with some of his colleagues. "It is you I want to talk to. In ten years these clowns will have gone, but you will always be there. You're the real power, the only man I want to negotiate with."

It is wrong to suppose that the Communists do not want détente; on the contrary, they would like to see it strictly applied. Détente, for them, means increased cooperation with Western managers, but a cooperation totally unaffected by the contingencies of political decisions. It is all very well to keep up a façade of ideological rivalry in order to lay increased stress on economic integration, but do not let the one influence the course of the other.

The slogan "Peace through trade" now upheld by the Vodka-Colanizers is strangely and disturbingly like the slogan "World peace through world trade" invented and promoted in 1933 by Thomas Watson, the founder of IBM, on his election to the Chamber of Foreign Commerce. Watson himself appears to have experienced no ideological conflict but betrayed an assiduous interest in the development of international politics. A close friend of Eisenhower, whose simple, optimistic outlook he shared, Watson met many heads of state in the years between 1927 and 1943 and formed a close friendship with Chiang Kai Chek. He criticized Communist Russia but warmly supported Benito Mussolini as the man who had succeeded in "bringing Italy out of chaos" and hailed his achievements. Four years later Hitler awarded him the Order of Merit of the German Eagle with star. Relations between the two men were warm, and with IBM established in Nazi Germany, they had considerable interests in common. At the beginning of 1938 there was another meeting in Berlin. On Hitler's assurance that there would be no war, Watson expanded his operations in France and bought new offices on the place Vendôme.

When war was declared he transferred IBM's European interests to a holding company in Geneva directed by Werner Lier, a captain in the Swiss army. Dr Otto Kriep was responsible for the firm's German activities. IBM was considered an important factor in the Nazi war effort.

Thomas Watson was waiting cautiously to see what would happen. After Pearl Harbour, however, in 1942 he completely reoriented the activities of his US group. With a 94% share in the Munitions Manufacturing Corporation, he manufactured bombers, heavy guns and parts for aeroplane engines. This effort on behalf of the free world brought him more than $200 million profit. Meanwhile, the Swiss holding company continued to receive profits from IBM's German operations. With remarkable ingenuity, Werner Lier established a series of channels by which these frozen profits could be sent out of Switzerland through the US embassy at Vichy.

Even then the IBM spirit, which makes all its employees identify with the firm, was working efficiently. During a raid over Sindelfingen, Frank MacCarthy, personnel manager of Canadian IBM and a bombardier in the Royal Air Force, dropped his bombs anywhere rather than hit his supposed target, the IBM factory.

IBM's French offices at Corbeil-Essones near Paris were administered by SS Captain Westerholt. Twenty years after the war, one of the longstanding board members was able to contentedly recall "the large number of former German leaders devoted to IBM and their continued interest in protecting a precious part of our patrimony."

Under every régime, the exploitation of men near power had been part of the basic strategy of large firms and of the psychology of their managers. Wars or changes of régime are perceived as merely temporary phenomena, requiring great adaptability so that business efficiency will be impaired as little as possible.

After the Liberation in France, therefore, IBM appointed as its new head baron Christian de Walder, who was chosen for his title, his connections with the Resistance and his friendly relations with general de Gaulle. Until his retirement in 1973, de Walder provided an effective counterweight to the confused moves towards national independence manifested by the Fifth Republic, since it was in France that IBM had tightest control of the computer market, with a two-thirds share. This proportion was much higher than its fraction of the market in the US. Firms like IBM made judicious use of local personalities without adhering in any way to national rules and regulations; and it is this which goes a long way to explaining their extraordinary vitality.

When IBM engaged in negotiations with Soviet Russia in 1949, at the height of the cold war, it was still only a modest American company with an annual turnover of $125 million. Today it enjoys a monopoly position, with over 300,000 employees and a turnover of more than $9 billion on which the Soviet leaders are relying to try and revitalize the Russian economy and keep themselves in power.

IBM's activities are not exceptional. In 1923, Primo de Rivera's Spain gave Sosthene Behn, the founder of ITT, his first break by granting him exclusive rights to provide all telephonic installations in the Iberian peninsula. The small, bankrupt Puerto-Rican company he had bought a few years before was now entering the hallowed halls of international trade. Before long, Behn's liking for authoritatian régimes was confirmed. On 4 August 1933 he was the first US businessman to be received at Berchtesgarden by the new Reich's chancellor.

On the advice of Hitler's economic adviser Wilhelm Keppler, Behn entrusted the management of his German companies to banker Kurt von Schroeder of the Stein Bank, who later became an SS general and a major financial backer of Himmler's Gestapo. Behn also profited from his relationship with Gerhardt Westrick, a well-known lawyer and influential member of the National-Socialist Party who made frequent trips to New York. There Westrick would stay in the Waldorf Astoria and go to meet Behn in his Louis XIV office at ITT headquarters which was dominated by a portrailt of pope Pius XI hung alongside the firm's motto "In the service of men and of nations." In 1938, with the agreement of Hermann Goering, the ITT subsidiary Lorenz bought a 28% share in Focke Wulf, whose fighter planes were to cause serious damage to allied convoys and weapons. Germany's entry into the war did nothing to alter Behn's strategy. In 1940, after an audience with Hitler, he agreed that Jews should be removed from senior management positions in his European companies. A few weeks later Westrick met Behn and Henry Ford in New York. The automobile manufacturer was also a familiar face in Nazi ruling circles. Nobody has forgotten the cheque for $50,000 he sent Hitler on the dictator's fiftieth birthday, with a telegram congratulating him on having set the country back on its feet. Westrick had been authorized by Foreign Secretary von Ribbentrop to ask Behn and Ford to do everything they could to persuade Britain to surrender. The two businessmen did actually take a step in this direction in communications with Churchill and Anthony Eden.

In 1941, stimulated by its Swiss rival Hasler's refusal to work for Germany, ITT stepped up the total of exports from its Swiss subsidiary to the Third Reich. Between 1941 and 1944, over half the product of its Spanish factories went to support the Nazi war effort. Although there was some criticism from American politicians, Behn knew that he could count on the total support of the military, a breeding ground for future directors of ITT with its hierarchical, authoritarian structure. While Focke Wulff planes were machine-gunning convoys and troops, Behn's American laboratories succeeded in developing the high frequency "Huff Duff" sonar system used to detect German submarines. Morality had triumphed and in 1946 Harry Truman himself presented Behn with the medal for merit, the highest civilian award, for his contribution to the military effort. From this unassailable position, ITT even managed to obtain $27 million damages from Washington, $5 millions of which were for the damage done to the Focke Wulff factory, American property bombed by allied planes.

As ITT has become a symbol of the financial firmament, it is worth examining more closely. With 430,000 employees in 800 companies based in over eighty countries and an annual turnover of over $8.5 billion, it is certainly an impressive institution. Its activities in Chile, Spain, South Africa and Brazil are well known. But if one goes beyond these ideological black holes, it is ITT's connections with the Communist states which give the firm its extraordinary scope. In this respect, the links between Harold Geneen, ex-president and managing director of the group, and Leonid Brezhnev are exactly like the relations of his predecessor Sosthene Behn with Adolf Hitler. What else could one expect?

Since 1930 General Motors and Ford have dominated the world market in all-surface, all-purpose utility vehicles. For their directors the only difference between the Ford T in which the nomadic American unemployed of the Great Depression journeyed after work and the grey-green trucks made for the Wehrmacht, was a difference in model. Their vision of the world, its rhythm determined by the speed of the production line, appeared to be confined to a series of highways and parking lots which had to be filled according to the likes and needs of local customers. Their philosophy had evolved from managerial methods which viewed the state as a sales zone. A few weeks before the outbreak of the Second World War, Henry Ford voiced his principles, which were as sturdy as his automobiles, "We do not regard ourselves as a national company, but solely as a multi-national organization."

When Hitler started his own game of Monopoly in 1939 and landed on the Polish square with his first move, the chancelleries and parliaments of Europe became so many fear-ridden chicken coops. But even then, Alfred Sloan, president of General Motors, curtly reassured his anxious stockholders with "We are too big to be inconvenienced by these pitiful international squabbles." Indeed, the largest firm in the world played an essential part in preparing Hitler's trans-European safari. In 1929 the American company became 100% owner of Opel. In 1935, at the request of the Nazi high command, Opel's offices in Brandenburg concentrated on developing a new heavy truck which was to be "less vulnerable to enemy air attack." From 1936, the German army was equipped with the Opel Blitz, production of which accelerated rapidly.

Moved by this gesture, in 1938 Hitler pinned his Eagle of the First Class to the lapel of General Motor's executive head. At the same time, Ford was opening an assembly plant in a Berlin suburb. According to American army intelligence reports, these buildings were designed to produce troop transports for the Wehrmacht.

In early 1939, seven months before the outbreak of war, General Motors converted the 432 acres of the Opel establishment at Rüsselsheim to manufacturing military aircraft. Between 1939 and 1945 these factories alone manufactured and assembled 50% of all the propulsion systems for the Junker 88, regarded by aviation experts as "the best bomber in the Luftwaffe."

On the ground General Motors and Ford subsidiaries produced 90% of the three-ton "Mule" half-tracks and 70% of all the medium tonnage heavy trucks supplied to the armies of the Reich. The English secret services regarded these vehicles as "the backbone of the Germany army's transport system." American involvement in the war made no difference in this case, either. The firms never deviated from their original strategy.

On 25 November 1942, the Nazi government appointed Carl Luer manager of the Rüsselsheim complex. But the Darmstadt provincial appeal court ruled that "this administrative decision would not affect the authority of the directorial board. Managerial methods and staff would remain unchanged."

Indeed, Alfred Sloan and his vice-presidents, James B. Mooney, John T. Smith and Graeme K. Howard, remained on the General Motors-Opel board throughout the war. Moreover, in flagrant violation of existing legislation, information, contacts, transfers and trade continued to flow between the firm's Detroit headquarters and its subsidiaries both in allied countries and in territories controlled by the Axis powers. The financial records of Opel Rüsselsheim revealed that between 1942 and 1945 production and sales strategy were planned in close coordination with General Motors factories throughout the world, in particular with General Motors Japan in Osaka, General Motors Continental in Antwerp, General Motors China in Hong Kong and Shanghai, General Motors Uruguay in Monte Video, General Motors of Brazil in Sao Paulo and the American mother company. In 1943, while its American manufacturers were equipping the

United States Air Force, the German group were developing, manufacturing and assembling motors for the Messerschmitt 262, the first jet fighter in the world. This innovation gave the Nazis a basic technological advantage. With speeds of up to 540 miles per hour, this aircraft could fly 100 mph faster than its American rival, the piston-powered Mustang P 150.

When the whistle blew for the end of the game, General Motors and Ford rushed back to their dressing rooms to ask the American government for compensation to offset the damage done to their installations in the Axis countries by allied bombing.

In 1967 justice was finally done. General Motors received $33 million in the form of tax exemption on profits for the "troubles and destruction occasioned to its aeroplane and motorized vehicle factories in Germany, Austria, Poland and China." Ford, on its side, managed to extort just under $1 million for the damage done to its military truck production lines in Cologne.

When Alfred Sloan retired in 1956, after thirty-five years at the head of General Motors, he seemed the perfect candidate for the position of undisputed patriarch of the American extreme right. An austere and angular man who neither smoked nor drank, he bore all the stigmata of those mystics of free enterprise who adopt their wives after marrying their industries. His intellectual attitudes are a marvellous illustration of the psychology and motivation of his fellow industrial giants. Though his mind is swift and athletic in the economic and trade spheres, it becomes paraplegic when he has to deal with the political and social development of his country. He finds any potential factor of change disturbing. Sloan hated all minorities, whether they be Liberals, "Blacks" or Jews. He was anti-union and used a private police force recruited by the Detroit Mafia to break strikes and put down protest movements among his 700,000 employees.

For Sloan the election of Franklin D. Roosevelt was a victory for a leader of the Communist Internationale, and the New Deal looked like the biggest attempt at forced collectivization since the October Revolution.

In 1936 a Treasury Department enquiry revealed that over the previous three years Sloan and his wife had managed to avoid paying $1,921,587 in taxes. In an attempt to avoid prosecution, the Detroit emperor created a foundation and allocated it $10 million. This gave him a completely legal means of continuing to evade taxation and, at the same time, of applying his full financial strength to fighting liberal extremism.

To this end Sloan financed several suspect campaigns, such as Dr Fred Schwartz's hysterical "anti-Communist christian crusade" or the publication of a decidedly Fascist broadsheet called *Human Events* in collaboration with the Life Line Foundation of Texan oil millionaire L. H. Hunt. So, when Sloan retired in 1956 it was to leave the business world but not to abandon any of his ideas. After an enquiry in September 1964, B'Nai B'Rith, the Jewish antidefamation league, named him chief financial supporter of the National Education Program directed by George Benson, president of Harding College at Searcy, Arkansas. This program, to which Sloan contributed $500,000 included the issuing of films and brochures intended to "support free enterprise and prevent the economic action of the government leading to Socialism and Communism." According to B'Nai B'Rith, a large part of the material used was inspired by the writings of Robert Welch, founder of the John Birch Society.

Today Sloan's successors are negotiating with the USSR for the construction of the biggest heavy-truck factory in the world.

The most popular toys sold in Soviet department stores last Christmas were little tankers made in West Germany and unmistakeably painted in Exxon and Shell colours. Socialist virtue was finally paying homage to "capitalistic and monopolistic vice," by conferring the rights of citizenship on the two oil giants whose activities outside East

Europe are still regularly and vehemently denounced by the Communist authorities and their fellow strugglers in the Western Communist Parties.

Deterding, the founder and managing director of the Anglo–Dutch company, Royal Dutch Shell, was also a victim of pro-Nazi fever. In 1936, after thirty years at the head of his group, he retired to Mecklemberg in Germany, from where he paid frequent visits to Holland in an attempt to emphasize cooperation between the two countries. When he died, memorial services were held for him in all Shell offices and Hitler, Himmler and Goering attended his funeral.

At the present time, Exxon and the other branches of the Rockefeller group are working with Communist ventures just as they continued to cooperate throughout the Second World War with the powerful Nazi chemical group, IG Farben, theoretically dismantled in 1945. After the invasion of Europe, Exxon continued to honour agreements signed in 1926 for the exchange of information and the development of cooperation. The company appeared to be following Hitler's progress with a benevolent and all-seeing eye. When German oil reserves looked too low, Exxon and General Motors combined with IG Farben in 1935 to build tetra-ethyl factories in Germany. This gave the highly mechanized Nazi war machine a plentiful supply of synthetic fuel.

The German chemical industry perfectly illustrates the unchangeability of business enterprises and of economic power as compared to the ephemerality of the human species. For the last hundred years, these firms have lived unshakeably on through all kinds of political régimes and all kinds of conflict, keeping structure and power intact.

In 1870 Hoechst made a green dye for the gowns of the Empress Eugenie and a red dye for soldiers' trousers, while BASF devoted a large part of its activities to the manufacture of synthetic indigo.

Before long this marriage of science and technology was accompanied by a new policy of rationalization.

In 1905, Karl Duisberg, president of the third chemical giant, Bayer, suggested forming a cartel. In 1916, the newly created IG Farben devoted itself to the intensive production of asphyxiating gases destined for large scale extermination operations among the enemy trenches. At the end of the First World War, it was English and American capital which helped the company to develop. IG Farben stocks worth several million pounds were held by various transatlantic banks including the Rockefellers' Chase Manhattan, the Morgan and the Warburg. As soon as the trust was formed, the firm directed its research towards means of achieving total self-sufficiency in raw materials. In 1913 work began on finding a substitute for Chilean nitrates. In 1919 Fritz Harber discovered a method of obtaining nitrogen from the air. In 1921 the group's factories were working on the production of synthetic nitrate for the manufacture of explosives.

In 1925 the company occupied a dominant position in world chemical markets. In 1926 it joined forces with the two largest German explosives manufacturers, Nobel Dynamite and Koln Rottweill, both of which had numerous subsidiaries abroad.

In 1932 IG Farben became the largest chemical power in the world. It controlled 400 German companies and 500 trading ventures, owned its own railways and coal mines and had factories in several dozen countries. The 500 largest wealth-producing firms in Western Europe and the United States were linked with over 2,000 agreements with the German group, which employed the largest number of highly skilled researchers and technicians ever to work for one company within modern economic history.

The German economy was totally dependent on IG Farben and no government could hope to stay in power without its cooperation. The Nazis' decision to make Germany an impregnable economic fortress would never have come to anything but for the kindly reception accorded it by the directors of a firm which had always supported the National-Socialist Party.

IG Farben's technical vitality and commercial strength enabled it to make many more discoveries, such as the hydrogenization of coal to produce oil, and the production of synthetic rubber from coal, which increased its independence from foreign raw materials.

Karl Duisberg, president since the formation of the cartel, died in 1936. He was replaced by Karl Bosch, a technical expert who sat on the boards of a number of foreign companies, including US Steel, Du Pont of Nemours and Standard Oil of New Jersey.

When Bosch died in 1940 he was succeeded by Nazi leader Karl Krauch, whose appointment symbolized the close cooperation between the top industrialists and politicians of the Third Reich, and, beyond that, the intimacy between IG Farben and the Nazi régime.

Thirty years on it is as if the last hundred years had never happened. The allies may have broken up IG Farben in 1945, the government may be Social Democrat rather than National Socialist, but, thanks nowadays to Bayer, Hoechst and BASF, West Germany still has the most powerful chemical industry in the world. BASF employs 110,000 people and has annual sales figures of £3,675 million; Bayer has 169,000 employees and annual sales of £3,255 million; Hoechst employs 18,200 workers and makes £3,815 million in profits. The three firms are linked by about forty joint-venture agreements, so there is no real competition between them. By comparison, the largest English chemical company, Imperial Chemical, only has a turnover of £3,100 million, while the American number one, Du Pont, manages £3,250 million.

Long service at the directorial level gives the German firms another advantage. While Imperial Chemical has had at least a dozen directors since the end of the war, Karl Winnacker, appointed director of IG Farben in 1941, went straight to the chairmanship of Hoechst immediately after the war and he is still in the same job.

In a chemical industry characterized by a high level of concentration, there appear to be more mergers in West Germany than anywhere else. IG Farben's three offshoots are now rebuilding the firm's prewar empire even more speedily by buying up, taking over and eliminating more vulnerable companies.

In a German nation theoretically divided into two rival states, these firms have succeeded where politics could not. Willy Hoerkens, director of Hoechst, recently said in Vienna that the Communist countries, including China, were demanding "the creation of giant chemical projects with German firms." As Hoerkens saw it, "the construction of large new factories should be 'speedily and discreetly' discussed between political and industrial leaders, and should function according to the system of co-production in which the private capitalist firm and the Communist state enjoy equal power."

At the present time West Germany is Comecon's largest trading partner, and BASF, Bayer and Hoechst send 26% of their exports to the German Democratic Republic.

In 1950 a whole political and cultural structure was established to justify the cold war and US anti-Communist strategy. A psychotic atmosphere which nurtured all forms of opportunism was developing in America. Robert Kennedy made his political début in one of the commissions of "red-hunter" Joseph McCarthy; Richard Nixon asked for and was given the head of Alger Hiss.

At that time, the future pro-détente men, Rockefeller and Ford, were using all the strength of their foundations and all available information channels to convince the American consciousness that Stalin's aims posed a serious and imminent threat to the free world. A whole system of values based on a rejection of totalitarianism was developed in this way, with the cooperation of well-known writers, influential journalists and reputable academics. The Harvard Business School, the temple of American academic conservatism and the intellectual voice of big business, was a symbol of this defensive, doctrinal intransigence. Its directors were still a long way from the peaceful change of plumage which now leads them to develop schools of management in Socialist countries and to help train Marxist managers. While American Defense Secretary James Forrestal leapt forty feet in the air from the balcony of his apartment shouting "The Russians are coming!" Alfred Krupp was returning to his directorship after a short absence spent in the Nuremburg court room and the cells of Spandau prison. This punctilious man, whose industrial empire had been symbolically dismantled at the end of the Second World War, now became a valuable auxiliary to the allied governments. He owed his remission to John MacCloy, the American High Commissioner for Germany and a former businessman with US Steel. It had been thanks to him that the American iron and steel number one continued to reap considerable profits in Germany during the war, by maintaining its factories in the Ruhr.

Krupp left prison on 3 February 1951, with 36 billion francs pocket-money in damages. It was hoped that his company would be able to build a wall of industrial combines and blast furnaces strong enough to keep the Federal Republic independent and safe from the objectives of its Communist neighbours. Alfred Krupp found a drained and anaemic company, employing only about 1,200 men. Nine years later the firm had 110,000 employees and a turnover of more than 520 billion francs. Through a family holding Krupp even succeeded in regaining control of his steel works which he had agreed to hand over to allied management.

The Essen firm had another victory to its name. In 1953, it was the first European company to gain a foothold in the Communist countries. This rare achievement no longer appears to worry anybody, however. Krupp's position as number one free-shooter is particularly commendable in that he snatched the title from a serious contender, Pr Valetta, a former private adviser to Mussolini and managing director of Fiat.

For its part the former arms manufacturer of Fascist Italy had experienced none of the political difficulties which occasionally accompany a return to a peacetime economy. Fiat's production lines switched directly and easily from machine guns to frigidaires and cheap automobiles. Valetta watched over the interests of the Italian company like a cardinal de Richelieu, and completed the education of the future boss and acknowledged heir, Giovanni Agnelli. At that time the powerful head of Italian industry was just a young playboy, almost nothing like the present firm supporter of Enrico Berlinguer and the new Communist Party strength. Present-day realities had not altogether taken shape. Traditional attitudes to trade still prevailed and there was no need for the chief protagonists to adjust their views.

But when Willy Brandt finally knelt before a Polish monument erected to the memory of the victims of Nazi crimes, exhausted by his race against time to complete the *Ostpolitik*, he found that his own companies Hoechst and Krupp had arrived there fifteen years before him. And these were the same companies which had installed the gas chambers and used concentration camp labour. The German chancellor's presence beyond the Oder–Neisse line was a fine example of the way diplomatic symbols can be used to assist the dynamics of development. Richard Nixon's presence in Moscow at that time similarly emphasized the irreversible bankruptcy and impotence of a political power which could only disguise its own uselessness by tagging along behind the impregnable strength of business and justifying its new directions. This situation will provide Franz Joseph Strauss with food for thought for many years to come. However much the most anti-Communist of West German leaders cultivated Mao's friendship in Peking, he knows perfectly well that even the most impressive relationships are not

enough to build a future on. If electoral arithmetic had been on his side, a new nationalist Chancellor Strauss, the little darling of international business circles, would indisputably have followed the same tourist route as his Social-Democrat rival. A guided
tour from East Berlin to Moscow by way of Warsaw would have reached its climax
before the Nobel Prize jury in Stockholm where the international press would have
praised his courage and realism, forgetting that the growth of any political career
depends on funds from the big companies, all of which are now actively seeking détente.

Before the rites and necessities of conceptualization transform politicians of all sides
into dogmatists of reality, it is possible to encapsulate present developments in two
historical comments, one made over fifty years after the other.

Hidden in the third book of *Das Kapital*, Karl Marx, whose observation was never
anything but strictly scientific, admitted that "the American stock company is the best
and most interesting means of transforming private property into social property."

In 1920, straining to hang onto a revolution which was already slipping out of his
grasp, Lenin added his own incisive article of faith, "Production is of the essence;
democracy is a secondary notion which belongs only to politics."

With unity of time in its illusory sense of history, unity of place in its world revolution
and unity of action in its dictum "Workers of all countries unite," applied Leninism
masquerading as socialism is like the bad, supposedly daring tragedies which no one
has the courage to finish. Frightened by their own impertinence, the playwrights defuse
them instead of sprinkling them with all the ingredients of bourgeois drama. So behind
a curtain of temerity and intransigence, the end result is an attempt to edify monopolistic capitalism which is too centralized and coercive for its less strictly brought up
half-brother to enact. Differences in the final product arise solely from questions of
proportion; the ultimate aims are the same.

The gigantic production lines which Henry Ford II now proposes to build in the Soviet
Union and in several other Communist countries are merely a continuation of those his
father installed in the Moscow suburbs in 1922 at Lenin's request.

There will always be a bridge extended between capitalist business and Communist
state ownership, two equally centralized, hierarchical and authoritarian powers with a
common love of secrecy among their leadership. 90% of the population are either ignorant of their decisions or powerless to affect them. In the West this percentage comprises
both the electors and the elected, drawn together in an affecting model of democracy and
egalitarianism which reduces politics to a pool game. Whether Democrats or Nazis,
therefore, the natural development of these firms has always involved implantation in
the vast geographical expanse between Berlin and Vladivostok, where 400 million
people live together in the shadow of the Gulags. The European companies, being closer
and more aware of it, were the first to enter this potential market. But the East will
always address its appeals for Western technological aid to smooth out the rough edges
of its system over the heads of the men of power, even over giant figures like de Gaulle.
When seeking to nationalize Renault in 1946, the Free French leader, a firm believer in
the effectiveness of the decree, wanted to make the firm a symbolic instrument which
would mirror the industrial dynamism of France and the careful, efficient control exercised by the state over a public company.

The nationalist general's belief in the possibility of "moralizing business activities"
was very close to the cynicism of the CGT. The leaders of nationalized industries are
faced with a constant dilemma which it is easy enough to resolve. To ensure that such
firms are profitable and expanding, which as good patriots they must be, they will have
to overlook or even contravene the laws and the general interests of the country concerned. Constant adaptations must be made to suit market conditions and the behaviour

of private companies, or there is no hope of salvation. So these high-ranking civil servants are bound to make use of the fortunately ever more frequent absences of their political masters. When the general, thinking he was making great strides forward, went to the Soviet Union in 1963 to establish a foundation for economic cooperation, there was universal praise from the politicians for his boldness and his remarkable farsightedness. But in the middle of his tour, at the critical moment when he daringly suggested that Renault might build a factory on the banks of the Volga, his Communist audience merely nodded their heads politely but unimpressed. The French firm had been with them for over nine years.

Claims that the state-controlled automobile industry represents French interests and that the range of its activities throughout the world "answers both present economic needs on an international scale and the interests of the country in which it is located," are counter-arguments based on a pre-established but factually erroneous assessment. There is no real difference between Renault's establishment in Franco's Spain, its factory building in Papadopoulos's Greece and the behaviour of the privately owned multi-nationals, against which the French CP claims to be struggling so fiercely. How can such theorists say "We are going to struggle against capitalist monopoly in the automobile industry except in Renault"? Nonsense like this proves nothing, merely that its authors are mental anachronisms.

Citroën, which has benefited from considerable state credits, is investing 2.5 billion francs in Rumania. The industrial complex being built there will enjoy exclusive rights to manufacture a new popular touring model, and will reexport part of its production to the West. Official claims that it is destined to create employment in France are absurd. The new complex will provide 1,200 temporary jobs in France as opposed to 7,000 in Rumania, and the French personnel involved will be only managerial and engineering staff. In the end the 7,000 new Rumanian employees will create unemployment among Western production workers through the reexporting process. Moreover, there is nothing to stop the Citröen management from using the Rumanian factory to manufacture parts and spares which can then be incorporated into the Citröen lines in France. Some of the Fiat engines produced in Poland and Yugoslavia are already being used for Italian models from the Salerno factory, with a detrimental effect on local production and employment figures in Turin.

There is clear evidence that there is a massive migration of the automobile industry in capitalist countries towards the dictatorships. There are various reasons for this.

Firstly, automobile manufacture lies half way between modern and traditional industry. Labour costs in the form of wages and national insurance still account for 30% of the unit production cost. This is an extremely high proportion compared to the 5% labour costs of the oil industry, the 2% of the petro-chemical industry and the 8% of the chemical industry, etc.

Secondly, it is a labour-intensive rather than a capital-intensive industry. Total automation can never be achieved, since the thousands of separate parts involved in assembly have to be fitted by tedious, repetitive, piecemeal, human labour.

Finally, it is a socially vulnerable industry, dominated in most European countries by political unions, usually under Communist control, with a grass roots membership increasingly composed of migrant workers, economic refugees from underdeveloped areas who are much more like the capitalism-oppressed proletariat needing an emancipating Communist revolution. This is certainly the case with the French CGT union in Renault and the Italian CGIL within Fiat. Both are Communist controlled, as are many of the members of the car workers' union in British Leyland, not to mention increasingly militant shop stewards in the auto plants of Spain, Germany and the Netherlands.

The only way to continue this "exploitation of man by man" is by transferring these industries to countries where there is no right of strike, countries which the dogmatists still see as the highest expression of Stalinist Communism.

	Bulgaria	Yugoslavia	USSR	Hungary	East Germany	Czechoslovakia	Rumania	Poland
Fiat		X	X	X		X	X	X
British Leyland	X	X	X		X	X		X
Citroën		X		X		X	X	X
Daimler Benz	X	X		X	X		X	X
General Motors	X	X	X	X				X
Volvo	X	X	X	X	X	X		X
Renault		X	X	X		X	X	X
Ford		X	X	X		X		X
Toyota			X	X			X	X

The French Communist leader George Marchais's attacks on the scurrilous activities of the big oil companies are difficult to take seriously as are most Communist railings against the "oil monopolies". Shell and BP own a large number of service stations in Hungary and Rumania. Moreover, the Compagnie Française des Pétroles and the Polish government oil and petrochemical department have joined forces in a consortium which is to build a fertilizer complex at Halidia in India. There are many such examples. Exxon, Gulf, Socal and Mobil, etc. are all established in the East and expanding rapidly.

2.

From Military Confrontation to Economic Concessions

Important changes seldom have much to do with official dates. Kruschev's report on Stalin's crimes at the 20th Congress of the Russian Communist Party has never been seen as a major event, except by a few survivors who finally found the courage to discard their crutches and try to walk unaided. When he waddled onto the rostrum "Mr K." was still only a subordinate who had spent too long in humiliated subservience, and was trying to assert himself in his new job by discrediting his former boss. His aim was a simple one: to make the politics of one man, to which he had subscribed, look like a sore, a historical mishap, on the face of an otherwise healthy system. Opportunism and denunciation are two of the great qualities of Communist leadership. Kruschev denied Stalin in just the same way that Berlinguer, Marchais and Carillo are now rejecting Moscow. The trashcans of history are there to be filled. But these three men, who are now trying to look like democrats, once made their living out of zealously and loyally supporting the perversions of a régime which was an affront to human dignity. The Communist Parties have always had a name for tale-telling and obscurantism, and it was easy enough to say that all the revelations concerning Russia were merely slander from the CIA.

And yet, it must have taken amazing political impassiveness to stomach the great purges of 1936, the swastika blowing in the wind on Moscow airport to welcome von Ribbentrop and then the postwar swoop which brought the Soviets a string of new countries, now empty of any hope of democracy.

Kruschev's churlish declamation was received with some embarrassment, but hardly hailed as a revelation. Thorez, Togliatti, Duclos and Pajetta had all known everything about father Joseph's methods of government for a long time. Their only reaction was to question the advisability of revealing his simple ways to a prejudiced world. It is superficial nonsense to describe this period as the "phase of destalinization," since that would imply that some crisis and subsequent readjustment had taken place. As it was, no sooner had the doors closed on the last guests to leave the 20th Congress, than Kruschev gave his army a tank ride through the streets of Budapest. The Hungarian uprising was put down as mercilessly as the workers' rebellions in East Berlin and Poland had been three years earlier. Santiago Carillo in Moscow approved. So did the French and Italian CPs. To this day nobody can deny that, in their anxiety to please, Marchais and Berlinguer accepted the policy of acquiescence adopted by their leaders. The CPs are introverted worlds, aware only of the conflicts which arise from their own internal tensions.

Twelve years later détente has replaced the cold war. A two-sided, warlike view of problems has apparently given way to a more sophisticated approach based on stabilization and a reduction of conflict. But all that has really happened is that we have Brezhnev instead of Kruschev and Prague instead of Budapest, and both these acts of suppression have been watched with the same indifference by the West. In fact it is not really a geo-political or moral problem.

During the last thirty years relations between the United States and the Soviet Union have been characterized by threefold rivalry, on the military, economic and ideological planes.

The Cuban crisis of 1962 appeared to be both the first nuclear duel between Moscow and Washington and the last threat of direct confrontation between the two super-powers. While the Russians were dismantling their missile bases in Cuba, Kennedy and his advisers wiped their brows and agreed that the stakes were too frightening to be connected with an irresponsible activity like politics. The American administration and the Soviet Politburo signed more and more agreements. In 1963 there was a nuclear test ban treaty; in April 1964 an agreement to reduce the production of radioactive material; in January 1967 a demilitarization of space. Of course, none of this had any effect on the volume of arms being manufactured and sold. The armaments industry was high on the list of trade priorities. In 1975 the joint turnover achieved by Western and Soviet military industries amounted to $300 billion. The cost of equipment supplied to NATO rose to $150 billion, and for the Warsaw Pact to $110 billion. The remaining $40 billion could be accounted for by various deals with Third World countries, for one of the salient characteristics of underdevelopment today is undoubtedly "tank fetishism."

In the United States there are 5 million people serving in the armed forces or as civilians attached to the Pentagon. A further 4 million work in the defense industries which, by a system of subcontracts, fuel 10,000 small ventures and several more million employees. The Defense Ministry can rely on the services of 400 members of pressure groups, senators and congressmen who have infiltrated key organizations such as the Atomic Energy Commission, the Senatorial Committee of Foreign Relations and the House of Representatives Committee for Foreign Relations. 6,000 people work in public relations, promoting the latest model of missiles or recent modifications to nuclear warhead firing systems. The twenty largest arms companies maintain vast offices and large payrolls in Washington, among them Lockheed, General Dynamics, General Electric, McDonnell, Rockwell International, Northrop, Hughes Aircraft and Boeing.

More than 10,000 high-ranking officers, former Pentagon officials, work directly for an industry which appears to the Western world to be at once totally private and totally dependent on government finance. If firms like Lockheed or General Dynamics appear to run at a loss, it is not because they are sinking but because they used financial tactics of this kind to obtain increased aid from official circles. It is easy enough to understand why this bargain has been struck between the manufacturers and the politicians. In the present world crisis, the arms sector is one of the few national industries whose results are still reflected in a country's balance of trade figures. So, in exchange for export subsidies, foreign trade ministers can have the fleeting satisfaction of being able to balance their books.

Firms like these, which work according to all the laws of trade, operate in a wide variety of markets. The Americans deal with Iran, the South American dictatorships and the Arab Emirates, the French and Italians with South Africa and Brazil. Fiat, the largest Italian arms manufacturer, works primarily for NATO, even though an essential part of its activities involve Communist East Europe. The same is true of Vickers in Great Britain. All the American companies which flooded the Vietnamese market are now involved in the Vodka-Cola process. Schmidt, Carter, Giscard, Callaghan, Palme, *et al*. may say that they favour disarmament but it is hard to believe them when they are totally bound up in this policy of military proliferation.

Corruption, though loudly decried, plays a very minor part in this particular race for profits and the extreme sophistication of the products which could exterminate humanity rules out the possibility of any war between the two big powers. The basic aim is to win contracts for the manufacture of equipment which will be obsolete by the time it is put into service and will have to be replaced immediately. There is very little difference in the East where the military establishment is one of the three pillars of the régime, together with the Party and KGB. It has direct control over an essential part of Soviet industry, owns its own factories and research laboratories and has priority claims of the budget. "Guns or butter" is a delightful expression but completely unrealistic. A consumer goods industry can hardly stand up to the new diplomatic language surrounding arms sales. Efforts to influence politicians have as much effect as a shot from the latest bazooka. Iraq, Cuba, Syria and Angola have all succumbed to the flowery phrases reinforced by arguments of ideological solidarity. "First we talk, then you kill and afterwards you pay."

On 25 February 1976 the State Department admitted that since 1972 a United States firm had been manufacturing miniature ball bearings in the Soviet Union which were basic to the guidance system of multiple warhead MIRV ballistic missiles. The decisions to break with the policy of embargo had been based solely on considerations of trade. According to the Pentagon, several Italian and Swiss companies, contractors for NATO, at the same time, were manufacturing similar parts and had been supplying the Soviets for several years.

It is the Western rocket merchants who are having to respond cautiously to the eager advances of the Communist military. The Red Army leaders are demanding the creation of co-production agreements between their ventures and the Fascist military lobbies who have the up-to-date technology. But, restricted by political stipulations, the Western companies can only come to temporary trade deals. In 1975 Rolls Royce signed a $160 million agreement with Peking for the sale of fighter plane engines. Shortly afterwards, China bought helicopters from France. According to the Institute of Strategic Studies in London, the Chinese régime's air force consisted merely of a few Migs left behind by the Russians at the end of the fifties, which would make little impact in the event of an airborne offensive from Moscow.

The Chinese would also like to buy anti-submarine installations, anti-tank guided missiles and, more especially, electronic equipment from the United States. This would be a decisive step towards technical re-colonization, a prospect not cited in the *Thoughts of Chairman Mao*.

However, the standard argument used on both sides by the defenders of East–West trade that the establishment of economic interdependence would make war impossible is not entirely justified. The Communist world and the West are both basically looking to optimize their economic positions through a fully armed détente. Détente may reinforce the trade in arms, but, paradoxically, by supplying equipment to customers who are also ideological enemies, it increases the risk of local wars in areas which are already unstable. Satellite conflicts between provincial powers which are still moved by ideological motives may well escalate and lead to armed intervention to protect vital economic interests. Such is the case with South Africa, where the multinationals' investment amounts to $35 billion. East–West integration involving arms companies increases the proliferation of both traditional weaponry and tactical nuclear arms. The real danger for the future lies in atomic weapons becoming commonplace and in the highly standardized regulations governing their operation. When the big powers tacitly decided to exclude armed conflict from their quarrels, they could still continue to fight it out on the economic and ideological levels.

The race for Stalin's office in 1953 resulted in a victory for Kruschev after Malenkov, who looked like overtaking him, had been tripped in the last lap. Malenkov had been foolhardy enough to disparage the sacrosanct dogma of "priority for heavy industry." As

he saw it, consumer goods should be developed to meet the needs of a people bled white
by the whims of the late dictator. All "Mr K." had to do was to stand on tip-toe and
denounce the heresy of such a rightist attitude and the top job was his. Then, safely in
office, he could almost immediately start work on the policy recommended by his opponent.

Kruschev was a blundering pioneer, whose stop–go policy resulted in a succession of
feeble attempts to reform and abrupt halts. But his chief mistake was to launch into a
thundering polemic on the superiority of the socialist economic system which "in fifteen
years will have more than overtaken the United States." As the years have passed his
speeches have grown sadly out of date, especially now that the Soviet régime appears to
have jettisoned all its previous links with the modern industrial system. It is one thing
to be overtaken, however, and quite another that everybody should know about it. A
good many members of the Soviet leadership resent the humiliation which has resulted
from Kruschev's rash words.

In 1957, when he launched his *sputnik*, Kruschev was already suffocating on his
political deathbed, the space project one of his dying breaths. Dazzled by the automative
processes used in American industry and agriculture, he was accused by his enemies of
being indecisive and irresolute. His appeal to his capitalist rivals came too late to
prevent his fall in November 1964. Indeed, his successors countersigned his death
certificate by reproaching him for his "complaisant attitude towards the imperialists."
The Brezhnev–Podgorny–Kosygin *troika* represented a return to the Stalinist tradition,
as far as we can see. As men of classical education, Brezhnev and his peers rehabilitated
Jdanov, the protector of arts and literature whose "flawless" aesthetic taste had transfused decades of Communist intellectual life. At the 25th Congress, it was Yuri Adopov,
chief of the KGB, who argued in favour of an extension to détente in a speech which
emphasized just how closely the repressive machine is linked to the chief political
decisions of the régime. Every prisoner in the Gulag must have warmed to his words.

Before long, however, Brezhnev was manifesting the same embarrassing tendencies
as his predecessor. It would appear that collaboration with capitalist firms and requests
for their technical know-how have a dangerous fascination for the Communist leaders.

Since then there has been no more talk of economic rivalry. In the latter years of the
Kruschev régime, in any case, Marxist ideas about the incomparable advantages of
nationalization of the means of production had finally died the death. Nobody, unfortunately, had raised the minor question, "Whether the business be private or nationalized,
how does it profit the worker who is subjected to the same authoritarian labour methods
in either case?"

Since the first principle of historic materialism is that the real is more important than
ideas and institutions, there is nothing to stop its proponents taking a few liberties with
dogma "to make it more lucid."

By the early sixties it had become perfectly clear that the policy of large transfers of
resources between various sectors of the economy was impracticable. The phase of
"extensive" industrial growth relying chiefly on an increase in the number of workers,
had to give way to a phase of "intensive" growth based on increased productivity and
improved use of existing resources. After three years of internal discussion, Kosygin
announced the establishment of economic reform at the plenary meeting of the Central
Committee in September 1965. It appeared that a compromise had been reached between the supporters of a highly centralized administration and the economists Liber-
man and Birman who were behind the new development.

Manufacturing, construction, transport and trade ventures were bound by a new
system of management, planning and economic incentives. The basic changes involved

a rehabilitation of profit as a criterion for measuring the performance of an enterprise, a further decentralization of investment and the introduction of a capital charge. In practice the essential characteristics of the Soviet system had changed very little and the improvements made by the party diehards during the 1965 leap forward severely limited the impact of the new measures. Moreover, under pretext of maintaining an equal balance between central authority and decentralization, the control exercised by central ministries and planning agencies had been preserved intact, and managerial initiative and decision-making at the factory level curtailed. In 1965, 25,000 ventures, representing 70% of Soviet production, were affected by the new measures. By the end of 1970 this figure has risen to 41,000 ventures and the 1971-1975 plan anticipated the whole economy, apart from collective farms, being involved. The USSR remains a citadel of conservatism in the midst of a tightly controlled Comecon. It is difficult to convince a central bueaucracy entrenched behind its power that the only way to hang onto its privileges is by changing the industrial environment. The army itself, which receives preferential treatment under the system, is reluctant to advocate any radical decentralization which might threaten the defense sector's priority position. In certain cases, centralized control of the economy is an advantage, particularly in the exploitation of the vast deposits of natural resources which require summit level management, especially as far as investment and transport policies are concerned.

Finally, the Soviet leadership has reached the age of the computer, but a generation too late. Dazzled by the vast computer programs adopted in the West it believes that they offer the means of achieving increased efficiency in central planning. Gosplan officials will be able to tap a few keys and acquire all the information they need to pass on their instructions.

This appears doubtful on two counts. The system will never function in a satisfactory way in the absence of objective economic criteria based on real trading relations. At the present time giant computers have been removed from all decision-making centers in the United States. All they had done was to produce a bewildering increase in the number of incorrect solutions and approximate estimates.

These dinosaurs of the electronic era have been replaced by minicomputers working on specific problems within the actual factory, which can be integrated directly into the production process like any other machine tool and operated by IBM-trained secretaries. Faster and more complex than the larger models, they will be used not to find mathematical solutions for all the wider problems, but through access to a limited range of information to take immediate decisions.

Looking enviously at these products, their noses pressed against the window pane, the Soviets are less bothered by the question of whether they ought to buy them than by anxiety as to whether the West will agree to sell.

Until now, IBM, like most of its capitalist colleagues, has been saying "No." Trade deals, discounts and long-term payment facilities are out. The USSR, that failing limited company, whose 250 million stock holders have had their attendance fee pinched by the management board, will have to yield part of its sovereignty if it wants to receive any aid in future.

Already at the last Party Congress Brezhnev was complaining about the opposition to his demands for a revision of the Constitution. The very minor alterations he has in mind are intended merely to allow privately owned means of production to function throughout Soviet territory. Groups of experts have been working on this problem in the silence of the Kremlin for two years.

Vladimir Zagladin, a member of the central committee, can of course voice polite concern about our ill health, stating that "socio-political instability has become a permanent phenomenon in the West, where it is virtually impossible to find any man now prepared to defend capitalism as the best social system in the world." What the noble comrade Zagladin appears to have overlooked, however, is that collaboration with the capitalists and the application of the co-production system have made his country the first in the world where all class struggle has been eliminated at the top. He is perfectly right to insist on the social damage wrought by the system flourishing in the West, which permits claims and struggles for the preservation of civil rights and the improvement of living conditions. And it is quite apparent that the Communists are prepared to agree that their own model should be exported, since the perfect universe for the Overworld would be a combination of Western economic efficiency and the totalitarian social organization of the Socialist states.

By the summer of 1976, the Comecon countries' debt to private firms had risen to $60 billion, and the Soviets' standard of living was still patently lower than that enjoyed in most satellite countries. A curious triumph for a Socialist doctrine which uses the ruined remains of its ambitions as a podium.

Détente provides an excuse for intensifying the ideological struggle, the only area in which the Communists can plan an offensive without fear of failure.

When Boris Ponomarev, the Politburo member in charge of relations with fellow Communist Parties, fires his blanks at the capitalists, he creates his own unreal "Wonderland." Comrade Boris thinks that "a simple comparison between the situation in the Socialist countries and the state of crisis in the capitalist countries is bound to have an effect on the consciousness and militancy of the workers. Millions of men are convinced that the miseries they endure are inherent in the very nature of capitalism. In fact, at the same time, developing socialist society experiences neither unemployment nor inflation nor financial upheavals." We have only to look at Ponomarev and his contemporaries to understand. Grey and weary-looking men in their sixties, they all seem to enjoy the prospect of retirement. There is no reason why these old gaffers, now materially comfortable after careers bound by the Marxist slogan as they clambered their way up the administrative hierarchy, should compromise the situation by spilling the beans about emperor Brezhnev's new clothes. The Soviet system is a long-service award and the Kremlin a gerontocracy which, according to Brzezinski, "is evidence of a process of political degeneracy."

The leaders of the Western Communist Parties who are the real "social cases" in power are in an even worse position. Now out of favour, they appear to be unusable outside the party and would be very difficult to reemploy elsewhere. So, since all career-making requires elasticity and political strategy is a shifting terrain, they move from one side to another, clinging onto whatever dogmatic handhold projects at the time.

It is very unfair to accuse the Communists of having no sense of public relations or of front-page exploits when they have orchestrated and managed two large-scale publicity operations in the space of one year. At Helsinki, an eminent international tribunal awarded Moscow total control of those states which it had been using to billet its troops since 1946; in June 1975 the conference of brother parties in East Berlin furnished ample proof that the Western CPs wished to be independent. The polite and obliging lads who had trotted along the outside of the sidewalk to prevent Brezhnev being splattered with mud from the wheels of revisionist vehicles, now declared themselves prepared to make use of the rush-hour and swing him out into the middle of the road. This statement of intent would have been infinitely more significant and credible if the Western Communist leaders had followed their argument through. Anyone who says that France is not Czechoslovakia and that Bulgaria bears little relation to Italy, should also add that East Germany, Poland and Hungary have nothing to do with Moscow, and that the desire for independence must be viable for all the satellite countries. East Germany was a judicious choice for this conference. The party of Erich Honecker, first secretary of the East German CP, is Moscow's mailbox. Apparently the wall had to be built to protect the country from an invasion by thousands of unemployed Westerners who camp out by Check Point Charlie hoping to find work in the East.

Through this conference, a microcosm of democracy in the midst of a restrictive world, the Communists were able to restate their strategy of increased political détente between governments, further economic integration with businesses and the maintenance of the social *status quo* in the East.

At the same time, each party tried to outbid the other on the ideological level in a way which grows increasingly extreme and ridiculous as collaboration between supposedly inimical systems grows.

As he boarded his plane after the conference, Georges Marchais was free to declare that he aimed to "gather all the active forces of the nation against the barons of big capital." There was no law to stop him saying so. In fact the development of communications and the demands of the democratic political game have forced the Communists to disassociate themselves from anything which might stand in their way. The Nazi leaders at Nuremburg in 1946 were able to try and convince the court that they knew nothing about the concentration camps. In 1976 even a very badly informed Communist cannot deny the benefits of the psychiatric hospitals, the Gulag rest homes and the "social security" system set up by the KGB.

It has taken the French CP twenty-five years to abandon the notion of the dictatorship of the proletariat, which places it chronologically in second to last position after the Portuguese Party and before the Japanese. It is not exactly what most of us would call progress.

The hand Georges Marchais extended towards the Christians was met by the arm of François Marty, archbishop of Paris, raised in a gesture of protest against French arms sales. As long as they stick to moral principles, both these men are sure of their ground, trained as they were in churches which have become bastions of conservatism. But it will be very hard for the French cardinal to justify the Vatican's position as one of the main stock holders in the Italian arms companies and a shameless speculator which works with the atheistic Marxists to increase its temporal wealth.

The legendary independence of the Italian CP goes back to Palmiro Togliatti and Luigi Longo. The upmarket braggarts of the via delle Bottege Oscure have always approved the major decisions taken by Moscow. Whatever Berlinguer's present beliefs, he is following in the footsteps of some suspect forebears. In 1945 the Czech Communist leader Clement Gottwald declared "Our Communist Party will have to follow a democratic and a national revolutionary road." In 1946 his colleague in Poland, Gomulka, added "Popular democracy in Poland will never be the equivalent of the dictatorship of the proletariat. Our democracy will not be the same as Russia's." In Hungary that same year Rakosi said "We cannot build socialism unless we look for a national road, free of any tactical consideration."

These three statements are hard to overlook, even if the secretary of the Italian CP is reduced to using the pathetic argument of the geographical distance between Moscow and Rome. Whether it sits under the umbrella of NATO or in the shade of the Warsaw Pact, the CP never changes the colour of its skin. It is ridiculous to call a party authoritarian when it wins 15% of the vote and liberal when it wins 30%. During the recent electoral campaign, much was made of the moderate tone of the Italian CP, but there was no mention of the fact that it still adheres to the rule of democratic centralism which makes it as resistant to any kind of national democracy as the Eastern European parties. But apart from a handful of people who are way behind the times, nobody any longer believes that the Soviets want to lower their iron curtain over Naples. The problem is a different one altogether.

In fact Eugenio Peggio, the Italian CP economist, is partly right when he says "Italy's economic crisis is not an invention of the capitalist world, but an objective event." But he does not go far enough. The country is suffering from a curious surfeit of unemployed workers in search of bosses who have gone up in smoke. Italy's financial and industrial potential is scattered over Poland, the USSR, Hungary and the tax havens, leaving the less mobile work force stranded on the Adriatic beaches. Fiat, Pirelli and Montedison are not knocked out but simply "out," and the CP will have to restore a secure social climate before Northern European and international capitalists can be persuaded to invest there again. We shall then witness the creation of a society ruled by slogans in which the men who turned out in their thousands from Turin to Naples to demonstrate against American aggression in Vietnam will be advised not to strike for the sake of production, accept unemployment for higher productivity and wage freezes for stimulating investment.

Then we shall see what the official left wing, which can hardly open its mouth without invoking the "people" and the "workers" actually thinks of public opinion. For 80% of the people in the world, whatever régime they live under, are completely void of power and vulnerable to every kind of manipulation. The Tonkinese peasant and the Milanese millworker are never doers, rarely fought over, but just excuses.

3.

Vietnam and Chile: Two Profitable Obstacles to Détente

Without wishing to offend the sensitive souls among us, Vietnam was never a victory for indignation over the cynicism of governments. When Nixon was elected in 1968, Howard Hughes, who had helped finance the Republican campaign, told his right-hand man Robert Maheu, a former member of the FBI with Mafia connections, to "Go and see our new friends in Washington, see what they can do to prolong the war."

Hughes's words were merely a more paranoid version of what was in all the industrial bosses' minds: the desire to continue reaping record profits from a war which was a gold mine to the business and military worlds. Every plane shot down meant another $50 million cheque for Lockheed or Rockwell. So, however just and heroic the struggle of the Vietnamese people, it seems unlikely that their efforts alone were enough to secure the orderly withdrawal of American forces. It is possible to believe in the strength of ideology as it is in the existence of the Holy Trinity, but neither of these concepts are any more than palliatives to facilitate intellectual digestion. Unlike inflationary and tax-ridden America, Vietnam offered private enterprise a total of $150 billion, though nothing to anybody else. The US business world had never known it so good.

On 20 April 1972, however, Kissinger's Boeing left Andrews airbase in total secrecy for a discreet airport near Moscow. Soon after his arrival a convoy of limousines reached the Lenin Hills and Dom Pyroma, a luxury retreat for Soviet leaders. So completely secret was this visit kept that neither the American ambassador in Moscow, Jacob Bream, nor brigadier-general Brent Scrowfort, attaché at the White House, knew about it—although Scrowfort was working on preparations for Nixon's next visit to the Soviet capital. Over the next four days Kissinger and his assistant Helmut Sonnenfeld had meetings with Brezhnev who was flanked by his Foreign Affairs Minister Andrei Gromyko, Soviet ambassador to Washington Anatole Dobrinin and special adviser on foreign policy Alexandrov.

These discussions marked the first phase of American disengagement from South East Asia. Kissinger suggested that the United States might agree to the establishment of a ceasefire if those North Vietnamese forces which had "entered South Vietnam since the beginning of the spring offensive were to withdraw." This was the first indication that Washington was prepared to allow North Vietnamese combatants to remain in the South. Reinforcements of 30,000 to 40,000 men had come South since the offensive, but there were already over 100,000 men established south of the 17th parallel.

Kissinger asked Brezhnev to inform Hanoi of the new American position. Then, after a rushed visit to the Kremlin on his last evening, he returned to Washington, only to leave again on 1 May for a secret meeting in Paris with the North Vietnamese negotiator, Le Duc Tho.

In fact, Vietnam was beginning to look increasingly like a stumbling block to détente. In 1970 the Russians had started discussions with Henry Ford concerning the construction of the largest truck-manufacturing factory in the world at Kama River. But the

Detroit firm had been forced to accept the Pentagon's refusal of this project on the strategic grounds that the trucks might be sent to Hanoi.

The Russians hoped to make Kama River the most enormous industrial complex ever. A new town was to be built for 250,000 people, 600 miles east of Moscow on the banks of a tributary of the Volga. It was envisaged that by 1980, when the complex was running at full capacity, it would produce an annual 150,000 trucks and 250,000 diesel engines, in a desperate effort to bridge the gap between the Soviet Union and the United States. In 1971 the USSR had 4.6 million trucks as opposed to 20.2 million in the US. Some Russian models, like the Gaz 5, had been manufactured according to exactly the same specifications for over twenty-five years. The Kama River operation was to cost $5 billion, and, as Moscow saw it, the success of the project depended solely on financial and technical help from the United States. Nobody in either the Kremlin or the White House was prepared to lose one rouble or one dollar for Thieu and Pham Van Dong. A hundred contracts worth over $500 million had already been signed with forty companies. The Chase Manhattan Bank was prepared to provide $80 million to finance American exports to Kama, and IBM was ready to sell 11 million dollars' worth of giant 370 computers for the Kama foundries. But because of the political situation, some credits were still blocked. Restricted by a need for discretion which reduced their business efficiency, these firms had to act through their European subsidiaries.

The yawning gap between ideological differences and economic facts had to be bridged. It was difficult for American and Russian leaders to sell the new era of cooperation when they were still supporting opposite sides in Vietnam.

Though 1972 was electoral year, Nixon was hoping for great things from his official trip to Moscow scheduled for mid-May. Once reelected, he planned to develop a whole strategy of economic agreement with Leonid Brezhnev. That is why the military counter-offensive mounted by Hanoi at that time was such an embarrassment. On 5 May, at 11 o'clock, Kissinger and his assistant Alexander Haig, who became commander in chief of NATO forces, went to the President's office for a meeting of the National Security Council, consisting of CIA boss Richard Helms, Secretary of State William Rogers, Pentagon chief Melvin Laird, Finance Minister John Conally from Texas and Vice-President Spiro Agnew. Nixon had decided to abandon Vietnam, but only after working out some semblance of a political solution. A military surrender would be a loss of face in the eyes of potential voters. Having decided to order massive bombing of North Vietnamese communication lines and the mining of the port of Haiphong, the President hesitated only to speculate about Moscow's reaction. The Soviets would hardly be able to celebrate over a corpse and might feel obliged to cancel Nixon's trip to Moscow as a sign of solidarity with the North Vietnamese Communists. Kissinger was told to sound out his friend Dobrinin, whom he called from the Oval Office. Dobrinin got in touch with Moscow and two hours later the answer came: the summit would not be cancelled. At 1 p.m. Nixon gave the military the order to begin operations, and at 9 that evening he appeared on television to announce his decision.

Sixteen days later, accompanied by Kissinger, he dined at Dom Pyroma with Leonid Brezhnev, Podgorny, Kosygin and Alexandrov. The discussions started at 8 and broke off at 11.30 so that the guests could go into dinner. As predicted, Soviet reservations about the American military reaction were muted. Kosygin merely expressed the fear that Russian shipping might be affected by the bombing of Haiphong. Not one of the leaders appeared to consider the Vietnam war an obstacle to détente which, according to Brezhnev, "continues to develop." The self-congratulatory diners' club thought that the sandal-shod troops and the resistance relay teams in South East Asia had been running the race for far too long.

The second meeting on Vietnam took place the following afternoon between Kissinger and Gromyko. Once again, the former Harvard professor ran circles round the principles of diplomacy which the American Executive had until then strictly upheld. He announced that the United States was prepared to agree to the creation of a tripartite electoral commission with representatives from the Saigon régime, the Vietcong and neutral forces. An amazed Gromyko said, "I would like to be completely sure that I have fully understood what you have told me."

"Absolutely," replied Kissinger, "I'm talking about the formation of a tripartite commission."

On 26 May the two men met at the Kremlin to discuss the possibility of suspending the bombing of North Vietnam, even without the liberation of American prisoners of war, which had until then been a precondition of any such move.

The same day, in another room, William Simon, Secretary of State at the Treasury, and Nicolai Patolichev, Soviet Minister of Foreign Trade, signed the first Soviet–American trade agreement. Nixon promised to get Congress to agree that Russia should be granted most favoured nation status. And it was then that Nixon and Brezhnev decided to set up the US–USSR Trade and Economic Council and to increase bilateral economic exchanges.

On 30 May, the last day of the official visit, the two leaders decided that Nicolai Podgorny, President of the Supreme Soviet, should go to Hanoi to try and win the North Vietnamese leadership over to the new American proposals.

On 16 June, Podgorny landed in Hanoi, while Kissinger flew to Peking. On his arrival, Kissinger had a four-hour meeting with Chou En Lai. The diplomat gave way to the historian as he tried to persuade the Chinese leadership to follow Moscow's example and discreetly pressurize the Vietnamese Communists into greater flexibility. But Kissinger's Chinese audience was still shot through with ideology and the discussions required delicate handling. Chou En Lai who had no desire to make things any easier for Moscow, remained evasive and disinclined to play the go-between. China could not influence the Vietnamese leaders, he said, and in any case "history and time are already against the United States, and Communism will eventually hold sway not only in Vietnam but also in Cambodia and Laos."

Despite Chou's reservations, it does look as if Peking exerted some diplomatic influence. At the beginning of July, Maurice Schumann, the French Foreign Minister, met Mao Tse Tung who told him that Mme Binh, the North Vietnamese Foreign Minister had agreed to abandon her demands for Thieu's resignation as a precondition for any talks. Mao must have explained to Mme Binh that at certain tactical phases, compromise was inevitable. Schumann immediately passed the news on to the Americans. Hanoi agreed to a secret meeting between Kissinger and Le Duc Tho on 19 July. These discussions came to nothing, however, since both sides refused to budge. Kissinger went straight from Paris to Saigon where he prevailed upon Thieu to start looking for a settlement. In this way the Democratic candidate, McGovern, who supported a speedy solution to the conflict and an abandonment of the South Vietnamese régime, would no longer be able to claim that Saigon was an obstacle to peace. Once reelected, said Kissinger, Nixon would promise to continue supplying aid and military equipment to Thieu.

Kissinger's task was to obtain a decent interval for Saigon between ceasefire and total collapse. When the slow death rattle came, no one must suspect that the patient had died of neglect.

In the plane taking him back from Saigon to San Clemente, where he was to tell Nixon about his talks, the presidential adviser confided to his colleagues "We cannot

allow Vietnam to poison us for another four years. This problem must be settled between the November election and the president's inauguration for his second term at
the beginning of January." A little later during the flight he added, "One thing is
certain: we must finish with it, forcibly, once and for all."

When the helicopter landed on his San Clemente lawns, the most expensive President
in United States history came out to greet Kissinger. Despite his success, Nixon appears
to have retained his *Wanderlust*. A number of Presidents have owned a second residence, but under Nixon the White House was totally decentralized. There were three
offices in Washington, two at Camp David in Maryland, two at San Clemente, one at
Key Biscayne in Florida and one at Grand Coy, a Bahamian island belonging to Swiss-
born industrialist Ablanap. Every time he moved to one of his nine residences, the
President was accompanied by 200 people. In the air a C141 equipped with ultramodern communications systems kept him in constant contact with his staff. A few days
before departure the secret services would ensure that the airports were safe. Doctors
would check that local hospitals had sufficient quantities of blood plasma in Nixon's
group. On take-off and landing, airports would be placed in a state of alert. Teams of
crack shots, rescue helicopters and bomb disposal squads would be mobilized.

Five Boeing 707s, sixteen helicopters, seven Lockheed Jetstars piloted by Air Force
teams, two armour-plated Continental limousines each costing $500,000 and thirty
other automobiles driven by military chauffeurs were reserved for Nixon's use. Even on
private journeys his family and staff only ever used government transport. The presidential family budget rose from $148,000 in 1968 to $640,000 for the 1973 tax year.
Nixon was paid an annual salary of $200,000 plus an expenses allowance of $90,000. He
also had access to a "special projects" fund of $1.5 million, from which he appears to
have drawn considerable sums. Throughout history, political powers all over the world
have emitted a stench of corruption. But the gold-digging atmosphere which prevailed
under the Republican administration was unprecedented. Bob Haldeman's determination to "sell the President" was the promise of an expert. As former director of a well
known advertising agency, he had promoted Disneyland, high recommendation to any
politician, and certainly enough to make him Kissinger's opposite number as far as
domestic policy questions were concerned. Using all the linguistic resources of the
mediaman, Haldeman glamourized Nixon's image in the same way that a Hollywood
studio graphic artist draws a cartoon character.

While George McGovern, the penniless and inept Democratic candidate, strode along
the New York sidewalks with his team, exchanging autographs for a few dollars, the
man who wanted to buy Nixon had to go to the Committee for the Reelection of the
President. Director Maurice Stans, who had resigned his post as Trade Minister, and his
assistant lawyer Herbert Kalmbach had set the reserve price pretty high.

At the same time Nixon was assuring his citizens that new laws adopted were
"guarantees against abuses of electoral campaigns and will make it possible to increase
public confidence in the integrity of the electoral process by giving it all the facts
about methods of financing." At least $60.2 million were collected between the spring
of 1971 and the last few months of 1972, not to mention the illegal contributions from
such people as Armand Hammer, Robert Vesco and Thomas Jones, president of
Northrop.

And, for that matter, Tom Pappas, a Greek millionaire who supported the colonels'
régime and owned several "Esso Pappas" refineries in Greece. His solid support for
Nixon at the extreme right of the Republican party helped the Communist leaders,
officially banished from the country, to do good business at the time of the military
dictatorship.

In fact the Communists had long since developed great flexibility in dealing with the totalitarian dynamics of their accomplices. Thus it was that in 1969 Vishiani paid an official visit to Franco's Spain at the head of a Soviet delegation. A few months later massive imports of Polish coal helped to break the miners' strikes in the Asturias. In 1971, Soviet–Franquist joint ventures were established in Spain in shipping, fishing and distribution. A few years ago Spain equipped several shoe factories in Russia, which now produce more than 2 million pairs of shoes a year. At the present time Spain's involvement in the USSR is extending to frozen fish supermarkets, restaurants and cafeterias near the Olympic complex planned for the 1980 Games. The 183 ventures involved in these operations import both technology and labour from Spain and were begun when the Soviet ideologues and Carrillo were calling Spain Fascist. The Fascist partner didn't seem to mind a bit.

In 1970 alarming reports were beginning to reach Washington and the headquarters of the big companies. The impending Chilean presidential elections due to be held on 4 September looked like being a victory for the Socialist candidate Salvador Allende and his left wing coalition which included the Communists. For the American directors such an eventuality was infinitely more serious than the establishment of the Castro régime. Cuba was still no more than a barge anchored off the coast of South America and supplied by the USSR. But a Socialist Chile might become an example, a refuge and a base for the Latin American revolutionaries hunted down by counter-guerilla forces trained in the Panama bases.

At the time of the 1964 Chilean elections, the Christian-Democrat candidate, Eduardo Frei, had received $5 million from the Kennedy administration. The money had been conveyed to him by fathers Wekermans and Vizzard, two Belgian Jesuits from Santiago, who had met the young Justice Minister, Bobby Kennedy. This upright representative of a spotless régime was then engaged in a pitiless struggle against the Mafia. And it was then that he met Sam Giamcano and Santos Trafficante, two of the Cosa Nostra bosses in the Caribbean, with a view to asking them to arrange the killing of Fidel Castro. From all the evidence, this idea had been originally conceived and supported within the Kennedy administration by McNamara. Though preparations had been underway since 1962, the project never came to anything. The Dallas bullet pipped the Havana bullet at the post, and Johnson showed no immediate desire to restart an operation in which McGeorge Bundy, Dean Rusk and all the Vodka-Colanizers now exiled in Moscow had been involved. One man had taken an active part in organizing this political encounter. This was John MacCone, director of the CIA; and six years later nothing had changed. MacCone was as interested in Chile as he had been in Cuba, but he had left his job with the secret service for the board of ITT. According to their own estimates, ITT's interests in Chile amounted to $150 million. Certainly it employed 6,000 people there. MacCone sent $350,000 to the extreme right wing candidate, Jorge Alessandri, former President of the Republic, leader of the Fatherland and Freedom movement and a local director of ITT; a further $100,000 went to the Christian Democrats.

On 4 September Salvador Allende came out in front, but, unfortunately, with only 35% of the overall vote. His election had to be ratified three weeks later by a congress of the Chilean parliament. On 13 September Augustino Edwards arrived in Washington from Rome. Edwards was the richest man in Chile, with a bank named after him, a television station and the largest daily newspaper in the country, the ultra-conservative *El Mercurio*, which had been violently opposed to Allende throughout the campaign. Edwards was a board member of IBEC, the Rockefellers' many-faceted group with considerable interests in Latin America as well as investments in Communist countries.

On 14 September the Chilean businessman met Nelson Rockefeller, who was flanked by his son Rodman, president of IBEC, and Nancy Maginess, Kissinger's future wife. Edwards was pleading a simple case: namely that the United States had to intervene before Allende's political victory was legally recognized and the harm done. The socialist leader had fought his campaign on the issues of nationalization and Chilean independence from foreign capital.

On the next day, 15 September, at 10 a.m., Augustino Edwards met his old friend Donald Kendall. For in the narrow international association of global managers, the Chilean sat on the board of Pepsi Cola, as vice-president. The route Edwards followed for his American tour is very revealing. He began by meeting the key figures of multinational economic activity. It was not until 1 p.m. on 15 September that he had his first words with the political leaders. Kendall had organized a lunch with Justice Minister John Mitchell, a close friend of Nixon, and Henry Kissinger who was then chief of the National Security Council.

At 4 p.m., Edwards was taken to see CIA boss Richard Helms, later ambassador to Iran. At 7.30 all these people met at the White House. Helms later stated that in his opinion "this meeting was arranged because of Edwards' presence in Washington and following Kendall's words to the president concerning Edwards' view of the Chilean situation."

Nixon returned from an official visit to Rumania. Ceausescu and Brezhnev supported Allende, but since they were committed to the policy of détente, they cooperated with Kendall and Harold Geneen. This difference between the political and the economic was fatal for the Chilean Democrats. Nixon received a report dated 12 September from his ambassador in Santiago, Ed Korry, putting the chances of using the Chilean army to change the situation as "non-existent." On the evening of 14 September, shortly after the meeting between Edwards and Nelson Rockefeller, there had been a session of the "40 Committee," which authorized secret operations abroad. Despite its name, this council set up in 1969 in pursuance of decision 40 of the National Security Council had only five members: Kissinger, Under Secretary of State Joseph Sisco, Richard Helms, Under-Secretary for Defense William Clements, and general George S. Brown, chairman of the Joint Chiefs of Staff. In a funereal atmosphere, these men had put forward various suggestions, including the spending of $250,000 on bribing Chilean members of parliament to oppose Allende's ratification. But there was general consensus that such a proposal was unrealistic and that it would be better to wait for the President's decision rather than prolong the discussion.

During a meeting in the President's office the next day, Helms jotted down a random selection of Nixon's comments. "One chance in ten perhaps, but let's save Chile ... Not concerned by the risks implied ... Ten million dollars, more if necessary ... Full time jobs and the best men we have ... Make their economy groan."

The President appeared "hard" according to Helms, who received an order to work with certain factions of the Chilean armed forces in preparing a *coup* against Allende. This operation, which Kissinger called "track 2" was to be organized solely by the CIA, unknown to the State Department and the Pentagon.

When the meeting came to an end at about 11.30 p.m., two directors of a soft-drinks manufacturing company had succeeded, or so they saw it, in steering the official policy of the American government against a democratically elected régime attempting an experiment in socialism.

Within ITT, Harold Geneen entrusted John MacCone with liaison between the company and the CIA. The two institutions worked together on a vast billboard campaign with pictures of Soviet tanks entering Santiago as they had driven into Prague in 1968.

In October, while on an official visit to Moscow, Nixon learnt that the *putsch* mounted by the CIA had failed and had ended in the assassination of the chief of the general staff, Rene Schneider. Credit diplomacy then took over from wasted bullets, and, when Salvador Allende spoke before the general assembly of the United Nations two years later on 4 December 1972, he was already a marked man, politically. The international banks had reduced their credit facilities to Chile from $300 million to $17 million. Direct American investment had fallen from $1 billion in 1969 to less than $100 million. The Swiss banks played an important part in this strangulation policy. The International Trade Bank at Geneva, owned by an extreme rightwing Chilean family, provided a link between the opponents of Popular Unity and the international financiers. Eduardo Frei, leader of the Christian Democrats and ex-President of the Republic, Jorge Alessandri, representing the extreme right, and Orlando Saenz, chairman of the Chilean management association, made frequent trips to Switzerland during the years 1972 and 1973 to meet representatives from this bank. And, according to Colby, director of the CIA, "the sums necessary (for repression) were conveyed through the banks of Europe."

In this financial wilderness, attempts to stir up sedition and civil war increased. In 1971 *El Mercurio* received $700,000 from the "40 Committee," with another $900,000 in April 1972. In answer to Allende's accusations that the paper was promoting extremism, a vast press campaign was put together in Europe and Latin America. A total of 726 articles and editorials supporting the conservative daily were published. Hard hit by nationalization, ITT and Anaconda, which had owned Chilean copper mines, were developing a whole subservice strategy. The top men of International Telegraph and Telephone were working in close collaboration with Kissinger's assistant, General Haig, and Peter Petersen, banker, presidential adviser and Trade Minister, to undermine the Chilean régime. According to an American Senate report, Kissinger and his staff were under continuous pressure from President Nixon, who was impatiently demanding immediate and definitive results. Between 1971 and 1973, $11 million were spent on toppling the government of Popular Unity.

President Allende's appeal for help from the international community from the rostrum of the UN in 1972 appeared ludicrous. With great dignity he declared "I accuse ITT before the conscience of the world of having tried to provoke civil war in my country, which means total disintegration in any land"; but the microphones into which he was speaking and the amplification system bearing his anguished appeal to the ears of the other delegates had all been manufactured and installed by ITT.

Similarly, when he tried to rally political support, his audience consisted of ordinary consumers who hired Avis automobiles, stayed in Sheraton hotels, built themselves Levit houses, or bought Oceanic televisions, all of which companies belong to ITT. It was hard to understand the conflict between supplier and buyer and certain people took Allende's accusations in the same way as they would a man's claiming that his telephone wire was trying to strangle him.

In his search for support, the Chilean leader left New York for Moscow, where he was greeted on the airport runway by the whole Soviet leadership "moved" by his sufferings. They all restated the "unfailing collaboration of the USSR in the just and progressive struggle of the Chilean people against Fascist and imperialist schemings by the great North American monopolies." But Brezhnev was too sensitive to admit to his guest that three days before his arrival the Soviet Union had signed a vast ten-year trade agreement with Frank Barnes, the company vice-president, for ITT. Geneen's company had been working with Moscow since 1968. It had supplied the Russian airports with reservation and communication systems and had been established in almost all the Communist countries since 1955, well before the Chilean *putsch*.

What we have to remember is that the development of détente had to be sold to the public as quickly as possible, and that Saigon and Santiago looked like troublesome detours from the Moscow–Washington highway. On 13 January an agreement was reached concerning Vietnam.

> The United States have assured the democratic republic of Vietnam that they will withdraw from South Vietnam, during the twelve months following the signing of the agreement, all their civilian staff working in the armed forces of the republic of Vietnam. They have also assured the republic of Vietnam that the majority of these people will have left in the first ten months. These assurances concern all those government employees whose chief activities are connected with the armed forces of the Saigon régime.

The American negotiators made sure that the text as a whole contained as many linguistic ambiguities as possible. Marooned in his presidential palace Thieu watched the Americans piling up heaps of new equipment around him as they left. It was as if he had been left on a desert island with a pile of cans and no can-opener. But his mind was on his luxurious dwelling in Paris and his secret, drug-running-funded bank accounts in Switzerland.

After that, it took the Hanoi marathon-runners only fourteen months to enter the South Vietnamese capital, rename it Ho Chi Minh City and reeducate the population: a superb victory for intransigent socialism jealously guarding its national independence. However, the corrupt puppet government in Saigon had granted the big American companies concessions to exploit the oilfields in the gulf of Saigon. Not only did the Communist leaders agree to honour these contracts, despite their discreditable origins, they even pestered Washington to deliver the promised American economic aid. Wriston, boss of the First National City Bank, Clausen of the Bank of America and Rockefeller of the Chase Manhattan, went to Hanoi, after having financed the massive destruction of the country. On several occasions, *Nhan Dan*, the party daily newspaper, pointed out the differences between "the realistic attitude of the American commercial world and the manoeuvrings of the politicians." But then Leninist-comrades, especially the Asian strains, cannot be expected to know of the vast holdings of these banks in the armament industry, even less their sway over politicians.

On 11 July 1974 the Hewlett Packard Company and the Soviet Committee for Science and Technology signed a five-year trade contract. The agreement was signed by William Doolittle, vice-president of the American firm, and concerned the manufacture and sale of measuring instruments, electronic medical equipment and computers. The American Under-Secretary for Defense's company had already been working with the Soviet Mashpriboringtoig and Electronogtechnika trade organizations for over ten years.

On 27 July Rockwell International (which makes rockets, fragmentation bombs and missiles) sold the Soviet firm Technopromexport four isolation chambers for nuclear power stations. On 21 September 1973 Rockwell signed a protocol with Avia Export saying that the equipment produced by the firm could be used in the Yak 40, a Soviet medium distance plane with thirty-one seats. Rockwell was to build the plane in the United States. On 19 October 1973, Rockwell sold Technopromimport 250 machines to be used in the construction of "high tension power stations." (Rockwell belongs to Rockefeller interests.)

In early November 1973 twenty Soviet aviation experts led by Stephen Kadishev, first vice-minister of Aviation, spent three weeks in the United States totally incognito. They paid lengthy visits to the factories and laboratories of the five largest Pentagon contractors, Boeing, General Electric, Lockheed, McDonnell–Douglas and Pratt and Whitney. This trip was arranged by the American Aeronautics and Astronautics Institute, following the Avia Export-Rockwell agreement for the Yak 40. The Communist officials were particularly interested in the ARTS2 electronic radar systems manufactured by Lockheed.

Six weeks before this trip, Allende had finally been murdered, weapons still in his hand, because he had placed too much faith in the virtues of democracy, and the Chilean military were now hunting down the last centers of Marxist infection with flame throwers.

On 17 October 1973, Pinochet declared "True nationalism does not consist in rejecting foreign capital." As far as this view was concerned, he gave the economic policy of the new régime into expert hands. The Minister of the Economy, Fernando Leniz, represented the country's upper middle classes. A close friend of Augustino Edwards, he had been chairman and director of *El Mercurio*, and, like his friend, sat on the board of IBEC, Chile. The Finance Minister, Jorge Cauas, had been exiled in the United States during the Allende interlude and had worked for the World Bank. Pinochet's economic adviser Jaime Guzman, a former scholar at Columbia University, was a member of the extreme rightwing Fatherland and Freedom terrorist organization. At the end of October 1973, Ismael Huerta, the junta's Foreign Affairs Minister went to the United States to justify the violent *putsch*. During his visit he attended over 120 meetings with representatives of American and Canadian banks. After Huerta's trip, the Manufacturers Hanover Trust, which had been the first to withdraw from Chile in 1970, granted $20 million to the country's central bank. As vice-president James Green said, this loan had "more to do with psychological aid and an expression of trust."

A syndicate composed of the Banker Trust, the Irving Trust and the First National City Bank offered credits of $150 million. The Bank of America and the Chase Manhattan formed another syndicate with a view to aiding the junta. Dow Chemical sent a technical team to check the condition of its two Santiago factories and to prepare for its return. It was followed by General Motors, Dodge, Textron, General Electric and General Tire and Rubber Company. The junta announced that the man dealing with its "public relations" in the United States would be Henry Gardner, retired vice-president of the powerful Anaconda group which mined the Chilean copper deposits.

The junta could count on support in its campaign to attract foreign capital from the influential Council of the Americas. Directed by David Rockefeller, this organization calls itself the "chief spokesman for American business in Latin America." Over 200 multinationals, representing 80% of investments south of the Rio Grande, are members.

In February 1974, this council arranged a schedule for Fernandez Leniz who had come to seek financial aid in Washington. On 4 February the Chilean Minister for the Economy met 100 directors of the big companies at a luncheon in New York. In May 1974, according to the *Pentagon Reports*, Chile became one of the chief buyers of American arms. With an armaments expenditure of $68,194,000 the country ran a close second to Korea and just outdistanced Brazil.

The Chilean junta is an amazing anachronism. Pinochet appears to think that a pre-Keynesian economic program will make him into another Franco. The financial doctrine of the military régime was developed by Chicago University professors led by George Schultz, Nixon's Finance Minister and a notorious Vodka-Colanizer. The man responsible for liaison between Santiago and the ultra conservative Middle West University, which is totally Rockefeller financed and controlled, is Arnold Habergen, director of the establishment's Latin American programs. Habergen, a former economic adviser to the Brazilian government, has delivered several speeches in Chile's Catholic

University, the most reactionary in the country. In July 1974, the junta invited him to address the annual conference of the National Association of Industrialists. On arriving in Santiago, Habergen stated "I think it is important for this country to understand the Brazilian example and to improve and apply it here." During his speech at the conference, he added "I am surprised that Chile has been able to find a way out of economic chaos so quickly and at a relatively low cost." Among his audience sat Pinochet, alongside the Peking ambassador to Santiago.

4.

Détente in Doubt: The Jackson Amendment

When American politicians learnt of the results of Nixon's trip to Moscow in May 1972, one man at least was strongly critical of the preferential economic relations offered to the Communists. By opportunely linking his basic convictions and his career hopes, Henry Jackson threatened the entire Vodka-Cola organization from within. And yet the Democratic senator from Washington State was undoubtedly one of the least charismatic figures in American political life. Then sixty-three years old, his Norwegian origins were reflected in his deliberate manner and his apparent lack of energy. But despite his sententious and monotonous line of argument, Jackson held one trump card, his extraordinary stubbornness. The two pillars of his faith were the Jewish cause and anti-Sovietism. In 1945, as a young congressman, he had visited Buchenwald shortly after its liberation. From that moment he had been a loyal and all-out defender of Israel. His attitudes and actions in foreign policy matters placed him very clearly on the right. Obsessed by national security during the fifties he expressed a doctrine which his parliamentary colleagues ironically called "the $23 billion calculated risk." In an interview to the *New York Times* on 19 November 1957, he had suggested that the country should agree to a massive increase in the number of nuclear missiles and that their manufacture should become an integral part of current production processes, on a par with refrigerators or barbecues.

Jackson had a decisive influence on the growth of the military industrial complex, and at least two men regarded him as the architect of American strategic strength. These were vice-admiral Hyman Rockover, father of US naval nuclear strength and long-standing mentor and superior to Jimmy Carter, and Air Force general Bernard Schreiwer who was in charge of the intercontinental missile launching bases.

Jackson's friend Nixon had long shared the Democratic senator's obsessions about the Red Peril and his desire to see the military warlords playing a more decisive role. However, when the reelected Republican President swam elegantly onto the shore of détente in 1968, Jackson watched incredulous as he receded into the distance; his pockets were still loaded down with missiles and his bedraggled cold-war finery had become a burden.

At the time of the South East Asia war Jackson suggested using tactical nuclear weapons to bring the North Vietnamese to the negotiating table. In 1969 the *New York Times* revealed that he had used his position as a member of the Senate Commission on the Armed Forces to help the Pentagon keep secret the exact cost of American anti-guerilla chemical and bacteriological war. Eight months later it was finally disclosed that $1 billion had been spent in one year on the research and development of what were basically anti-civilian weapons.

But Jackson's main claim to fame was his support for the trading policy of Boeing, the largest employer in his state with a payroll of 75,000 and nearly $5 billion in annual sales. The Seattle firm has dominated the world civil and military aviation market for some years. Since lack of credit facilities interrupted work on the SST, the American rival to Concorde, Boeing has been working on a bomber equipped with nuclear missiles.

At the present time more than half the commercial aircraft flying throughout the world are manufactured by Boeing, which can also offer its customers a wide choice of merchandise from long-haul 707s and Minuteman intercontinental ballistic missiles, to SAM short-distance nuclear missiles launched from FB111 fighters and costing $1 million a piece.

Like most of the big companies, Boeing is controlled by a financial group which includes the First National City Bank, the Morgan Guaranty Trust, the lawyers office of Sherman and Sterling and the Chase Manhattan Bank, which holds 8.7% of its stock.

Jackson is a regular contributor to the *Seattle Argus*, the aviation firm's newspaper. In the sixties he asked the federal government to grant additional credit facilities so that Boeing could build the new giant B52 bombers used so effectively in Vietnam. (Thirty of them were shot down in eleven days.)

Grey-faced Henry J. Jackson, however, was not just a sad little nobody. He was racked by ambitions to be President. In 1970 three Boeing directors, William Allen, George Wuyerhauser and William Reed, arranged a huge dinner at the hotel Olympio in Seattle, for which the guests paid a total of $200,000 to further Jackson's political hopes. Boeing also gave Jackson access to the Rainier, the millionaires' club of Washington State.

In 1972 his presidential run was stopped at the Democratic investiture after disastrous results in the primaries. Several company officials had followed him around during his electoral wanderings. In Wisconsin they had even used the firm's travellers cheques to buy space for him in the local paper.

Rendered temporarily idle and purposeless by this defeat, Jackson continued to mutter his suspicions about Nixon's détente policy and the Republican administration's excessively permissive attitude towards the USSR. Then, out of the blue, a dispatch from the Tass news agency in July 1972 gave him a cause to fight for.

In a brief announcement, the agency revealed that the Soviets were instituting an emigration tax, which meant that any Jew wishing to leave the country would have first to reimburse the cost of his education. Some would-be emigrants might be compelled by this discriminatory measure to find sums up to $30,000.

Jackson immediately called the office of Abraham Ribicoff, Democratic senator for Connecticut and an influential member of the Jewish Lobby. Ribicoff was not there, but Jackson had a long discussion with his legal assistant Morris J. Amitay who had once worked with Kissinger. "It is terrible, Morris," said Jackson. "If the Norwegians had taken a decision like this a generation ago my parents would never have been able to come to the United States."

As Jackson saw it, the path ahead lay clear. The Soviets had to be forced to make humanitarian concessions in exchange for the trade benefits resulting from the Nixon–Brezhnev agreement signed two months earlier. He was sure that there would be considerable support from a public well aware of the Jewish problem and always ready to express concern at any legal twists perpetrated by the USSR.

In early August he met Jacob Javits, the Republican senator for New York State. Javits carried the Zionist flag within the American political machine, but was also, and more particularly, an important business lawyer with connections with Nelson and David Rockefeller who forced him to jettison his political convictions. If he supported Jackson's suggestion of linking the purchase of technology with the emigration of individual people, even Jewish people, he would be compromising the whole strategy of trade with the East, possibly irremediably. Javits therefore chose to take up a position of evasive approval. However, events were moving fast. The American Jewish Committee, the powerful anti-defamation league B'Nai B'Rith, thirty-two other Jewish organizations and 200 local Zionist agencies invited Jackson to speak at the national conference on Soviet Jewry. On 26 September 1972, the Washington State senator declared, "The time had come to place our highest human values above trade in the dollar. Do you know what you have to do? I'll advise you. Support my amendment and hold firm."

Javits turned pale. This direct appeal to an earnest and determined grass-roots to take militant action might well arouse a vast, uncontrolled movement which could soon spread outside the American Jewish establishment. Javits tried to persuade the conference to adopt a more flexible approach, but it was a wasted effort. The delegates declared themselves massively in favour of the amendment. Every American Jew was asked to write to and telephone his own senator and demand action.

While Jackson and Ribicoff were leading a campaign to rally support, Javits, Stuart Symington and various other congressmen whose names appeared on every petition on behalf of Israel, were working to stop them. They expressed further objections that such an amendment might endanger peace. This argument appears to have struck a chord with several Liberal congressmen. However, when the irritated Jackson called him on 2 October to tell him which five senators were sponsoring his amendment, Javits was won over. The opportunist had triumphed over the man of conviction. The evening before, Jackson had had a long meeting with Nixon. Both had agreed that the question of Jewish emigration should be kept out of the presidential campaign. In exchange Nixon agreed that certain conservative Republican senators, like Storm Thurmond, would support the amendment. For, at that time, the Republican President scarcely believed that his former accomplice's efforts would come to anything.

When the amendment was officially introduced on 4 October, it was signed by seventy-six senators. As it stood, the document attacked the very *raison d'être* of détente: money. It said, in fact, that "no communist country which denied its citizens the opportunity to emigrate, whether by taxation or other means, would be authorized to benefit from most favoured nation status."

For some years the USSR had been grounded just outside this system of fiscal lockgates which enabled a country to export its products to the United States under preferential conditions. This meant, for example, that Russian caviar in New York was subject to a 30% tax, while Turkish caviar, benefitting from most favoured nation status, was only taxed at 5%.

Up until then the United States had applied this preferential treatment to 130 non-Communist countries, adding Poland and Rumania to the list in 1971.

For the Vodka-Colanizers, making the USSR a most favoured trading nation was more than just a symbolic move. It meant that products belonging to the capitalists, which were manufactured in the East according to the co-production system or imported on a compensation basis, would be liable to considerably less import duty and thus more profits. The big firms stood to profit twice over, first by using the Soviets to manufacture their products at cheap rates or to sell cheap imports, and secondly by obtaining preferential fiscal treatment for these same products from their own government. Cheap components could be incorporated in products produced in the US as well.

Jackson's ally in the House of Representatives was Charles Vanik, a member of the powerful Ways and Means Committee, whose grandparents had emigrated from Czechoslovakia. On 18 January 1973, one thousand American Jewish leaders publicly voiced their support for the projected amendment. Jackson could also count on support from the unions. Committed to a policy of defending employment in the USA, the central AFL–CIO was disturbed by the flow of investment towards the East and recommended the adoption of protectionist measures. Moreover, the eighty-three-year-old union leader George Meany, a virulent anti-Communist, was only too glad to be given a chance to torpedo a détente which he described as "damned business" and "appeasement for dictators."

On 22 January Nixon sent Peter Flannigan, his adviser on trade affairs and a director of the Dillon Read bank to see Jackson. Flannigan was to restate the position of the Republican administration, which regarded the granting of most favoured nation status to the USSR as a duty.

On 7 February Vanik introduced the amendment to the House of Representatives with the support of 289 colleagues.

Nixon reacted by trying to isolate Jackson on the right wing. Ultrareactionary senators like Ben Blakeburn from Georgia or Barry Goldwater from Arizona, the unlucky presidential candidate in 1964, were now members of the Vodka-Cola camp and described the amendment as "an error which can only have adverse effects on the economic expansion of the United States," and on Soviet emigration policy. As Goldwater saw it, any attempt to intervene in the national affairs of a country like the USSR and impose some humiliating reform was bound to fail.

Alarmed by reports from Soviet ambassador in Washington Alexander Dobrinin, the Kremlin asked for explanations. In late February Charles Colson, the corrupt presidential assistant who emerged from the Watergate scandals as a repentant and religious man, went to Moscow. Officially, he had gone to negotiate the setting up of offices for American companies in the USSR. In fact Colson went first to see Gromyko and then Kosygin, with lengthy explanations of the legislative tangles.

Shortly afterwards Vladimir Alkhimov, assistant Minister for Foreign Trade and co-chairman with Donald Kendall of the recently created US–USSR Trade and Economic Council, took advantage of a trip to Washington to meet senator Wilbur Mills, chairman of the Ways and Means Committee. The general attitude reflected by Mills was scarcely encouraging. If the emigration tax was not annulled, at least 350 congressmen would vote the amendment in.

In any blackmailing scheme, there is often an attempt at seduction before the threats start. In March Dobrinin invited Jackson to the Russian embassy. For the first time the diplomat suggested that his country's placing a large order with Boeing might offer a means of honourable withdrawal from the amendment. Some days later the directors of the Seattle firm received a letter from the Soviet organizers of the 1974 International Aeronautics Exhibition, stating that they were prepared to increase the size of the pavilion reserved for the company. Aware that large sales were at stake, some of the Boeing directors expressed increasingly critical, if private remarks about Jackson who was also under pressure from a number of the businessmen contributing to the Democratic Party. They all intimated that Jackson's political career and presidential hopes for 1976 were dependent on how quickly he could bring this untimely move to a halt.

On 18 April Nixon invited Jackson to the White House. The President was already experiencing the first symptoms of the Watergate disease, an infection resulting from the solitary exercise of power which finally produces behavioural problems.

Without showing him any documented evidence Nixon told Jackson that on 16 March and 10 April he had received "communications from the Soviet leaders" to the effect that the emigration tax was to be suppressed. "As a consequence," added Nixon in a jovial tone, "my diplomacy makes the amendment pointless."

After a long silence Jackson replied, "Mr President, if you believe that you must be blindfold." The next day, with that feeling for the terse statement which is the hallmark of the great man, he added "I am holding firm".

The idea that the most important act of economic cooperation ever undertaken between two absolute powers could be compromised by a single man, and a rather obscure and undeniably stubborn senator at that, was an interesting paradox as well as an encouraging sign for democrats everywhere. But there was no way that the Overworld leaders, with their combined infiltration and integration systems, could have foreseen their plans being so irrationally and illogically thwarted by mere human ambition.

Nixon then tried to bring about a split between Jackson and the Jewish community. On 19 April he invited fifteen leaders of Israeli organizations to his office, including Max Fisher from Detroit who had financed his reelection, Jacob Stein, president of the conference of the largest American Jewish organizations, and Charlotte Jacobson, vice-chairman of the National Conference on Soviet Jewry. The American head of state voiced his agreement with some of the amendment's objectives, but added "Jackson is a hawk and Brezhnev will never yield to public pressure." There could be no point in aggression, in any case, when the Soviets had promised, as he had already told Jackson, to suppress the tax on emigration which had caused the whole conflict. Emigration to Israel would be able to continue and to increase from 32,000 to 35,000 people a year, an appreciable improvement on past figures.

Back in Fisher's office, the group issued a communiqué congratulating the President on his achievements. No mention was made of the Jackson amendment. Ten days later the group asked that the American Jewish community "should agree to a fresh delay for thought before supporting the Jackson–Vanik amendment."

In the face of this statement, an extraordinary meeting of the New York Conference on Soviet Jewry was convened. Jacob Stein and Charlotte Jacobson were in a minority. Any backsliding on the part of congressmen previously in favour of the amendment was immediately dealt with. James Corman, Democratic representative from California, who appeared suspiciously lukewarm as the months passed, told how "on several nights I was continually harassed on the telephone by people asking me why I had decided to sell out the Jewish cause."

In mid-September, after a meeting of the US–USSR Trade Council in New York, Kendall sent cables to sixty-five directors of banks and big companies, asking them to ensure "by whatever means, the funeral of the Jackson–Vanik project." Kendall and his friends were unaware that the text of the cable had been intercepted by a pro-Zionist employee of the US–USSR Trade Council, who sent a copy to senator Abraham Ribicoff's assistant, Richard Amity.

The next day the front page of the *Washington Post* read "The big companies are pressurizing the Capitol to support trade with the Soviets."

Furiously angry, Kendall said "Jackson is aiming for the presidency in 1976, and his amendment is simply a means of winning support from George Meany by helping him to destroy Soviet–American trade."

With the Yom Kippur war, American Jews temporarily shifted their priorities to the survival of Israel. Kissinger, who was trying to find a diplomatic settlement to the conflict, thought that the amendment was an obstacle to the conclusion of an agreement. On 23 October, Leonard Garment, a former associate of Nixon in Mudge Rose who had come to the White House as legal adviser to replace the "criminal" John Dean, invited Jacob Stein, Max Fisher and Richard Haas to a meeting with General Alexander Haig two days later. At the last moment Kissinger came back from Moscow to take Haig's place. The head of the State Department painted his guests a disturbing picture. Apparently Brezhnev had sent Nixon "an aggressive warning," indicating that he was prepared to send Soviet troops to the Middle East to "stop Israeli violations of the Truce." According to Kissinger, "whatever the aims of the United States and Israel, there will be no peace if the USSR is opposed to them." The chief of American diplomacy considered it totally inopportune to aggravate this climate of tension by opposing the application of the trade agreement. Furthermore, he suggested to the Jewish leaders that the amendment be withdrawn from the House of Representatives and kept in the senate. He promised that the administration would grant no new credit facilities to the USSR until the senate had validated and ratified the trade agreement the following year. Fisher, Stein and Haas considered Kissinger's approach "sensible, realistic and honest."

On 5 November, a meeting took place in Jackson's office. With the help of detailed notes, Haas summarized the Secretary of State's words. "All the same", he added, "it is important if Kissinger assures us that his negotiating position would be strengthened by a simple delay on the amendment." Later in the discussion Stein said "Trying to get the Jews out of Russia is a tasteless game if its only consequence is a weakening of the US position in the Middle East talks."

A strained Jackson interrupted him, "I cannot guarantee you in writing that there are no risks involved in supporting my initiative, but you are naïve to suppose that suppressing it would strengthen Israel's security. If we give up now, the Russians will profit by it."

Then, addressing the whole gathering, the Democratic senator added "the administration has always manipulated you. The only means of ensuring that the Jews leave the USSR is by supporting my amendment against anything and everything."

When the meeting ended Stein and Haas left quickly on the pretext that they had to catch a plane back to New York. On the way to the airport, however, they stopped at the White House to report what had been said at the meeting to Peter Flannigan and Helmut Sonnenfeld, State Department number two and Kissinger's closest colleague.

On 11 December the House of Representatives adopted the amendment by 319 votes to 80. In the Senate Jackson could count on the help of at least seventy-nine senators. Threatened with impeachment, Nixon had become the phantom of a White House deserted by all those now facing trial on charges connected with Watergate. In this atmosphere of governmental vacancy Jackson was eager to widen his support for the next presidential campaign and might well have been prepared to make concessions, especially as a poll among businessmen conducted by *Business International* revealed that there was total hostility to his initiative. 236 bosses from 220 companies declared themselves in favour of conferring most favoured nation status on the USSR unconditionally. Jackson found it hard to ignore manifestations of ill humour from the men who form the life-support systems of all political diehards.

In early January 1974 Kissinger had dinner with Jacob Javits. The Republican senator thought Jackson would only be stopped if the ground was cut out from under his feet. If Kissinger would agree to work with him on the Jewish emigration policy, Javits would do all he could to rally support for him in the Senate.

On 29 January Jackson's assistant, Richard Perle, informed William Eberle, Under-Secretary for Trade, of his boss's latest position. If the Russians would give the administration an assurance that they would grant 100,000 visas a year and stop all their bureaucratic red-tape, Congress would agree to extend the relevant trade privileges to the USSR.

In the meantime Peter Flannigan had been removed both from the negotiations and from the White House, following his involvement in corrupt deals concerning the sale of ambassadorial posts to wealthy Republicans and ITT's bending of the anti-trust regulations. His later appointment as ambassador to Madrid was turned down by Congress.

The first meeting between Jackson and Kissinger took place on 6 March 1974. The two men quite openly hated each other. Kissinger saw Jackson as the mole-hill which had appeared in the middle of his otherwise level and faultless career. The Democratic senator, whose intellectual life had always been focussed on bare essentials, thought that the convolutions of the Kissingerian mind must be concealing dark and evil tendencies, which of course it did.

At all events, Henry the "jet-age diplomat" had received favourable impressions from his first conversations with the Soviet leaders. They would be prepared to authorize the annual emigration of 45,000 Jews, one and a third times the 1973 figure and double the 1974 figures.

"Too few," replied Jackson, who also expressed a desire that people would be authorized to leave not just from the big conurbations like Moscow, Kiev or Leningrad, but also from the outlying Republics. Jackson also demanded that Kissinger should confirm the agreement concluded with the Communist leadership in writing. It took four months of negotiations to achieve a satisfactory opening sentence. "We are informed that ..." "We are confident that ..." "I have reason to believe that ..." were all suggested. Then on 15 August, after a dinner at the White House with the new President Gerald Ford, Jackson, Ribicoff and Javits, Kissinger agreed to his opponents' "We have received assurances that ..."

Six weeks earlier on 2 July Ernest Bouillion, president of Boeing, had signed a cooperation agreement in Moscow for the creation of a joint venture in the Soviet Union to manufacture jet engines for long-haul commercial aircraft.

On 20 September Gerald Ford had two meetings, the first with Jackson, the second with Andrei Gromyko. The next day, during a long conversation with his Soviet counterpart, the Secretary of State set out the form of the agreement. Two letters were to be written. In the first, addressed from Kissinger to Jackson, the Secretary of State would confirm the assurances he had received, first "that the repressive measures adopted against people wanting to emigrate would be violations of socialist law and their application repressed," and second that "the tax on emigration will be speedily suspended."

The letter ended "We foresee that the rate of emigration from the USSR will soon exceed its 1973 level and will correspond to the number of demands for exit visas."

In the second letter, addressed from Jackson to Kissinger, the senator would restate the essential prerequisites for any agreement. First that there must be no persecution of those who wish to emigrate, or of their families. Second, visas will not be refused to those who have had no access to classified information over a period of three years. Third, that the minimum rate likely to appease the American Congress was 60,000 departures a year.

On 26 September Mike Mansfield, leader of the Democratic majority in the Senate, asked Kissinger during a private conversation whether he had really got the USSR to agree to the annual departure of 60,000 people.

The Secretary of State refused to answer.

Nevertheless, on 18 October, the exchange of letters took place. Jackson looked as smug as a man who has bought a black market ticket for the baseball game, not realizing that it will never take place. In exchange for the assurances Kissinger had obtained from the Soviets, Congress approved the new trade agreement permitting the administration to grant the USSR non-discriminatory tariff treatment, although various additional regulations restricted the application of full concessions. This meant that the Soviets and the Vodka-Colanizers who relied for their expansion on cheap official credits, had only $300 million in the name of the Export–Import Bank to finance their operations, a derisory sum compared to the amounts of liquid funds actually needed. The decision was described by Kissinger as "stupid and regrettable." It also rather clumsily placed the USSR in a position of being tested. Eighteen months later, in

February 1976, Congress would be able to go back on their agreement if the Communists had not kept their promises. Taken as a whole the measures appeared over-
draconian to the Soviets who were disappointed by how little they had been granted in
the way of credits.

The humiliated Russians were quick to react. In early December, there was a session
of the Central Committee of the Russian Communist Party following the Vladivostok
summit between Gerald Ford and Leonid Brezhnev. Shortly afterwards, on 18
December, the Tass news agency revealed that Kissinger had lied, and had kept quiet
about a letter Gromyko had sent him the week after Congress adopted the new trade
measures. The Soviet diplomatic chief vehemently denied ever having furnished the
least assurance and affirmed that the alleged promises on emigration were equally
false. On the contrary, said Gromyko, all his conversations with the American Secretary
of State had suggested that the demands for visas would continue to decrease.

President Ford signed the new trade law on 3 January. On 4 January the *Washington
Post* revealed that "Moscow is envisaging reopening the question of its trade relations
with Washington." Congress seemed suddenly to have grown dizzy with its own temerity and worried that it might have gone too far. When Kissinger told congressmen that
the amendment was a permanent obstacle to a reduction in tension they all listened
contritely. And when on 10 January the Soviet government rejected the agreement as
unacceptable, Jackson found himself wandering aimlessly about with his amendment in
his hand, like a kid on the beach looking for a pool to sail his new boat in.

On 21 February Vladimir Alkhimov and Donald Kendall, co-chairmen of the US–
USSR Trade Council, held a conference in Washington. The Communist leader declared
that "the principles of the Soviet régime are not for sale." The *Red Star*, the organ of the
Russian army, violently attacked Jackson as the man who had decided to serve the
three Leviathans of oil, aviation and Zionism, and whose "only political creed is anti-
Communism." This was an amazing misunderstanding on the part of Karpovich who
wrote the article, since the majority of the oil and arms companies and the big banks
most firmly established in the Communist states sympathized with Soviet arguments
and were fiercely anti-Jackson.

It appeared that Jackson had been wrong to believe that principles and self-interest
could be reconciled. Two years later, in 1976, the senator from Washington State had
only a walk-on part in the great electoral spectacle, with a two-second appearance in the .
New York primaries. His amendment achieved a drop in Jewish emigration figures
from 35,000 in 1973 to less than 13,000 by the end of 1975.

In March 1977 the World Jewish Congress, the largest international agency of organized Jewry and the primary source of finance and funds for Israel and Zionism, attacked
the USSR for mounting a renewed wave of anti-Jewish harassment and repression. In a
strongly-worded communiqué, the Congress accused the Soviet Union of mounting the
campaign in response to the heightening clamour in favour of East-European dissidents
in the West.

Illustrative of the growing separation of the protest movement against violation of
civil rights and individual liberty and economic cooperation was the announcement,
almost simultaneous with the World Jewish Congress protest, of an accord signed by
Vishiani for the USSR State Committee for Science and Technology and Edgar M.
Bronfman, chairman of the giant liquor multinational, Seagram Co. Ltd. of Montreal
and New York. The two put their signatures to an agreement for cooperation and
research in the food and drink industry. One provision of the accord covers a Soviet
technique for recovering a high-protein residue, left after molasses is distilled into rum.
The residue is converted into swine and cattle feed. To date, North American experi-

ments with molasses residue have failed to make it appealing to cattle. Because the Canadian firm and its New York-based subsidiary, Jos. E. Seagram and Sons Inc., own the Paul Masson Vineyards of Saratoga, California, the accord may also cover wine-making, a field in which the USSR Ministry of the Food Industry, already the world's leading producer of sparkling wines, wants to expand. Imports of Soviet spirits are also involved.

Considered as unrelated and irrelevant to the agreement, was the fact that Edgar M. Bronfman is the International Treasurer of the World Jewish Congress, and Vishiani a high-ranking official of the KGB, the agency implementing the alleged "pogroms" against the Jews.

Now that the amendment has blocked credits through official channels, the big banks have turned to the Eurodollar market. Consortia of American, European and Japanese and Communist banks are formed to raise the money necessary to finance their operations in Europe and Asia. In this way they can also avoid the restrictive measures imposed by national governments. Similarly, American companies looking for liquid funds are now forming joint ventures with European firms. Thus, on 30 October 1975, a partnership of Entrepose, subsidiary of the French Vallourec group, and Armand Hammer's Occidental Petroleum sold 900 million dollars' worth of engineering and know-how to Techmashinimport for a 2,400 km ammonia pipeline to be constructed between Togliattigrad and the port of Odessa. Vallourec will also supply 400 million French francs' worth of steel pipe line. The French government is granting this project 1 billion francs in financial aid.

Part V

The publicists of détente never cease to point out the favourable accompaniments to such a development, in an effort to win over public opinion. Just as a commercial promotion campaign never mentions the dangers, defects or useless nature of what it is trying to sell. The "refreshing break" for Coca-Cola parallels the descriptions of the brimming vitality of the "Pepsi generation."

Thus détente is justified as the surest means of avoiding a nuclear confrontation.

In the same way numerous elegant valuations are elaborated around the central theme of a convergence between the two systems. With certain modifications, these theories put forward an extremely simple proposition: that each of the two systems would tend to assimilate the best characteristics of the other, stripped of faults and deficiencies. So the argument moves towards a positive synthesis, which holds on the one hand that the economic chaos and injustice caused by the monopolistic market economies of the capitalist system would be modified by the extension of common ownership of the means of production and by social planning. On the other hand, the salient features of the Communist régimes, such as political authoritarianism and the curtailment of individual freedom, would be countered by an extension of personal liberty on the Western pattern.

The influence of the capitalists and their bankers pursuant to their entry into the Eastern economies hardly argues in favour of such a probability. On the contrary. Their agreements with the Fascist leaders before them have never altered the nature of the régimes themselves.

The modern capitalist enterprise, integrated within a multinational company system, is by nature authoritarian. There is nothing in its structure or its fundamental aims to suggest that it would pioneer or implant freedom or democracy in the USSR or among its satellites.

The Communist régimes certainly do not include among their fundamental objectives the suppression of a capitalist system dominated by these companies which have become their natural contractual partners. Why should the USSR seek to encourage nationalization of ITT, IBM and the Chase Bank when it is benefitting from growing profits with their help in the Soviet Union or in joint projects in the Third World?

Trade union independence and the basic freedoms are rejected and despised by both sides of the Vodka-Cola camp. That is why a *negative* convergence seems infinitely more likely, emphasizing the authoritarian characteristics of both systems.

This section displays our deep scepticism of official theories of positive convergence. The negative development has already been realized at national level in Italy with the "Historic compromise" strategy of the Italian CP, which is seeking direct participation in government. The party is staking its future on the success of the local version of détente, or Vodka-Espresso. The American power élite, and especially the Trilateral Commission group, consider this experiment as a regional phenomenon, but a desirable one for the Vodka-Cola movement. It would be illogical for President Carter to continue cooperation with the Eastern countries while refusing to adopt a similar conciliatory attitude towards an Italian CP which became part of a coalition government.

What is more, the USSR has unconditionally supported the stance of the Italian fraternal party in pursuance of a global strategy where economic interests are apparently decisive.

Agnelli and all the chiefs of Italian industry support the CP. Even the organs of the major media (*Stampa, Corriere della Sera, La Republica, Espresso, Il Mondo*, etc.) have supported Berlinguer and his friends throughout the land during the June 1976 elections.

The Party has always maintained very close links with the multinational companies established in Italy. The CP itself is a vast capitalist enterprise, thanks to its numerous commercial firms, fully tied into big banks around the world through the tax havens.

The strategy is to promote the CP to join the government as a stabilizing force, to control the more militant elements in the trade unions and extend Euro-Communism.

Just like the leaders of the USSR, the Italian Marxist *apparatchiks* extol the virtues of the big companies, declaring them to be free and private partners. But despite the breadth of the operation, nothing proves that the negative aspects of this convergence will not provoke an adverse reaction on the part of ordinary citizens. It is difficult to sell the average citizen Vodka-Espresso.

Like the Italian Communist Party, the French CP has a vast network of commercial companies involved in East–West trade. Its banks and enterprises have made it a major contributor to the workings of French capitalism. The comrades' trips to Moscow are financed by Coca-Cola and advertisements for the big companies in the Party newspaper. These are just some of the "secret" links between the "revolutionary" party and the Vodka-Cola multinationals.

1.

Convergence

In 1964, in the middle of the Vietnam War, Brzezinski and his stooge Huntingdon published a study entitled *Political Power, U.S.A.–U.S.S.R.*, on the existing manifestations of convergence between the two systems. As they saw it, there was no likelihood of economic similarities extending to the establishment of multi-party democracy in the USSR. In 1968, Brzezinski enlarged on this argument in a series of articles published in the CIA-financed magazine *Encounter*. It is worth pointing out that this specialist in Soviet–American relations, who joined Hubert Humphrey's electoral staff as foreign policy adviser a year later, was well known in the Eastern bloc as an anti-Communist thinker. On 19 August 1969, Radio Moscow even went so far as to accuse him of collaborating with the American secret services in fostering the Czechoslovak "counter revolution." (It just so happened that Brzezinski was married to the great niece of Beneš, former president of the Czech Republic, and had been teaching at Prague University during the spring of 1968.) *Kommunist*, the Soviet Central Committee review, also attacked him in September 1973. "As for the anti-Communist Brzezinski, he expresses 'the modest hope' that there should be room in the Soviet Union for both a socialist economy and private enterprise capitalism, with an eventual 'radical reform' of the socialist system." We mention this only to emphasize the curious background to our fairy story about Coke, the puppet, going to live with Vodka, the animal trainer, after long fears that it would be eaten by his bear. Brzezinski may have swivelled politically as quickly as his chair in the White House basement, from which he now directs the National Security Council, but he is only too well aware of the situation he has to deal with.

In 1970 he published *Between Two Ages, or The Technocratic Revolution*. Although the title and the author's name together sound like some kind of joke, the book was a first serious attempt to assess the sudden invasion of technological power, and its disruptive effect on political systems and foreign relations. It also pointed out the basic difference between Brzezinski and his colleague Kissinger. Although both men had been trained in the same school to juggle with similar concepts and support identical interests, the one had chosen to follow the path of Metternich, the other of Norbert Wiener.

In a necessary transition towards the denationalized and anti-democratic age, Kissinger's reassuring views were welcomed by the political commentators' Internationale. He travelled the route of the classical foreign policy broker from Peking to Helsinki by way of Paris and Moscow, even though some of his fellow travellers arrived with their pockets stuffed full of unfilled order books. His statement on 17 May 1975 that "the real problem of the future will be economic" was perfectly correct. It was also an admission that his days as a salary-earner at the State Department were numbered. The departure of this chubby little man marked the end of an era. There would be no further need for the epicurean intellectuals who stumbled their way from Clausewitz to Spengler as they gunned down the old order.

As Brzezinski sees it, the present "predominance of technical and economical factors" is a far more important and dramatic turning point in our history than the French Revolution or the accession of the Bolsheviks. Carter's man of ideas is contemptuously filling in the trenches dug by the old guard of the rival systems. He has all the facts at his fingertips to create an impeccable pedigree for present developments. "Soviet economic development between 1917 and 1930 was basically reliant on the technological aid of the United States. At least 95% of the industrial structure of the USSR received assistance from them."

On 12 April 1976 president of Occidental Petroleum Armand Hammer and a relaxed Brezhnev signed a $20 billion agreement for the construction of fertilizer factories. Brezhnev laconically described Hammer as "a man who helps me and whom I help."

Hammer's activities have always bordered on political and legal conspiracy. Oblivious to his élitist Soviet friends' totalitarianism and disregard for civil and human rights, he has equally shown total unconcern about the régimes and dictators which became his associates: Kadhafi in Libya, militarists in Latin America, etc. With equal disdain he evaded and circumvented laws and regulations of the capitalist world in his operations. In addition to his conviction for making unlawful contributions ($54,000) to the campaign of fellow Vodka-Colanizer Richard Nixon, the US Security and Exchange Commission, the ineffectual regulatory agency of the New York Stock Exchange, accused Occidental of distributing more than $650,000 in illegal gifts and political contributions at home and abroad. At least $400,000 of this was alleged to have been distributed to foreign political leaders, government officials or officers of state owned companies between 1969 and 1970. One can readily imagine the real amount being many times more than the "proven" figure. Hammer's "investment program" in the Soviet Union, the SEC revealed in May 1977, coincided with the discovery that Occidental Petroleum had set up two secret companies in Europe and then funneled profits from them into clandestine Swiss bank accounts and secret cash kitties for illegal campaign contributions (New York Times, May 4, 1977). The SEC stated they could not account for all the profits generated by the two companies, and that of the $200,000 alleged profit at least $165,000 was deposited in two numbered bank accounts in Switzerland. Which still leaves all the other many tax havens where Oxy Vodka-Cola profits may be hiding skimmings of profits from American tax collectors and public awareness, and available to finance lobbying campaigns for East-West trade and granting MFN and credits to the Soviet Union.

The fertilizer deal set the seal on fifty-seven years of economic cooperation. Armand Hammer's father, an emigrant from Odessa and founder-member of the American Communist Party, had known Lenin since 1907, and financed the Soviet Liaison Bureau in New York, which was run by one of his friends Ludwig Martens. When Trotsky landed in the United States to look for financial support, Hammer was there to greet him. And when the future head of the Red Army left New York again on board the SS Christinia on 27 March 1917, it was with a Canadian passport supplied by Hammer. One of his uncles had handled Ford Motor Company interests in Tsarist Russia. In 1922 Armand Hammer held negotiations with Lenin and Mikoyan in Moscow to keep Ford production lines running in the new Communist state.

In 1920 John Rockefeller's Chase Bank negotiated the creation of a Soviet–American Chamber of Commerce with the state-controlled Prambank. When this institution was opened in 1922, it was run by René Schley, one of the vice-presidents of the Chase Bank. Together with the Equitable Trust Company, another Rockefeller interest, the Chase appears to have been heavily involved in credit deals with the new revolutionary régime in Moscow. In 1925 it negotiated the financing of American cotton and machine-tool exports to the USSR. Three years later it was severely rebuked by American patriotic organizations for raising loans for the Russians in the United States. According to a State Department report, "Kuhn Loeb and Co., the biggest New York financiers, are helping to finance the first five-year plan, and have acted as a deposit bank for the Bolshevik government which transferred to it over 600 million roubles in gold between 1918 and 1922."

When it became clear that the Romanovs were losing whatever crumbling power they still had and that the Kerensky government was merely a stop-gap, Max Warburg and Jacob Shieff, the two principal stock-holders in Kuhn Loeb, worked in an official partnership with John Rockefeller and John P. Morgan, to finance Lenin and his group. According to the *Washington Post* of 2 February 1918, the Morgan Bank had spent at least $1 million on the men who were nationalizing the means of production. On 14 June, 1933, Louis McFadden, chairman of the House Banking Committee, stated "The Soviet government has received funds from the American Treasury, through the Federal Reserve Board [the American central bank]. The Federal Banks have cooperated in this operation with the Chase Bank, the Guaranty Trust Company and other big New York banks. If you open the books of Amtorg, the Soviet government trade organization in New York, Gostorg, the general office of the Communist trade organization, or even the central bank of the USSR, you will see how much Russia has profited by this drain on the American Treasury. These operations benefitting the Soviet state bank have been conducted by its correspondents, the Chase Bank of New York and Kuhn Loeb and Co."

Offering credit to a régime in the early stages of industrialization was a shrewd manoeuvre. It is only now that the Communist leaders are beginning to realize that technology is not neutral but bought and sold as part of a whole strategy of economic domination which makes ideological attitudes redundant.

After the Revolution, Standard Oil of New Jersey bought 50% of the vast oil concessions in the Caucasus which had once belonged to Alfred Nobel and had, in theory, been nationalized. In 1927 Standard Oil of New York built a huge refinery in Russia. Soon afterwards, the New York company and its subsidiary, Vacuum Oil Company, reached an agreement with Moscow on marketing Soviet oil in Europe, for which a loan of $75 million was granted to the Communist government. This would seem to support Brzezinski's ironic conclusion that "Investing in countries which later become political enemies had always been one of the characteristics of the capitalist era."

When Kruschev's future ally David Rockefeller left the Kremlin after his first meeting with the Russian leader in 1964, he declared to an anxious public, "That was the most intensive conversation I have ever had. But we know each other. We have been used to working together for a long time."

In June 1944, after several trips to the Kremlin, the immensely wealthy and influential Democrat Averill Harriman was quoted in a State Department report as saying "Stalin recognizes that about two thirds of the biggest Soviet ventures were built with financial or technical aid from the United States."

Relaxing between purges in the calm of his apartments, the former seminarist from Georgia, who supported one-country socialism, admitted "We should have combined the revolutionary conscience and American capitalist efficiency."

The coercive and all-pervading political power in the East has drained the life-blood from an economy too dependent on doctrinal decisions. Simultaneously the dynamism of the Western industrial sector has been accompanied by an identity crisis among national governments. The West today is confronted by a two-tier global economic system.

1. *The multinational level*. The world economy is controlled by about one thousand

companies which work hand in glove with about thirty or so big banks. These firms handle about four fifths of total world production and owe their strength and prosperity to the fact that they have bypassed the market economy and the phenomenon of competition. Three companies monopolize the computer industry, seven the oil, seven the paper, four the computers, three the photography, eight the rubber, 150 the chemical and nine the automobile industries, etc., etc. General Motors could certainly teach Gosplan a thing or two about planning. Even the most ardent supporters of free enterprise must admit that cartelization is here to stay and that the concept of competition is too damaging, inefficient and expensive to be practicable today, as John D. Rockefeller so often declared.

So while the Common Market complains about American protectionism with regard to imports of European cars, it also asks that the Japanese should voluntarily reduce the volume of their automobile, electronic and textile exports which are now flooding the European market and creating unemployment. But why should Ford and Fiat want to engage in dangerous competition when it would only result in disrupting national economies and creating social upheavals? Imagine what it would mean if a firm like IBM which employs 300,000 people throughout the world, went bankrupt; or General Motors with its 800,000 workers and 75 billion dollars' worth of assets in dozens of different countries. Even the indirect effects would be catastrophic. What is more, theoretically competitive firms like these actually work together through thousands of joint-venture agreements governing the use of existing sales outlets, the establishment of new markets and the sharing of available capital.

The business enterprise is no longer the single, independently productive entity it once was. Anti-trust laws are still ineffective and, in many cases, inoperable. Take the European chemical firms, for example. The links and agreements between them are reducing their numbers considerably. How can you ask partners to compete? The seven supposedly competitive, major oil companies are bound together by over 20,000 agreements. With legislation lagging behind the activities of the multinationals, some people are pinning their hopes on the medium sized businesses which they see as the last symbol of national economic independence. But technology is dependent on investment and all existing capital is totally monopolized by the big companies which control the distribution and sales networks. In the OPEC countries, for example, the major companies have as much power as they have always had, except that it now lies in their control of commercialization and transport. Also, the medium sized companies are too small or capital starved to engage in large scale projects and must choose between subcontracting work within the industry (as in the automobile sector) or extreme specialization and the production of a very limited range of articles. The only way they can finance expansion into the international markets is by merging with or selling out to the multinationals. By creating a vertical chain of operations in this way, companies like Renault or Volkswagen can not only keep up the appearance of a free market economy, but also use whatever realizable assets the smaller firm brings with it, so as to avoid borrowing capital.

2. *The national level*. Although we still have a system of separate and supposedly competitive national economies, they too are largely influenced by the activities of the big businesses which work in twenty or thirty currencies a day. National political powers have too narrow a sphere of influence to be able to control firms which carry out their forward planning and decision making on a global scale. Imports, exports and competition with the United States have become meaningless terms when all the big European firms have long established links and cooperation agreements with their US "rivals". State control is one of the finer intellectual concepts of recent years. But state

and government are abstracts. All that really exists is a group of people affiliated to political parties who are subject to the same basic forces whatever their creed.

It is naïve and shortsighted to hold up increased state interference in the economy as a progressive move on the road to convergence. On the contrary, all that this "socialization" does is to emphasize the shortcomings of politics, which must accept big company strategy. For the past thirty years political power in Italy has been shared by the public and private sectors of industry which finance the political parties and can make or break governments. With slightly less Latin *brio*, a similar situation pertains in all Western countries. With national fiscal systems favouring capitalist interests, present-day management techniques can be directed towards increasing cash flow, the basis of investment, and severely curtailing net profits which would otherwise be lost to the company in the form of dividend payments. Fiat, Montedison, Volvo and all the oil companies have financed their investment and their staggering expansion almost exclusively through their enormous cash flow, while recording minimum net profits so as to avoid taxation. Tax-dodging, like the oldest profession in the world, will never be eradicated. Any government looking to achieve true equality for its citizens would have to alter the laws so that everyone has the same opportunity to defraud. Even the most "progressive" of governments, however, will never have any real control over investment, capital and profits, but will confine their activities by imposing indirect taxes on consumer sales. After all, in a democratic society, the tax imposed on half a pound of butter ought to be the same for the millionaire as it is for the working man.

On a more serious level, the way in which the big companies take available capital out of the national framework to reinvest it through a global system is highly inflationary. For many years only about 15% of the employees of the big Dutch multinationals like Shell, Unilever, Philips and Akzo, have actually been working in Holland. With over half its assets in the US, BP is no more British than Exxon. As this multinationalization continues, sovereignty is eroded and ideology becomes a wide mesh through which capital flows unimpeded. Along with the present large scale move to the Eastern bloc we have factory closures, increased unemployment and threats of dumping in the West.

Fiat, Montedison, Pirelli and the state-owned companies which have already transferred the bulk of their activities to other countries are working Italy as if it were a mine to be exploited until its last seams have run dry. Fiat is only an Italian company in Turin. Otherwise it is an international group based on IFI, the Agnelli family's holding company in the tax haven of Luxemburg. Similarly, Michelin, the jewel of the French CNPF, is only French in its Clermont-Ferrand factories, just as it is Canadian and American in North Africa. But decisions affecting all its tyre factories in eighteen different countries are taken in Basle and Bermuda where a holding company, whose profits are never repatriated to France, controls Michelin's finances. Existing legislation is used to isolate the power of ownership of the business. As they become multinationals, the big companies are forced to practise methods of money management which contravene the present out-of-date laws. For short periods company wealth may be based on speculation rather than production. At one time, the Italian state-owned company, Montedison, earned more through speculating on the money exchanges than through its profits on sales. Today its holding company has become a financial colossus. Real power is with the banks, and unless their activities can be controlled any attempt to nationalize is bound to fail. When Lenin described the advanced stage of imperialism as a period of financial hoarding, he could never have imagined the complex and sophisticated way in which power is manipulated through stocks and the creation of holding and finance companies in the tax havens. Banks are merely money-processing industries. The governors of the Bank of Ten (the central banks) admitted that in 1971 they speculated for their clients (the national banks) exactly like private financiers, and this despite all regulations governing that highly speculative and uncontrolled market of 400 billion hot dollars, the Eurodollar. Even the Communist financiers are gleefully dirtying their hands in this area.

If the franc devalues, Michelin can use telex and telephone to speculate on the Eurodollar so that none of its assets which are quoted in French francs will fall in value. By using the wildly inflationary Eurodollar system in which money can be created over the telephone, the multinationals are able to bypass national monetary restrictions, secure in the strength of the forward-purchased currency. In an interview in Basle, former governor of the Bank of England Sir Leslie O'Brien admitted that central banks connived in such operations. "We cannot act. If we were to control Eurodollar operations in the City, they would move to Hong Kong or Singapore." But Karl Marx was seriously mistaken in thinking that the capitalist's sole concern is to hoard profits for his own enjoyment. Today wealth is no longer subject to estate duty but to taxes on capital. Private personal fortunes are obsolete.

Similarly, the new global system has blurred the distinction between state-run and private banking. There is a large number of nationalized banks, but, like governmental politics, they are forced to accept the dictates of modern finance and operate exactly like the private banks. At the present time, multinational production and banking finance are organically linked in an osmotic process. In West Germany three merchant banks own 70% of all shares with voting rights. In Britain 200 firms are responsible for 85% of all production, and the 150 which achieve 75% of all exports are dependent on fifteen big banks. In the United States five of the 13,000 banks hold 52% of all banking assets; nine banks own 90% of the oil industry, 66% of the iron and steel industry and engineering firms and 75% of the chemical industry.

The expansion rate of the one thousand firms dominating our economic system is limited only by the amount of capital available to them. In the future, the chemical and plastic sector will need to make four times its present investment. In Rome in 1973, David Rockefeller estimated that over the next ten years the oil industry would need to invest 1,300 billion dollars, which is roughly the equivalent of the American GNP. For these firms, it is capital invested in new technology, and not labour, which increases productivity.

Of the vast finances demanded by research and development costs for new techniques and machinery, 90% can be raised through cashflow methods. There is evidence of this in the permanent pressure on prices, as companies try to increase their profit margins. This chase after capital is the source, and the only source, of our present inflation. But there is a great deal at stake. In fifteen years time, 80% of all products manufactured and sold by the chemical industry will be new discoveries which do not exist today. At one time it was industry which exerted pressure on science. Now science has become a pre-production force.

As far as management is concerned, every dollar spent on wages is a dollar lost to investment. Every wage rise won by the unions eventually leads to fewer jobs. This is inevitable. The stand for full employment is much like the obstinate heroism of the Japanese soldier who continued his war in the Borneo scrubland until 1976.

It is ridiculous to say that a reflationary policy will help to reduce unemployment when the new capital injections go to the big companies' foreign subsidiaries and when unemployment is bound to become a face of capitalist expansion.

The fifty biggest firms in the US represent a wide cross-section of industry from oil and automobiles to electronics and chemicals, and there seems little to distinguish between them in terms of their sales figures. But if we look at their numbers of employees and the ratio of assets to individual worker, we get a very different picture. As far as assets go, Exxon is the world number one with $42 billion, and yet it has only the 13th largest work force (133,000 including management). General Motors comes second in assets ($32 billion) and first in the size of its labour force (740,000). If we exclude management and stick to the shopfloor, this means that one new job costs $750,000 in Exxon as against $30–35,000 in a traditional industry like General Motors. Similarly, Texaco Oil has fourth largest sales ($23 billion) but 33rd largest labour force (76,000); Mobil comes fifth in sales ($19 billion) and 37th in labour force (75,000); Standard Oil of California sixth in sales ($167 billion) is 96th in labour force (40,000). The most striking example of this disparity is still provided by the Anglo–Dutch group Royal Dutch Shell. Most of its staff work in its headquarters in London and the Hague. But most of its profits are earned in the United States where it has the seventh largest turnover ($8 billion) and the 125th largest work force (32,000).

In the same way, national trading figures have long since ceased to reflect the activities of the big companies. Since production, sales, profits and dividends are now distributed right across the world, national balance of payments figures, which reflect none of this international trade, are condemned to showing a permanent deficit.

To say, as some people do, that the Communist countries offer capitalist companies only very limited scope for the creation of new production and marketing set-ups is like diagnosing a patient as "suffering just a little bit from cancer." It is impossible to say exactly where a dynamic process like this will end. Constant readjustments will be required, but we can be sure that it will continue, partly because of its political implications and partly because of the calibre of those involved. The firms moving in to the East are those responsible for 75% of industrial activity and 85% of exports in the West. Some of the banks established in Communist countries control the 500 biggest American companies which employ 75% of all industrial workers. Together these banks control 80% of the assets of the Western financial world.

The Communist leaders hoped that the multinationals' presence in the Eastern bloc would strengthen their position and help their industry to catch up with the West. There is still an enormous gap between research and its industrial application in the East. According to the economist Trapeznikov, 98% of Soviet researchers in 1967 were still in scientific institutes, while over 70% of their American counterparts were working directly for related industries. He also estimated that about half of Soviet discoveries were obsolete by the time they reached the production line. In some cases over ten years had elapsed between the original discovery and its application. Conscious of this problem, Soviet officials tended to attribute it to bad coordination between the various research organizations, many of which work along totally independent lines. On the level of the individual enterprise, there was often little incentive to introduce new technology for managers far more concerned about keeping up with the production rates set by central planning. In certain sectors, mini-computers for example, there is a twenty or twenty-five years technological gap between the West and the East. The reason why the Soviets are interested in increased cooperation with the West is that many of the large and technologically backward sectors of industry are vitally important for the Soviet economy. Over the next twenty years, the main task of the Soviet government will be to exploit the enormous natural resources of Siberia. There will also be a need to improve production of consumer goods in the near future.

The Soviet manager, trying to demonstrate his efficiency within the bounds of quantitative planning, was like someone trying to tap-dance on an ice rink. In a system of state monopoly where power and industrial control remain in the hands of the administration and the Gosplan officials can juggle their figures about in a totally abstract way, Soviet management has been undergoing an identity crisis. This new class has been conscious of its historical potential but has enjoyed none of the power associated with its position. It knows what has to be done but has no tools to do the job. That is why Soviet managers have all worked so meticulously to undermine the set standards by reductions in production and systemized go-slows which have only added to the inherent inefficiency of the Soviet economy. Where consumption and the market economy are unknown, they could see no point in exacerbating their own problems by exceeding production figures.

As the years have passed and the problems increased, more and more managers have taken to extolling internationalism. Their spokesmen in *Voprosy Ekonomisti* have written "Management methods are similar in form and content in all societies, and the principles of management are common to all modes of production." The call for even a partial return to the laws of the market economy reflected two basic objectives. First, the need to reorganize a system of production which had always overlooked the 250 million consumers, now growing increasingly intolerant of their poverty-stricken state. Second, on the more political level, the managers hoped to win official recognition for the increasingly preponderant influence of technicians, rather than ideologists, on the running of business. Naturally enough, however, there was no desire to compromise the coercive and totalitarian spirit of the régime. In the small ventures founded by Lenin and some of his associates in 1917, today's young, pragmatic, ambitious and efficiency-conscious managers, who admire Western-style management, have been finding it increasingly hard to work under the watchful eye of the older directors who have been with the venture since the beginning and may only have reached their present positions because they knew the founder. Souslov's or Pelche's sentimental stories about how store-keeper Lenin laid out his shelves or made his deliveries, merely irritate Vishiani's friends. The new generation are impatient and ready to shout "Death to the old men." As they see it, the store is delapidated and smelly, the stock unsellable and the managerial methods calamitous; what is more the staff, who are admittedly very badly paid, are blithely following their own paths into chronic absenteeism. The young men want to change the old bazaar into a supermarket, to replace the cash register with electric calculators and the oil lamps with neon lighting, and to bring in an even stricter system of staff discipline. But none of this can now be done, as long as the Communists limit their relations with the capitalists to strictly commercial deals for the purchase of patents and licences they are incapable of using. In order to reap the benefits of technical innovation, the Russians will have to enter more fully into the system designed by and for the capitalists, who want to retain control over their own know-how. Business and technology are now totally interconnected and interdependent. "If you take my technology, you take me." Even Vladimir Ilich Lenin, who never wasted an opportunity to remain silent, said "There is one force superior to the desire, will and decision of any government or hostile class; and that is world economic relations."

ITT (Chile) and Dow Chemical (napalm in Vietnam) are no longer content to remain in the East for the four months it takes to complete a single deal, but are successfully negotiating long-term contracts. Nor are they prepared to discuss technological aid without cooperation or co-production deals in which they are virtually equal partners with the Communist enterprise. At the same time the Soviets are having to pay for the establishment of this infrastructure by reexporting part of their production to the West. What is more, they can only market their own products through the capitalist companies' sales outlets. So, if we agree with Lenin that "politics is the concentrated expression of the economy," Zbigniew Brzezinski's statement that "the transition to a technological society will become the essential, determining factor in changing society as a whole," becomes equally valid.

As the Socialist state is forced to make further concessions, cohabitation with the multinationals imposes a serious strain on the overall picture of Soviet Communism. Some barren, unrealistic and bureaucratic thinkers suggest that present developments only affect the technical infrastructure and leave the main framework unchanged. Other more entertaining and even less convincing theorists reason that the Communists are killing the capitalists with kindness and that "the development of regular cooperation between the multinationals and the Socialist countries could deal an appreciable blow to the monopolies' domination of world markets." There is an obvious answer to this argument. How can the establishment of monopoly companies in enemy countries, which are new territory to them, affect their strength on Western markets? Is IBM, which dominates the computer market, any weaker because it has signed twenty-five joint-venture agreements with East European countries? Has the Chase Manhattan Bank, with its involvement in the arms and oil industries and its 175 odd branches in seventy countries, gone into a decline since it opened branches in Moscow, Prague and Warsaw? And, by the way, how is it that the "cold and implacable" monsters of Communist slogan writing are oppressors of the working classes in the West and respectable industries dealing in neutral technology in the East?

In an attempt to blur the edges even further, the Western Communists sometimes change their terms of reference, so that relations between the multinationals and the Communist régimes become totally justifiable economic cooperation between capitalist and socialist countries. But this kind of reasoning is false. Companies which are multinational monopolies in their activities in democratic, racist or Fascist states, cannot suddenly be labelled states, just because they are negotiating transfers of technology with Moscow and Budapest. The least national, but most nationalistic of all Communist parties, the French, are guilty of just this kind of chauvinism in their economic terminology.

The truth of the matter is that East–West integration is unjustifiable in terms of Marxist principles, but inevitable in the face of facts, and it gives rise to apprehension and tension. If there were no revolutionary struggle against the big companies in the West, there would be no need to preserve the Western Communist parties simply in order to heckle the Social Democrats. As it is, these firms are putting the Western system severely out of joint and causing almost continual political and social crises, partly because of their move to the East. And that being the case, all the *apparatchiks* can indulge in their taste for ideology by drawing a veil of modesty over the Rockefeller–Brezhnev liaison and letting off a whole firework display of glittering rockets about "the decline of capitalism" and "the alienation of the workers by twenty-five financial groups." An excellent way to disguise the truth while trying to preserve some superficial rivalry.

On both sides the state is hand in glove with the companies. The impotent politicians of the West stand idly by while the big firms commit their frauds, ignore the law and make thousands redundant, and go all out to woo the directors whom electioneering makes into a threat to democracy and civil rights.

The all-powerful but spastic Eastern régimes are forming partnerships which fly in the face of all the sacrosanct principles used to justify their existence. There is an increasing tendency to base commercialization, management, calculation of profits and decision making on capitalist methods. Those enterprises cooperating with Western firms are growing progressively more free of control from the Party and of planning imperatives. The Communist half of any joint venture is totally integrated into the

Western business system which is amoral, humanly corrupt and indifferent to human and social values. Communist banks cooperate in the same way with their opposite numbers in the West. With their offices in the tax havens, they can join in all kinds of shady or criminal deals, contribute to inflation and ensure that nothing is ever repatriated to the Socialist workers back home. As accomplices of the multinational industrial and financial system in which their businesses are developing, the Communist Party leaders have far too much to worry about without trying to plan some kind of revolutionary strategy. The writings of Zaradov or Ponomarev about the "imminent end of capitalism" are part of the standard propaganda supplied to embassy waiting rooms. They could not really want to destroy a system which they need so badly. In any case, the global managers do not take these manifestations at all seriously; very often they know nothing whatever about them.

The Eastern countries are setting up growing numbers of Foreign Trade Organizations, which are really enterprises or groups of enterprises working independently of central planning. These FTOs have considerable administrative autonomy and can negotiate and sign contracts directly with capitalist companies in the name of the Minister of Industry. Although this autonomy from state control is a blatant infraction of the principle of state monopoly, the FTO system is widely accepted in Hungary, Yugoslavia, Rumania and Poland, and about to be applied in Czechoslovakia. It has also been the subject of long discussions in the USSR.

The objectives of these ventures are no longer determined by the centrally planned society but by criteria much closer to capitalist principles. Their flexibility and freedom to make decisions should place them in a better position to negotiate with Western firms for the development of long-term relations and joint-venture agreements within Communist countries, in which the private companies enjoy the same rights of ownership and decision making as their Marxist partners. Structurally, the FTOs are organized to meet the demands of the multinationals, with which they hope to do business. All this looks very much like an attack on the sacred dogma of centralism and an adulteration of socialism, as the venture turns towards the dominant principles of the market economy without losing any of its authoritarianism.

Negotiations tend to follow a set pattern. The FTOs start by demanding that any licences they buy should be freely available to all relevant ventures throughout the country, as laid down by socialist legislation. The capitalists then refuse and limit the use of their licences to one, or at the most three or four, ventures. Finally, the Socialist state, anxious not to endanger the agreement, allows its laws and its sovereignty to be compromised. When dealing in up-to-the-minute sectors of highly specialized equipment, the Western managers may refuse to grant licences at all and insist on forming new kinds of partnerships in which their specialized technology remains under their control.

Further problems arise from the contrast between these small islands of sophisticated technology and the state of Communist industry as a whole. Most of the factories are old, with out-of-date machinery and appalling productivity shortfalls. Such things tend to slow down and endanger cooperation. The efficiency imperative is bound to demand maximum quality control over all aspects of production and the Western partner will insist on being totally involved in the different phases of the operation.

To accommodate these enclaves which are bound by none of the basic laws regarding the application of socialism, the Communists have had to perform a rather pathetic cosmetics job on them. Legally the Rumanians treat these ventures as totally independent companies, separate from the system. To keep up the illusion of "nationalization of the means of production" the Hungarians have decreed that such ventures could not be productive enterprises and have created artificial holding companies to negotiate for and on behalf of the Communist business. In this way, the actual machinery continues, in theory, to belong to the state and under exclusive control of the Party. But minor semantic distinctions, like using the word "consultant" to describe a manager does not disguise the true situation. The end result of co-production operations is profits for the capitalists, and this means that the socialist enterprises are involved in creating the surplus value which Marxism regards as the basis of the capitalist class's exploitation of the worker. To avoid calling a spade a spade, we may term this profitability, efficiency or the use of resources, but the net result remains the same. Moreover, the big companies insist that Western accounting systems be used in joint ventures, so that they can exercise more effective control. Little wonder Rumania has been granted most favoured nation trading status by the US and been so warmly greeted by Carter in Washington.

The ideologists must be wondering: what price Stakhanovism now? It is one thing to ask the simple-minded and the dedicated to stiffen their sinews, furrow their brows and follow the example of the "hero of labour" in helping to build the régime for totally non-monetary reasons. But how do you motivate the appallingly low-paid workers in a joint venture when they know that half of the profits are going back to the capitalist camp?

These enterprises are legally constituted on a basis of 51% for the Socialist state and 49% for the private partner. But that is just window-dressing. In fact the management board consists of equal numbers of representatives from both sides, each with a right of veto. It is even laid down that certain decisions must be taken unanimously.

The Socialists have made further legal concessions. Out of date laws are temporarily suspended until they can be amended, and are replaced meanwhile by the terms of the contract made with the capitalist partner.

Trade between the West and the Socialist economies may be decreasing, but only because the co-production system is replacing traditional exports. In an interview in the *U.S. News World Report*, David Rockefeller joked about his meeting with the Polish Party Secretary, Edward Gierek.

> Imagine, he'd never met a real live capitalist before. We discussed what had already been done in other countries and projects which might be of interest to us. Shortly afterwards I learnt that he had met a group of American senators and had told them that following our conversation he was going to recommend new Polish laws on joint ventures which would be more generous than in other socialist countries.

> *Question*: Why are companies so interested in these joint ventures?

> *Rockefeller*: Because these arrangements offer the opportunity of re-establishing certain kinds of profit.

On 26 June, 1975, Poland obtained $240 millions credit from the Chase to develop its copper resources. It had created a precedent by authorizing experts from the American bank to make detailed checks on its finances through documents previously regarded as state secrets.

While Donald Kendall was using the Brazilian footballer Pele to promote Pepsi in a vast publicity campaign throughout Yugoslavia, Dow Chemical and Tito's government were signing the biggest joint venture contract ever concluded with a Socialist country.

The Yugoslav head of state himself had negotiated this agreement, which proved highly interesting for various reasons. First of all, it underlined the futility of career-making and of the concept of national autonomy. At the age of eighty-three, twenty-six years after extricating himself from the influence of Stalin, the old Resistance fighter, who symbolized the struggle against the invader, had surrendered unconditionally to a notoriously reactionary and viciously anti-union company. Dow Chemical had also contributed a great deal to the American war effort in Vietnam, and had helped to produce the napalm which rained down over the South-East Asian fields beloved of progressive minds like Tito. Secondly, the Yugoslavs agreed that the board of the complex should be organized on a 50/50 basis, and that every year the American company should buy back 150 million dollars' worth of production for export to the West. Financial support for the deal came from Kuwait and Libya.

Arthur Koestler tells how, during his travels in Russia in 1931, he was struck by the disparity between reality and the ideological interpretation of it. As he visited areas suffering from a famine which cost thousands of lives, the local newspapers devoted their front pages to celebrating the abundance of the mythical harvest and the enthusiasm of the dying agricultural workers. Nothing has really changed. The "directive" still reigns supreme over the actual experience, but the large-scale tragedies have given way to the petty, daily dramas of the shopping basket. The Russians deny the existence of inflation in their country as vehemently as any criminal about to break into a confession. Indeed, the prices fixed by laws do remain stable. It is the products which change. They no longer exist. There is sad evidence of this inflation by scarcity. In over fifteen regions of present-day Russia, people are queuing outside the bakers where the yellow posters fixing bread at the 1954 price still hang on the walls, but where there is no bread to be bought. There is also a large number of products which are never bought because they are too shoddy or do not answer consumer needs. A socialist system in which production is geared solely to the central plan hits the consumer harder than anyone else. He has no choice but to indulge in the delights of the black market, apparently the only thriving element in the Communist economic system, or to cultivate a kind of underfed thrift. Deposits in the savings banks have now reached 80 billion roubles, while the value of stocks in shops and factories only amounts to about 50 billion. All reports reaching the West support the argument that the East European states are suffering from signs of political instability, as illustrated by the rebellion in Poland and the embryonic crises in Hungary and Rumania.

By introducing Western technology in their countries, it seems that Gierek, Kadar, Ceausescu and Brezhnev are desperately boarding a life-raft which may well disintegrate under them at any moment. They will have to abandon the dogma of full employment. The only reason why the ravages of unemployment have not yet hit Eastern Europe is because the administration has refused to recognize it. Any man or woman without a job has been described as "being reassigned", a state which may last for years. With sly cunning, the legislative has devolved responsibility for this painful problem onto the individual venture rather than the state. The manager has a duty to provide his workers with financial assistance; and this means that they may be reemployed in less skilled jobs. The Soviet press is full of examples of technicians and engineers working as semi-skilled or manual labourers.

The problem posed by ventures which are both non-productive and over-manned was neatly solved by Kosygin in his appeal at the 25th Party Congress for greater efficiency and increased quality control at every level.

Between 1971 and 1975, $207 million were spent on improving existing ventures. Of this sum, 1 billion roubles was used to replace unusable equipment. Nearly 20% of the new machinery and equipment installed in the USSR over the last five years has been imported. If they are hoping to see these technological changes through to the end, the Eastern managers are bound to aggravate the structural unemployment to a fantastic degree. If profitability is to be the new criterion, technical innovation will make much of the labour force redundant. Paradoxically, however, the men of technology will be hampered in their vital effort to set up new ventures by a shortage of qualified staff, since the relatively low level of education does not match technical demand.

The future of the USSR may depend on how soon Soviet technicians can be trained to suit the standards of capitalist management, and on sending vast troops of emigrant workers to Albania and China.

There is no doubt, however, that the future success of the phenomenon will be largely the concern of the managers. Even if legal ownership remains in the hands of the Western bank and the Eastern government, management is bound to seek maximum freedom and power of decision-making so that it can determine its own objectives and profitability. Only the size of the profits made will be controlled by the owners.

In these areas, it will be the technicians, and not the financiers, who lay down the law.

Peter Nehemkis, a professor at the University of California specializing in international trade negotiations and a consultant to several multinationals, has emerged as a champion of such manipulation. "Is it right to invite a congressman to give a speech to a trade association and to pay him $5,000 when everyone knows he has nothing to say? Isn't it a subtle form of corruption?"

Nehemkis thinks that many companies operating abroad have no choice and should not be condemned on that account. Indeed he thinks "the consequences of refusal could be disastrous. The first people to suffer from this strict code of conduct would be the workers and the shareholders." As he sees it, such practices are accepted in all markets, including the Communist countries. Not long before, in fact, a Soviet businessman had been shot for accepting $150,000 from a Swiss company. Enquiries made by the Securities and Exchange Commission (SEC) have confirmed the existence of this kind of insinuation. The SEC had documented evidence that the General Refractories Company of Philadelphia had paid one Rumanian official $250,000 through a holding company registered in Switzerland. On further enquiry it was revealed that at least four of the shareholders in Establishment Sanbil, a Geneva holding associated with General Refractories, were residents of two East European countries. In a letter, one of General Refractories' lawyers even stated that one of these people was a "member of a Communist government." General Tire and Rubber also admitted on 13 March that it had access to a secret fund of $1 million, most of which was used to ensure that Arab and Communist negotiators suppressed their misgivings and their scruples.

There is no denying the Communist élite's fervent and legitimate desire to preserve a social distance which entitles a Soviet Party official to privileges equivalent to thirty times the income of a skilled worker. According to a confidential study drawn up in the McKinsey Office, the Soviet oligarchy is composed of a few thousand "dear comrades" who are extremely jealous of their power and as concerned with higher living standards as the provincial bourgeois hankering after the delights of life in the capital. These include 95,000 CP officials, 60,000 trade unionists, journalists and leaders of Komsomols, 53,000 academicians, scientists and artists, 50,000 diplomats, KGB agents, directors of farms, combines and factories. In this bloated counterpart to the Western Overworld, thousands of people are furthering their careers in the grey area surrounding the few dozen men with real power, and following the currents of conformism, opportunism and complaisance.

There are signs of convergence, but they are totally negative. Communist countries may be drifting into a kind of capitalization, but only by using all the resources of their

totalitarian system. Laws on profits, investment and capital may be broken to benefit
the minority, but the social structure remains intact. If there are no strikes in the
Eastern bloc, it is not because they are forbidden, but because the class struggle has
been eliminated. In this socially harmonious world, the idle, easy-going unionist is an
integral part of the system. The leader of the trade union movement is a member of the
central committee and even, on occasion, of the Politburo. The former union leader
Alexander Chelepin, for example, was previously director of the KGB where he managed the Gulags, in defense of the workers.

The Soviet managers within the Foreign Trade Organizations, who are almost all
Party members, also belong to the same union as their workers. They are therefore
organically associated with the monopolies against which they are assumed to be
fighting in the West, and are collaborating in operations which lead to unemployment
for Western workers.

Logically, one would expect to find Western trade unionists sitting on the boards of
enterprises in the East, so that they could defend themselves against the decisions
taken by those of their managers who are established in Socialist countries. How otherwise can they protect their position in the United States, when decisions affecting their
future may be taken secretly and unilaterally in Prague?

Pravda may call for a general strike in the West, but the big companies will continue
to go Eastwards, knowing that they will benefit a) from a system of low wages, which
attract investment, and b) from authoritarian, hierarchical methods aimed at optimum
efficiency and production.

Today Fiat is asking the Italian government to set up tariff barriers against the
cheaper, more competitive Fiats manufactured in Poland. Apart from the fact that
cost-prices may be up to 40% lower there, the idea of stock-piling in countries where
production levels are not controlled by free workers must appeal to any far-sighted
manager as a possible weapon with which to break strikes and encourage submissive-
ness in the West. However, if a Western trade unionist were to appeal to his Hungarian
or Polish comrades to close a factory established in their countries, they would simply
reply, "That is economics; trade unionists have nothing to do with that."

This defensive argument is also used by the capitalist bosses. Talks with the unions
are confined to the subject of wages. Profit and investment are economic questions to be
handled only by management.

Signs of convergence in the West are equally sombre. Now that they are making such
headway in the Socialist countries, and forming partnerships with Communist governments, the men of the Overworld are hardly likely to start socializing their system. The
Nobel Prize-winning economist Jan Tinbergen, who chants the liturgy of convergence,
argues that there is increasing evidence of incomes policies being introduced, which
implies a socialization of the régime. But this is a nonsense. The system leaves profits,
production, business and taxes unfettered. In fact the only thing which is socialized is
earned income. What we are seeing now is a desire to establish a system of
authoritarian control over collective bargaining and to legislate about the right to
strike.

Laws imposing permanent and authoritarian limitations on collective bargaining are
already being passed in England. Tomorrow it will be Germany and France. The Overworld is steering national politics in this direction in several countries. What more
perfect than a system in which the unions are forced to police their own membership and
keep tabs on threats of uncontrolled initiative?

No government or Party, especially a Socialist one, can exert any influence on the
companies. Nationalization is absurd. Refuse to grant one company cheap credit

facilities for implantation in the East, and a rival company will obtain them from elsewhere and steal the market. Every head of state is bound to serve the interests of his national enterprises, which are still linked to those companies which serve their own interests first. Where strong-arm tactics are called for, politics do not appear to go very far.

As investment in the East increases, there will be a temptation to control the resultant tensions, difficulties and unrest in the West by law. In a climate of inflation, unemployment and dumping, worker–management relations will be regulated in a first step towards the suppression of rights and of liberties. In Italy, the economic power base already controls the political parties which, in turn, rule the unions. As billions of dollars are invested and vital technology transferred, the interests of the élites on both sides have more and more in common. With so much at stake, existing pressures on our institutions will be aggravated. By lobbying, by contributing financially to the parties and by ensuring that their friends hold governmental posts in the cabinet, the banks and the multinationals will be able to influence political decisions in such a way that their dealings go unchallenged. With their common love of secrecy, both Communists and capitalists will do everything possible to keep the details of their collaboration secret from the public. And the critical factor in this development is that this deliberate form of intimidation will only have any effect on our vulnerable democracies. The Soviets cancelled the BBC director-general Sir Charles Curran's visit to Moscow after British television had broadcast an interview with Solzhenitsyn. As the Communist leaders see it, the only way to preserve good relations with Great Britain or any other Western democracy is by suppressing any communications medium hostile to the USSR. Richard Davy, *Sunday Times* correspondent in Moscow, has pointed out that the Russians think that the Western media, like their own, should serve the politics of the age.

2.

Agnelli and the Communist Party

One August night a small group of men idly made their way across a deserted Rome to Castelporziano, the summer residence of the President of the Republic. There they intended to assume a mantle of power which appeared to have well and truly disintegrated already.

The politicians were then enjoying a holiday from the delights of the inter-party coalition game. But when they returned the conspirators planned to suspend parliamentary immunity and to send all left-wingers to concentration camps. In strict accordance with the tried and tested rules of the *Blitzkrieg* the *coup d'état* was to be quick and merciless. Colonel of the Carabiniere Salvatore Peccorella was to deal with the presidential guard, and a commando force armed with weapons with silencers was to wake the President. Giovanni Leone would then be forced at gunpoint to announce the dissolution of parliament, the resignation of the Rumor cabinet and the formation of a new military and technical government. To give this night-time raid some semblance of legality, the President would be told to state that he was "surrendering at the request of a qualified delegation of military men, senior civil servants and industrialists" who had "sworn to stand aside so that Italy could be saved from the self-destruction of its institutions." He was to be replaced by Randolfo Pacciardi, an old man of seventy-eight, who had previously led the Republican Party and held the post of Defense Minister. Pacciardi had also founded the "New Republic" party and had since 1943 been a creature of the Americans, working actively with the OSS.

The new government was to base its program on a few basic but fixed principles, the prevailing concept being that of a "strong régime." The military powers had to be recognized as the sole legitimate force until the crisis affecting the country had been dealt with. There would therefore have to be loyalty to the armed forces and recognition of their predominant role within the constitutional system. There would have to be one union, and the administration would have to be purged of dissidents. Further plans included outlawing all rightwing and leftwing extraparliamentary groups and arresting militants and ring-leaders to be sent to special camps. There would also be immediate trials for politicians convicted of breaking common law. The whole country would have to be galvanized to support these initiatives with civilians being organized into paramilitary groups as the need arose.

Despite financial backing from "international circles," this particular outbreak of blight came to the same kind of tragi-comic end as many an Italian comedy.

After two years, Luciano Violante, a judge from Turin with avowed Communist sympathies, had worked his way painstakingly through twenty-five files of evidence and uncovered the two men behind the abortive coup.

The political mastermind was the rather unstable Edgardo Sogno. Then sixty, the anti-Fascist Sogno was a former hero of the Resistance and leader of the Liberal Right, who had founded the anti-Communist Peace and Freedom movement in 1954. He had also been ambassador to Burma before being recalled by the then Prime Minister Aldo Moro who thought him "lacking the necessary resolution and prudence."

On his return to Italy, the apprentice *caudillo* became a minor fanatic, bombarding his former contacts in the business and political worlds with requests for help in establishing a Second Republic in Italy, in order to "defend democracy." Looking like a cross between Franco and Charlie Chaplin's dictator, Sogno had always been regarded as a reliable friend by the English and American secret services. He was on extremely close terms with John Volpe, former American ambassador in Rome who appears to have known all about his plans.

While Sogno belonged to the realms of wild obsession and political sectarianism, his accomplice Luigi Cavallo was little more than a professional provocateur. In 1944 the Americans began using their information services to develop a political and union-based anti-Communist strategy in Italy. They enlisted the help of a number of willing or frightened politicians who continued to reinforce these prefential links between their own parties and the US over the years.

Cavallo may have been only an accomplice but he soon proved to have enormous skill as a quick-change artiste. In 1944 he was working for Edward Philip Scicluna, a naturalized English Maltese, who dealt with union matters for the OSS within the new allied military administration set up in Piedmont at the time of the Liberation. Scicluna was also advising Fiat on union questions. Cavallo then managed to win the confidence of the Communists, became a Party member and even managed to be appointed *Unita*'s correspondent in Paris at the height of the cold war. When he was finally unmasked and expelled from the Party he went straight to work for colonel Cellerino, Fiat's head of security services. His new job was to strengthen the anti-union strategy instigated by Valetta, then regent of the firm, whose blatant Fascism had been conveniently overlooked by the Allies. Clare Booth Luce, American ambassador in Rome, regarded Valetta and Fiat policy as "a test of the methods to be used to contain the red peril."

As Cavallo appears to have seen it, the simplest way to do this was by creating commando forces to attack Communist workers and by making life very uncomfortable for anyone attempting to utter leftwing views within the firm.

In 1956 Cavallo became Turin organizer of Sogno's Peace and Freedom movement. From shortly after until Valetta's death, he directed *Tribune Ouvrière*, an expensive illustrated magazine full of overwhelmingly anti-union propaganda which was distributed to about 50,000 Fiat employees.

It would be wrong to suppose that the abortive *coup* mounted by Sogno and his pal was merely a pathetic move on the part of two anti-Communist crusaders clinging to their beliefs in a world of scepticism and irony. Behind them stretched a whole network of tacit complicity from every shade of the Italian political spectrum.

Financial backing came from the Industrial Union of Turin and the Neapolitan lawyer Antonio Lefevre, now fleeing prosecution for his activities as principal intermediary in the Lockheed bribery scandal. Lefevre had often played the middle-man. A few months before, he had helped the Fribourgs' powerful, East European-oriented American company, Continental, to sell 200 million lires worth of cereals to an Italian state company in extremely suspicious circumstances. Shortly afterwards he negotiated the building of a grain-carrying ship with Finmare, an IRI company, again on Continental's behalf. The president of Finmare, Camillo Crociani just happened to be the other Lockheed defendant who also indulged in the delights of Vodka-Giani.

On 12 May 1976, Sogno and Cavallo were arrested. That evening, Giovanni Agnelli's private jet landed at Rome airport from Athens. The Fiat boss was greeted by the little judge, Luciano Violante, and by an unusually large contingent of policemen "in case he was attacked." Throughout his investigations Violante had been turning up evidence of Fiat influence and involvement in the case, even of Fiat empire methods.

Just before the presidential elections in 1971, the Agnelli Foundation had published a study entitled "Five by Five." This two-tier document saw an immediate need for a power group to be set up so that a strong President might be elected. In the longer term, it would be necessary to work out some political and philosophical basis for the establishment of a Second Republic. This new form of government was to be presidential on the surface, although the real political power would be concentrated in the hands of the business managers, the military and civil services. Urbaldo Scassellati, the author of "Five by Five," was a Catholic traditionalist, connected with the right wing of the Christian Democrat Party and general secretary of the foundation. He was also a much-heeded adviser to Giovanni's younger brother, Umberto Agnelli, appointed managing director of Fiat in 1971.

Vittorio Chiusano, Scassellati's predecessor, had also worked on the project in the initial stages. A member of the directorial old guard formed during the reign of Valetta and on close terms with Amintore Fanfani, Chiusano held two key posts, as secretary to the Fiat board and manager of the firm's external relations. It was he who was responsible for all contact with the political forces and the press. He was also political adviser to the two Agnelli brothers and always regarded the foundation as a vital socio-cultural instrument.

This institution had been opened on 6 December 1966 by the newly appointed Fiat director Giovanni Agnelli who had an abiding enthusiasm for the "model company." He hoped to use the foundation as a means of achieving "the most far-reaching integration between political, military and economic powers and scientific research" along the lines of the American foundations.

There were frequent "cultural trips" to the United States. Flanked by Chiusano and Scassellati, Agnelli visited the best known of the US research centers and think-tanks. He was especially interested in the work on conditioning and the social research undertaken by the American army, the State Department and the CIA. But despite, or perhaps because of, its attempts to model itself on the American pattern, the foundation never managed to achieve its end of finding a sociological justification for the industrial activities of the group.

Chiusano provided judge Violante with an important lead in his case. A faithful and over-zealous employee, he appeared to be taking up the traditionalist's view against his bosses' progressive attempts to follow the general trends of an open society in the hope of influencing them. In his nostalgia for the days when a certificate of baptism was one of the prerequisites for a job with Fiat, Chiusano belonged very much to the Valetta school; though, to be fair, this approach had been warmly welcomed by Agnelli.

Chiusano was much in favour and many of his arguments were undoubtedly well received by Agnelli, who then appeared to be arguing the progressive's case. Above all, Chiusano was quite well acquainted with Sogno and Cavallo and shared their "dyed in the wool" views on the decline of the West.

Between 1971 and 1975 the two conspirators received the bulk of their financial support from Fiat. In his search for subsidy Sogno could count on Liberal senator Manlio Brosio to put in a good word for him to Chiusano. During those four years of enlightened despotism, Chiusano transferred 400 million lire from the firm's special funds, which he handled, to the two conspirators. At regular intervals Sogno used to trot innocently along to the Turin Credit Bank to deposit his checks from Fiat central funds.

When Violante asked him about this at Fumicino Airport, a relaxed Agnelli confirmed that it was true, but added "That money was used exclusively to finance the

Liberal Party which had been founded by Sogno, and the funds were transferred quite independently by Chiusano."

However, when further enquiries were made of Giovanni Malagodi and Augusto Bignardi, president and secretary general of the Liberal Party respectively, a very different picture emerged. The two men were amazed.

"The party has never received a penny from Sogno. On the contrary, he owes us 100,000 lire."

From 1970 to the end of 1974, Fiat continued to pay Cavallo's salary. In 1971 he directed a broadsheet entitled "Initiatives Syndicales," printing the names and first names of the "most criminal" trades unionists and suggesting that the workers should lynch them.

In the autumn of that year, he brought about a merger of the Turin federation of the neo-Fascist MSI movement and an employment office working for Fiat. However strange the contrast between Agnelli's deliberately Democratic and leftwing exterior and Cavallo's obsession for denunciation, the Fiat board must have known about what he was doing.

In fact, judge Violante's unexpected attack on the figure unanimously regarded as the strong man of Italy was part of a whole CP strategy. Obviously there was no question of arresting Agnelli, merely of compromising him. This was the pre-electoral period and his younger brother, Umberto, had declared his intention of standing as a candidate for the new-look Christian Democrat Party. The Communists were extremely anxious to avoid the majority Catholic Party undergoing a revival or swinging, however superficially, to the left. They feared that once the old pawns had gone, the Christian Democrats might look much more attractive to a fickle electorate. Since Umberto was a symbol of this new life-blood, involving his brother in the Sogno–Cavallo scandal was a means of checking any such development. Worried by a possible loss of credibility, Giovanni Agnelli was aware of the implications. He banished Chiusano to Paris to direct Fiat France and began to recruit new, younger managers. He also bought himself some expert help in the shape of blue chip investments like former Finance Minister Bruno Visentini who had been president of Olivetti and vice-president of the state-owned IRI group, and Guido Carli. The announcement that the former governor of the Bank of Italy, a symbol of public service and stalwart resistance to the power of money, had actually joined the Fiat empire came as a shock to the Italian powers.

Giovanni Agnelli was engaged in a crucial two-tier operation, which was attentively followed by his fellow industrialists Leopold Pirelli, the Buitoni brothers, Guiseppe Pellicano, director of the Swiss Brown Boveri group and Roberto Olivetti.

Italy is one of those countries where efficient management requires a politician's temperament. With the whole parliamentary system and the center–left coalition threatened, Agnelli realized that, paradoxically, the capitalist system could only survive if the Communist Party came to power.

He also shared his friend David Rockefeller's views on the necessity of world government and thought that Enrico Berlinguer's party was large enough to make Italy the first Western bridgehead in the process of integrating the Communist élites into capitalism.

At the same time, and with Carli's help, Agnelli the "attorney," as some commentators called him, was reorienting the activities of his group and packing his bags to leave Italy. The Italian miracle worker of the sixties was no longer the pin-up of the Overworld media. For some years, the man who symbolized industrial vigour in Italy had been diversifying and multinationalizing, abandoning his bases in Milan and Turin for the Eastern European markets and a firm foothold in the United States. And all this had been done with the blessing of the CP which stood to benefit directly from this new commercial policy.

With 71% of Italian light automobile production and 94% of truck registration already under its belt, Fiat could not afford to rely on expansion in the automobile market.

At the present time, Fiat, together with its factories abroad and its subcontracting firms, produces 2 million automobiles a year and has a labour force of 450,000. It has 100% control of Lancia, 50% of Ferrari, 40% of the French truck manufacturer Unic and its German opposite number Magirus Deutz. It is estimated that a total of 2.5 million people, i.e. 13% of the Italian working population, are working directly or indirectly for the Agnelli group. No other private organization in our industrialized societies appears to enjoy such relative power.

The company makes no concessions to morality. It produces 200,000 automobiles a year in Brazil and 400,000 in Spain, through its 37% share in SEAT. But it also has production lines in Poland (160,000 automobiles annually) and in the USSR, notably at its giant Togliattigrad complex, which produces nearly 700,000 "Ladas" (a copy of the Fiat 124) every year.

That Fiat represents 230 companies scattered around the world makes little difference, the real financial strength of the Agnelli group is a masterly example of fiscal imbroglio. All the capital of IHF (International Holding Fiat), for example, which is based at Lugano in Switzerland, belongs entirely to the Agnelli family.

But the Agnellis have manipulated their personal fortune in an even more cynical way. Since 1968–1970, the family has deliberately moved its patrimony to the United States via Luxemburg, while continuing to step up its cooperation with the CP in Italy. This transfer of wealth was organized by an expert, Gian Luigi Gabetti, former managing director of Olivetti–Underwood in the United States. Gabetti was assisted by Agnelli's private lawyer, Pasquale Chiomenti, now being sought to face charges of fraud.

In 1970 a company called IMO (Investment Immobiliere) with $500,000 capital was set up in Luxemburg, the tax haven in the heart of the EEC. In 1972 IMO changed its name to IFI International which was quoted on the Luxemburg stock exchange as having $65 million capital. The holding company held 80% of the shares, the remaining 20% being distributed between various reliable banks like Lazard Frères, the Warburg, the Lambert Bank of Brussels and the Chase Manhattan. With all the shares belonging to the Agnellis, the family can retain a 26% control of Fiat Automobile and therefore of IHF. Naturally enough, none of the tax restrictions to which Fiat employees are subject apply here. Then there is IFI Turin, the largest Italian shareholder in Fiat, which also owns an 11.5% share in Rinascente department stores, 15.3% in Fabbri editions, the Juventus Football Club of Turin and the big daily *La Stampa*, as well as various other publications, including *Playboy Italiano*. IFI Turin's 48 billion lire share capital is divided into ordinary shares, all held by the Agnelli family, and preference shares, posted on the stock exchange. In 1973 Fiat offered its shareholders a farcical dividend of 30 lire for every three shares, on the grounds of circumstantial difficulties and losses suffered by the group.

In July 1973 the second phase of the operation began. The basic idea was that IFI should become completely independent. It was therefore proposed that one IFI International share should be exchanged for twenty-five IFI Italy shares. In 1974 there was a repeat offer of one IFI International share for fifty IFI Italy shares; and finally, in October 1975, one IFI International share for thirty IFI Italy shares.

Total separation of the two financial membranes was completed by an increase in IFI

International's capital which rose in three stages from $65 million to $82 million to $94 million to $175 million. Finally, Agnelli family control over IFI Italy dropped from 80% to 46%, but this was a totally meaningless tactical withdrawal since real power had now moved to Luxemburg.

The Agnelli family had broken all previous records and scaled the heights of immorality. Carlo Dona Cattin, the leftwing Christian Democrat Minister of Industry had already foretold this eventuality a year earlier, when complaining that the Agnellis were "about to own a finance company, in a tax haven, with capital greater than that of Fiat." The assets held by IFI International amounted to over $300 million, half in bearer shares and half in ordinary shares. The building sector alone accounted for $134 million, with the two principal investments being Corporate Property Investors, a company dealing mainly with tenement building and shopping centers, and Blackwell Land which owns 10,000 hectares of arable land, chiefly in Arkansas. But IFI International also has interests in Eurafranc, a French holding with insurance interests, and Euralux, a European finance company specializing in construction with assets in both Germany and France. It is through Euralux that the Agnelli family has come to own important property in Paris. IFI has holdings in Bantham Books, the powerful American publishing house and vast property holdings in the US as well as in Cinzano and, following an agreement with Edmond de Rothschild, in the Club Méditerranée. In Latin America Fiat's industrial empire is expanding rapidly, notably in Brazil and Chile, and in Quebec it is already one of the largest property-owners and primary building contractors for the provincial government.

At the same time, "Giani" Agnelli was been working with Gabetti to sell off various sectors, including the 19% of ordinary shares and 26% of preference shares IFI previously owned in RIV–SKF, the largest Italian ball-bearing manufacturer which were bought back by the Swedish SKF group.

For a dreamer like Agnelli, this marked the end of a page of history. It had been by selling some of the RIV shares in 1965 that Agnelli had finally removed the old autocrat, Valetta. RIV was part of the Agnelli brothers' personal inheritance. As a result of the deal with the Swedish company, Giovanni and Umberto had been able to appreciably increase their package of Fiat shares and force Mussolini's former adviser to go.

In July 1976, a month after the elections, Giovanni Agnelli sold 52% of his shares in the shaky-looking SAI insurance company which had recorded losses of 50 billion lire for 1975. Rafaele Ursini, who bought them, was vice-president and managing director of the Liquigaz group, which has 36.3% control of the American Ronson group and 35% of the once Vatican-owned Ceramica Pozzi. More importantly, Ursini had been protected by Vincenzo Gazzaniga, nicknamed "the Cardinal" and former boss of Esso Italy, who was involved in various corruption and bribery scandals. During his years as president of the Italian oil consortium, Gazzaniga had financed various political parties, and had helped the CP especially by buying full-page advertisements in its daily newspaper, *Paese Sera*. Ursini had also partnered Sindona in the US and had obtained numerous services from the latter's finance bank in Geneva.

A successful career often depends on whatever image the public chooses to give you. Agnelli's right arm, Guido Carli, for example, has always been the enigma of the financial gossip columns, the intransigent man, the man whose sixteen-year struggle as governor of the Bank of Italy almost saved the lire. After a discreet career in the public service, Carli took on a totally different role in the private sector on 4 December 1974.

Following a meeting of the Fiat board, the ex-governor of the central bank found himself in charge of a financial holding called Impresit based in Holland. Officially Carli was to ensure the construction and installation of hydro-electric, thermo-nuclear and electro-nuclear power stations, motorways, airports and harbour stations in countries outside Italy. In fact Impresit was using Carli's experience of financial markets and money management expertise to practise a policy of large-scale tax evasion; plans were afoot to open a branch in Curacao, the West Indian tax haven. Agnelli was also using his Arab contacts to involve Impresit in recycling the petrodollar. Despite the fact that his son-in-law was a self-confessed Zionist, he managed to swing deals of this kind with those most revolutionary of the Arab states, Libya and Algeria. Agnelli and Carli also drafted a financial scheme to form a single holding company, which would unite Impresit, ITAS (another member of the Fiat group), and—amazingly—Generale Immobiliare.

At this point, the story becomes rather disquieting, and Sindona's statements acquire a whole new significance. It was Carli who destroyed the Sicilian's financial empire and forced him to abandon his finest creations, including the construction company which was bought by a group representing both Agnelli and CP interests. With hindsight, what appeared then as a clumsy, if well-intentioned, initiative looks much more like a deliberate conspiracy today. Moreover, in April 1976, Carli received his first introduction to the comforts of the international banking boards with his appointment to the foreign consultative committee of the giant Chemical Bank, a US Rockefeller establishment. His fellow committee members included George Ball, director of Lehmann Brothers, and, like Agnelli, a member of the Trilateral, who worked as foreign policy adviser to Jimmy Carter. Throughout the American electoral campaign Ball had continued to reassure the Italian communists that the Democratic candidate and his entourage were well disposed towards them. Shortly afterwards, Carli became financial consultant to the First Boston Corporation of New York, which handles the sale of Chase Manhattan shares to the public. Through the First Boston, the Rockefellers exert considerable influence over two vital organs of the American media, the *New York Times* and the CBS Television Network, both of which were to play an important part in the Italian operation.

Carli was also on close terms with the directors of the Bank of America, one of whose branches, la Banca di America e Italia, is the biggest commercial bank in Italy outside the public sector. All these establishments are firm followers of Vodka-Cola strategy. So, we can see a two-faced shadow cabinet emerging in opposition to the empty Italian government, the one face represented by the Communists and the other by Agnelli and his right arm, Guido Carli. Carli, whom Agnelli had appointed head of Confindustria, the Italian employers' association, in 1976, was to deal with integration between Agnelli's group, Italian financial circles and the American Vodka-Cola camp. Agnelli would be dealing with the political matter of cooperation between the multinational capitalists and Berlinguer's party. Vodka-Cola-Italiana.

The fact that all the prevailing economic and spiritual forces in Italy are following, willingly or otherwise, in his wake, makes the way ahead even easier for Agnelli. There is no longer any distinction between the public and private sectors. At the present time Montedison and IRI hold shares in Agnelli, and vice versa. The various elements of the financial web completely overlap. Moreover, by replacing Sindona, Agnelli has become official financier adviser to the Vatican, which has interests in both Fiat and Montedison. None of the Vatican men are taken in when Berlinguer reaffirms his "respect for all the democratic rights and for individual and social liberties, including religious freedom."

All Agnelli has to do is banish this thimbleful of diehards from active politics. During the months leading up to the legislative elections, Agnelli's press blatantly concentrated its attacks on the right wing of the Christian Democrat Party, emphasizing its corruptability and incompetence. Whilst eliminating his former allies, Agnelli was also broadening his strategy of monetary manipulation. In 1975 he created another financial holding in Holland, Iveco of Amsterdam.

One of Iveco's major concerns is the Fiat–Allis company, also based in Amsterdam, which has given the Italian financier a foothold in the American market for cranes, tractors, bull-dozers, generators, pumps and turbines. In 1974, Fiat acquired a 65% share in the US firm Allis Chalmers, and Giovanni Agnelli became president of the company. By the end of that year, the Fiat–Allis factories had produced 13,476 units with a value of $598.5 million. This made Fiat–Allis third largest earth-moving equipment manufacturer in the world, alongside International Harvester and John Deere, the numbers one and two being the American Caterpillar Company and the Japanese Kamatsu.

At the same time, Agnelli was developing the arms production sector of Fiat, which is one of the largest contractors to NATO. In 1975, this gun trading accounted for over one tenth of the income of the whole group, and since that total amounted to 3,893 million lire, we have yet another clear indication of Fiat's hold on Italian life. The arms sector had originally been set up by Valetta, who immediately won unconditional collaboration from SIFAR, the Italian counter-espionage agency. Some years later, the symbiosis between the two was institutionalized with the creation of the REI (Economic and Industrial Research). Valetta appointed one of his trusted friends, Renzo Rocca, head of REI and set him up in a Fiat-owned apartment in the via Barberini. This gave the firm's directors a means of bringing pressure to bear on public authorities, and access to the most compromising and confidential information. Rocca died mysteriously in 1968.

Shortly afterwards, general Giovanni Allovena resigned his post as head of SIFAR and entered Fiat as a concessionary. Allovena had drawn up a detailed card index on thousands of journalists, priests, trade unionists and politicians with progressive views. He also had very close connections with neo-Fascist circles, and in late 1969 he set up the Committee for the Election of Richard Nixon, which won support from Agnelli.

Agnelli's links with the secret services and the military chiefs have given Fiat the opportunity to market an extremely wide range of material. In 1969 it offered the Ministry of the Interior an armoured car equipped with gas grenades and machine guns. This vehicle had been designed for the maintenance of public order and was described for publicity purposes as "usable in towns for street demonstrations."

Fiat has total control of Whitehead Motorfides, a firm specializing in the manufacture of mines and torpedoes. It also supplies engines, drive belts and suspension systems for the German "leopard" tanks which are fitted with nuclear weapons, and sells the F 104 Starfighter in Italy. Its aviation sector, Finora, has manufactured 170 types of machine, and sold 500 of its most popular model, the Fiat G.91, to NATO, Israel, South Africa and Portugal (for its colonial wars).

Since 1968 Fiat has been involved in the MRCA program for the construction of a European combat plane in collaboration with the United States. In this area it has been working with Aeritalia, an IRI company directly controlled by Finmeccanico, whose boss, Camillo Crociani, is on good terms with the Italian CP. Through Selenia, another IRI company in which it also has a share, Fiat supplies radar detection equipment for aeroplanes, missiles and land and sea firing systems.

Agnelli also maintains his preferential relations with the military by regularly employing the services of a certain number of big guns.

In August 1976, the economic daily paper *Il Fiorino*, which had once been linked with Sindona, drew up a balance sheet of Russo–Italian economic cooperation. It took as an example the medium-sized venture Coe e Clerici, which had succeeded, by its own efforts, in raising the value of its deals with the Soviets from $760,000 to $150 million in the space of fifteen years. What the article failed to mention was that the enterprise belonged to Ugno Rattazi, husband of Susanna Agnelli, who, together with her two brothers, played an active part in the management of the family patrimony.

Indeed, the Agnellis have their moments of staggering false modesty. They are able at one and the same time to arm our Western defenses with their weapons, to lead Italian investment in the totalitarian states of the East and to create huge numbers of unemployed, all without provoking any comment whatever from the unions or the Communist Party.

There are times, however, when Agnelli sets himself up as a severe critic of the unfair competition practised by the state-owned companies which he considers to be "cheating" in the free competition game by receiving public subsidies. This is an interesting approach, in view of the fact that Italy is unanimously regarded by the international community as financially insolvent, socially unstable and economically on the brink of chaos. Even so, the big banking houses, headed by a consortium of the Chase Manhattan and the First National, are increasing their credit facilities and long-term loans. This philanthropy must be contagious, since the Italian state, itself on the edge of bankruptcy, has been granting large loans to the USSR. And who benefits? Energetic Giovanni Agnelli, for these loans enable him to finance the construction of his factories in Poland, Hungary and the USSR. Agnelli's activities in this area demonstrate two of the advantages of multinationalization:

1. the opportunity to find backing for his extremely profitable financial policy from private banks and state credits;

2. the means to overtly defraud the national tax collector by sending profits earned abroad to the tax havens rather than to Italy.

Italy and Agnelli have always been front-runners in the policy of extending credit to the East. In 1961, when most of the Western countries were cautiously taking up their "wait and see" positions against the Communist world, the Rome government granted the USSR $100 million credit, an extremely high figure in Italian terms.

Five years later, Italy financed the giant 700,000-automobile Fiat factory at Togliattigrad with further credit of $363 million to be repaid over fourteen years.

In July 1974 the Chase Manhattan Bank and the First National City Bank granted $790 million and $637 million respectively to an Italy generally regarded as on the brink of Communist domination. For a couple of shrewd financiers like David Rockefeller and Arthur Wriston, this might seem a strangely inconsistent move were it not for the fact that like their comrades in the Bildeberg, the Trilateral and the Council on Foreign Relations, they were fervently hoping that the political presence of the Communist Party would be a moderating factor.

To return to Agnelli, however, he appears to have made his final exit from the long dark tunnel of the Italian economy by way of the Libyan oil wells.

On 1 December 1976, backed by their two financial experts, Cesare Romiti and Gian Luigi Gabetti, the brothers Giovanni and Umberto announced their plans to the press at Turin. Their new scheme was the result of eighteen months of secret negotiations and the most brilliant means yet conceived by the Italian Vodka-Colanizers of extricating themselves fully and painlessly from the Italian mudbath.

Agnelli had had to find the best way of withdrawing from the automobile sector, which was still a source of chancy profits and social headaches. With the Italian state so much in the red that it could not even begin to offer compensation for nationalization, the only hope was the petrodollar. Former governor of the Bank of Italy Guido Carli, then working for Agnelli at the head of the Impresit Construction Co., confirmed as much. He had negotiated several important agreements with the Libyans and they appeared to be attracted towards their old Italian colonialists, who were still their number one trading partners. It would be a sweet revenge for the nationalist leader Kadhafi to appropriate whole areas of an Italian economy, shaky as it was.

In June 1975, Agnelli had gone to Moscow, apparently on a routine visit to talk to German Vishiani about increasing production at Togliattigrad from 700,000 to 1 million vehicles a year. But, more importantly, he had met an emissary from Kadhafi who was a member of the Libyan revolutionary council and a director of the Libyan Arab Bank. Agnelli was accompanied by the business lawyer Sargent Shriver, Kennedy's brother-in-law and ex-American ambassador to Paris, who directed the Kaplan Fund, a foundation identified as working with the CIA. Throughout the subsequent negotiations Agnelli was supported by the Italian CP's principal intermediary for trade operations with the East, Savoretti. Here, too, Rome was proving to be an experimental laboratory for the Vodka-Colanizers in their attempts to graft two apparently disparate elements together. On the one side there was the tired, political, economic and social fabric of Italy with its old traditions; on the other, the incoherent and power-hungry Libyan leader with his revolutionary speeches, his strict adherence to the Koran, his subsidies to the terrorists and his surplus petrodollars.

The Italian Communist Party enthused over the project from the outset. Not only did it strengthen the Party's political penetration of the industrial establishment through active involvement in major triangular projects, but the Party stood to benefit financially.

The ICP was the only political Party with which Agnelli discussed the project before initiating contacts with Kadhafi. Agnelli, in fact, had secret discussions with Sergio Segre, the Party's Foreign Minister, and it was subsequently a mission of the ICP which journeyed to Tripoli on Agnelli's and FIAT's behalf to open negotiations with Kadhafi. Commercially the ICP benefited in two ways: one, from a percentage of the bilateral deal with the USSR, and two, from a Libyan concession to a trading company of the Party for exclusive imports of a series of Italian products. Under such circumstances, Agnelli has little fear of being attacked or exposed in regard to his "arriverderci Italia" protected as he is by his Communist Party partner against any leftist attacks.

Agnelli had come up against the same problem as all the top men of Italian industry from Cefis of Montedison to Pirelli and Buitoni: namely, where to find the necessary credits to speed up their advance and integration into the East. The Russians would agree to increase capacity and production at their Fiat factories, but only in exchange for investment credits at an extremely low rate of interest. There was no point in looking to an Italian government which was itself drawing on credit lines and sending President of the Council Andreotti on frequent visits to Washington. In any case, a public which had been subjected to austerity measures would never agree to the capitalist superman Agnelli being granted subsidies so that he could go and build an exact replica of his Piedmont factories on the banks of the Don.

Only Kadhafi, with his 2 million inhabitants and his $10 billion a year in oil revenue, was in a position to back the application of any such scheme.

The negotiations started. The chief Libyan representative, Prime Minister Ahmed Jalloud, Kadhafi's "companion in the revolution," was assisted by the governor of the Libyan central bank. Their opposite numbers were the English representatives of the Franco–American Lazard Frères Bank, which handles the personal interests of the Agnelli family.

With exemplary coolheadedness, a financial establishment whose directors are self-declared and militant Zionists was negotiating with the Arab state most fiercely opposed to Israel's existence.

Carli favoured a speedy decision. The Soviets would be quite prepared to accept any agreement which would tie the USSR closer to the Libyan leader at a time when the Russians were losing ground in the Middle East.

Prime Minister of Malta, Dom Mintoff offered his services. He had links with Gabetti, the boss of the Italian cooperative Communist league.

But nothing positive came of this initiative. Tensions within the Fiat board exacerbated. To give himself more time for his political scheming, Agnelli had appointed a college friend of his younger brother Umberto and Turin industrialist, Benedetti, to head the automobile group. This young and dynamic figure was closely linked with pro-Israeli business circles and had rejected the Kadhafi plan out of hand when it was first mooted among the directors. A month later he resigned, without giving any explanation.

By the end of 1976 it had been agreed that Fiat was to extend the USSR $415 million credit by way of Libya, to be spent on increasing production at the Fiat factories in Russia making the 124 and 127 models. The interest rate on repayments was a ridiculous 5%.

Moreover, as Agnelli was departing over the Italian border, Kadhafi was passing him on the way in to occupy the remains of what had been a traditional-type economic empire so shortly before. Agnelli had sold a 10% share in Fiat to the Libyans for $410 million, of which 180 million went to buy 30 million new Fiat stocks from Agnelli's private holding.

This deal was far more than a simple case of technical and financial acquisition. Control of Fiat meant a major political influence. The Libyans had bought much more than a 10% interest. They were now entitled to one place on the directorial board and to two places on the five-man managerial committee which was responsible for all decision making. Considering that two of these five members were the Agnelli brothers, we have a clear idea of how much power and influence was coming to the Arab directors.

Some days before the agreement was announced, Ted Kennedy arrived in Rome where he stayed with Agnelli and met Sergio Segre and Pajetta of the Italian CP. Jimmy Carter had sent him with a message of appeasement to the Communist leaders, but also to find out how the Fiat–Libya negotiations were going. On 30 November 1976, the day before the contract was announced, David Rockefeller himself dined in Turin with Agnelli who had just returned from a Moscow meeting with Kadhafi, in Russia on an official visit. The Libyans had reached a secret agreement with Brezhnev, providing among other things for:

1. Complete rearmament of the Libyan army by the Soviets.

2. Immediate delivery of sixty SAM 2 and 6 missiles, twenty patrolling planes armed with missiles and 300 T 62 tanks to add to the 700 already delivered.

3. The purchase of seventy-five Mig 23s and twelve reconnaissance aircraft.

4. Expert Soviet guidance in reorganizing the Libyan army and increasing manpower from 22,000 to 30,000 soldiers and from 2,000 to 4,000 marines.

5. Harbour facilities for the Russian Mediterranean fleet and construction of safe anchorage.

Libya was to provide all the finance. So, while promoting the Soviet military presence in North Africa, Kadhafi was at the same time becoming one of NATO's chief manufacturers of military equipment through his involvement in Fiat.

The Soviet–Agnelli agreement dealt with various sectors. It was decided, for example, that Allis Chalmers (a 100% Fiat group) and the Soviet Ceboksalg should build a giant complex on the Volga for manufacturing earth-moving equipment, from diesel tractors to scoops and bull-dozers. The planners are hoping that an initial output of 5,000 units a year will soon be stepped up to 100,000 with 50% of this earmarked for export. Part of production will go to pay back Agnelli and Kadhafi.

Agnelli does not have to worry about abandoning Italy to his Communist partners and to future under-employment. He now has a worldwide chain of solidarity behind him, from Kadhafi and Brezhnev to Tito, Boumedienne, Gierek, Kadar, Ceausescu, Geisel and Pinochet.

As far as the Libyans are concerned, this deal has given them a fine introduction to international realities. The Arab Libyan Bank has also acquired an interest in the Fiat holding Impresit, in order to finance a number of projects in "racist and colonialist" South Africa.

3.

The Vodka-Espresso Operation

When he arrived in Moscow on 15 July 1975, at the head of a Party delegation, Gian Carlo Pajetta, the historic leader of Italian Communism, was greeted with a ritual 21-gun salute. But this ideological homage did not cover the rift between the Soviet Politburo and the Berlinguer group. Constantin Zaradov who was covering the visit for *Pravda* that day, began his article with a confused interpretation of a text by Lenin and ended it with a veiled, but severe, condemnation of the line of "historic compromise" being followed by the Rome Communists. Western governments and editorial offices were only too delighted with this flimsy broadside. Reading between the lines, every paragraph betrayed Brezhnev's further exasperation with the "original and independent experiment" being conducted by the champions of Eurocommunism.

A month earlier, the Party had made unmistakeable progress in the municipal elections and was increasingly emerging as a responsible body capable of administering local councils and governing regions. With no obvious successor to take the reins from the dying Italian body politic, and the country being torn apart by scandal, the Communists were conspicuous for their honesty and competence. Although its membership covers a wide range of social strata, the Italian Communist Party, or CPI, has never been a working-class party. Rather it is evidence of Western progressive intellectuals' curious leanings towards totalitarianism. In 1922, the English socialist writer H. G. Wells hailed the arrival of Mussolini as a man able "to instil the necessary discipline in such a corrupt country," while the liberal English Sunday *Observer*, now owned by the American Richfield Oil Company and Robert Anderson, admiringly described the dictator as a "human volcano." Even Churchill, addressing a delegation of Italian Fascists, said "If I was Italian, I would have been on your side from the beginning."

It would be interesting to study the myth of "political hygiene" as practised by the Western intelligentsia.

Be that as it may, this unconditional support for a politically acceptable and morally justified CP formed an appreciable part of Vodka-Cola strategy.

While Pajetta and his delegation were playing their walk-on parts in the Kremlin, two of the real actors in the drama, Zygmunt Nagorsky and Sergio Segre, were meeting in absolute secrecy at the Rockefeller Foundation-owned villa Serbelloni, near Bellagio on the shores of Lake Como. A former diplomat, Nagorsky was a high-ranking member of the powerful Council on Foreign Relations. As a specialist in Soviet–American problems, he had published a book entitled *Psychology of East–West Trade*, which laid stress on the vital convergence of interests between the Party chiefs in Moscow and the holders of real power in the West. Over the previous two years the CFR had devoted most of its working hypotheses to Italy. It seemed possible that any progress made by a "reformist" Communist Party might provide a factor of stability in this politically ungovernable country. This advance would also be basic to the strategy of economic cooperation and social control to be evolved in a preferential partnership with Giovanni Agnelli.

Sergio Segre arrived a little late that morning. He had just returned from East Berlin where he had been attending a preparatory meeting for the next summit of European Communist Parties. A fifty-year-old from Turin, Segre was the Italian CP's spokesman on foreign policy, a member of the central committee and a deputy since 1972. His stiff and formal appearance belied his inner tactical flexibility. He is said to have done more than anyone else to convince the leaders in East Berlin that they should support the *Ostpolitik* developed by that European champion of détente, Willy Brandt.

The project Nagorsky and Segre had come to discuss was the simple but explosive idea that the CFR should invite Segre to the United States. There he would be able to speak at various conferences and take part in debates, but his main objective would be to sell the American public the image of the "good" Communist on a semi-official visit to the US. Up until then Washington had always refused to grant official visas to leaders of Marxist parties. The Vodka-Colanizers then hoped to capitalize on Segre's trail-blazing visit by arranging a widely publicized trip to America by Berlinguer himself in the autumn. Berlinguer was to sell himself as the leader of a European Party which was "neither anti-Soviet nor anti-American." Such a declaration of proud, tactical independence and good neighbourliness would be bound to win open approval and clear away the last barriers to acceptance.

Detailed preparations for this influx of Italian Marxists had been underway since 1974. David Rockefeller's trusted adviser, Zbigniew Brzezinski, at that point still a non-political figure, had been working on the problem with support from the official Republican trio of Kissinger, Nelson Rockefeller and Ford. Now Carter's foreign policy adviser and Kissinger's successor on the National Security Council, Brzezinski was then director of the Trilateral Commission and making frequent trips to Rome.

The Trilateral Commission had its own mail box in Rome at the Instituto Affari Internazionali, 88 viale Mazzini. The chairman of the IAI, Altiero Spinelli, was a member of the Commission of European Communities, though he resigned in 1976 to stand in the parliamentary elections as a Communist; for in its apparently legalistic way, the CPI is prepared to tap out its message through all the existing institutional channels. When elections for the European Parliament are held in 1979, Berlinguer and the French CP leader Marchais are hoping to muscle their way into a supra-national capitalist organization which they have been happy enough to condemn until now, and which they would like to control themselves.

In November 1974, Brzezinski went to Rome for a conference on the future of American politics, but, more importantly, for two meetings with Segre arranged by Spinelli's institute. He also went to see Agnelli, a European member of the Trilateral, in his apartment a hundred yards or so from the Quirinal Palace. The Fiat directors have long maintained excellent relations with the men of the via delle Bottege Oscure. The Communist local government in Turin has been even more tolerant towards the firm than the previous Christian Democrat council was, despite the fact that the living standards of the working classes in Turin are among the worst in Italy. There is even a representative of the Fiat management on the town council.

Agnelli agreed to the choice of Segre, but thought that the delegation going to the US should be padded out, even if the star part went to Segre. The Communist leader must not look like a solitary figure brought over as part of a propaganda operation, but appear to be a representative of a *bona fide* political party surrounded by representatives from other democratic parties chosen from the whole Italian political spectrum, regardless of whether his political views differed from theirs or not. The only point on which the discussion came to grief was over the public role to be allotted to Agnelli. "Giani" hoped to join the delegation, and thereby plant the idea that Italy's future was dependent on the Agnelli–CPI diarchy. Brzezinski respectfully expressed some reservations about this view. As he saw it, any complicity between the Communists and their class enemy should be kept well hidden.

Some weeks later, when Andrei Gromyko was in Rome on an official visit, the Soviet ambassador to Italy arranged for him to meet Giovanni Agnelli, Sergio Segre, Petro Ingrao, the leader of the CPI left wing who was elected President of the Chamber of Deputies in 1976, Alberto Carpanna, one of the IRI bosses and Mgr Casaroli, the Vatican Minister for Foreign Affairs.

Two months later, Agnelli and Gromyko sailed out of Odessa on board the *Pushkin*, a pleasure cruiser kept for distinguished visitors. The Communist leader was delighted with Agnelli's pragmatic attitude. During initial conversations about the Italian situation, the Fiat boss expressed his view that the Christian Democrats were now a totally discredited political power and beyond reform. According to observers, Agnelli's attitude to his former allies struck Gromyko as very harsh. Their conversation then turned to Europe, to which Italy, somewhat ironically, had adopted a "Gaullist" posture, on the grounds that the formula of "Europe from the Atlantic to the Urals" was a judicious line to take.

Finally the two men exchanged a few remarks about Kissinger, whom they both knew well. The Soviet minister appeared slightly bitter. He regretted that the Secretary of State had not supported the policy of détente more vigorously and that he had merely described the Italian Communists' electoral victories as "an advance of anti-democratic forces which had to be taken into account." Gromyko thought this statement highly ambiguous and had come increasingly to the view that Kissinger was being blocked by a minority within the State Department opposed to the policy of cooperation with the East. That apart, when Agnelli returned to Milan it was with full support from the Soviet Communist hierarchy for a publicity campaign based on images such as: "Sit down to a plateful of spaghetti with a Communist and you'll see he no longer has a knife between his teeth"; or "They're really ravioli revolutionaries, much more capitalist pasta than revolutionary meat."

Within the party leadership things were more difficult. Berlinguer and Segre had to face active opposition from the fiercely Stalinist minority represented by Armando Cosutta, Gian Carlo Pajetta and even Napolitano, all of them members of the policy bureau. None of them had given any more than lip service to the form and content of the historic compromise. Berlinguer was well aware that he was gambling his political future on whether some unforeseen circumstance would threaten the new détente and Vodka-Cola strategy on an international level. For then his own situation would be shaky. He even knew that Moscow wished him to be replaced by Armando Cosutta, the CPI's manager of capitalist companies trading with the East. Cosutta was a party man totally trusted by the Kremlin, which when Berlinguer had been ousted would resume its previous strict orthodoxy and happily cast aspersions on any moves towards Eurocommunism, which it now condones despite appearances. On 20 May 1975, Segre received a letter at Party headquarters from the Council on Foreign Relations with detailed information about the arrangements for his American trip on 24–26 October that year. He was to have meetings with David Rockefeller, George Ball, Luigi Einaudi, a specialist in Italian affairs for the Rand Corporation, and several senators and members of the Trilateral Commission, including Jimmy Carter. On 25 and 26 October, he was to join in discussions on the following themes: the reasons for the change in Euro–American relations (political and strategic aspects); American involvement abroad and the political situation and development of political powers in Italy.

Several CPI experts began doing their homework on Segre's speeches.

For their part, Agnelli and Brzezinski had been drawing up a list of possible Italian delegates, which included Oddo Biasini, secretary of the Republican Party, Pietro Lezzi, the Socialist Party spokesman on foreign affairs, Flavio Orlandi, former general secretary of the Social Democrat Party and, of course, "Giani."

Agnelli had stubbornly refused to include any Christian Democrat delegates, but he did agree that two trade unionists should join the trip: Fabrizio Beduel of the CISL (with Christian Democrat leanings) and Mario Dido who represented the Socialist minority within the mainly Communist CGIL. Dido belonged to the tiny Socialist faction led by Ricardo Lombardi which favoured unity with the CPI, while accepting subsidies from Exxon and placing faction-leaders in banking posts.

The Nagorsky–Segre meeting by Lake Como had been arranged so that the two men could put the finishing touches to the epoch-making visit. Only about twenty people knew about it. The two men agreed that total secrecy should be maintained until the day before the visit.

On 10 September, however, the American ambassador in Rome, John Volpe, gave an interview which was to have far-reaching effects to the weekly *Epoca*. "Washington," he said, "will never tolerate Communist participation in the government of a member state of NATO."

At first sight there was nothing in the immediate political picture to warrant such a firm, if unexpected, statement. But, in fact, the irredentist minority in the State Department which opposed Kissinger's active collaboration with the CPI had known about the Segre operation and had immediately told Volpe. His interview was intended both to put the Secretary of State on his guard and to exert pressure on him.

The American ambassador was one of the most controversial figures in international diplomatic life. Set down in the midst of the Italian forest, he had devoted his time to tirelessly pruning the Communist tree. Nicknamed "Mr Golpe" by the leftwing Italian press because of his sympathies with Sogno, Cavallo and prince Borghese, Volpe was known to be a friend of Sindona and Mgr Benelli. Since taking up office in Rome in 1972 he had managed to transform his residence into a club for the nostalgic where reminiscences about the paramilitary Blackshirt processions vied with longings for the charms of the preconciliar church. He also supervised the various American information agencies in the country.

The son of an emigrant from the Arbuzzio, who had always been a Republican and an aggressive anti-Communist, Volpe had been interested in Italy since 1948 when he had owned a large construction business in Massachusetts. At that time he had belonged to the Sons of Italy, an organization with Fascist tendencies which CIA Report F 103918/113044 described as closely linked with the Mafia. 1948 was an electoral year for Italy, and Western strategists were afraid that it might swing too far to the left. Volpe sent a frenzied letter to the singer Frank Sinatra evoking the Communist threat to Italy and the recent spectre of Czechoslovakia. Shortly afterwards the Hollywood star told Minister Marshall that "Given Italy's dangerous situation, several big American stars are prepared to go and rally the Italian people during the first two weeks of April." People like Joe di Maggio, Jimmy Durante, Frank Capra and Arturo Toscanini were all, according to Sinatra, "ready to render an enormous service to democracy, and since they speak Italian there will be no language barrier. The journalist Ed Sullivan has contacted TWA which has offered to make a Constellation available for the trip."

In 1975 Volpe was experiencing all the discomfort of an outdated and rather rigid political posture. He was a firm believer in the old Italo–American tradition of US financial support for non–Communist political parties. Contemptuous of this attitude, Brzezinski retorted "A few million dollars do not change the life of a population of 55 million." Volpe even boasted that he had never had any contact whatever with a Communist or even a Socialist member of parliament.

David Rockefeller and Giovanni Agnelli both cordially despised him. *La Stampa*, the Fiat newspaper, had even expressed doubts about his "professional sensibilities." Kissinger had thought about replacing him on several occasions but had always deferred any decision because of the forceful minority within his ministry. In any case, he had never placed much trust in the ambassador's reports and had sent his personal adviser Arthur Hartman to Rome on various occasions. But despite Volpe's generally intolerable situation, this particular blow struck home and caught the whole Overworld on the wrong foot.

Kissinger could scarcely admit that he had connived in the Segre–Berlinguer business by disowning an ambassador who was only adhering faithfully to the terms of the official American position.

On 12 September, Giovanni Agnelli met David Rockefeller in New York during a reception for fashionable writers like John Updike and Truman Capote. The next day he went to see a disillusioned Kissinger who said "Nothing has changed since 1961. There is always a General Walker on duty ready to parachute 360,000 men into Italy to muzzle the reds."

In fact the ground swell threatening détente was coming not only from the State Department minority, but also from the Pentagon and the CIA. James Schlesinger, the former Defense Minister sacked by Ford, and Eagleton, the former head of counter espionage who had been dismissed by Nixon, publicly attacked the tolerant attitude of American diplomacy towards the Communists. Schlesinger revealed that his predecessors in charge of the Defense Department had insisted that figures published on the military potential of East European countries be systematically understated.

On 15 September, four days after Volpe's outburst, State Department spokesman Robert Funseth published a definitive statement, "The ambassador's speech precisely and completely represents the position of the United States, which does not intend to grant visas to leaders of foreign Communist Parties except in special cases."

Volpe's satisfaction was shortlived. Eugenio Peggio, an economist from the CPI, was authorized to attend an official meeting of the IMF for *Unita* and to spend a week in New York, Boston and Washington. For its part, the COFR immediately back-pedalled, with a statement that it had never taken much interest in the list of Italian delegates which it said had been drawn up by the IAI in Rome.

On Kissinger's initiative, high-ranking American State Department officials had been maintaining regular contact with Italian Communist leaders for some years. It was clear that the policy of détente approved by Washington since 1968 was giving the European Communists a cloak of respectability which even the efforts of the Berlinguer–Marchais–Carillo *troika* had never achieved before.

Kissinger could hardly continue his official mutterings about the Marxist tyranny when the American authorities had measurably increased their threshold of tolerance and connivance with regard to world Communism. Strictly speaking, Soviet–American relations could be made to look like the result of a coldly calculated strategy in which business relations were merely the consequence of a deliberate attempt to keep the balance and reduce tension. But nothing of the kind was possible with Eurocommunism. "Down with the masks. See what smooth and honest faces we have under our balaklavas." The Vodka-Cola experiment in Italy was cleverly based on psychological recruitment carefully tuned to local attitudes and conditions.

The only difference between Berlinguer and Agnelli is in their respective jobs; they both have the same attitude to their country. The only way to unite the Northern industrial electorate with the Southern population, for whom stagnation is relieved by a few small pockets of development, is by well-tempered propaganda.

The obvious first move is to sprinkle a little Marxism on the pasta of a basically Catholic population. You can bet that Berlinguer would tell his deputies to attend mass in their constituencies, if he could.

At the same time there needs to be an attractive brand image for external consumption. The fact that this takes the form of ready-made opinions on all the social problems now exciting the Western intelligentsia can be explained by the exclusive nature of the Italian Communist leadership. With middle-class intellectuals outnumbering working-class representatives on the central committee and the policy bureau by two to one, the CPI must be among the most élitist of political parties anywhere.

Take any subject—China, abortion, pollution, the damage done by plastic bottles, artistic creativity, relations with Christians, freemasons, divorce—the list is infinite, and the CPI will have some attitude or solution to offer. This tactical position is very different from that adopted by the French Communist Party leaders. They still give the impression that they are keeping vigil by Stalin's tomb, and that even when they do wander surreptitiously off from time to time to drink a whisky in a fashionable night-club they are haunted by the idea that the "little father of the people" might rise from the dead while they are away.

Enrico Berlinguer publicly supports the idea of a part-Communist government remaining within NATO, which is only to be expected now that the defense system inherited from the cold war has become ineffective.

The CPI has moderated its nationalization program, but then more than half the Italian economy is already controlled, hopelessly inefficiently, by the state, and merely serves as a provider of sinecures to the men who support the political parties. In any case, the private Italian companies are so deeply entrenched in the Communist countries that there would be little left to nationalize inside Italy. There is no point in the CPI going all-out to eliminate capitalism when Hungary, Poland and the USSR are looking for further investment from the West. Indeed, the Party economist Luciano Bara has said, "What worries us is not that the multinationals have established themselves in our country, but that they might leave!" The answer must be to develop a program in which further nationalization is halted and deficiencies in the public sector condemned, while private capital is accorded preferential treatment. But this supposedly "realistic" attitude is curiously like the stance adopted by the trans-Atlantic authoritaian régimes proliferating South of the Rio Grande. If president of Chrysler, John Ricardo, has specifically stated that, even with a Communist government, his firm will continue to work in an Italy where strikes are firmly rooted in the social tradition, then we can be sure that the big companies have considerable confidence in the ability of the party to control any excessive demands from their membership.

In the space of four years, both the public and private sectors of Italian industry transferred over 50% of their potential to the Communist world. The resultant unemployment and dumping have increased by 40% and will continue to grow. Unita may be ready to brand the monopolies as the worm in the working-class pear, but it never mentions the way Eugenio Cefis, Giovanni Agnelli or Leopoldo Pirelli go gallivanting off to Warsaw and Moscow, jettisoning some of their Italian workers as they go.

Segre and Berlinguer's abortive trip to America taught the Vodka-Cola strategists the valuable lesson that there was no point in launching a new detergent on the international market until it could be proved to work at home. And between September 1975 and the elections in June 1976, promotion of the CPI was based on its ability to clean up the country. Those dirt-greedy enzymes, Pajetta, Napolitano and Berlinguer, became indispensable adjuncts to every Italian political housewife. An intensive press campaign lasting nearly a year emphasized the Party's sense of national independence, its serious intentions, its moderation and, above all, its purity in the midst of prevailing corruption. The news of the scandals came not from party papers like *Unita* or *Paese Sera*, since that could have reduced its credibility, but from good, solid representatives of the bourgeois press like Agnelli's *La Stampa* and *Il Corriere Della Sera*, in which the Fiat boss also had considerable support. (It was not until the end of the electoral campaign that fifty of the *Corriere Della Sera* journalists who had done most to uncover the scandals compromising the Christian Democrats were revealed to be card-carrying members of the CPI.) Then there was the weekly *Espresso*, which was owned by Agnelli's brother-in-law Caracciolo, and the daily *Refpublica*, published by a company owned on a 50/50 basis by Caracciolo and one of Agnelli's cousins. Since then, Agnelli and the Vodka-Colanizers have become involved in further antics in the publishing world. Through Caracciolo, the Fiat boss has acquired a share in the big Communist daily *Paese Sera*, which recorded a 3 billion lire loss in 1976. The Agnelli group is supposed to have promised to respect the paper's general line, while appointing former director of the weekly *Espresso* Livio Zanetti as its new chief editor. This is real convergence. Presumably we can now look forward to a joint issue of the *New York Times* and *Pravda*.

The two main lines of argument followed in these articles were a) that practically all the people involved belonged to the Christian Democrat, Socialist and Social Democrat parties, and b) that most of them had important jobs in the public sector, which suggested that they had got where they were by political nepotism. In this way embarrassing questions about the Agnelli group's activities (tax evasion, etc.) could be avoided, while the honest CPI members who served the State so blamelessly at the head of Montedison, Olivetti or the IRI could be held up as potential saviours.

In the medium term, every Italian had to be persuaded that the familiar highways and byways of Italian politics were hopelessly polluted, so that he would rush headlong towards the great green spaces furnished jointly by Fiat and the CPI. Once the Christian Democrats and their Socialist and Social Democrat allies had been subjected to methodical mudslinging, the Communist Party would be bound to emerge as the only hope, even in the Sardinian and Sicilian provinces where country priests still wanted to put underpants on nude statues.

The Italian people were hardly likely to be shaken by the news that the main non-Communist parties were being financed by the CIA, merely surprised that the United States had tried to engage in undercover activities of this kind in a country where it is impossible to keep any information secret. Between 1948 and the present time, the Christian Democrats, Republicans and Social Democrats have allegedly received a total of $74 million between them, to prevent the Communists reaching the corridors of power. During the 1972 elections alone, the then ambassador Graham Martin is supposed to have distributed $9 billion among the center-left parties.

But at least the demonstrators could shout "Our laws are bought, our governments are sold," and it would look as if the CP was the only Party never to have yielded to the seduction of "foreign interests." After the local government elections in 1975, the liberal US daily *New York Times* recalled its Rome correspondent Paul Hoffman. A former officer in the German army, Hoffman had taken refuge in the Vatican at the end of the war and had remained a soldier in the cold war right up until his last dispatch from Italy. On his departure, Cyrus L. Sulzberger, the paper's leader writer who worked from Paris and Greece, took over coverage of Italian affairs. Sulzberger was a member of the CFR and as soon as he saw Berlinguer all his constantly demonstrated aversion for the Communists melted away. It was as if a racing correspondent sent to cover a Classic had fallen for some slender lady jockey. After following Berlinguer around, asking him questions and listening carefully to his speeches, Sulzberger came away with the impression that the Communist advance was due not merely to the erosion of the Church and the bourgeois parties, but also to the existence of a "Marxist movement, which supersedes all the other Western movements not only in terms of number, but also in terms of the quality of its union leaders and district managers." According to Sulzberger, Enrico is looking for a "Western Marxist rennaissance," and the CPI is inspired by Lenin's words that "Socialism is irreconcilable without democracy in two directions: on the one hand the proletariat cannot achieve the socialist revolution without a preparatory struggle for democracy and on the other, victorious socialism cannot consolidate its victory and guide the people towards the decline of the state without having achieved total democracy." "Berlinguer is determined to succeed in this rennaissance," concluded the admiring Sulzberger, in an article which obviously appealed to Brzezinski. This sudden suspension of the critical faculty in a man well enough aware of the methods used in the people's democracies, will come as little surprise, although we might question the advisability of using Lenin as a reference for democracy, even in a totalitarian argument post-dating the death of that high priest of the October Revolution. The *New York Times* also welcomed the comments of Zygmunt Nagorsky who attempted to argue that Marxism imported from the USSR and replanted on the shores of the Adriatic would bring "the seeds of a new socio-political current."

The complaisance of the American press knew no bounds. The financial weekly *Business Week* had a long interview with Giorgio Napolitano, the policy bureau spokesman on economics. "We are not opposed to the multinationals," he said. "Private enterprise will work better in a well governed Italy. . . . We will try to do something about absenteeism which we regard as degenerate and as a mistaken and unacceptable form of protest."

Using the energy crisis and the slump as an excuse, Fiat already had a crisis agreement which had been in existence since 1973 and which enabled the Communist trade unionists linked to Agnelli to tighten control over the workers.

As one meeting succeeded another, Berlinguer's statements appeared to be leading towards an Ali-like hyperbole along the lines of "I am the cleanest." Admittedly he had an impressive list of supporters. The Democratic candidate Jimmy Carter, governor of a Georgia where people must think of Italy as a place somewhere between Yugoslavia and Morocco, felt an irrepressible urge to take up a stance on a question which he obviously knew nothing about. But beyond Carter there was a long line of little nesting dolls, starting with Brzezinski who sat in his Trilateral Commission office in Manhattan near the UN building managing his whole foreign policy campaign. And after Brzezinski stretched a row of similar figures from George Ball to Paul Warnke, Cyrus Vance, Clark Clifford and David and Nelson Rockefeller. In a strange paradox, Kissinger the promoter of détente and much favoured in Moscow, was obliged "for electoral reasons" to look harshly on the progress of the CPI; while his opposite number Brzezinski, the most obliging of Berlinguer's public relations men, was officially rejected by the Kremlin as an anti-Communist ideologist.

George Ball, the calculating banker who had been Under-Secretary of State under Johnson, earnestly said that he had studied all Berlinguer's speeches and was virtually sure that the Italian Communists were trying to become as independent of the Soviet Union as they could. As he saw it, they were bound to come to power, and any attempt to intervene as ambassador Volpe had done, was merely meddling in a question of national politics which ought to be left to the Italians to solve. It is a pity that Ball never applied this political tolerance to Vietnam, where he advocated increased US intervention.

Similarly Frank Church, whose Senate commissions into the CIA and the multi-nationals included Rockefeller men like Charles Percy (ex-president of Bell and Howell) and Jacob Javits, implied that if the Italian Communists managed to become members of the great club of democratic governments, then Washington would undoubtedly agree to share the clubhouse with them. Even so, Berlinguer came dangerously close to catching his line on the thorns of unpleasant revelation when he cast out the statement that Church and his commission "Know as we all do that it is the greedy Christian Democrats who have received the money from the CIA, the oil companies and Lockheed."

At first sight, the aviation company scandal looked like a surefire winner for the CPI. In September 1975, president of the company Daniel Haughton, apparently a man of conscience, revealed that 14 billion lire had been spent throughout the world on "national political figures in a position to help promote and sell American machines." Before long the Lockheed operation had become required reading for all the front-line militants. With its reputation as a multipurpose provider, the company was used as a scapegoat through which to denounce the commercial strategy of all the multinationals in the West.

Berlinguer and Marchais could count on considerable support in their arguments from Church. The Billy Graham of the American legislature was a forceful exorcist, appealing to God to drive out the demon and the spirit of mammon from the minds of those servants of mankind, the big company bosses. Church divided the business world into black and white, into the good, honest firms which the last reaper will gather into his barn, and the tares which must be burned. This kind of absurd distinction is like trying to separate the lungs of a living man from the rest of his body. Bribery is an inevitable element of corruptive and secretive economic power.

But the range of diversity of Lockheed's financing activities was a windfall for the bourgeois scandal sheets and the party cells, not to mention the list of people involved who were all, from a Dutch prince consort to a former Japanese Prime Minister, members of the jet society and of a corruptible and business-oriented right wing.

In February 1976, after the first tidal wave of revelation had lapped at the steps of the Italian parliament, it withdrew to leave the usual débris in its wake. In this case the dross consisted of two ex-Defense Ministers, Luigi Gui and Mario Tanassi, who were later joined by former President of the Council Mario Rumor. Gui, who was Christian Democrat deputy for Padua and Minister of the Interior in the fourth Aldo Moro cabinet in early 1976, allegedly received $78,000 from Lockheed between 1970 and 1971. This sum was transferred to Ikaria, a Liechtenstein company, in connection with Italy's purchase of fourteen C.130 Hercules planes, worth $45 billion. Tanassi, Gui's successor at Defense, was national secretary of the Social Democrat Party and vice-president of the Council. He was alleged to have received $1,680,000 "for himself and his party" to complete the operation.

Before long the whole affair had passed from the marble halls of the ministerial offices and the corridors of parliament to the business world which sits perched on the shoulders of political power. The two main middlemen in Lockheed's Italian operations were the very wealthy Neapolitan lawyers Antonio and Ovidio Lefevre who shared luxury offices at 11 via del Nuvoto, Rome. According to the reports, Antonio Lefevre had claimed commissions from the aviation company out of all proportion to the services he had rendered, and had further links with a number of other multinationals. A graduate in maritime law, he was chairman of the Adriatic shipping line. He also used Italy's pro-Arab leanings to accompany his old college friend President of the Republic Giovanni Leone on several of his official trips to the Middle East, where concentrated wealth and political tensions suggested that the Lockheed directors might find an important market.

The Lefevre brothers also had chambers in an apartment on the piazza Fontanel la Borghese which belonged to the Bank of Italy and had been leased to Leone before he became President.

As pillars of the international *dolce vita*, the Lefevres led an ostentatiously high life. Antonio owned a complex of four villas linked by underground passages at Olgiata and one of the finest mansions on the Costera Almafitana at Capo d'Orso de Maiori worth over 1 billion lire. Meanwhile his tax returns for his earnings as a lawyer and university professor amounted to only 12 million lire.

The Ikaria company which Lockheed used for its deals with the Italian defendants, was one of the numerous branches of the Swiss multinational finance company Cogepro. Cogepro's Geneva offices at 92 rue du Rhone are in the same block as the European headquarters of the aviation company.

Cogepro covered all kinds of operations from promoting the French Secam colour television process in the US to purchasing as many Swiss restaurants as possible for a large Italian catering group. It was the managing director of Cogepro, Luigi Olivi, who received the cheque for $78,000 Lockheed sent to Defense Minister Luigi Gui. Olivi's brother Marcello was Christian Democrat deputy for Padua, the home town of the ex-minister involved and a member of the parliamentary Commission of Enquiry. A third Olivi brother had an important job in the Italian delegation to the European Commission in Brussels.

As the scandal unfolded it was as if a deck of cards had been tossed up in the air and fallen to reveal some of the court cards lying face up. Maria Fava, for example, had been a model member of the Rome administration who left her post at Gas and Electricity to become director of a ghost company called Comel on 25 October 1969. On 30 October 1971, three days after the contract for the Hercules C130s had been signed, she resigned from Comel which had been used as a cover for negotiations.

The day before the news broke, this attractive sixty-year-old left her Rome apartment at 78 via Savoia for an extended vacation on Capri.

On 16 February 1976, the deputy public prosecutor, Ilario Martella, led a routine interrogation of general Bruno Zatroni who had been head of the construction and armament sector of the Aerospace office at the time of the Lockheed negotiations. Zatroni is now president of Ciset, a company supplying electronic equipment to the armed forces.

On 17 February, the enquiry took a completely different turn and went far beyond the colourful world of petty Roman shopkeepers. It appeared that Maria Fava had been collaborating with the influential lawyer Vittorio Antonelli, whose office in the expensive Rome district of Parioli was working for industrial companies linked with the military. Antonelli was also a consultant and board member of various companies, including Elettronica SpA and Ciset.

Ovidio Lefevre was arrested; brother Antonio bought two first-class tickets for a flight to Bombay and fled with his wife. A warrant was then issued for the arrest of Maria Fava. But all the evidence pointed to one of the big bosses of state-owned industry, Camillo Crociani, president of the powerful Finmeccanica. Antonelli was his lawyer and all the companies involved either belonged to Crociani or were controlled by his group. On the evening of 20 February Antonelli left the prosecutor's office in handcuffs on a charge of perjury.

The net appeared to be closing in on Crociani, whose political history had always been somewhat suspect. In 1943 he had supported the Salo Republic before joining the Nazi

SS. He had then been arrested after the Liberation and condemned to death for collaborating before being granted an amnesty in 1946 "for services rendered to the Liberation forces."

Since then he had devoted all his attention to business. A fine figure of a man, he was reckoned by his friends as being capable of selling the Coliseum. An interest in electronics led him to play a modest part in the construction of the defense system planned by the Americans for the Atlantic Alliance. But he did not confine his activities to Italy. In the late fifties he began selling Western military equipment to Yugoslavia and in 1956 he sold surplus arms to the Arab countries just before the Suez crisis. Soon after that he created Industrial Import which became sole agent in Italy for the powerful American Westinghouse company and supplied precision instruments for civil and military aircraft.

With this ideal entrée to private industry and ruling political circles Crociani soon made friends with Emilio Colombo and the unavoidable Andreotti, Defense Minister in several governments. Crociani had always been a grateful supporter of the Christian Democrats and in 1965 he decided to move from commerce to industry by setting up his own business, Elettronica SPA at 650 via Tiburtina. It was then, however, that he began to set his heart on entering the nobility of Italian economics by becoming director of one of the powerful state-owned groups. With shrewd patience, he agreed in the first instance to accept the modest position of president of the National Institute for the Management and Improvement of Industrial Workers in April 1967. A year later support from Mario Rumor, secretary of the Christian Democrat Party, brought him the top job at Finmare, the IRI branch controlling shipping companies. That year he changed the name of his trading company Industrial Import to Ciset and increased its share capital from 30 to 500 million lire, 498 million being held by himself.

Once he had become head of Finmare, Crociani devoted his time not to managing the group in a responsible fashion but to using all the resources of a dominant economic position for deals of his own. Within a few years Finmare was close to bankruptcy. When its recorded losses reached 250 billion lire, Crociani asked the lawyer Antonio Lefevre to negotiate the sale of two of the finest Italian steamships, the *Michelangelo* and the *Raffaelo*, for a 2% commission. Lefevre started talks with the Arab company Interman, owned by the Middle Eastern financier Gaith Pharaon.

At the same time Crociani was leading the life of a Hollywood plutocrat with a luxury villa in Rome and a collection of modern paintings valued at over 2 billion lire. In 1970 he bought a historic thirty-hectare seaside estate at San Felipe Circeo from Count Galeazzi, the *éminence grise* of the Vatican. There he had a landing strip built for his personal helicopter and a private harbour large enough for about thirty boats.

Over the years all the leading lights of Italian high society, political and business worlds came trooping through the armoured gates of this estate to attend receptions which Crociani kept carefully hidden from the photographers.

To buy the 2 billion lire property, Crociani had created a 7 million lire fictitious company called Torre Cervia in Vaduz in Liechtenstein. On the surface, this company was sole legal owner of the estate, but then Torre Cervia's single director Antonelli leased Crociani the property for the derisory sum of 2 million lire a year.

In 1973 Crociani finally reached the Italian Overworld, where the men who head the most vigorous industries are given a free rein by the Italian government. Despite fierce opposition from a number of politicians worried about his free-shooting methods, Crociani was made president of Finmeccanica, the most powerful of the IRI industrial and financial groups. This appointment gave him control of about fifty companies, including Alfa Romeo and Aeritalia, and of the nuclear development project promised by the public powers. He began his new life by obtaining 150 billion lire state credit so that Boeing and Aeritalia could work on a mysterious plane called the 7X7. Crociani had a number of friends in the American business world and promised the Rome government that he would create 10,000 new jobs and a 200-seater, three-jet aeroplane with a 30% more economical fuel consumption. Such an aircraft would obviously find few buyers in the civil aviation market. The giant American company Boeing would have an 80% share in the business, with the remaining 20% being split between Finmeccanica and Fiat, the two shareholders in Aeritalia. This totally unrealistic scheme won approval from the Communists because of its job creation possibilities.

In fact Crociani was using Sindona's Banca Unione of Milan to make secret deposits which were then transferred to Switzerland. At the end of 1972, Finmeccanica had had deposits of 500 million lire in the Milanese bank. But by one year after Crociani's arrival, the new boss had 14 billion lire in his account, a sum which was withdrawn just before the crash.

To transfer his money Crociani also used the IBI, Finmeccanica's banking house and the Roman branch of the First National City Bank which has numerous offshoots in the Bahamas.

Naturally Crociani hung onto all his interests in private industry. Through Filipo Fratalocchi, manager of his company Elettronica, he manufactured and sold radar equipment to the Italian armed forces and to NATO.

In one year as head of Finmeccanica he managed to triple the group's losses which stood at $540 million by the end of 1975. But it was then that he signed his own death warrant by engaging in open confrontation with Agnelli and the private industrial sector over tenders for the nuclear power station program being planned by the government. There was a fabulous 20,000 billion lire at stake. Crociani opened this atomic war by suggesting that Westinghouse licences be adopted. He was still the American company's official representative in Italy. Fiat supported General Electric, in which the Rockefellers own a large share. But Crociani's chief rival apart from Fiat was the Swiss Brown Boveri group owned by industrialist Pellicano which had entered a consortium with German and American interests for the purpose. The Lockheed scandals exposed by *La Stampa* and *Republica* caught Crociani just as he was about to win contracts for eight 1,000 megawatt power stations. Four of them were to be built by Finmeccanica using General Electric's BWR system, while the remaining four were developed by a consortium in which Crociani's company had a 50% interest using Westinghouse's BWR system.

Agnelli stood to benefit twice over from the clean-up operation, first by removing his most dangerous rival and secondly by using Crociani to discredit both Christian Democrat methods and the activities of the state-owned groups. The Vodka-Cola business world gathered behind the Fiat boss who was also being given access to a big commercial market. Even so, it seemed a pretty flimsy argument on which to base a whole case, and the press appear to have been very selective in their indignation. How much should we make of the shady deals surrounding the purchase of those fourteen Hercules C130s when nothing at all has been said about the equally ambivalent negotiations between Lockheed and Fiat for Agnelli's company to manufacture 137 F104 Starfighters in Italy at 1 billion lire apiece?

While President of the Council Aldo Moro was sending ex-minister Emilio Colombo, one of the stalwarts of the Christian Democrat Party, to Washington to ask the American authorities to call a halt to the revelations, Crociani was flying off in his helicopter, taking with him his family and several cases of documents damaging to his former political friends, first to Switzerland and from there to South America. On 23 February when the IRI board were reading his elegantly worded letter of resignation, the *carabiniere* were breaking down the doors of his villa in Rome. But it was evident from the length of time the enquiry had taken to reach him and from the ease with which he had been able to leave, that Crociani had continued to use his influence and his friends in high places right up to the very end of his régime.

As far as the Communist Party and the Vodka-Cola camp were concerned, this would have been an ideal point at which to end the story with an edifying message about the morality of power.

But by now the tale was acquiring a life of its own. It transpired that Crociani had been able to leave Italy with a diplomatic passport given him in October 1975 when he paid an official visit to the USSR to make important economic agreements. The document had been granted him by the head of Information Services in the Ministry of the Interior, who was Enrico Berlinguer's cousin.

Various strong leads appear to emanate from the Crociani corruption case. The Finmeccanica president's social evenings at his Circeo villa were frequently, if discreetly, attended by the Soviet ambassador in Rome, Nikita Rijov, who soon became a personal friend of the former SS man. Their relationship dated back to the time when Crociani was head of Finmare but had become closer since his appointment to Finmeccanica. The shadowy middleman linking the Marxist diplomat and the Fascist sympathizer was Alexandrian-born Enzo Gomma, who had done much to build the CPI's economic strength, even though he did not figure on any of the party's ruling bodies. For Gemma was manager of Restital, an import–export company belonging to the Party which had been set up in Milan in 1966 and which dealt with all negotiations between Finmeccanica and the USSR or other Socialist countries. Through Restital, the Italian Communists were able to monopolize the huge number of deals made with East European countries. Since 1970 Italy has tripled its exchanges with the USSR, bringing the party considerable profits. For every contract made in the East Crociani, like any other capitalist manager, had to give Restital 7.5% of the turnover. Even in his days at Finmare he had entered into negotiations with Chim-Metal, another CP company representing Soviet interests, over the sale of the steamships *Michelangelo* and *Raffaelo*.

These kinds of deals emphasize the CPI's total integration into the suspect mechanics of a capitalist market which it claims to be fighting.

Since 1971, Restital, which deals with the promotion of Cinzano (a Fiat interest) in the East, has had two main offices, one in Rome and another in Milan. It also works with another CPI company, Sorimpex, which specializes in gold and precious metal deals between Moscow and the CPI. Restital has earned commissions from all the Italian industrial giants from Montedison to Fiat and Pirelli. In 1975 it expanded with the opening of two new branches at the hotel Ukrania in Moscow and at 17 Marzallkowska, Warsaw. It is extraordinary that the virtuous comrades who claim to be self sufficient in their press releases should turn up in so many controversial operations, however out of the way they may be. Two of the other Lockheed defendants, Maria Fava and Antonio Lefevre, for example, were on close terms with Alfonso Conte, the millionaire lawyer and Communist mayor of Frattaminore, a small district near Naples. Conte, who made large financial contributions to the Neapolitan CP was a friend of Giorgio Napolitano and of Carlo Obici, vice-president of the CP powerful cooperatives. He was a character wide open to caricature, riding round as he did in a Rolls Royce and having gold hammer and sickle motifs embroidered on the cushions of his yacht, while declaring only 31,810 lire to the tax inspectors for the year 1969. But this kind of behaviour was recognized and accepted by all the leaders of the CP. Above all, Conte was in touch with the most dubious elements in Southern Italy. Through Fava and Lefevre he dealt with the Milan directors of Sindona's Banca Unione, from which he obtained a number of loans to finance his property speculations and corruption activities. He even launched a development program without ever having obtained the relevant authorizations from the local town council, the regional department and the urban development office. Although the party faithful appeared to be limitless in their tolerance of him, it was caution which finally brought him down. Just before the legislative elections in 1976, it seemed likely that Conte's activities might be subjected to various judiciary enquiries and the Naples CP made him resign as mayor of Frattaminore on 2 April. As his former townspeople put it, "We have lost our 'little Crociani'."

The CPI owns a 243-office credit and insurance company called Unipol which does business with private financial groups and companies and cooperates with the Eastern European Insurance Company. One of the members of the Unipol board is an East German trades union leader. The league's chief retail outlet, however, is through the 477 "Coop" stores which had a turnover of 240 billion lire in 1973, as compared with the 432 billion of the Standa group.

Further evidence of the CPI's commercial and capitalist attitudes has been furnished by a minor scandal in Parma, where the town council was partly Communist. There, Renato Corsini, an important member of the local party, the former treasurer to be exact, was arrested for property fiddles. He had worked through a company called Siem Real Estate to support the purchase of large lots of land for the Cooperative league at a favourable price. Although the land was originally intended to be used for social services and leisure areas, the council had voted through a motion enabling the League to build apartment blocks on it.

Nonetheless, Galetti, the chairman of the Cooperative League, appears to have satisfied the requirements of the CPI's national leadership since it was decided that four import–export companies specializing in trade with the East which had been directly controlled by the CPI central office should be managed by the League. The companies in question were Bostifal, Esteuropo, Siteco and Italimpex. The league has also developed several local credit agencies in Emilia Romagna, though the real financial power of the Communist-controlled councils in Tuscany is still with Il Monte dei Paschi di Siena, directed by Berlinguer's cousin Luigi, a professor at the University of Siena. The two basic organizations of Italian financial politics are totally bound together. The Italian Central Bank and the Commercial Bank have their own union, the USPIE, to which 96% of employees belong and which is directly affiliated to the Communist-inspired CGIL rather than the bank workers' union. This means that the governor of the bank of Italy negotiates all union matters with a Communist representative. As well as this indirect control over Italian credit and finance policy, the CPI is also pursuing a course of commercial expansion.

On 9 September 1975, Galetti signed a collaboration agreement with Dom Mintoff the Labour Prime Minister of Malta. This gave the League and the CPI a sixth finger in the Third World pie to follow their construction of factories and commercial complexes in Somalia, Algeria, Mozambique, Tanzania, Angola and Guinea-Bissau. On each occasion, ideological solidarity was used as an excuse for further, more suppressive economic penetration. The Cooperative League has been used as a cover for various East European operations, while openly working with private commercial groups. In Malta, for example, it has been cooperating with Generale Immobiliare and Agnelli's Italstat holding company "on the development of those countries whose whole economic system we must rebuild," as Galetti put it. Within the party, this foreign trade policy is directly controlled by Berlinguer, Galetti and Tullio Vechietti, who is in charge of relations with other Communist Parties.

Since it has been recognized that political "education" makes life much easier for the leadership, the League has underwritten the increase in capital planned by the progressive publisher, Feltrinelli of Milan, to the tune of several billion lire.

Having thereby obtained access to what had until then been a bastion of the intellectual extreme left, the CPI and the League placed two of their own men in positions of trust. One of these, Giuntini, a party member, is responsible for the sales office of the publishing house. Feltrinelli and the League then launched a vast sales operation through the "Coop" stores, selling 60,000 copies of works by Engels, Togliatti and other CP leaders in the space of one month. The Party also has control of the Riuniti and Einaudi publishing houses. It was on Togliatti's orders that the parasitic economic machinery of the party was rebuilt immediately after the war, largely due to the financial support of industrialists who hoped to clear themselves of accusations of pro-Fascism. The first import–export company to deal with Stalin's Russia was Simes, set up following negotiations between Andrei Jdanov, a former Soviet Politburo member and Eugenio Rela, a friend of Togliatti who left the Party after the Hungarian Uprising in 1956. Since the cold war, the Communist companies have maintained warm and friendly relations with the big capitalists, as if they were no more than neighbours exchanging advice and assistance over the garden fence.

In the early fifties a large part of the Communist trade in Hungarian meat and Polish coal went to Valetta's Fiat as compensation from the new Communist régime in Poland for the 4,000 trucks and automobiles appropriated from Polski–Fiat factories. There were also discreet shipments of strategic equipment supposedly under embargo from the US to Western Europe and then on to the Eastern bloc. These deals were handled by Falchimex, a Communist company in Zurich. Collusion between the two sides has never been denied.

In 1950 the only Italian firm with which the East German government would agree to deal was the Party-owned Coecor company. During the same period, another Party-linked company, Nord-Express, was handling the majority of trade operations with Poland, for a 3% commission. There are certain companies now which appear to be private but are actually owned and controlled by Party members or sympathizers. Petro Sovoretti, for example, the president of Hovasider, a Milan, Turin and Moscow based company, is a Party member and a close friend of German Vishiani. An immensely rich man, with a personal fortune estimated at over $10 million, he has been involved in all the big Italian Vodka-Cola operations. As an official representative of Fiat, he played an important part in the creation of the giant Togliattigrad complex.

Control over the workers has also been growing tighter. In December 1976 a delegation of Soviet trade unionists visited Italy. They were led by Vladimir Afornin, political commissar for the Fiat factories at Togliattigrad, with backing from Oleg Avramenko, a former diplomat who directed the KGB services in Greece from 1956 to 1965 and in Italy from 1967 to 1970.

This did not stop comrade Adalberto Minucci from issuing a sharp rebuke to Carlo Donat-Cattin, Minister for Industry, for having suggested that the CP had really connived with Fiat by accepting 4,000 redundancies in the automobile industry over the previous few years apparently without a murmur.

In fact the CPI has been receiving increasingly solid support from the Vodka-Cola camp for some time. In July 1976, it reached the true hall of the gods when Sergio Segre had an article on "the Communist question in Italy" published in *Foreign Affairs*, the prestigious quarterly bible of the Council on Foreign Relations. Apart from a pleasant tourist guide to Rome, as a town which will always be "open to international businessmen even after the Communists are in power," the main body of Segre's article was a restatement of his party's intention to fight the "virtual paralysis of the state caused by tax frauds, illegal exports of capital and corruption."

Although the CPI publicly supports greater fiscal justice and tax reform, it actually works with the Christian Democrats to maintain the existing inequalities. Berlinguer's party may look like the only Italian political movement never to have experienced financial difficulties, but it was involved in one of the biggest commercial scandals of recent years, in which it behaved like any wild capitalist speculator.

For some years Italy has suffered a domestic meat shortage which has meant that in 1975, for example, it had to import 1.5 billion lire worth of meat from the EEC. However, the legislative yoke developed by the Commission in Brussels forces the member states to buy first from the community market to safeguard the common agricultural policy, even though prices may be 35–40% higher than on the world market.

It was by exploiting loopholes in the EEC regulations that the Cooperative League were able to carry on their ingenious operations with the East European countries.

The whole business started in 1971 when several of the directors of the CPI import–export companies, including Italcoop and Soresco, made a series of visits to East Berlin, officially to discuss opening retail stores in East Germany.

Shortly afterwards a secret agreement was signed between the Italian Foreign Trade Institute and the East German Nahrung Export company which had a monopoly of the meat trade and had worked with the CPI cooperative for some years. The Party's Committee on Foreign Economic Cooperation, led by Umberto Cardia, was directly responsible for coordination between the two sides.

The inestimable advantage of East Berlin was that it could export freely to West Germany without falling foul of EEC restrictions. So all the East German authorities had to do was to buy meat in Bulgaria, Hungary and Rumania at favourable prices and then nationalize it. The League could then forward the consignments to Italy where frozen meat from East Europe was offered for sale in Coop stores at the same price as meat bought from the EEC market.

This vast-scale fraud brought the CPI an alleged 40 billion lire and one martyr. The victim, Benito Gorghi, was a truck driver who was killed in suspicious circumstances in July 1976 by East German border guards at Hirschberger when bringing back a truckload of meat for the CPI company ARA.

Shortly before the elections, it was decided that a national committee of meat producers should be set up under the aegis of the League to represent organizations as disparate as the Communist-inspired Alleanza and the neo-Fascist-inspired Confagricoltura.

It was not until after the result of the 1976 elections had been declared that the public learnt that thirty-three Communists involved in the frauds had been imprisoned some months earlier. The chief companies involved in these deals were:

1. The STALCA of Turin, which sold boned and wrapped meat labelled "Moldavian" or "Carpathian" products. These practices resulted in arrest for director of the company Biagnini Bosco.

2. The Consorzio Caseifici Sociali of Modena, a member of the Communist Cooperative League. The directors had operated large-scale frauds by falsifying delivery notes on their fleet of refrigerated trucks bringing consignments from the Communist countries. Ten people were arrested, including Erte Righi, a party official from Modena and president of the Consortium. The CP managed to keep the charges secret. More than one billion lire worth of illegal trade was involved.

3. The ARIS (Azienda Regionale Incremento Selvaggina) of Bologna. This company organized what amounted to an airlift of poultry and meat imports from Rumania. The Tarom aviation company received $15,000 for every flight to Bucharest. ARIS succeeded

in adding $6 million to Italy's balance of payments deficit.

4. Meatimex (55 via de Marchi, Rome) imported meat from Bulgaria and Rumania. The company is a member of the Swiss Meatimex AG Chiasso group which has links with European capitalist banks.

5. Inalca (23 via Belvedere, Castelvetro), director Luigi Creminini. This company had an agency in East Germany and worked with the People's Bank of Modena.

6. BECA (via Nasi, Bologna). First set up in 1966, this company was directed by Bruno Fustini Faustini, the husband of Adriana Lodi, an important Party member. The company handled the importing and processing of frozen meat from East Europe, some of which was sold to Rinascente stores (a Fiat group).

7. SIBA (Societa Importazione Bestiame Allevamento, 3 via 4-Novembre, Brescia). The company was created in 1967 and directed by the three Balzarini brothers who imported products from Yugoslavia and Rumania.

8. Torresana Veneta Carni SpA. With its offices in Jesolo, a town administered by a left wing coalition council of the CP Socialist Party, the company illegally imported 110,300 kilograms of frozen meat from Rumania and Hungary to be stored in its refrigerated warehouses in San Martino Buon Albergo, a town in the province of Verona. Over 1 billion lire worth of trade was involved. Director of the company Bruno Tosi had two Rumanian middlemen, Dr Lupu in Rome and Mr Nirea in Bucharest. Nirea was director of a government agency. Most of the profits from these deals went into the Party coffers, with the remainder going to a ghost company which Tosi had set up in Liechtenstein. Bruno Pozzana owned a huge refrigerated complex at Palma de Mallorca where he stored some of the meat until it could be brought clandestinely back to Italy.

9. Coppe SRL, also with offices in Jesolo.

10. Comavicola of Milan.

11. The company belonging to the four Gallieni brothers.

12. Carpinetana of Emilia-Romagna.

13. Molteni of Arcore.

14. Miglioti of Cremona.

CPI cooperation with Italian industry in operations like the under-cover meat imports has resulted in further privileges and prosperity for the big companies, and total ruination for small-based Italian agriculture which has always been very shaky in any case. In 1965 Fiat reinstituted the antediluvian barter system with an exchange of 7,000 tons of Chinese pork (which proved unsellable on the Italian market) for deliveries of finished materials to China. Since then Agnelli has made the whole operation look more sophisticated. An importer named Franco Grosoli now buys meat in Shanghai and Canton and sells it on the European market. Profits from these sales are deposited with the Italian Credit Bank, one of the few institutes to work with the Chinese state bank. The money is then sent to Fiat to pay for orders lodged with the company by the Chinese government. Deals of this kind have so far accounted for over 18 billion lire worth of business.

CPI controlled commercial companies

1. Giza SPA, which belongs to two Communist industrialists, Pietro Gibertoni and Nelson Giovanardi. The company was originally set up at Togliatti's wish and specializes in agricultural equipment, textiles and food. It is divided into various subsections, some of which handle food and agricultural products, e.g. Euromilk (milk and milk derivatives). This company works with the USSR.

2, CIG, an industrial meat company.

3. CGIA, a commercial company specializing in agricultural industry.

4. The Cereto Alpi Laghi Correggese property companies.

5. Sipem, a construction company.

6. SVAR, a company for the development of the Apennine region.

7. SPAP has its headquarters in Milan and is oriented towards trade in food products.

8. LASA has its headquarters in Bologna and deals in imported and exported merchandise.

9. Italcontrol has its headquarters in Bologna and deals in imported and exported merchandise.

10. Pulital has its headquarters in Rome and specializes in trade with Bulgaria.

11. Stan Italiana specializes in the textile trade and the sale of machine tools. Its subsidiary, Lombarmet works in Emilia—Romagna and Lombardy. Stan works with Montedison and Snias Viscosa (IRI-Vatican) in the USSR and handles the sale of Italian technology to Communist countries.

12. Romintal, oriented towards trade with Rumania.

The following list of companies under CPI influence in Rome and the Emilia–Romagna region is by no means exhaustive. There are also many such companies in Milan, Turin and elsewhere in Italy.

CPI companies in Milan

1. Uff. Commerciale Cecoslovacco—via G.B. Morgagni 20
2. Carb. Fornit. Ol.—via G.B. Pirelli 19
3. ASCA—via Socrate 64
4. CBF—via Socrate 64
5. Dacia srl—via Torino 15
6. Trastecnica lic. Rapistal—via Brunelleschi 7
7. Ticino Ast (USSR)—via Carducci
8. GI de emme srl—via Cardusio 2
9. Elektrotecnic Export–Import—via Monero 17
10. Oselectric SAS—via Valtellina 20
11. Mire SAS—via Teodosio 61
12. Herhold—via G. Dal Verme
13. Nordimport Co. Gen. Imp. Pesce—via S. Mareo 44
14. Immobil Risorgimento Sestese
15. Cim. Meta
16. E. Gipi SPA Edit.—piazza Cavour
17. Picc. Immobil. Briantea
18. Immobil. SPA Edilia
19. Immobil Soc. Mi.
20. FIM—Co. ME
21. STIM Italiana—via Grandi 16
22. SIGMA—via Cassala 28
23. Soc. Nebbia.
24. SACET—via P. Luigi da Palestrina 2
25. Coopexim
26. Sacmi Imp. SPA—piazza Velasca 5
27. Edilmoscova—via Brera 10

28. Tecnider—via Santa Sofia 27
29. Italmex SPA—via Pitteri 62
30. Società FAR
31. Società CIEI
34. Società Sogeprim—via Lovanio 6
35. Società Import House
36. Società Coopexim–Import–Export SRL—via Famagusta 75
37. Società Ciech telex Polchem—via Valtorta 8
38. Società MEZ Italiana—Corso Buenos Aires 79
39. Società Europhon
40. Società Mazzotta—via F. Buonaparte 52
41. Rest Italia SRL
42. Società Novasider
43. Società Soresco—via Borgonuovo 15, viale Maino Hungheria
    Terimpex 6000 export agric. prod.
    Medimpex 2760 Roma—via Majno 38, Hunyadi Janos (Min. Water)
44. Società Romital SRL—via General Fara 28
45. Società Vitama SPA Macchine Utensili—viale Marche 97
46. Stan Italiana—via Melchiorre Gioia 57
47. Librerie Italiane Riunite—LIR—via Giulio Carcano 32
48. Società Orbis SRL (Uff. Viaggi Pol.)—via Londonio 8
49. Cominter Società Commerciale Internazionale—via Cino del Duca 12
50. Socomar—via Romagna 14, via Cerva 46
51. Imexo—via della Giustizia 9
52. Eastern Trade—via L. Anelli 1
53. Coe Henry & Clerici—Roma Tecnica SPA, via B. Oriani 47
54. Fiscambi—piazza Diaz 7
55. De Angeli
56. Katia, viaggi, via Borsani 4
57. Lombarmet SPA, via Giambellino 31
58. Stan Italiana SPA, via Mechiorre Gioia 57
59. Elektropol—Cantoni & Co, via Lomellina 20
60. Cornali Attilio—di Corn. Roberto & Co., SAS, via Fiamma 24
61. Schweppes Italia SPA, via Copernico 42
62. Meazzi SPA—via Bellerio 44
63. La Ducale di Nava Guglielmo—via Giambellino 15
64. Consorzio Vinicolo Sutti A. di Sutti A. & C. SAS—via Bartolomeo Panizza 5
65. Cosinter—via F. Turati 3
66. Novogem SI SPA—via Lorenzo Bartolini 39
67. Bolfram—Macchine Utensili—via Lancetti 33
68. Commental di Pastorino Gianni—via Ugolini 11
69. Articoli Novità ARNO SRL—via Caldara 13/7
70. SPI (Pubblicità)—via Manzoni 37
71. Italsug—via Andrea Doria 56
72. DIMAS SRL—via G.B. Pergolesi 9
73. Multimare di Vigano Paolo A. & C. SAS—via Monviso 77
74. Furcht & C. SRL—via Manzoni 44
75. Bulgaria SAS—viale Tunisia 24
76. Grocomac Internaz. SRL—via Oldrando da Tresseno
77. Comavicola

78. Centro Tecnica SPA
79. De Fonso & De Giorgio—via F. Colletta
80. Società Fima
81. Witox di C. Sanvitto & C.
82. CNC Gru Edilmac
83. Soc. Off. Meccaniche Tacchi Giacomo & Figli
84. Carle e Montanri SPA
85. CRF Tesmec SPA
86. Boltriret Machinery Ital.
87. Metecno
88. Enermac SPA—via Giambellino 39
89. SIMA
90. Forsind SPA
91. Ceram Soc. Off. Mecc. Nazani
92. Cofermet SPA S. Donato—via Politecnico
93. BM di G. Biraghi
94. Goldsmith Ital.—piazza Diaz 6
95. Co. Be. Ca. SRL—via Strigelli
96. Soicarni—via L. Palazzi 2/A
97. Viand Imprt—viale Molise 69
98. Patti—via Manzoni 35
99. F. Lli Arduini SNC—via Marzorati
100. Solfrene—via Palermo
101. Imex—viale Sabotino 19
102. Italturist Victor Pisani 16
102B. Italturist Victor Italia 6
103. Ghenimex
104. GRJBER Macch.
105. Librer dell'Amicizia—via Padova 84
106. Giulio Savelli
107. CIMA—via Carducci 2
108. Helber
109. CGE
110. FAMO
111. SAN Italiana
112. Stanislava Mesk—viale Papiniano 2
38B. Tavecchio—corso Garibaldi 35
38C. Elta SRL—via de Marchi 2
38D. Motomac
87B. SIPS
34B. Org. Internaz, Dorman's—via Statuto 8
34C. 3 Spiaggia SPA
32B. Off. Mecc. Zocca—piazza Diaz 7
113. Assicuraz. Unipol—via Unione 2
21B. Boomerang Ital. SRL
 3B. Beri Antonio SPA
75B. Loreto Supermarket Confez—via Brianza 6
75C. DSC SAS—via Tadino 60
73B. Winkler Ital. SAS
44B. Nimco SPA—via dei Giovi 6

45B. Vitali Macchine—via Maffucci 40
45C. Immob. Norina SPA
43B. Soresco SRL
66B. Komest SPA—via Cavalieri 8
67B. Bolfram SRL
114. Vittadello V. Giovine Italia 5
115. Soveco
116. Ferrochimetar
117. Antares Fos
118. Feltrinelli F. Lli—via Borromei 1B
43C. Sorimpex V. le Magno 38
114. I Vittadello Organizz. SAS
114. H. Moda Club Lord Alvit SRL
114. E. Drop SPA
114. D. Abital SPA
114. C. Vitadello SPA
114. B. Ind. Confez. Vitadello SPA
87C. SIPS Metecno—via Priv. S.Remo
73B1 Tasfa SRL
75C1 DSC SRL
75B1 Confez. Loreto SRL
38B1 Tavecchio SRL
35B. Ferraretti SRL—piazza Borromeo 12
119. Italcambio
120. Sytco SPA—corso Sempione 73
124. All Import
125. Bepi Koellinger automob.
126. Sovit Pesca
127. Romenia Real Estate Agency
128. Centro Est—viale Cenvoris
129. Grandi
130. Ital.
131. Unimax
132. Sibeca—via Mizzim 15
133. Ucimo—via M. Rona 21

CPI companies in Turin

1. Novasider.
2. Bazzani Pietro, Italian rep. for Russian clocks.
3. Piacentini Ing. & F. lli SPA, rep. for East German paraffin and vaseline.
4. Sclaverano Cav Giuseppe & C. SAS, Czech motocompressors.
5. Intersas. CP experts' office.
6. Unionfidi. Cooperative company offering credit to small and medium-sized businesses in collaboration with the San Paolo Banking Institute and the Novara People's Bank. Unionfidi guarantees credit lines up to 50 million lire.
7. Societa Eurofin. Financial consultant with branches in Sicily, Reggio de Calabre, San Remo, Bologna and Pisa.
8. Immobiliare Camera del Lavoro.

9. Società Fata. Exports spare parts to the USSR and has just concluded a $560,000 deal.

10. Gilardini. Exports to Poland and has just carried through two deals worth 324 million lire.

11. Famir di Rossetto and Co. Exports machine tools to Poland. Deals amounting to 824 million lire.

12. Gambia and Fiorito SPA.

13. Immofina. Recently increased capital from 1 to 1.5 billion lire. Vice-president of the company, Giulio Segre is brother of Sergio Segre, the CPI Foreign Affairs man. Giulio Segre also controls the Gilardini holding company.

14. Società Giuseppe Marchello. Presently negotiating exports of hydraulic drills worth 31 million lire to Yugoslavia.

15. Pianelli and Traversa. Exports aeroplane parts to USSR; deals amounting to 4 billion lire.

16. DEA (Digital Electronic Automation). Presently negotiating three-dimensional measuring instrument exports to USSR for 7 million lire.

17. Imeco–Tecmo. Specializes in aluminium, electronics and non-ferrous metals. Cerutti, one of the Party ideologists, plays an important part in company management.

18. COMAU.

19. Cooperative of Vittorio.

CPI companies in Rome

1. Tourist Romea SRL—piazza dei Cinquecento
2. Italcontrol—750 via Flaminia
3. Immobiliare Nuova Nomentana
4. CO Import–Export
5. Sias—via Maes 65
6. Motorest—viale Tiziano 3
7. Sigma—via Pereira
8. Sibicar. Branch of Balkancarimpex of Sofia (Bulgaria). Manufactures electronic machinery. Linked to Technopetrol, a construction company. Company chairman of Technipetrol, Adolfo Proino, is Italian representative of the French national bank, the Crédit Lyonnais. Another director, Armand Guilbaud, is European director of the Compagnie Française des Pétroles. Sibicar also works with CTIP (Technical Company of the Petroleum Industry), whose president is Vincenzo Gazzaniga. CTIP deals with construction of petrochemical complexes and is presently negotiating a large project with Algeria. Sibica and CTIP have part of their interests in the Bastogi financial holding company in Nassau, Bahamas.

The company is a member of the Communist Cooperative League and handles its foreign trade. It is presently working with Algeria on operations worth 21 billion lire.

9. Fotoreflex. Photographic and optical equipment. The company is a branch of the Polish Varimex company and was set up in 1973. Present director Beate Fritz is an East German.

10. Centro Product. Exports diesel pumps to Yugoslavia.

11. Antares Fos. Soviet photographic and optical equipment.

12. Uniexport Film.

13. Sarmi editions. Has published a collection of Berlinguer's speeches for the period 1969–1976.

14. Cedok. Czech tourist office.

15. Transworld Fuels. Subsidiary of Toys International SpA controlled by the financier Aron Benatoff. The company deals with import–export with Japan, Korea, Pakistan, Hong Kong and exports to Bulgaria.

16. Proveditoria Garibaldi. Offices in Messina. Imports Polish beer.

17. SMO. Works with an American company importing bananas from Somalia. When the Italian market was saturated most of the cargo had to be thrown overboard in the Bay of Naples.

18. Il Rinnovamento editions. Published the Communist daily *Paese Sera* and has now been taken over by the Communist Cooperative League after internal reorganization.

19. Comet. Soviet tourism.

20. Kaviar SpA. Linked with Restital, another Communist company in Milan. Kaviar imports luxury goods from Russia and East Europe. Managing director is Walter Borgato.

21. Immobiliare Marchini. Created when Generale Immobiliare was bought by the CP.

22. Sogene. Another Communist construction company. Recently laid off 86 workers.

23. Residenza Garden and Edilnova Romana. Two subdivisions of Sogene.

24. Italcid SpA. Film distributors. Has offices in its subsidiary Euro-Impex at via Rubicone 27.

CPI companies in the Emilia–Romagna region

1. Docks Cereali di Nuovo Porto di Ravenna SpA—via del Idrovora, Ravenna. Manages silos for grain and other agricultural products and has two ships, the *Giustiniano* and the *Teodorico*.

2. Cemamit (Cemento Amianto Italiano). Production and manufacture of construction materials (cement). Exports chiefly to France, Israel and the African countries. Linked with another Communist company, Giza, and works with the Banco di Roma (IRI) and the Banco di Santo Spirito (Vatican).

3. Italcommerce at Reggio nell'Emilia. Imports carpets, fabric, sporting equipment, synthetic furs from Czechoslovakia and handicrafts, porcelain and Vodka from Russia.

4. Pilota. Property company, manages commercial buildings.

5. Maglificio Sima SAS. Exports to Belgium and Eastern Europe. Recently sold machinery worth 125 million lire to the Yugoslav textile industry.

6. Emilia Tyre Company—Reggio nell'Emilia.

7. Emiltex—Reggio nell'Emilia. Manufactures and exports sports equipment.

8. Lux-Electron—Reggio nell'Emilia. Import and export of electric and electronic equipment. Sole agent in Italy for Czech products.

9. Export Carpi Maglieria—Reggio nell'Emilia. Import and export of hosiery.

10. Lady Jane. Ready-made men's and women's clothes and hosiery.

11. Simes—Modena. Imports metal bolts, fencing and girders from Prague. Exports shoes and clothing to Czechoslovakia.

12. Riva Calzoni SpA—Bologna. Recently exported a press for the manufacture of asbestos parts to Czechoslovakia in a deal worth 114 million lire. Also builds machinery for hydro-electric installations. The record profits earned by this company in 1976 enabled it to buy a Genoa company.

13. BGMSRL—Fiorenzuola d'Arda. Imports prefabricated housing, notably from Czechoslovakia.

14. Bartoletti SPA—Forli.

15. Corazza N. & C.—Bologna. Has exported 386,000 Swiss francs' worth of automatic machinery to Czechoslovakia.

16. Rosetti Marino and F.—Ravenna.

17. Società Sporghini.

18. AICA (Alleanza Italiana Cooperativa)—Bologna. Offers technical assistance and economic management for improving productivity of arable land.

19. Sacmi—Imola. This cooperative was set up in 1919. In 1974 it had a turnover of over 19 billion lire. Started by specializing in the manufacture of agricultural machinery and has since diversified activities. Now covers various fields from the manufacture of machine tools for the ceramics industry to hydraulic presses and bottling equipment. Has a highly vigorous export policy. Has sold 1 billion 575 million lire worth of exports to Iran; 152 million lire worth to Mexico and 1 billion 500 million lire worth to Australia, all in the first six months of 1976. Armando Sarti, one of the directors and deputy mayor of Bologna was recently elected Communist deputy.

20. Cetel (Ceramica di Telese SpA)—Telese. Ceramics.

21. Ceflacoop—Imola.

22. Calorlux—Bologna. Manufactures vacuum cleaners and electrical household goods.

23. PMS (Promozione Mazzotta–Savelli)—Bologna. Founded by two left wing publishers, Gabriele Mazzotta and Giulio Savelli, this new publishing house is thinking of coming together with the CP-controlled Feltrinelli office. PMS specializes in the publication of political works supporting Party arguments.

24. ICEA (Elettromeccanica)—Parma. Up-to-date technology, works with USSR.

25. Camst—Bologna. East European tourism. Director Vittorino Vezzili was deputy mayor of Bologna.

26. Cidif—Bologna. Film distributors working from and to Eastern Europe.

27. Compagnia d'importazione de prodotti alimentari, Dolciari, Vini, Liquori—Bologna.

28. Cofcoop—Cesena. Exports fruit and early vegetables. Was the subject of a judicial enquiry.

29. Nova Meccanica SPA. Manufactures machine tools and exports to South America and Eastern Europe. Manufactures various machines under the brand name Nova. Sales organization based on a close-knit network of agents in the main Italian towns.

30. Giuseppe Minganti—Bologna. Manufactures lathes and other machine tools. 40% of production is exported. Two chief directors, Zanotti and Giovanni Barbieri are Party members.

31. Finike Italiana Marposs SAS—Bologna. Set up in 1952. Produces and exports electronic equipment, and has branches in the US, Japan, Switzerland, Brazil, France and Canada. Also works for NATO and NASA. The plant at the Italian factory is worth over 2 billion lire.

32. Cooperativa Utenti—Bologna. Insurance company.

33. Autostar—Bologna. General representative for Daimler–Benz automobiles and parts in Italy.

34. F. Lli Rinauldi Import SpA—Bologna. Imports vodka. Director Mario Racca is a Party member.

Miscellaneous

1. Illadex SA—Lugano.

2. Scancov Transport AB. Joint Soviet–Swedish enterprise dealing in maritime transport.

3. Agrucosa—Spain.

4. Migros Italia. The CPI has interests in a chain of Swiss stores in Italy.

5. Animex. Company importing Polish meat.
6. Elopakitalia SRL
7. Doma Import—Pavia. Imports prefabricated housing from the USSR.
8. Morabito Salvatore—Reggio de Calabra. Agent and stores for pharmaceutical and dietetic products.
9. GIGI SPA—Naples
10. Valla Verde SRL—Perugia. Construction company.
11. Casa Turismo Toscana—Follonica.
12. Renzo Gabetta—Casteggio. Retails furniture and funeral parlour.
13. Martinengo Francesco—Cuneo. Agent for prefabricated housing.
14. Lazzio Doma SRL—Rome. Imports prefabricated housing from USSR.
15. Emildacia SNC—Piacenza.
16. Vima Sport SAS—Tezze sul Brenta.
17. Vittadello
18. Alvit SRL—Rome
19. Solimene—Vicenza
20. Italscambio—Naples
21. Costruz. Mecc. Lonatesi SPA—Lonate Pozzolo. Manufactures metal beams.
22. Officine Fiore—Ercolano
23. S. Andrea—Novara
24. F. Lli Schellino—Fotmigliane
25. Monopanel SPA—Travesio
26. Socomi SPA—Ronco Scrivia
27. Feltrinelli Masonite SPA—Bolzano
28. Nuova Centrale del Lotte SPA
29. Leporati Luciana
30. Incom
31. CAP
32. La Torre
33. Krcivoj Import–Export SRL—Brescia
34. Tobeca—Castelfranco
35. Centin Vittorio PD—Saletto di Montagnana
36. Randozzo—Palermo
37. F. Lli Catalani—Figline Valdarno
38. Zerbi Filli—Cermenate
39. Ronzoni & Perego—Cisano Bergamasco
40. Alca—Castelvetro
41. SCI—Tombolo
42. Pellini Igino F. Lli—Cremona
43. Cama SRL—Lucca
44. Gabbiano Brevetti SPA—Podenzano
45. Basso—Noventa
46. Morbidelli—Pesaro
47. Rapini—Pescara
48. Priolo—Trieste
49. Dukcevieh—Trieste
50. Dimarco—Viterbo
51. Libreria Italia–USSR—Genoa
52. F. Lli Fortunato—Nocera Superiore
53. Immobiliare Monfalconese. Construction company. Has built two large buildings

worth more than 1 billion lire, the CP headquarters and an apartment block in the commune of Monfalcone.

54. Astro E.—Udine. Construction company.

55. Agind. Branch of the Sepal group specializing in food products. Has sold 22 billion lire worth of exports to the Communist countries, notably to Bulgaria.

56. Citta del Mare—Palermo. Holiday villages in Sicily and Tunisia.

57. Loreti Gilberto—Spoleto. Brother of Lanfranco Loreti, commercial consultant to the CP in Spoleto, Gilberto Loreti handled the reorganization and cooperation between the Coop stores and the Standa stores in the Lazio and Ombria regions.

58. Issel. Exclusive importer of Bohemian glass. Value of articles sold varies from 150,000 to 800,000 lire.

59. SPA Rimorchi Bertola. Has exported trailers worth 200 million lire to Libya, Chile and Hungary.

60. Technicon. Recently exported steel-part manufacturing plant worth $9.5 million to Rumania.

61. Filli Devita. Recently exported animal slaughtering and meat processing equipment to Hungary.

62. Dolphin. Shipping agent. President Victor Levin was born in Moscow and has kept his Soviet nationality. Works with Sovinflot of the USSR.

63. Sagital—Genoa. Shipping agent

64. Mira Lanza. Chemical group which recently concluded a $20 million agreement with the Sodaso chemical complex in Yugoslavia. Mira Lanza will install a plant capable of producing 50,000 tons of detergent a year.

65. Lebole. Ready-to-wear clothing. Recently signed an important agreement with Rumania for the manufacture at reduced price of clothing stocks to be reimported to Italy.

66. EDG Impeuropex. Manufactures and exports electronic calculators.

67. Sovitalmare. The result of a merger between the IRI company Finmare and Sofrat in 1974. The new company with offices in Genoa is intended to play an important part in the expansion of maritime cooperation between Italy and the USSR.

Underlying the concept of the historic compromise which Berlinguer developed in 1973 and which has since been used as the basis of all CPI promotion, there is a glaring contradiction. The Communists say that the original idea was conceived as a means of avoiding Allende's tragic experience being repeated in Italy by bringing together as wide a range of social classes as possible within a Communist alliance. And yet the *compromesso istorico* relies on total collaboration with the same forces which were behind the fall of popular unity in Chile. The multinationals whose presence in Italy the Communist leadership hopes to retain are the very companies which cut production and credit lines in a country trying to achieve economic emancipation by way of a socialist experiment.

We should not assume that the Italian Communists are any more clear-sighted and realistic. At the present time the multinational bosses are haunting the via delle Bottege Oscure as eagerly as their Italian subsidiaries. A delegation from the General Electric group, in which Rockefeller interests are substantial, recently met members of the Italian C P Politburo to study the company's possible role in the development of the Italian nuclear program. The international business world is quite certain that the Party will come to power. Giorgio Napolitano may say that "big capital is bound to oppose a people's vote in favour of the CP," but this kind of statement is intended purely for national consumption. We should not take it any more seriously than the remarks made by Helmut Schmidt during the run-up to the German elections when, fearing that his Christian Democrat opponents might achieve a swing to the right with their anti-Communist campaign, he stated that his country would stop all financial aid to a red Italy. He never followed this up.

The future of the Italian experiment depends on a tireless search for financial support from the Vodka-Colanizers. In a country torn apart by crises, Western credits are increasing at the same rate as Italian industrial potential is leaving the country for the Eastern markets. In exchange for this support the CPI is offering guaranteed control of its membership and the unions as well as a pro-capitalist policy, while the Christian Democrats are gradually losing any influence over organized labour.

The austerity measures suggested by Andreotti's minority Christian Democrat government which impose the bulk of the financial burden on the working classes were totally approved by the Communists. But the situation is delicately balanced and outbreaks of strikes have shown that the grass roots response to decisions taken by the ruling Party organs is negative.

Following the Puerto Rico summit between Gerald Ford and seven Western heads of state, including Giscard d'Estaing, Schmidt and Wilson, it was decided that Italy should be given a great financial leap forward in the shape of 1,000 billion lire credit. It just so happened that this meeting was held in a luxury billionaire complex owned by the Rockefellers.

Berlinguer's statements to the effect that the CIA is opposed to a Communist government are merely rhetoric bearing no relation to reality. Indeed the intelligence agency produced a report which astounded the American politicians. The forty-five typed sheets (eventually condensed to fifteen) contained in this work came from the Rome section of the agency and its new boss Hugh Montgomery. An expert in Mediterranean affairs, Montgomery had done much to institute the military dictatorship in Greece in April 1967. He had abandoned the usual information channels used by the agency (the Church, the economic right wing, the middle classes and the neo-Fascists) to reach a fairly precise picture of the clearest tendencies to emerge from the main forces of Italian society. As a specialist in strong régimes, Montgomery thought that Communist participation in government was "not merely probable, but desirable."

The whole situation can be encapsulated in the ironic, accurate and epigrammatic words of one Italian weekly newspaper: "Rockefeller pays; Agnelli collects; Berlinguer rules!"

The French Communist Party's Financial and Commercial Enterprises

Befitting the second largest Communist Party in the West, the French CP like its Italian counterpart, has created a vast "capitalist" network of enterprises. A symbol of this commercial activity is Jean-Baptiste Doumeng, who gained particular public notoriety for his deals in EEC-subsidized butter on behalf of the USSR, and describes himself as "the richest Communist in the world." Although his claim might be challenged by several better known global financiers whose recent activities seem to jibe equally well with the current spirit, if not the dead letter, of Soviet Marxism, Doumeng's way of dispersing the European Community's "butter mountains" certainly proves he has flair as a capitalist entrepreneur.

The operation of the European Common Agricultural Policy regularly deposits some 400,000 tons of surplus butter annually at the feet of the EEC Commissioners. Produced under tax subsidy, this surplus is then stored to prevent a fall in market price. Doumeng, twenty-two years a Communist and a member of the National Committee of the Party, is well equipped to appreciate the wilder excesses of economic "planning." Accordingly, he has made rich pickings by buying off the mistakes of the bureaucrats in Brussels to feed the faces of their counterparts in Moscow. Even a general outcry from his fellow Europeans, mostly unable to afford the artificially inflated price of the Commission's butter, was unable to prevent consumption of his most recent deal. No less than 75,000 tons of butter were purchased at subsidized EEC prices and transferred to the USSR through comrade Doumeng's intermediacy at just a quarter of the price demanded of would-be European consumers. Of course, a large commission is earned by Doumeng's commercial cooperative for the French Communist Party.

Doumeng is an old hand at these matters, and sits at the center of a web of over fifty French trading firms. The two largest holdings of this empire are Interagra and Ucaso-Toulouse, which between them turned over $2 billion in 1976, mostly from trade with the East. The Doumeng group, at the service of the Party in France as in Moscow, extends into virtually every current and potential area of East–West commerce.

Interagra	Agricultural commerce
Ucaso	Agricultural commerce
Sica	Agricultural commerce
Seav-Interagra	Agricultural equipment
Cari	Agricultural cooperative
Sica Be-Py	Groups a number of agricultural and financial companies
Sica Engrais	Fertilizer
Cama	Agricultural machinery and supplies
Socopa	Meat marketing
Union Nationale des Caves Coopératives	Wine trade

Union du Sud-Ouest	
Alimentation	Food marketing
Cave Cooperative de Noe Capens et Longages	Wine
Cooperative Ucavin	Wine
Sapvin	Wine
Viandest	Distribution of Eastern meat products
Comptoir Agricole Français	
SA Jacques Esterel	Clothing
Sophima	Clothing trade
CED (Cie Européenne de Distribution)	
Boropa	
Intra-Robuste	Commerce in Eastern agricultural produce
Baccot-Vanier	
Les Silos du Sud-Ouest	
Negocoop	
Activ-Auto	General trading, especially in Soviet tractors
Frantorg	In partnership with several other CPF financial holding companies to promote sales of French produce in the East
Agro-Equipment	Cattle trading
Sibelor	Wine import/export
Sovimex	Rumanian tractor imports
Cie de Tracteurs universal	Hungarian tractor sales
Dutra-Robuste	Czech machinery
Copon	Meat packing
Boucheries de l'Europe	Printing and paper
Dussac	East—West African trading
Ipitrade International	Insurance
Gar	Development company
Les Eleveurs du Sud-Ouest	Grain trading
Société Céréalière J.A. Goldschmidt	Meat trade
SVP	Czech tractor imports
Zetor	Air charter/hire company
Uni-Air	Holding company and consultancy
Sepromec	

Associated with his enterprises in the Cie Européenne de Distribution (CED) is no less a pillar of capitalism than Guy de Rothschild and director of the Rothschild Bank, Michel de Boissieu. But for the "red millionaire" the bank of choice is France's very own "red bank," the Banque Commerciale pour l'Europe du Nord (BCEN), or Eurobank, which provides a base through which the "Gnomes of Moscow" accumulate and manipulate their increasing stake in Western capitalism. Equally impressive are the Communist Party secret dealings with the UK management side of the Rothschilds.

Originally founded in 1867 and taken over by the post-1917 Soviet régime, the Eurobank has become in recent years a major conduit for East–West commerce and for the funding of the French CP. Owned and controlled by the Russian State Bank (Gosbank) and the Russian Foreign Trade Bank (Vnechtorgbank), this bastion of revolutionary morality turns in a good profit from its diverse operations in the West.

With a turnover exceeding 1,361 billion francs in 1975, it produced post-tax profits of 40,187,000 francs. This performance shows it to be no slouch in accumulating the currency of exploitation, since its income now exceeds even that of the French subsidiaries of the major American banks such as the Bank of America, Citibank or the Morgan Guaranty Trust.

Perhaps the thinking of Eastern détentists runs along the lines: Why strive to conquer capitalism when with a little ingenuity one can simply *own* a growing part of it? Certainly, the flexible skills of the comrade bankers at BCEN have already proven a boon to the global aspirations of big Western multinationals, by way of their greatest creation—the Eurodollar. The expansion of international operations among (particularly American) major companies, which revived after the Second World War, led to problems of overseas financing and capital shortages in new local subsidiaries by the mid-fifties. The creation by BCEN of a dollar pool outside the USA not only removed substantial liquid funds from the control of the American government during the cold war of ideologies, but also made available the necessary mobile capital for the next stage of economic development at the level of reality. Christened the Eurodollar market by the grateful financial community in honour of its creator, the Eurobank, this fund has been a fountainhead for the globalization of business activity in recent years, dragging laggard ideologists in its wake towards détente. It is held to exceed $400 billion as of January 1977.

The same transferability of assets has enabled the BCEN to multinationalize its own operations by participation in sister banks in Luxemburg, London and Switzerland. There it links strongly with the overseas branches of the Communist state trading organizations, on whose behalf it is a virtuoso performer of the disappearing tricks developed by the trading banks to protect their clients' income. Its size, flexibility and contacts have made it an inviting partner for numerous leading banks of avowedly capitalist persuasion, in consortia which finance the entry of Western firms into the Soviet enclave. Its associate deals cover everything from the sale of wheat to the construction of turnkey chemical plants.

In his book, *Les Finances du P.C.F.*, Jean Montaldo quotes multiple cases in support of the thesis that the funds accrued by such operations within the BCEN have boosted the flagging financial fortunes of the French Communist Party for many years, by way of "anonymous" donation. Apart from the happy growth of Party deposits within the Eurobank, its trade-union creature, the CGT, has held the vast bulk of its funds in parallel accounts with the bank, as have the following commercial enterprises of the Party:

Sorice	Industrial and commercial trading company
Cifal	Holding company for French–German trade
Cofrosid	Engineering
Trans Tour	Travel, transport and tourism agency

Several publishing houses:
Editions Sociales
Editions Vaillant
CDLP
Editions de la Nouvelle Critique
Club du Livre et du Disque Sociétique
The Doumeng group (see list, pages 307–8)

If the ubiquitous presence of enterprises controlled by the French Communist Party in the field of "information" is supported entirely by self-financing from sales of its literature to an eager populace, it is beyond comprehension why the Party has not long since been swept to power by popular acclaim. For to maintain such a media empire on a commercial basis, each French man, woman and child must maintain a personal secret library of Communist literature. At least thirty-nine Party-controlled publishing houses, twenty-five printing companies and thirty-two bookshops are the more visible examples of Communist commercial enterprise, providing outlets for its six daily newspapers, thirty weeklies, thirty-three magazines, eleven technical journals, forty-four local publications, plus countless "occasional" offerings. Behind the propaganda barrage operate some three or more finance, property and trading companies which provide more solid backing in the capitalist hinterland. Recent publications put the total number of Party-owned enterprises at over 320.

With such investments in the fabric of French capitalism, and with direct and dependent linkage to primary financial organs of East–West commerce, the French CP is doubly bound to its slogans. Trade is good for détente and détente is good for profits.

There are five mixed Soviet–French companies in France in which the French Communist Party is a partner. The import of Soviet goods into France, outside of co-production-related imports, is largely done by these joint companies. This also applies to a major share of exports especially of raw materials, consumer goods and agricultural products:

Actif-Auto	Tractors, land and street building equipment
Stanko-France	Machine tools and equipment
Slava	Watches, instruments, equipment
Sogo	Chemical and pharmaceutical goods
Rusbois	Wood and paper products

This CP East European capitalist commerce is, nevertheless, a lesser part of the total French involvement. By far the greater portion are the co-production deals by the leading multinationals, private and state-owned, which the French CP daily denounces as the enemies and exploiters of the working class, of which the Party claims to be the champion.

Through the nexus of the Soviet-owned BCEN, which is completely and extensively interconnected to most of the large French private banks, especially Paribas, the Communist Party's commercial operations overlap the private sector's in many areas. This is inevitable perhaps, given that almost 75% of the 100 firms which dominate and monopolize most of French industry are profoundly engaged in co-production projects in Eastern Europe. Below is a list of some of such deals. It is emphasized that all, or nearly all, are based upon co-production and/or counterpurchase which entails the receipt of goods produced by low-wage, non-union workers sold on the French domestic and export markets. The examples listed include only the most important. Total projects exceed 500, including many carried out jointly with subsidiaries of US firms in France. An important number are East–West production projects between the Soviet Union and fully-owned US subsidiaries. American firms utilized their French subsidiaries to circumvent US trade and credit restrictions on such trade.

Examples of some French co-production deals

Companies	Production	Communist partner countries
Creusot Loire	Metallurgy	East Germany, Poland Rumania, USSR, Yugoslavia
Schneider	Iron and Steel	Poland, USSR
Vallourec	Steel tubing	USSR
Aerospatiale	Aircraft	Czechoslovakia, Rumania, USSR, Yugoslavia
ELF	Petrochemicals	Bulgaria, Rumania, Czechoslovakia
Compagnie générale d'Électricité	Electrical equipment	Czechoslovakia, Hungary, Poland, Rumania, USSR, Yugoslavia
Citroën	Vehicles	Hungary, Poland, Rumania, USSR
Péchiney-Ugine-Kuhlmann	Chemicals, metals	USSR, Yugoslavia
Rhône-Poulenc	Chemicals	Poland, USSR
Saint-Gobain	Construction materials	Bulgaria, Poland, Rumania, USSR, Yugoslavia
Thomson Brandt	Electronics computers	Hungary, Poland, Rumania, USSR
Renault	Engines, machine tools	Hungary, USSR
Nicolas	Heavy trailers	Poland
Oreal	Typewriters	Bulgaria
SACMM		Poland
Alsthom (linked with Compagnie Generale Électrique)		
Amtec France (linked with Litton US)		USSR
Atelier et Chantiers de Bretagne (linked with Chantiers de Saint Nazaire et Penhoet)		

Deliveries of complete (turnkey) factories based on payment through co-production

Compagnie Centrale d'Études Industrielles	Carbon sulfide	Poland
Ensa ($ 30 million)		USSR
Gexa ($ 25 million)	Fertilizers	Hungary

The most important agreements reached between 1970—1976
for the establishment of factories in the east

Creusot Loire   2 ammonia plants worth $ 250 million

1)   5 drying installations for natural gas — capacity 15,000,000,000 m³ per annum
                              cost 53 billion old francs

2)   factory for reconstituted tobacco   — capacity 10,000 tons per annum
                              cost 11 billion old francs

Aluminium Péchiney in cooperation with Creusot Loire
     installation beside the Black Sea of an aluminium production plant — capacity
     1 million tons per annum

Technip

1)   in Czechoslovakia petrochemical complex worth $ 300 million

2)   in USSR   De-sulphurizing complex for natural gas at Orenburg
                    Two aromatics production complexes, intended for Polyester
                    fiber manufacture at Ufa and Omsk

Speichim

1)   in USSR   Construction of three fertilizer plants, capacity 800,000 tons
                    all on counter-purchase deal

2)   in Yugoslavia Construction of plastic products factory under licence from
                    Rhône-Poulenc

Citroën
     in Rumania   Joint venture producing 130,000 cars per annum

Joy
     in Poland   Manufacture of transportation for copper mines

Berliet
     in Poland   Omnibus assembly

Logabax-CII
     in Poland   Licensing agreements with the Polish firm Mera Blonie for the
                    manufacture of computer peripherals, for re-export to France

Amtel Providence

in USSR   Two petrochemical complexes worth $ 250 million

Rhône-Poulenc

in USSR   Rhône-Poulenc has signed a contract worth close to 6 billion
               francs ($ 1.2 billion) with the Soviet Union. The agreement
               calls for the Franch group to supply installations for the
               production of chemical products, notably fertilizers and
               insecticides. The Soviet Union will also increase its purchases
               of Rhône-Poulenc products over the next ten years. In return,
               the French company agreed to buy certain products for its
               own needs from the Soviet Union over the next few years,
               but did not elaborate which items or for what amounts.

French banks

Bank	Number of Western countries in which they are established	Communist countries in which they are established
Banque de Paris et des Pays-Bas (Paribas)	10 countries — 14 branches	Hungary, Poland USSR, Rumania, Yugoslavia
BNP	24 countries — 35 branches	Bulgaria, Poland, Rumania, USSR, Yugoslavia
Compagnie Financière de Suez	14 countries — 16 branches	Poland, USSR
Crédit Commercial de France	6 countries — 7 branches	Bulgaria, Poland, Rumania
Crédit Lyonnais	33 countries — 35 branches	Bulgaria, DDR, Poland, Rumania, USSR, Yugoslavia
Société Générale	20 countries — 30 branches	GDR, Poland, USSR

Conclusion

Contrary to claims made in Vodka-Cola propaganda, Brezhnev has repeatedly declared that for the USSR détente has nothing to do with convergence between the Communist and Capitalist systems. And since on the question of Soviet détente aims, Brezhnev (and not Brzezinski) is still the primary source, it is his position which must be accepted. At the 26th Congress of the CPUSSR in February 1976, he declared " . . . no one should expect that because of the détente Communists will reconcile themselves with capitalist exploitation or that monopolists will become followers of the revolution . . . we make no secret of the fact that we see détente as the way to create more favourable conditions for peaceful socialist and Communist construction."

This is the core of Soviet strategy and its dimensions remain global, to be extended whenever and wherever it is tactically possible and expedient. Soviet spokesmen repeat continuously that détente is exclusively a matter of governments and does not apply to relations with social forces, ideological movements, the intelligentsia, or trade union organizations with whom ideological crusades and confrontations continue. It is also explicitly non-applicable in situations of continued support and encouragement for sympathetic and allied nationalist and revolutionary movements around the world: Portugal, Spain, Angola, Ethiopia, etc. It also does not apply in the case of the Soviet orchestrated Eurocommunism, a public relations symphony to the glories of independent social-democratic Communism in Western Europe. After all, acceptance of East Euro-Communism by the capitalist West makes a similar acceptance of West Euro-Communism politically and logically necessary.

Peaceful co-existence, as détente is still called in the Soviet Union, has been a long-standing strategy of the USSR going back to Lenin's NEP period of the twenties. Other brief periods of warmer relations, such as during the alliance against Hitler's armies and the Krushchev peaceful co-existence campaign (before he blew it with his Cuban missile gamble), merely confirm that it has always been a lasting and essential component of the Soviet Union's geo-political "Weltanschauung."

But peaceful co-existence has always been only one side of a double-tier, obverse-faced policy, designed to permit unofficial ideological and political aggression (the USSR itself has never been involved in an offensive war against the capitalist empire) at one level, and simultaneous and parallel, peaceful co-existence for securing capitalist credits and technology at another. Such a split-level policy involving peace and co-existence through an Eastward flow of capitalist goods, technology and know-how at the conscious and formal plane simultaneously with under-cover Westward-oriented ideological and political campaigns to obliterate capitalism and instal socialism, has remained the cornerstone of Soviet strategy. Such a two-tier policy, simultaneously pacific and adversarial, makes entirely credible a statement of Brezhnev to the effect that "Strict observance of the principle of non-interference in the affairs of other states and respect for their independence and sovereignty are one of the essential conditions of détente." It is entirely credible and applicable at the upper tier of public, Eastward-oriented détente based upon the innovation of co-production and its barter-based variations. But it is equally totally lacking in credibility and inapplicable to the Soviet Union's lower tier Westward-oriented ideological and political offensives.

It is the discovery of economic cooperation and co-production which has made the latest period of peaceful co-existence more plausible and more solid than earlier ones. For the "different social systems" of Eastern Europe, the first phase has been a remarkable success. In Kissinger fashion, it has permitted stripping away the moral and human opprobrium against the Eastern régimes, such as criticisms of absence of human rights, repression of individual liberties, denial of legitimate trade unions, plural-party political systems, etc. They are now merely Communist régimes with "different social systems." There is now no better or worse, no evil or virtuous, merely "different." In economic Vodka-Cola jargon the systems are referred to in neutral, balanced terms of "centrally planned" and "market economy" systems. Such cold war, pejorative appellations as authoritarian, capitalist, dictatorships, etc., are henceforth banished or submerged in the flood of Vodka-Cola syrup.

Perhaps the most salient statistical criterion of the East-bloc countries' first phase success is the rapid pile-up of cheap (6% to 7% rates of interest) credit-debt to the West of around $60 billion; a debt representing the value of technology transfers in money terms. Given the thick cover of secrecy maintained over such data, the real level of debt is probably considerably higher than $60 billion. Another credit indicator is the rise in Euro-currency (probably the most pernicious and speculative money market in the history of modern capitalism) credits to Communist countries. From a total of around $38 million in 1970, such Eurodollar credits increased to $66 million in 1971, to $273 million in 1972, to $779 million in 1973, to $1,238 billion in 1974 and $2,597 billion in 1975 (Morgan Guaranty Trust). These credits or debts of détente represent eagerly sought technology needed to bolster and strengthen faltering economies; technology, as Brezhnev says, to "create more favourable conditions for peaceful socialist and Communist construction."

He has reason to be optimistic, for this time the upper-tier part of his strategy has a real chance of proving viable, in contrast to the past ephemeral manifestations of détente. Through cooperation and co-production, capitalist enterprises are acquiring an ever-growing stake in the maintenance and continuity of the existing régimes despite their autarky, lack of exportable goods, and non-convertible currencies. Large-scale capitalist profits in hard currencies from the sale of low-wage Communist production facilities have provided the key to capitalist profits missing in the past. It is the key link of the systems and the bond of their growing interdependence. Comrade Brezhnev and his élitist, authoritarian colleagues, as partners of the monopoly–capitalist enterprises, can confidently expect the kind of sympathy and comprehension that only important debtors receive from Western bankers anxious for the prosperity of their client so he can meet interest charges and repay his loans. A violent and abrupt change in the régime would be likely to result in the replacement of the current crop of non-elected élitist usurpers, and the repudiation of their international treaties and other obligations, especially contracted debts. Why would a Russian worker who chased the régime out of power want to honour the debts of his previous non-mandated oppressors? And what a trauma the prospects of independent trade unions with the right to strike would provoke, given that the elaborate superstructure of co-production depends on the prevailing low wages and depressed living standards of workers in the Soviet bloc.

The future can be expected to repeat the past in respect of the influence of capitalist investments upon authoritarian economies. Instead of inducing liberalizing and democratizing pressures and movements, it will, on the contrary, strengthen existing totalitarian political régimes. Names such as Standard Oil (now Exxon, and numerous other fictitious, independent oil companies), IG Farben (now Bayer, Hoechst and BASF), ICI, Unilever, Shell, Philips, Michelin, Goodyear, Du Pont and hundreds of others have invested, flourished and grown in symbiotic cooperation with virtually every oppressive, racist, undemocratic régime on all continents and throughout modern history. Spain, Portugal, the banana republics of Central America, Chile and other Latin-American military juntas, racist African régimes and the authoritarian, repressive military dictatorships of many African and Asian states are evidence of the amoral, apolitical proclivities of the multinationals and their apolitical, amoral status quo supporting managers. With considerably less authoritarian strength and less concentrated central power surrounding them than is the case in Eastern Europe, the multinational enterprises and banks still did nothing to induce or catalyse liberalizing or democratizing tendencies in their host countries. On the contrary, they willingly or complacently helped strengthen and sustain the existing régimes as all law-abiding corporate citizens must. Hard empirical facts and experience rule against any possibility of it being otherwise. The oil companies, General Motors, ITT, IBM, Fiat, Krupp, etc., are not going to do anything for democracy and human rights in the Soviet Union, Poland, Czechoslovakia that they did not do in Franco's Spain, Salazar's Portugal, Papadopoulos's Greece, Pinochet's Chile, or what they haven't done during their long presence in the undemocratic, feudalistic, oil-producing sheikdoms of the Middle East. By nature of the systems in operation and their own intrinsic logic, they will become the props and supports of the régimes, not their reformers or transformers. On the other hand, their physical presence in East-bloc countries makes possible the growth of the latter's influence upon Western institutions and policies. Communist debt is growing at the rate of between $1 billion and $1.5 billion per month. It will soon exceed $100 billion. At such astronomic levels, the debtor possesses considerable pressure, especially if willing to brandish the threat of default. Common interests would easily perceive anti-Soviet, anti-Communist criticism as destabilizing and harmful to the framework of détente, thus to be eliminated or suppressed. There are already many examples of the most reactionary and élitist officials and managers attacking critics and opponents of détente in support of the USSR and the East European régimes. Instead of liberalization in the East-bloc countries, the trend could more likely be to curtail economic and political liberties in the West. Just as the socialization of all essential means of production is perhaps a necessary condition of socialism, but not sufficient to ensure optimum welfare and optimum human values, so political democracy in the West is a necessary but not sufficient condition to ensure optimum economic and social liberty and justice. The conjunction of two authoritarian economic systems, the Eastern Communist state monopoly organizations and the multinational companies and multinational banks, through co-production will override and most likely dominate the increasingly fragile political democracies. There is but a slight potential for greater freedom and liberty in the Communist countries as a result of détente; there is, however, a very real potential for a gradual but steady erosion of political liberties and freedoms in the West.

President-elect Carter has announced a foreign policy which calls for a strong defense capacity and for the maintenance of adequate military preparedness as a position of strength to continue and advance détente. For the political-military complex such a policy is ideal. On the defense side it means massive armament spending and military procurement contracts for the large multinational armament companies and thousands of related subcontractors. On the détente side it means increasingly lucrative profits from cooperation and co-production deals, even joint-ventures, on the territory of the alleged enemy against whom the defense contracts are intended.

Power is by definition a multi-dimensional system. Only a fragile, weak organization is simple and obvious. Cultivating ties and relations with all sides is a basic principle of power techniques. But there must surely be few examples in history or in politics where working simultaneously with friend and foe in armaments on such a scale has been declared official state policy.

The Vodka-Cola generation of the American foreign affairs establishment and its trilateral extension of élitist academics, bankers, journalists and politicians, advance theories of optimistic convergence in order to sell their questionable product. Like the commercial advertising promoting Vodka and Cola drinks, the emphasis is entirely on the positive potential of convergence. Seldom is there any discussion of the possible dangers or negative consequences, just as in the TV commercials and media advertisements there is never any reference to the possible harmful effects of the caffeine and caramel colouring contained in the Cola drinks, nor to the effects on the liver and other organs of Vodka's high-proof alcohol content.

In general, two broad theories of convergence are propagated in the West. Both are based upon the hypothesis that radical technological or technotronic change work to correct the defects and shortcomings of each system by substituting the best features of one another. One school holds that the Communist and Capitalist systems will change by adopting the positive features from each other and discarding the negative ones. Central planning of the Communist system will extend through exposure and cross-breeding to the Capitalist system and weaken the power of free market monopolies and privileges, especially the power of the military-political complex. In the East, the introduction of market economy privileges for consumers will modify the excesses of the authoritarian, centralized administration. Symptoms of this hybridization in the West, according to this theory, are evident in:

- The extension of the mixed public–private economy and growing importance of the public sector through nationalization of parts of industry and finance.
- Importance of the national budget in national income.
- Large-scale social insurance and health programs.
- Indicative economic planning by governments, and imperative planning by large-scale enterprises.
- Increasing public regulation of prices and wages, interest rates and money supply.
- Socialization of transport, publicly supported housing projects and service sectors.
- Greater fulfilled expectations for material creature comforts and individual consumer goods, like cars, appliances and foreign travel, inducing relaxing of administrative centralism.

The corresponding rub-offs on the Communist economies are numerous. Here are some of those most often cited:

- Growing acceptance of consumer sovereignty and choice in retail markets.
- Greater authority and decision-making delegated to industrial management with a corresponding weakening of arbitrary central authority.
- Restoration of the functions of profits, interest and cost of capital.
- Use of monetary rather than quantitative aggregates in planning.
- Restoring currency convertability as a final step in discarding autarky.
- Freedom of the consumer market to determine preferences to which the authoritarian central planning authority merely balances out supply and demand through adjustments in prices, quantity and quality of products.

The second and more recent theory seeks to attribute convergence not to exogenous synthesis but to endogenous restructuring of industrial society. It contends that through the technotronic revolution already under way, radical transformation of both economic and political systems has begun. The particular and differentiating characteristics of both the Communist and capitalist systems will necessarily be mutated into completely different social systems closely resembling one another in essential aspects and qualitatively different from the two original models.

To buttress this endogenous theory, a number of modern industrial issues are cited: universal impact of the scientific and electronic age; the gigantic size of modern enterprise necessary to achieve economy of scale, high productivity and low unit labour costs; the consequent vast amounts of investment capital required both technological and financial; long and medium-term planning necessary at both enterprise and national levels to administer and manage the extremely complex modern economy; the domination of the economy by science-based industries, which will be capital and not labour intensive. These technological or technotronic parameters, the theory goes, will be imperative and determinant upon both systems requiring them to discard their Communist and capitalist specificities and replace them with identical modern, technotronic system components. As in the earlier theories, all of this radical transformation is in some unexplained way supposed automatically to turn out positively for society. The new emerging systems, it is assumed, will discard their worst political and economic authoritarian features and substitute quantitative "scientifico-technical" ones programmed to produce maximum welfare for the greatest number.

Another version of the technotronic convergence theory contends that technically qualified managers with a monopoly over information and specific skills are wresting authority and control from the Communist Party *apparatchiks* and from Western banks and insurance companies. This theory is especially popular among managers and academics, who are or aspire to become consultants to managers. In Eastern Europe, convergence theories have been proposed, which see a form of market socialism evolving—market freedom and consumer choice and sovereignty coupled with central administrative steering of the production and distribution functions legitimized by the continued social or state ownership of the essential means of production.

But all of these theories of convergence share a common defect. They are all abstract models with limited relevance to reality, especially the reality of power and how it functions. This aspect of economic behaviour is always ignored for obvious reasons. Though they have specific knowledge and skills, operational management seldom has any real political power in a company. Its allotted sectors of authority are subservient to effective power of ownership and control vested in the banks, fiduciary holding companies or other power groups. Power structures vary considerably according to different types of enterprise as do forms of control and ownership. They are too complex and varied to define simply and abstractly. Nothing in the system proves the inevitable dominance of technical knowledge and skills over ownership and financial control. Similarly, the technocratic managers in the Eastern systems do not wield much influence on major policy options of a strategic nature. No matter how complex and large modern enterprises become, the specialized and segmented sectors of operational managers or scientist-employees will never permit them to dictate to the centers where real overall power and control is concentrated. The technology and structure of industry has changed drastically over the past decades in such branches as petroleum, chemicals, engineering, transportation, communications, etc. Banking, finance and credit institutions have been radically transformed as well. Major modifications have occurred in the mode of ownership, especially through domination of the Western economies by multinational companies. Nation states are losing control over their economies to the new global system of the multinationals. Despite these profound and far-reaching changes of structure and technology, real power and control in the enterprises remains essentially with the same families, banks and combines as in the past. If anything, they are stronger and more concentrated than before. Rockefeller, Du Pont, US Steel, Mellon, Fiat, Shell, Unilever and the fifty leading banks of the world continue to rule over their technologically transformed empires. One merely needs to compare the ownership and control of the oil companies, the chemical, rubber, pharmaceutical, electronic and space industries of the world to appreciate that real power and control has not been substantially transferred or distributed in the West.

The picture is even more clearly defined in respect of the Communist régimes where the real power and control by the Party, army and secret police has not been modified or weakened through the introduction of computers, atomic energy, telecommunication and space-age technology. If anything, through planned, widespread application of computers and the centralization of data and decision-making in administrative and production systems, central authority is in the process of recovering the minimal authority it delegated to operational management a few years ago in the Soviet Union.

The optimistic premises of convergence theory could, however, prove correct. There is nothing theoretically which rules out an optimistic development. It is just that it is not supported by convincing historical or empirical evidence and does not merit a high probability rating. In fact, positive convergence is most likely improbable, a point of view shared by most objective analysts and the majority of industrialists involved in cooperation deals with East-European trusts.

Negative convergence possibilities

1. Transfer of investment and technology to East-European countries to dump cheap-wage, co-production imports on domestic and export markets.
2. Closure of Western domestic and foreign subsidiary plants to flee strong, militant trade unions, evade stringent regulations of pollution emissions, work hazards and occupational health.
3. Gradual dismantling of regulation and control of monopolies and trusts due to the growing number of joint partnerships with Communist state-monopoly organizations.
4. Strengthening of attitudes for greater limitation upon freedom of trade unions, including limitations upon the right to strike, under influence of exposure to East-European practices and partner's union-free structure.
5. Intensification of propensity to secrecy and exclusion of external influences in industry due to the fact that for the Eastern partner it would be illegal to reveal economic and industrial data, classified as secret state information.
6. Western management will be put under pressure by Communist state partner to influence official policy to stop anti-détente, anti-Communist, anti-authoritarian opposition.
7. Growing number of Eastern Communist firms and banks will retain influential lobbyists, important law and public relations firms to promote support from parliaments, governments and mass media close to big business.
8. Strengthening of business philosophy in regard to labour, wages, work organization, prices, money, etc., along the lines of the philosophy of Communist state partners.
9. Use of Communist state-owned banks both in Eastern Europe and in the West to guarantee maximum secrecy and safeguards against revealing profits, currency speculation and other monetary operations for purposes of tax evasion.

10. Guarantees against nationalization in any country by counter-threats to go East to join nationalized state enterprises.
11. Integration and assimilation of top industry officials, lawyers, etc., in Vodka-Cola élite and philosophy.
12. Propagation of new thinking in élitist circles that industry and economic development require more stable, more authoritarian political systems, based upon technologically competent planning, free of disruptive, destabilizing influences of excessive democracy in the system.
13. Strengthening of élitist influence over parliaments, media and academe in promoting an uncritical and packaged propaganda package for selling the philosophy of détente.

Vodka-Colanization has not developed in a natural environment. It is an environment which was created, promoted and expanded by the creative efforts of a very small number of people and power institutions. For 99.9% of the world population, like 99.9% of the East-European, West-European, and American people, have in no way been involved or consulted. In no Western parliament to date has there been a really serious debate on détente nor on the implications of co-production systems upon which it is based. It is probable that members of parliament, even most cabinet ministers, have remained uninformed, given the secrecy and mystery which has enveloped the process. It has remained a matter for the élitist professionals and not for the public. Fundamental decisions on the expansion of co-production and economic détente involve only a very small handful of East–West élitists. It is such control and direction of the development of détente by a small group of power merchants on both sides which makes the prospects for positive convergence unlikely and the prospects of a process of negative convergence more probable. Under the guidance of these power élitists, some of whom have been described in this book, détente has to serve narrow, vested interests, not broad social objectives.

This could result in a hybridization and consolidation of the worst features of both systems rather than the reverse. Why could the interaction and cross-breeding not produce a tougher, more authoritarian, more unjust, more repressive species than what now exists? Some of the more negative characteristics are the system's strongest dominant genetic qualities. The legally authoritarian and monopolistic Foreign Trade Organizations under the central authority of an absolute dictatorship and the large multinational enterprises which are intrinsically hierarchical, authoritarian and secretive in their operations are both aggressively opposed to any external regulation of their activities. As the two principal parties to co-production functionally and ideologically are not structured along the lines of optimum social welfare and maximum human values, their combined net influence is more apt to justify a pessimistic and negative rather than optimistic and positive evaluation. Nothing is yet finalized and irreversible. But the negative aspects need open and public examination and debate alongside the flood of positivism churned out by the profiteers of détente.

The danger is that as the number of Vodka-Cola co-production deals and joint ventures grow, pressures will rise against criticism or opposition to détente, thus stifling and assimilating public and democratic discussion. It is in the hope of contributing to open and democratic debate of the issues that this book is written.

Index